INTRODUCTION
TO ENGINEERING
DRAWING

INTRODUCTION TO ENGINEERING DRAWING

SECOND EDITION

The foundations of engineering design and computer-aided drafting

Warren J. Luzadder, P.E.
Purdue University

Jon M. Duff, Ph.D.
Purdue University

Prentice Hall, Englewood Cliffs, New Jersey 07632

Library of Congress Cataloging-in-Publication Data

Luzadder, Warren Jacob.
   Introduction to engineering drawing : the foundations of
engineering design and computer-aided drafting / Warren J. Luzadder,
Jon M. Duff. -- 2nd ed.
      p.   cm.
   Includes index.
   ISBN 0-13-480849-5
   1. Mechanical drawing. 2. Computer graphics.   I. Duff, Jon M.,
1948-   . II. Title.
T353.L884 1993
604.2--dc20   92-4006
                                            CIP

Acquisitions Editor: Doug Humphrey
Editor-in-Chief: Marcia Horton
Production Editor: Bayani Mendoza de Leon
Marketing Manager: Tom McElwee
Interior Designer: Kenselaar Graphics
Cover Designer: Wanda Lubelska
Prepress Buyer: Linda Behrens
Manufacturing Buyer: Dave Dickey
Supplements Editor: Alice Dworkin
Editorial Assistant: Jaime Zampino

Printed in the United States of America

10 9 8 7 6 5 4 3 2 1

ISBN 0-13-480849-5

Prentice-Hall International (UK) Limited, London
Prentice-Hall of Australia Pty. Limited, Sydney
Prentice-Hall Canada Inc., Toronto
Prentice-Hall Hispanoamericana, S.A., Mexico
Prentice-Hall of India Private Limited, New Delhi
Prentice-Hall of Japan, Inc., Tokyo
Simon & Schuster Asia Pte. Ltd., Singapore
Editora Prentice-Hall do Brasil, Ltda., Rio de Janeiro

To
Engineering Drawing Teachers
past and present,
especially F. W. Duff

Contents

Preface xi

PART 1
Graphics and Engineering Design

1 Introduction 3

2 Design Process and Graphics 11
A Design Process 11
B Implications of Computer in Design and Production Processes 31
C Patents and Design Records 33

3 Computer-Aided Design and Drafting 37
A Fundamental Practices of CADD Drawing 38
B General Steps—CADD Drawing 53

PART 2
Engineering Drawing Fundamentals

4 Freehand Sketching 59
A Sketching and Design 59
B Sketching Techniques 62
C Multiview Sketches 64
D Sketching in Isometric and Oblique 66
E Sketching Applications 70

5 Engineering Geometry 73
A Plane Geometry—Engineering Constructions 73
B Geometry and the Computer—Plane and Solid, Two- and Three-Dimensional 88

6 The Theory of Shape Description 95
A One-Plane Projection—Pictorial 95
B Coordinate Planes (2-D) Projection 96
C CADD Construction Planes 100
D Coordinate Axes 101

7 The Theory of Size Description— Dimensions and Notes 108
A Fundamentals and Techniques 108
B General Dimensioning Practices 112

**PART 3
Engineering
Drawing
Applications**

8 Multiviews 127
A Multiview Projection—Coordinate Plane Method 127
B CADD Strategies for Principal Views 130
C Projection of Points, Lines, and Planes 131
D Conventional Practices 145

9 Auxiliary Views 152
A Primary Auxiliary Views 152
B Secondary Auxiliary Views 162

10 Sectional Views 163

11 Pictorial Views 174
A Axonometric Projection 175
B Oblique Projection 184

Appendixes

A Glossary of Terms 190
1 Shop Terms 191
2 Computer-Aided Design Terms 194

B **ANSI Abbreviations** 197

C **Millimeter/Inch Tables** 199
1   Inch-Millimeter Table 200
2   Inch-Millimeter Table 201
3   Decimal Inch-Millimeter Table 202

D **Engineering Drawing—Instruments, Equipment, and Lettering** 203
1   Manual Drawing Equipment and Its Use 203
2   Computer-Aided Drawing Equipment 220
3   Technical Lettering—Manual, Mechanical, and CADD 231

Index 240

Exercises

Preface

Welcome to the second edition of *Introduction to Engineering Drawing*. This text continues to respond to the demand for a short, concise, self-contained text and workbook that can be used in an introductory course in engineering drawing. It covers the theory of engineering drawing as a method of describing and analyzing geometric shape in the form of orthogonal, pictorial, auxiliary, or sectional views. This text provides the means by which engineering drawing fundamentals may be taught as a precursor to a course in engineering design or computer-aided design and drafting. When engineering drawing principles are taught first in a one or two hour course, CADD equipment can be better utilized in later courses with these fundamentals well in hand.

Introduction to Engineering Drawing is not intended to be an exhaustive reference on the subject. Rather, it fills the need for quality instruction in the core of engineering drawing while providing sufficient laboratory exercises for students to see the theory in practice. This edition features an enlarged selection of problem sheets with an emphasis on introductory and developmental activities. The sheets themselves are now a translucent material, more suitable for light table grading, and encouraging more professional student solution. For those who desire a text that can be used in a multicourse sequence in engineering drawing or drafting technology, consider *Fundamentals of Engineering Drawing*, 11th edition, by Luzadder and Duff.

Introduction to Engineering Drawing is organized such that a student acquires an understanding of the functions of engineering drawings within the engineering design process, the types of drawings that are produced, and the methods by which they are made. With this as background, the theory of multiview drawing and size description is presented along with freehand, mechanical, and CADD fundamentals. Lastly, specific applications of engineering drawing—pictorials, sections, auxiliaries, and assemblies— complete the instructional section.

Contained in the appendix section is valuable information of a supplementary nature. A glossary of terms, a list of abbreviations and symbols, conversion tables, lettering techniques, and a description of common equipment are included. Completing *Introduction to Engineering Drawing* are laboratory exercises which reinforce the information presented in the instructional chapters. These problems are time-tested—chosen to demonstrate the major teaching points of each chapter. With the additional introductory problems in this edition, you may find little need to supplement the problems with ones from other sources. The problems include fractional inch, decimal inch, and metric problems for both freehand and mechanical solution as well as several assignments suitable for CADD.

The authors would like to thank the many contributors recognized in *Fundamentals of Engineering Drawing,* 11th Edition, from which *Introduction to Engineering Drawing* was constructed. The same careful treatment of basic subject matter and many familiar problems have been kept, but the authors have organized this text in a such a manner that engineering drawing is available to a wider audience than ever before. Special thanks go to Carol Hoffman of the University of Alabama for her suggestions on this second edition, to Craig Miller of Purdue University for his numerous comments and evaluations on the text and work sheets, and to Raquel Russel who assisted in the preparation of the manuscript.

W.J.L.
J.M.D.
Purdue University

INTRODUCTION TO ENGINEERING DRAWING

PART 1

GRAPHICS AND ENGINEERING DESIGN

The IBM Interactive Graphics Display System unlocks man's imagination. With the IBM system product designs can be prepared and plots and maps displayed in their expected form. Under program control data can be entered, displayed, and modified as needed by using the light pen, program function keyboard, or alphanumeric keyboard.

Technical drawings may be created by techniques similar to those used at a regular drawing board. Drafting requirements for arcs, lines, dimensioning, notes, automatic scaling, parts lists, and three-dimensional pictorials are fully met in accordance with ANSI drafting standards by the applications program. (*Courtesy IBM Corporation*)

Introduction

1.1 *Brief History of Drawing*

For almost twenty thousand years a drawing has been the main way that ideas have been communicated. The first drawings were made even longer ago, when prehistoric man tried to communicate ideas by marking in the dirt floors of caves. It is natural for humans to graphically draw their ideas because *drawing is a universal language.* Even today, when some drawings are made by computers, this is true. The first permanent drawings, made on the rock walls of caves, depicted people, deer, buffalo, and other animals. These drawings were made to express emotion and record experiences, long before the development of writing. When writing developed, drawing came to be used primarily by artists and engineers as a means of showing design concepts for pyramids, war chariots, buildings, and simple mechanisms.

One of the earliest drawings, found in Mesopotamia, shows the use of the wheel about 3200 B.C. The drawing depicts a wheelbarrow-like mechanism being used by a man to transport his wife. This early drawing was a crude picture, without depth or perspective. Another example of early drawing is a floor plan of a fortress made on a clay tablet around 4000 B.C.

At the beginning of the Christian era, *Roman architects* had become skilled in making drawings of proposed buildings. They used straight edges and compasses to prepare plan (top), elevation (front and side), and perspective views. However, the theory behind engineering drawing, the theory that enabled architects to depict views on various planes, was not developed until the Renaissance period. Even though *Leonardo da Vinci* was probably aware of these theories, his classical training as an artist influenced his engineering drawings like the one shown in Fig. 1.1. No multiview drawings (top, front, side views) made by Leonardo have been found. He knew the value of pictorial drawing in showing how parts of a mechanism fit together. It is interesting to note that even in this day of space travel, engineers continue to use pictorials to supplement multiview drawings (see the pictorial drawing of Skylab in Fig. 1.2).

Most of the very early drawings still existing today were made on parchment, a very durable type of paper. Although the paper that was developed in Europe in the twelfth century made the use of drawings more prevalent, the paper was too fragile. Of the thousands of engineering drawings of fortresses, buildings, and mechanisms made during the twelfth through fifteenth centuries, only a few exist today. Pictures made into pottery, carvings, and weavings were more permanent than paper drawings, and many of these artifacts have survived.

4

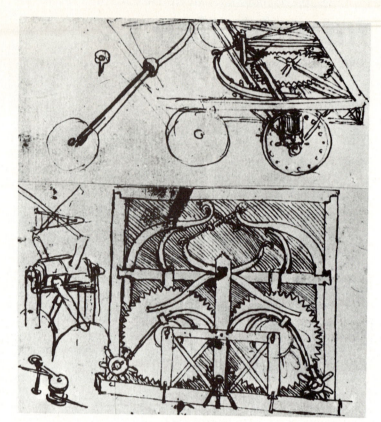

FIG. 1.1 Idea sketch prepared by Leonardo da Vinci (1452–1519). Leonardo's "automobile" was to have been powered by two giant springs and steered by the tiller, at the left in the picture, attached to the small wheel. (*From Collection of Fine Arts Department, IBM Corporation*)

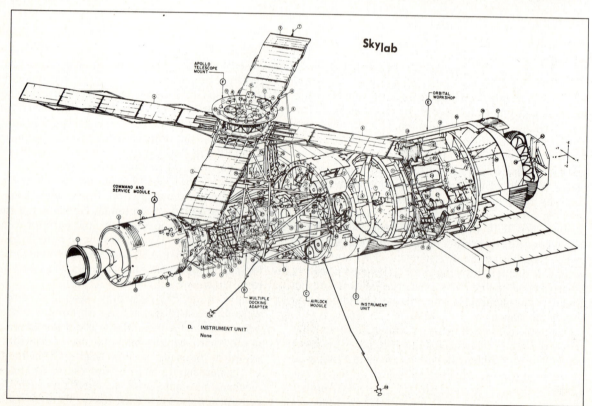

FIG. 1.2 Skylab—manned orbital scientific space station. The Skylab was designed to expand our knowledge of manned earth-orbital operations and to accomplish carefully selected scientific, technological, and medical investigations. (*Courtesy National Aeronautics and Space Administration*)

1.2 Interrelationship of Engineering Drawing and Design

Engineering design uses engineering drawing as the way to communicate and document ideas. Engineers, drafters, and other members of the design team must work closely on the design project and speak the same language: *the language of engineering drawing.* A design engineer, though not responsible for the actual production of the drawings, must be able to read and understand all aspects of the drawing. At the very least, the design engineer must be able to make clear, concise sketches that can be given to technologists and drafting technicians for the actual preparation of the drawings.

Any person on the design team who makes engineering drawings must combine *classroom study* of engineering graphics with *practical experience* in company methods, standards, and practices. This knowledge may include such things as manufacturing methods, numerical control, and digital computer applications (Chapter 1–5 and 12–18).

Engineering drawings present technical information to tens or even hundreds of individuals who may be engineers, managers, suppliers, machinists, installers, or repairmen. All need engineering drawings to complete their tasks. For this reason drawings must conform to *exacting standards* for their preparation and understanding.

Engineering drawings are documents that change. During the life of a drawing, there may be changes in the design, materials, suppliers, and uses of the product. These changes must be noted and recorded. Very often a single drawing may be used for a whole family of parts. Consequently, engineering drawings must be made with materials and equipment that allow for clean and efficient changes. (See Chapter 2, which covers equipment and materials.)

1.3 Engineering Drawing Today

The design team is often made up of individuals from many different disciplines. A project manager assembles a team to accomplish a goal such as building a bridge, designing a car, or placing scientific equipment on the moon (Fig. 1.3). In general, the design team is comprised of three groups of individuals, each having particular knowledge of engineering drawing: (1) engineering designers, (2) engineering technologists, and (3) engineering technicians.

Designers and technologists think about the way that a mechanism or product works and how it can be manufactured or built. These individuals must have a working knowledge of engineering drawing to be able

FIG. 1.3 The Lunar Rover. The photograph shows the Lunar Rover taken to the Moon by the Apollo 15 Mission. It is parked near Mount Hadley in the right center background. The Lunar Rover is one of man's most noted innovative designs. (*Courtesy National Aeronautics and Space Administration*)

to direct drafters in the preparation of final drawings. The final drawings follow preliminary design sketches that the designer may have made. Such design sketches must follow the basic rules of engineering drawing so that it will be easy for the drafter to turn rough sketches into final drawings.

To be effective, the engineering designer and technologist must have skill in three areas of communication: (1) English, both written and oral; (2) symbols, as used in science and mathematics; and (3) engineering drawing, both sketching and interpreting drawings.

A drafter must be able to assemble written, numeric, and graphic information and make final drawings. These drawings are called ''working drawings'' because they are the drawings from which the product is made. The drawing must convey *shape, size,* and *manufacturing information* needed to fabricate the parts and assemble the structure. This must be done with knowledge of company practices and national and international standards such as those of the *American National Standards Institute* (ANSI) or the *International Standards Organization* (ISO). Because ANSI standards govern the preparation of engineering drawings, drafters must keep up to date with the latest published standards.

Engineering technicians, assigned to aid the engineer or to work in production, must have considerable knowledge in preparing engineering drawings. Those working with the design engineer may be called on to solve problems graphically or prepare working sketches within their own areas of expertise, such as electrical, structural, or mechanical systems.

1.4 Engineering Drawing and the Computer

Engineering drawing is a *graphic language* that allows humans and computers to work together. The computer has made the current period one of revolutionary change in how engineering drawings are made, stored, and printed. The emphasis in engineering drawing today is on conveying design information efficiently to a design team that may be in widely separated locations. The saying ''a picture is worth a thousand words'' has never had more meaning than today.

Computers understand numbers and are able to print information in the form of numbers—rows and rows of numbers, page after page of numbers. But humans, who find it easier to understand words and pictures, call on graphic computers to take these numbers from the *data base* and show the drawing they represent (Fig. 1.4). Engineering drawings prepared with the aid of a computer are important as a means of visually checking the numbers for correctness, since it is much easier to check a picture than fifty pages of numbers.

These computer-assisted drawings take on two general forms: (1) a chart (graph, plot, or diagram); or (2) a picture showing the shape or size of the object.

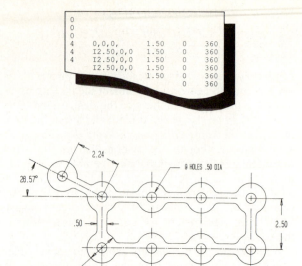

FIG. 1.4 Numeric data base and its graphic representation. The set of numbers which defines the geometry of an engineering design is ''read'' by the CADD program and displayed in the form of an engineering drawing.

With either form, the designer is trying to determine whether or not the *computer model* satisfies the design criteria. To do this, the designer must be able to read the drawing and understand shape, size, and manufacturing information as it is represented. The principles of engineering drawing, the accepted ways of drawing standard features such as bolts and springs, and the methods of specifying size are discussed in Chapters 2 to 5 and in Chapters 13, 14, and 21.

With powerful computer-aided design (CAD) systems, drawings on paper may not exist. Instead, drawings may appear on computer monitors where they are corrected, updated, and evaluated.

1.5 Computer-Aided Design Drafting (CADD)

It might be helpful at this point to make a distinction between *computer-aided design* (CAD) and *computer-aided design drafting* (CADD). CAD is an analysis technique, a way of *modeling* the performance of a product before it is actually built. Paper drawings may not be necessary in the design phase. The ideal situation is one where the numbers controlling the machines produce the same geometric description for making the parts as was used to describe the design. To coordinate the workers manufacturing the product, engineering drawings are required.

Every point on an object has its own unique location, or ''address,'' in space (see Chapter 4). Together, the addresses of all of the points on an object form the data base for that object. Two-dimensional objects have two-dimensional data bases. Three-dimensional objects have three-dimensional data bases. The size of the data base (the actual volume of numbers) and not the physical dimensions of the paper determines the size of the drawing. A CADD drawing's size is determined by

1. Dimensionality (three-dimensional data bases are larger than two-dimensional data bases for the same object),

2. The size of the object (large objects contain more points),

3. The detail of the object (the more detail, the more points).

The following is a brief overview of important concepts in CADD. For more extensive information refer to Chapter 17.

With CADD, the computer can easily present individual components of a product separately by placing each component on a different layer, the computer version of clear plastic overlay sheets. Layers can be selected for viewing in any combination.

CADD programs allow the designer to select the units of measure (such as inches or millimeters) for the data base. The image can be displayed larger or smaller, depending on the level of detail desired. This does not affect the actual size of the object defined by the numbers in the data base; rather, it enables you to view the object close up or from farther away. If the data base itself is changed, the object is said to have been *scaled*.

CADD systems can be very accurate. Accuracy is determined by the total number of individual points that the computer can keep track of at one time. It is not uncommon for a CADD system to be capable of accuracy to 1/1000th of an inch and still allow a designer to work in a space 30 miles on each side. The greater the accuracy, the smaller the available work space. The smaller the accuracy, the larger the work space that can be defined.

This flexibility allows for the design of both large and small projects on the same system (Fig. 1.5). It is possible to work on the overall design of a very large space station and a computer chip for the station's electrical system on the same computer terminal. Once it took hours to describe the geometry of even the simplest part. Today, with more sophisticated and "user-friendly" CADD programs, a complex design can be defined in a fraction of the time previously required.

The role that drawing plays in the design process is changing with the increased use of computer-aided machines and processes. Companies that continue to make engineering drawings without the aid of computers use drawings for the actual production of parts and for the assembly and checking of the final product. These manual drawings become the basis for all subsequent documents prepared for manufacture, distribution, and service of the company's product. There is no master set of numbers describing the design; so the drawing, in this case, is the data base.

Companies that build a computer data base of the part use that set of numbers to generate all engineering documents necessary during the lifetime of the design. This includes engineering drawings, instructions for numerically controlled machine tools, quality control, assembly, marketing, maintenance, inventory control, and accounting. There is a fundamental difference between manual drafting and CADD. *In CADD, all doc-*

FIG. 1.5 Minicomputer interactive computer graphics system. (*Courtesy Computervision Corporation*)

uments go back to the same numeric data base for information, assuring accuracy and completeness. In manual design, a drawing may be made from a previous drawing which was made from an earlier drawing, and so on. The chance for error with manual design and drawing is much greater.

1.6 How CADD Drawings Are Used

If the data base contains the representation of a part's geometry in the memory of the computer, *any and all views of that geometry are available* to the designer. To make an engineering drawing of the data base, the form must be displayed in a position that reveals the desired views (Fig. 1.6). When a CADD system is used, like lines will be the same thickness on every drawing, lettering will be the same regardless of the drafter, and other manual-skill operations will be made consistent. Prints are made only as a verification of the data base or for locations where a computer terminal is unavailable.

Although this difference appears to be a conflict of manual versus computer drawing, the use of engineering drawings is not an either-or situation. Industries will continue to use both paper and computer drawings side by side. Paying attention to drafting standards will assure that the two can be used interchangeably. The structural steel industry, for example, makes use of CADD data bases for design and analysis, but will continue to make extensive use of manual drawings or printed copies of computer drawings for the actual fabrication of structures. Why? Because a drawing is much easier to carry than a computer terminal as you climb the superstructure of a bridge.

1.7 Computer-Aided Design and Manufacturing (CAD/CAM)

Manufacturing companies are becoming increasingly interested in linking design and manufacturing to reduce production time, cut drawing room costs, simplify production planning, and increase accuracy. An integrated *CAD/CAM* system *shares the data base* created during the design phase (Fig. 1.7). *Computer numerically controlled* (CNC) machines were developed before CAD and required a separate data base. If the machines could recognize this data base, why not create the original description of the part geometry in the same form, avoiding the costly process of translating manual drawings into a CNC data base? The coupling of these two activities became CAD/CAM—the marriage of computer-aided design and computer-aided manufacturing. Whenever computers are widely used for manufacture, the term CAM is used. This applies to the planning and production processes, inventory control, and for the programming of numeri-

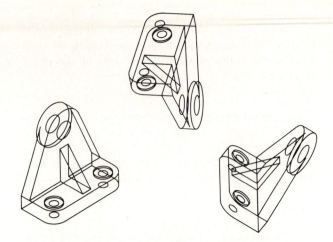

FIG. 1.6 Multiple views from the same data base. Once an object is described in a numeric data base, *any* view of the geometry is possible. (*Courtesy of Mike Gabel, Department of Technical Graphics, Purdue University*)

cally controlled machine tools, to be discussed in Chapter 18.

CAD/CAM can be thought of as being divided into the following four general areas:

1. Engineering design
2. Design drawing or design drafting
3. Planning or scheduling
4. Fabrication or machining

CAD/CAM is part of the complete integration of manufacturing, a process known as computer-integrated manufacturing (CIM). CIM integrates the manufacturing process from product planning through design, CADD, production, materials handling, inspection and quality control, and assembly.

In the future, small but powerful computers will control machines on the production line. These computers will in turn be controlled by larger computers

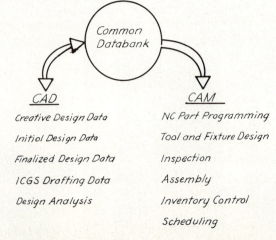

FIG. 1.7 Work flow in an integrated CAD/CAM system.

which assign to them specific tasks, route materials to each work station, and keep track of inventory. These intermediate computers will be controlled by even larger computers which coordinate activities between departments.

The chapters in this text are limited to the CADD aspects of CAD/CAM. Students who are interested in becoming drafting technicians must learn the fundamentals of engineering drawing before they enter the work force and become members of the total CAD/CAM team. As a member of that team, an understanding of the overall picture of CAD/CAM is essential.

1.8 International System of Measure

Although the *metric system* was legally approved for use in the United States by an act of Congress more than one hundred years ago (1866), it has not been widely adopted because its use was never made mandatory. Most industrial and trading nations use the metric system. To compete in a world market, many American companies had to convert to metric measurements. Companies such as General Motors, Ford, IBM, 3M, Navistar, John Deere, Caterpillar, Honeywell, McDonnel Douglas, Rockwell International, and TRW have or are currently converting to the Système International d'Unités (SI) or metric system.

Total conversion will not come about immediately for much of American industry. Acceptance of ISO standards is a slow process. The ANSI standards continue to be translated into metric; therefore, this text will include problems in both the metric and English systems. Just as use of computer graphics is not an either-or situation, many companies that have essentially "gone metric" continue to use the English system for some fasteners, pipes, drills, and bearings. The appendices of this text contain numerous conversion tables as well as metric parts tables. In the revision of this text the authors have been guided by the current ANSI metric standards and by the metric design and drafting standards furnished by General Motors, John Deere, Navistar, and IBM.

1.9 The Educational Value of Engineering Drawing

By studying engineering drawing, a student becomes aware of how industry communicates technical information. Engineering drawing teaches the principles of accuracy and clarity in presenting the information necessary to produce products (Figs. 1.8 and 1.9). It de-

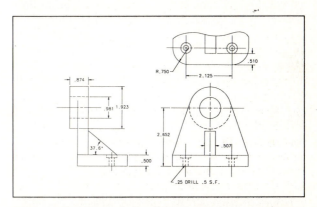

FIG. 1.9 An engineering detail drawing prepared using a CADD system. This drawing represents the mathematical description of a machine part in standard form, easily understood by engineers, technologists, and technicians.

FIG. 1.8 Classroom laboratory showing microcomputer workstations for the use of beginning students. Computer, monitor, digitizing board, and digital plotter can be seen. (*Courtesy of Professors Birchman and Sadowski and the Department of Technical Graphics, Purdue University*)

velops the engineering imagination that is so essential to a successful design. Finally, in learning the techniques of engineering drawing, you will find that something very important has happened: it has *changed the very way that you think about technical images* and that, more than facts and figures, will stay with you throughout your career. It is ideal to master the fundamentals of engineering drawing first and to later use these fundamentals for a particular application, such as CADD. The deeper your understanding of the fundamentals, the more command you will have over whatever engineering drawing tools you have available.

1.10 Organization of Text

The purpose of this text is to present the *grammar and composition* of engineering drawing, much as an English text presents the grammar and composition of our written language. With study, engineering and technology students will eventually be able to prepare satisfactory engineering drawings and, after some industrial experience, be capable of directing the work of others.

To organize study, this text has been separated into the following topics:

• Engineering Design and Graphics

• Computer-Aided Design and Drafting
• Engineering Drawing Fundamentals
• The Theory of Shape Description
• The Theory of Size Description
• Multiview Drawing
• Auxiliary Views
• Sectional Views
• Pictorial Drawing

Most of the material in this text concerns the preparation of machine drawings. This may not seem to be of immediate interest to students studying construction or architectural or electrical technologies. Knowing the methods used in machine drawings, however, prepares the student for later specialization. A discussion of several of these specialized fields is presented in this text after the fundamentals of engineering drawing have been studied.

The same argument applies to CADD. A student who is not thoroughly versed in the fundamentals of engineering drawing simply becomes an operator of the CADD system, unable to use the computer as a design tool. Space problems, such as the clearance between a wheel and a fender or the true angle between a turbine blade route and the axis of an engine, can be solved by computer solution only if the fundamentals of engineering drawing have been learned.

Design Process and Graphics

A DESIGN PROCESS

2.1 Design

In the dictionary, design is defined as follows: (1) to form or conceive in the mind, (2) to contrive a plan, (3) to plan and fashion the form of a system (structure), and (4) to prepare the preliminary sketches or plans for a system that is to be produced. *In engineering, design is a decision-making process used for the development of engineering systems for which there is human need* (Fig. 2.1). To design is to conceive, to innovate, to create. One may design an entirely new system or modify and rearrange existing things in a new way for improved usefulness or performance. Engineering design begins with the recognition of a social or economic need (Fig. 2.2). The need must first be translated into an acceptable idea by conceptualization and decision making. Then the idea must be tested against the physical laws of nature before one can be certain that it is workable. This requires the designer to have a full knowledge of the fundamental physical laws of the basic sciences, a working knowledge of the engineering sciences, and the ability to communicate ideas both graphically (Fig. 2.19) and orally. The designer

should be well grounded in economics, have some knowledge of engineering materials, and be familiar with manufacturing methods. In addition, some knowledge of both marketing and advertising will prove worthwhile, because usually what is produced must be distributed at a profit. Proficiency in designing can be attained only through total involvement, since it is only through practice that the designer acquires the art of continually providing new and novel ideas. In developing the design, the engineer or engineering technologist must apply his knowledge of engineering and material sciences while taking into account related human factors, reliability, visual appearance, manufacturing methods, and sale price. It may therefore be said that *the ability to design is both an art and a science.*

Creative persons will almost never follow a set pattern of action in developing an idea. To do so would tend to structure their thinking and might limit the creation of possible solutions. The design process calls for unrestrained creative ingenuity and continual decision making by a free-wheeling mind. The total development of an idea, from recognition of a need to the final product, does appear to proceed loosely in stages

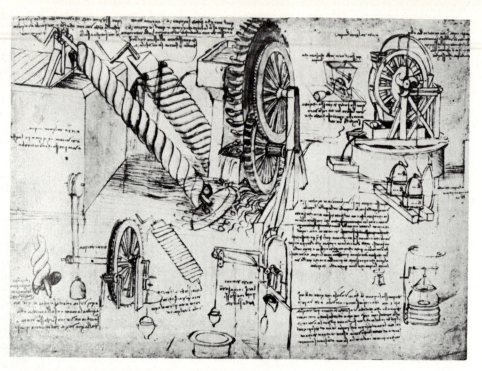

FIG. 2.1 Archimedean screw and wheel. Sketch showing Archimedean screw and wheel by Leonardo da Vinci (1452–1519), engineer, scientist, and painter. (*From Collection of Fine Arts Department, IBM Corporation*)

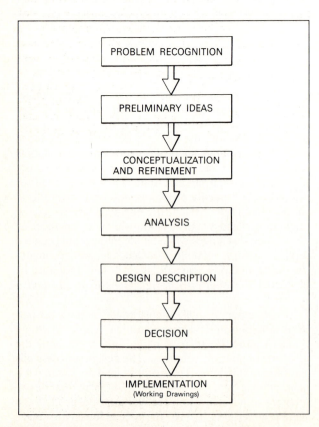

FIG. 2.2 The design process.

that are recognized by authors and educators, however (Fig. 2.2).

Creative thinking usually begins when a design team, headed by a project leader, has been given an assignment to develop something that will satisfy a particular need. The need may have been suggested by a salesperson, a consumer, or even an engineer from another company now using a product or a machine produced by the design team's own company. Most often the directive will come down from top management, as was the case with the development of the electric knife some years ago. Although it is always pleasant for an individual to think about the careers of famous inventors of the past, and dream of the fame and fortune that might await the development and marketing of an idea, the fact is that almost all new and improved products, from food choppers to aircraft engines, represent a team effort.

2.2 *Design Synthesis*

The process of combining constituent elements in a new or altered arrangement to achieve a unified entity is known as *design synthesis*. It is a process that involves reasoning from assumed propositions and known principles to arrive at comparatively new design solutions to recognized problems. The synthesis of systems for simple combinations as well as for complicated assemblies requires creative ability of the very highest order. The synthesis of both parts and systems usually requires successive trials to create new arrangements of old components and new features.

Proof of this point is the Land camera, once considered by many people to be an entirely new product. In reality, the camera represents a combination of features and principles common to existing cameras to which Mr. Land added several new ideas of his own, including a new type of film and film pack that for the first time made it possible to develop film and pictures within the camera itself. Land's design activity no doubt started with a recognition of the need and desire that people had to take pictures that could be seen almost immediately. The early automobile is another example that bears out the fact that old established products have features that are used as a starting basis for a new product. For example, at the turn of the century the automobile looked like a horseless carriage; the horse was taken to the barn and a motor was added in its place.

2.3 Design of Systems and Products

In general most design problems may be classified as being either a *systems design* or a *product design,* even though it may be quite difficult in many instances to recognize a problem as belonging entirely to one classification or the other. This is due to the fact that there often will be an overlap of identifying characteristics.

A *systems design* problem involves the interaction of numerous components that together form an operating unit. A complex system such as the climatic-control system for an automobile (heating and cooling), a movie projector, a stadium, an office building, or even a parking lot represents a composition of several component systems that together form the complete composite system (Fig. 2.3). Some of the component systems of an office building, aside from the structural system itself, are the electrical system, the plumbing system (including sewers), the heating and cooling systems, the elevator system, and the parking facilities system. All of these component systems, when combined, will meet the needs of a total system; but usually the total system design will involve more than just a technological approach. In the design of composite systems for use by the public, as in the design of a highway, an office building, or a stadium, the designer must adhere to the availability of funds. One must build into the design the safety features that are required by law and, at the same time, give due consideration to human factors, trends, and even present-day social problems. In many cases, a designer will find that there are political and special-interest groups that limit the freedom of decision making. Under such conditions the designer must be willing to compromise in the best interests of all concerned. This means that a successful designer must have experience in dealing with people. Social studies courses taken along with and in addition to the scientific courses offered in engineering colleges and technical schools will prove to be helpful.

Product design is concerned with the design of some appliances, systems components, and other similar unit-type items for which there appears to be a market. Such a product may be an electric lock, a power carjack, a lawn sprinkler, a food grinder, a toy, a piece of specialized furniture, an electrical component, a valve, or other item that can be readily marketed as a commercial unit. Such products are designed to perform a specific function and to satisfy a particular need. Total product design includes not only the design of an item, but the testing, manufacture, and distribution of the product as well. Design does not end with the solution of a problem through creative think-

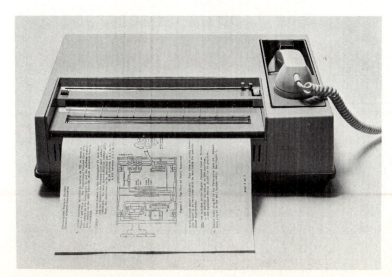

FIG. 2.3 Telecopier transceiver. This transceiver sends and receives a letter-size document or drawing. (*Courtesy Business Products Group, Xerox Corporation*)

FIG. 2.4   An entirely new concept for the electronic control of automobiles is illustrated above by an artist's rendering. Many additional drawings of a more conventional type will be needed to make the idea a reality. The trailing car is equipped with a transmitter (at left) which projects an invisible beam at the car ahead. The taillights of the car in front, which does not have to be especially equipped, reflect the beam back to a receiver (*right*). A computer "reads" the signal and adjusts brakes and accelerator automatically so that a preset safe following distance will be maintained. (*Courtesy Ford Motor Company*)

ing. The design phase for a product to be sold on the open market ends only when the item has received wide acceptance by the public. Of course, if the item being designed is not for the consumer market, the designer will have less reason to be concerned with details of marketing. This would be true in the case of components for systems and for items to be used in products produced in finished form by other companies.

After initially recognizing a need or desire for a new product, the creative individual enters the next step in the design procedure—the *research and exploration* phase. During this phase, the possible ways and the feasibility of fulfilling the need are investigated (Fig. 2.4). That is, the question is raised at this point as to whether the contemplated product can be marketed at a competitive price or at a price the public will be willing to pay. Except in the case of the public sector, where a system is being designed under the direction of a government unit (Fig. 2.5), profit is the name of the game. A search of literature and patent records will often show that there have been previous developments with the possibility of infringements on the design and patents of other companies. The discovery that others already may have legal protection for one or more of the possible solutions will tend to control the paths that innovative thinking may take in seeking an acceptable design solution. Although freewheeling innovative thinking is the basic element of successful design, the experienced engineer never fails to consider known restraints when he is brainstorming possible solutions. In addition to avoiding patent infringements, the designer must be fully aware of possible changes in desires and needs, and give full consideration to the production processes. Also not to be overlooked in the decision-making stage are the visual design (styling aspects) and the price range within which the product must be sold.

The ultimate success of a design is judged on the basis of its acceptability in the marketplace and on how well it satisfies the needs of a particular culture. In these latter decades of the twentieth century, we have added to these judgments a requirement that what has been created must not damage the physical environment around us, an environment that has been rapidly deteriorating because of some past technological advances. New requirements are being prepared and approved in rapid order that set standards to reduce if not eliminate pollution. These restrictions were almost unknown to the creative designers of the first half of this century. Today, it has become almost mandatory for a designer selecting a material or an energy source to ask if the material can be recycled and whether any residue discharged into the atmosphere is damaging to life.

2.4   Innovative Design—Individuals and Groups

In the past there have been several creative individuals, working almost alone, who have created products that have advanced our culture, products for which people still have a great desire. Examples of such products are the printing press, the steam engine, the gasoline engine, the automobile, the telephone, the phonograph, the motion picture camera and projector, the radio, the television, and many more. These individuals were keen observers of their culture, and they possessed inquisitive attitudes that led to experimentation. Some called them dreamers. If so, their eyes were wide open, they worked long hours, and they persisted in making a new try after each failure. Their fame and their fortune, although rightly due them, resulted from the fact that each brought forth a new product or system at a time when it would be readily accepted and when it could be more or less mass-produced. These people possessed a good sense of timing

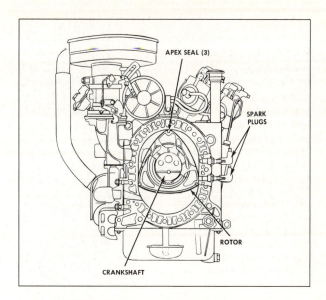

FIG. 2.6 Wankel (rotary) engine. Because of its different mechanical configuration, a variety of new and different mechanical problems have been encountered that have been subject to extensive research and development. (*Courtesy General Motors Corporation*)

FIG. 2.5 NEMO on the ocean floor. NEMO is a 168-cm-diameter sphere of acrylic plastic. The sphere is constructed from twelve identical curved pentagons. The capsule, with 63.5-mm walls, is bonded with acrylic adhesive. One of the first uses of NEMO will be as a diver control center at points of Seabee underwater construction sites. In operation, the manned observatory is lowered into the sea from a Navy support vessel, with the crewmen flooding the ballast tanks for the descent. NEMO operates independently, controlled by an array of pushbuttons (forty-one) linked to a solid-state circuitry control system. NEMO has been designed for a normal stay underwater of 8 h. Under emergency conditions it may remain submerged for as long as 24 h. (*Official Navy photograph. Courtesy The Military Engineer Magazine*)

conduct extensive searches of current literature and patent records, and to hold numerous discussions with knowledgeable experts in seeking the guidance needed for making necessary decisions.

The most widely used of the group-related procedures is known as *brainstorming*. In applying this procedure to seek the solution to a design problem, a group of optimal size meets in a room where they will be relatively free of interruptions and distractions. The people selected should be knowledgeable, and there should be no one assigned to the group who might take a strong negative attitude toward the design problem

and they were not afraid of failure or ridicule. They belonged to the age in which they lived.

At present, it is the practice of large industrial organizations to use group procedures to stimulate the imaginations of the individual members of the group and thereby benefit from their combined thinking about a specific problem (Fig. 2.6). Within the group, the innovative idea of one individual stimulates another individual to present an alternative suggestion. Each idea forms the basis for still other ideas until many have been listed that, it is hoped, will lead to a workable solution to the problem at hand. This group attack on a problem produces a long list of ideas that would be difficult for a single individual to assemble in so short a time (Fig. 2.7). A single person attempting to solve the problem alone would find it necessary to

FIG. 2.7 A Picturephone is shown in use. (*Courtesy American Telephone and Telegraph Company*)

to be considered. Usually, group size ranges from six to fifteen persons. If the group consists of fewer than six people, the back-and-forth interchange of ideas is reduced and the length of the list of ideas, which will be the basis for eventual decision making, is shorter. Conversely, should the group be larger than fifteen, some individuals who may be capable of making excellent suggestions will have little chance to talk. Also, very large groups tend to be dominated by a few individuals.

During the brainstorming phase of design, no appraisals or judgments should be made nor should criticisms or ridicule of any nature be permitted. The group leader, who should be a capable person, will encourage positive thinking and stimulating comments, and will discourage those who many want to dominate the discussion.

The ideas and suggestions of the members of the group should be listed on a chalkboard, and, no matter how long the list, none should be omitted. All ideas should be welcomed and recorded. After the meeting, all the ideas presented may be typed and reproduced for the information of the group and for reference at later discussions.

As the list of suggestions lengthens, several possible solution patterns usually emerge (Fig. 2.8). These in

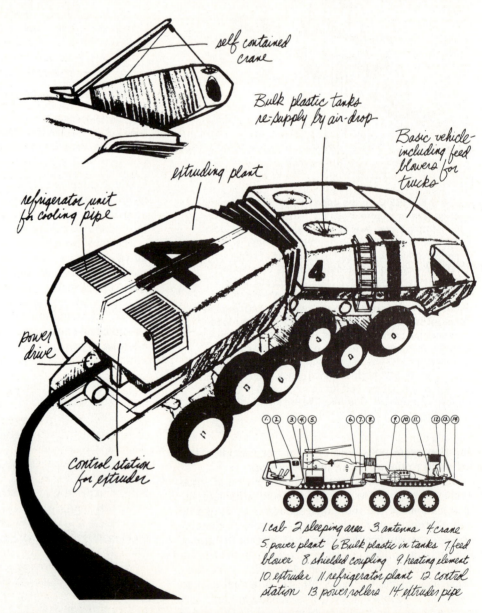

FIG. 2.8 Design of a self-contained pipe layer. It is intended to facilitate irrigation of large tracts of desert land. The equipment as designed is capable of transporting sufficient bulk plastic to lay approximately 2 miles of plastic pipe from each pair of storage tanks. Tanks are to be discarded when empty and replaced by air drop. (*Courtesy Donald Desky Associates, Inc., and Charles Bruning Company*)

turn lead to still more suggestions for other possible combinations and for improvements to likely solutions to the design problem.

One or two lengthy brainstorming sessions can result in several acceptable design solutions that represent the combined suggestions of the individuals in the group. Making a group evaluation of the ideas that have evolved from brainstorming is another matter, however, because no one member feels completely responsible for the results. The major weakness of any group procedure, such as brainstorming, is that individual motivation is dampened to some extent. Because group procedures are productive and have become widely used in industry, however, there have been studies made that will, it is hoped, lead to changes that will minimize this recognized weakness and improve group effectiveness. Means must be found to raise the motivation of each participant to the highest possible level.

2.5 Creation of New Products

A product or a system may be said to have been produced either through evolutionary change or by what appears to be pure innovation. The word *appears* has been used appropriately, because few, if any, products are ever entirely new in every respect. Most products that appear to have drawn heavily on innovation usually combine both old and new ideas in a new and more workable arrangement. A product of evolutionary change, however, develops rather slowly, during a long period, and with slight improvements being made only now and then. Such a product may be reliable and virtually free of design and production errors, but the small amount of design work involved, done at infrequent intervals, will never really challenge a creative person.

In today's competitive world, when products are produced for worldwide consumption, evolutionary change is hardly sufficient to ensure either the economic well-being or even the survival of those companies that seem to be willing to let well enough alone. Rapid technological changes coupled with new scientific discoveries have increased the emphasis on the importance of new and marketable products that can gain a greater share of the total market than is possible with the product the company may now be promoting. In meeting this need for new and marketable ideals, the designer will find that one's innovative ability and one's experience and knowledge are being taxed to the limit and, because one may in a sense be stepping into the unknown, some risks must be taken.

The unusual characteristics that seem to be a part of the general makeup of every outstanding designer are the following:

1. Ability to recognize a problem

2. Ability to take a questioning approach toward all possible solutions

3. Possession of an active curiosity about a problem at hand

4. Innate willingness to take responsibility for what one has done or may do

5. Ability to make needed decisions and to defend those decisions in writing and orally

6. Possession of intellectual integrity.

William Lear, one of the most prominent designers of the last three decades, spent his entire working life discovering needs and then finding ways to fulfill them. In the case of the development of the eight-track stereo tape, he was working from economic considerations that required more repertoire on tape without adding more tape. This meant either running the tape slower or adding more tracks. The practical answer from Lear's viewpoint was to add more tracks. In addition to the Learoscope, an automatic direction-finder for use on airplanes, Lear is responsible for the development of the car radio, the automatic pilot, the Lear jet plane, and more than 150 other inventions. A few years ago, he began development work on the problem of steam-powered automobile engines. Lear's inventing was done when surrounded by many people with considerable knowhow. His work involved the gathering of a maze of information and ideas from which he could pick out the salient facts and discard the unimportant ones, while always keeping the goal in mind and solving the problem at the least possible cost.

2.6 Background for Innovative Designing

Designing should be done by people who have a diversified background and who are not entirely unfamiliar with the problem at hand. As an example, even though the design of a product may be thought of as being in the field of mechanical engineering, a designer with a knowledge of electrical applications and controls will find it a distinct advantage since many of our present-day products use electric current as an energy source. When a design group is involved, it is important that the mechanical engineer and others should have at least some understanding of the electrical engineer's suggestions. This added knowledge will enable them to modify their thinking about a product that is largely a mechanical device. Examples of these products include electric locks, electric food choppers, and electric typewriters.

The background required will vary considerably depending on the field in which the individual works. For example, a person who may be designing small household appliances would probably never need more than the knowledge acquired from his basic engineering courses, whereas a designer in the aerospace field would need a background based on advanced study in chemistry, physics, and mathematics. Conversely, there are respected and competent designers in industry who have had as little as two years of technical education. With this limited training and several years of on-the-job experience, these men and women have become able to design complex solutions.

Because of the increasing complexity of engineering, the rapid development of new materials, and the accumulation of new knowledge at an almost unbelievable rate, it has become absolutely necessary for engineering design to become a team effort in some fields. Under such conditions, the design effort becomes the responsibility of highly qualified specialists. A project requiring designers of varied specialized backgrounds might need, for example, people with experience in mechanical, electrical, and structural design and persons with considerable knowledge of materials and chemical processes (Fig. 2.6). If it is decided that styling is important, then one or more stylists must be added to the team. A complete design group for a major project could include pure scientists, metallurgists, technicians, technologists, and stylists in addition to the designers.

Finally, graphics must not be overlooked when one considers the background needed to become a successful designer. Anyone who hopes to enter the field of design, other than as a specialist, must have a thorough training in this area. A working knowledge of all of the forms of graphical expression that are presented in this text is required along with the ability to explain the design orally and in writing in preliminary and final reports. The methods used for the preparation or oral and written reports are discussed in Sec. 2.24.

2.7 History and Background of Human Engineering

Human engineering is a relatively new area in the field of design. To simplify matters we might define human engineering as adapting design to the needs of humans; that is, we engineer our designs to suit human behavior, human motor activities, and human physical and mental characteristics. The applications of human engineering apply not only to machine systems and consumer products but to work methods and to work environments as well. In the early years of its development, human engineering was concerned mainly with the working environment and with the comfort and general welfare of all human beings. As time passed, designers came to realize that more than just safety and comfort should be considered, and that almost all the designs with which they were concerned were in some way related to the general physical characteristics, behavior, and attitudes of people. At this point, designers began to include these added human factors in their approach to the solution of a design problem so as to secure the most satisfying and efficient relationship to machines.

It is in the area of human engineering that an engineering designer must adhere to the input of specialists who may be involved in a wide range of disciplines. These disciplines may be industrial engineering, industrial psychology, medicine, physiology, climatology, and statistics. Stimulated to a great extent by the space program, scientists from all of these disciplines have, together and separately, become deeply involved in basic research and laboratory experimentation, which has led to a continuous input of new human-machine information into design. Although in the past human engineering has been associated mainly with industrial engineering, industrial psychology, and industrial design, designers in all fields of engineering must now not only be knowledgeable about the principles of human engineering but they must be capable of using these principles and related information whenever they are developing a product that involves human relationships.

Typical body dimensions, representing an average-size person, are used when a product is being designed for general use. The measurements of typical adult males and females, as determined from studies made by Henry Dryfuss, may be used for most designs requiring close adaptation to human physical characteristics. Because many designs involve both foot and hand movements these average body dimensions, as tabulated, include arms, hands, legs, and feet along with other parts of the human body. Data relating to body proportions and dimensions are known as anthropometric data. Information relating to body proportions may be obtained from *The Measure of Man,* Whitney Library of Design.

The first known serious studies of the human body were made by Leonardo da Vinci. To record his studies for his own use and for the use of others, he made some of the finest and most accurate detail sketches and drawings of the human body. These drawings show even the intricate details of muscle formation. His work, done in defiance of the laws of his time, is still used today in several textbooks. Da Vinci's studies of the human body mark the beginning of the science of biomechanics (Fig. 2.9).

From the time of Leonardo da Vinci until early in the twentieth century, very little work was done toward the development of this science. This lack of interest in people and their relationship with equipment and tasks to be performed was due largely to the fact that from the beginning of the Industrial Revolution (which many people say began with invention of the steam engine patented by James Watt in 1769) until the early 1900s, the interest of designers was centered mainly on the creation of new products and the raising of production efficiency to the high levels needed to compete in world markets. Until about 1900, revolutionary change was the order of the day and there was very little time available for consideration of the human anatomical, physiological, behavior, and attitude factors that have now become the basis of our present human-machine–task systems. Even though our computer-programmed numerically controlled machine tools permit us to do almost any task with only mini-

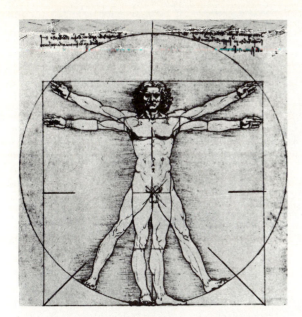

FIG. 2.9 Human proportions and body dimensions as illustrated by Leonardo da Vinci (1452–1519).

mal human intervention, people are still needed in most of our human-machine–task systems and they must be taken largely as they are. In our designs we must not overlook even the possibility of boredom, for a person who becomes sufficiently bored might just "pull the plug," and everything would stop.

2.8 Human Engineering in Design

There are several factors in human engineering, other than human anthropometric measurements, that must be dealt with in design. These factors include motor activities (Fig. 2.10) and body orientation; the five human senses (sight, hearing, touch, smell, and sometimes even taste); atmospheric environment, temperature, humidity, and light; and, finally, accelerative forces if they are exceptional and are likely to cause undue physical discomfort.

During the first half of this century most of the research done in human engineering, aside from the anthropometric studies already mentioned, was directed toward: work areas and the position of controls; physical effort and fatigue; and the speed and accuracy to be expected in the performance of particular tasks. Finally, when it became evident that this was not enough, industrial engineers and industrial psychologists turned their attention to the more complex activities of the average human being. These new studies dealt primarily with receiving information through sight and sound, the making of decisions in response to stimuli, and, finally, the performance in direct response to these decisions.

The study of body motion deals primarily with the

effective range of operation of parts of the body, usually the arms and legs, and the amount of body force a human being may reasonably be expected to exert in the performance of an assigned task. For example, many time and motion studies have been made of the range of operation of persons performing given tasks while seated at assigned work areas. At the same time, in many of these studies attention has been given to the location and the amount of force required to operate levers and controls in relation to the size and strength of the operator.

Vision is an important factor in all designs where visual gauges or colored lights on control panels are a part of a control system that involves manual operation or, in the case of numerically controlled machines, monitoring for manual intervention at specified times. Control panels for such equipment must be designed to be within the visual range of the average person, and distinctive colors must be selected and used for the colored lights. The colors selected must be easily recognizable and must be capable of quickly attracting the operator's attention. Not to be overlooked is the fact that vision studies have produced much new information for use in highway design. From these same studies have come new ideas for our highway warning and information signs along with suggestions for their placement.

When a designer must consider the working environment as a part of the total design, that environment includes

1. Temperature
2. Humidity
3. Lighting
4. Color schemes
5. Sound.

These are a few of the factors that also deserve full consideration in the design of a large industrial plant, a particular work area in a plant, the cockpit of an airplane, or the cabin of a space vehicle.

The overall environment and the design of the working areas and the living quarters of the undersea laboratory shown in Fig. 2.11 were based on human requirements. The design of any undersea craft or laboratory involves problems that are similar in many ways to those encountered in the design of space vehicles, in that an artificial living environment must be created and maintained for extended periods of time. This requires a self-contained atmosphere. The members of the crew also must have ample space in which to work and live under climatic conditions that duplicate those on land. Crew members must be able to perform their tasks under normal lighting conditions, and they must be able to see to the outside. Aside from the design of features and components that are related directly to the performance of the research assignments, the overall development of the undersea craft can be said to be based on the physical needs and the psychological attitudes and reactions of human beings.

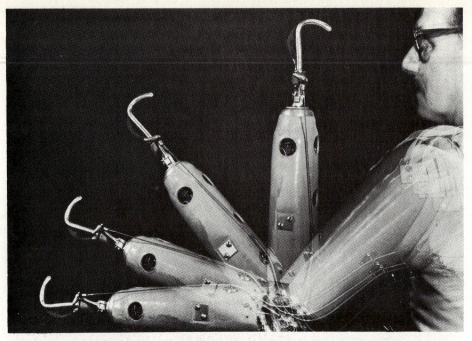

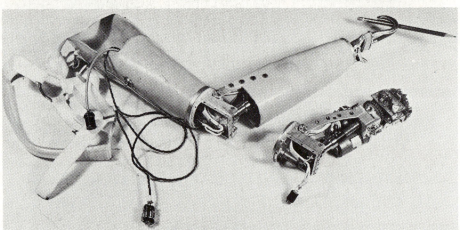

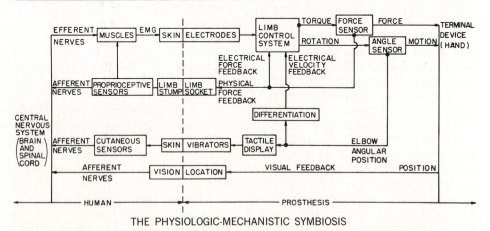

THE PHYSIOLOGIC-MECHANISTIC SYMBIOSIS

FIG. 2.10 Boston Arm. The range of movement of the Boston Arm is demonstrated in the upper photograph. The arm, developed as a joint project of Liberty Mutual Insurance Companies, Harvard Medical School, Massachusetts General Hospital, and the Massachusetts Institute of Technology, acts as does a normal arm through thought impulses transmitted from the brain to existing arm muscles. The design of a product for the handicapped can provide much satisfaction to the designer. (*Courtesy Liberty Mutual Insurance Companies*)

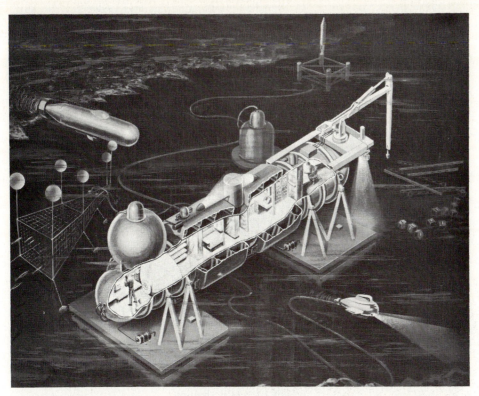

FIG. 2.11 Artist's conception of Atlantis undersea habitat. The project was to be designed and developed as a joint project of the University of Miami and the Space Division of Chrysler Corporation. The project goal was to explore the continental shelf along our coasts. (*Courtesy Space Division, Chrysler Corporation*)

Human engineering is applied to a wide range of consumer items. Automobiles (Fig. 2.12), refrigerators, furniture, office equipment, lawn mowers, hand tools, and like items have long been designed with human factors in mind.

The automotive industry, as it designs and redesigns cars with human factors in mind, is producing cars in accordance with stricter government safety regulations.

AIR-BAG/SEAT-BELT RESTRAINT SYSTEM
WITH STARTER INTERLOCK

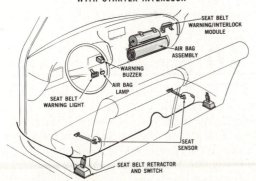

FIG. 2.12 Major elements of an air-bag–seat-belt restraint system by the Ford Motor Company. The air-bag assembly and the seat-belt starter-interlock components are identified. (*Courtesy Ford Motor Company*)

Under pressure from consumer groups and organizations interested in safety and in protecting our natural environment, there has been an increase in governmental laws and regulations. Many of these laws and directives provide controls in the field of human engineering. In the case of environmental pollution, automobile companies, acting to meet regulations set forth by the Environmental Protection Agency, developed several devices to reduce undesirable pollutants at a scheduled percentage rate to produce an almost pollution-free car. In the interest of safety, some type of passive protection system, such as the air-bag device shown in Fig. 2.12, will probably be added.

These government laws and regulations have come into existence because of a growing interest on the part of the general public in human engineering. Designers in the years ahead must be fully cognizant of all such regulations and must be willing to abide by them or seek to have them changed should they appear to be unreasonable or impractical.

2.9 *Visual Design*

Visual design includes the use of line, form, proportion, texture, and color to produce the eye-pleasing appearance needed to bring about the acceptance of a consumer item. Without this acceptance there would

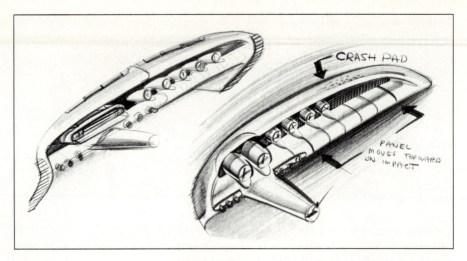

FIG. 2.13 Design sketches for dashboard panel. (*Courtesy General Motors Corporation*)

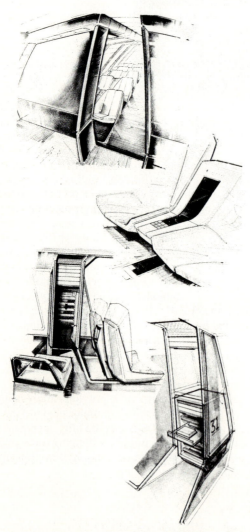

FIG. 2.14 Styling design sketches prepared for the ill-fated U.S. supersonic transport. These studies project the visual appeal of proposed interior design details. (*Courtesy the Boeing Company*)

be no profit, and even though the item might otherwise have been carefully engineered, it would soon disappear from the marketplace. The sketches shown in Fig. 2.13, for the dash panel of an automobile, tastefully combine these visual elements into an attractive design. An illusion of depth has been obtained by means of pencil shading.

Because styling is now recognized as being one of the most important factors in sales, many engineers have come to accept the role of industrial designers in the development of a consumer product, particularly when they are employed by a company that is small and cannot afford to employ one or more trained stylists. Large companies, such as the Ford Motor Company, General Motors, and the Boeing Company (Fig. 2.14), having styling divisions. Medium-size companies often turn to nationally known organizations to get needed help; the industrial design is then done under contract agreement. Many books have been written about aesthetics that have proved to be helpful to engineers. At present, design engineers, who have been trained largely to solve technical problems, are reading more about styling, and they are considering the eye appeal and the overall appearance of products as part of their engineering interests.

2.10 *Constructive Criticism*

There are people who seem to find it easier to criticize than to mix praise with alternative suggestions. In any group meeting a critic should show respect for good ideas and be able to offer constructive suggestions. If there is to be feedback, which it is hoped will lead to the introduction of more ideas, the discussion must be free of any harsh criticism. Harsh criticism may cause a sensitive person to assume a defensive position or to withdraw almost entirely from participation in group action. It is the responsibility of the project leader to prevent this from happening.

2.11 Recognition of Need

A design project usually begins with the recognition of a need and with the willingness of a company to enter the market with a new product. At other times an idea may be initiated and developed by an individual who either seeks personal economic benefits or who seeks to solve some social or environmental problem. In either case, the identification of the need in itself represents a high order of creative thinking, and the search for a solution to the need requires considerable self-confidence and inner courage. As can be easily observed from reviewing the achievements of our distinguished inventors of the past, those who are closely attuned to life around them become aware of needs or less-than-ideal situations that are worthy of their attention.

It is important that a proposed design project have clear and definite objectives that will justify the money and effort to be expended in product design and development. The statement defining the objectives should identify the need and state the function the product is to perform in satisfying this need. The identification of the need may be based on the designer's personal observations, suggestions from sales people in the field, opinion surveys, or on new scientific concepts. The identification of the design problems involved in creating the needed product comes later in the design process.

2.12 Formal Proposal

The statement covering the recognition of need can be used as a basis for a formal proposal that may be either a few short paragraphs or several typewritten pages. A complete proposal may include supporting data in addition to the description of the plan of action that is to be taken to solve the problem as identified (Fig. 2.15). The report should have the same general form as other technical reports and might include a listing of requirements and possible limitations as then recognized. In preparing the report one should keep in mind that the proposal, when approved, gives the broad general parameters of an agreement under which the project will be developed to its conclusion.

2.13 Phases of Design Process

Many people in the past have prepared outlines of the steps that can be followed in the process of design (Fig. 2.16). They have prepared these outlines to give some semblance of order to the total design process from the point of recognition of the need to the point of marketing the product. One must recognize, however, that there are actually many combinations of steps in the overall procedure, with no single pattern either the best or the only combination. The design procedure

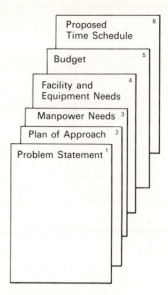

FIG. 2.15 Elements of proposal.

required in many cases can be very complex, and successful designers have found different ways to achieve their goals. The phases of design, as recognized by these authors, have been listed here in sequential order to provide some degree of direction to students who are making their first attempt to design a product under a contrived classroom situation, however. More experienced persons may find it desirable to alter this outline to make it more suitable to their own method of designing.

The basic phases in the design process are

1. Identification of need
2. Task definition (goal)
3. Task specifications
4. Ideation
5. Conceptualization
6. Analysis
7. Experimental testing (Fig. 2.23)
8. Design (solution) description
9. Design for production.

Phase 9 (implementation) is not usually a primary concern of a designer. Also, the designer may or may not give some thought to manufacture, distribution, and consumption of the product. Consideration of these factors may be thought of as being the tenth, eleventh, and twelfth stages of total design.

2.14 Task Definition— Definition of Goals

Briefly stated, *task definition* is the expression of a commitment to produce either a product or a system that will satisfy the need as identified. By means of

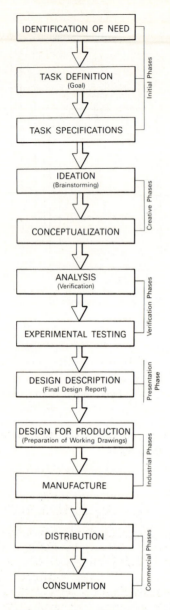

FIG. 2.16   Basic phases of total design.

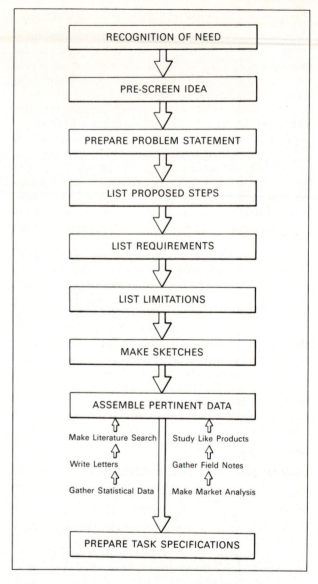

FIG. 2.17   Initial steps of design process.

broad statements, the product and the goals of the product are identified. The statements, as written, must be clear and concise to avoid at least some of the difficulties (often encountered in design) that can be traced directly back to poorly defined goals.

Even though it is probable that the person who has initiated the project has already gathered some pertinent information and has some preconceived ideas, it is desirable that this material not be included (Fig. 2.17). It is better to present the goals in terms of objectives and then allow the designers to pursue the project in their own way, as free of restrictions as possible. The task definition should be included in the proposal.

2.15 *Task Specifications*

This is a listing of parameters and data that will serve to control the design. This stage will ordinarily be preceded by some preliminary research to collect information related to the goal as defined. In preparing the task specifications, the designer or design group lists all the pertinent data that can be gathered from research reports, trade journals, patent records, catalogs, and other sources that possess information relating to the project at hand. Included in this listing should be the parameters that will tend to control the design. Other factors that deserve consideration, such as materials to be used, maintenance, and cost may also be noted.

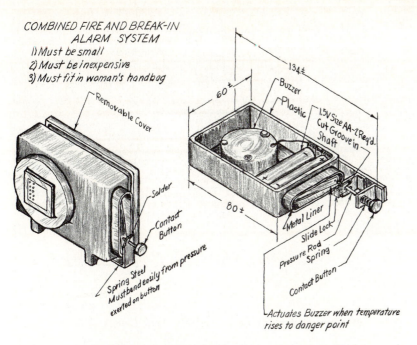

COMBINED FIRE AND BREAK-IN
ALARM SYSTEM
1) Must be small
2) Must be inexpensive
3) Must fit in woman's handbag

FIG. 2.18 **Idea sketches for small portable safety alarm that will give warning for both fire and attempted break-in.** (Dimension values are in millimeters.)

2.16 *Ideation*

The ideation phase of design has been discussed for group procedure situations in Sec. 2.4. It is recommended that readers review this discussion to refresh their memory regarding brainstorming procedures. It is important to remember that often a lasting solution to a problem has resulted from a creative idea selected from several alternative ones (Fig. 2.18). The likelihood of finding an optimum solution is greatly enhanced as the list of possible alternatives grows longer. Truly great creations are possible when someone's imagination is allowed to soar with little restraint, either when working alone or with a group. If engineers on a design project can set aside their engineering know-how and blind themselves, at least temporarily, they will be in the right frames of mind to meet almost any challenge. This is the mood and the mental approach for great discoveries. Some call it ideation; others have called it *imagineering*. If we can learn to open up our engineering minds to new approaches to our technical problems as well as to our existing problems of air pollution, industrial waste, transportation, and even unemployment, there is no limit to what we can accomplish.

This open-minded *imagineering* approach to problems must be tempered with a sense of professional responsibility. It is no longer acceptable to solve an immediate problem using a solution that in years to come can endanger the environment. Imagineering is engineering for the total well-being of humankind and all other living things.

2.17 *Conceptualization*

Conceptualization follows the preliminary idea (ideation) stage when all the rough sketches (Figs. 2.19–2.21) and notes have been assembled and reviewed to determine the one or more apparent solutions that seem to be worthy of further consideration. In evaluating alternative solutions, consideration must be given to any restrictions that have been placed on the final design. It is at this stage that the preliminary sketches should be restudied to see that all worthwhile ideas are being included and that none has been inadvertently overlooked. At no time during theis phase should designers become so set in their thinking that they do not feel free to develop still another and almost entirely new and different concept, if necessary. They should realize that it is more sensible to alter or even abandon a concept at this stage than later, when considerable money and time will have been invested in the project. *The conceptualization stage of design is that stage where alternative solutions are developed and evaluated in the form of concepts.* Considerable research may be necessary, and task specifications must be continually reviewed. As activity progresses, many idea sketches are made as alternative approaches are worked out; these approaches are evaluated for the

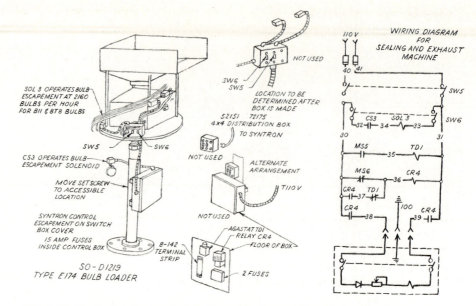

FIG. 2.19 Portion of design sketch. (*Courtesy General Electric Company***)**

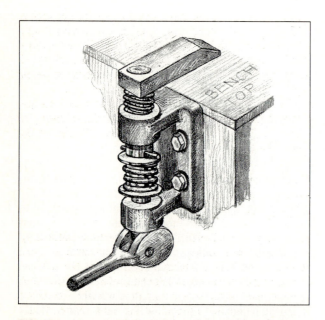

FIG. 2.20 Idea sketch for quick-acting machine clamp.

FIG. 2.21 Idea sketch showing remote control system for motor boat.

best possible chance of product success. It is not necessary at this stage of the design procedure for any of the alternative solutions to be worked out in any great detail.

2.18 Selection of Optimum Concept

As the design of a product or system progresses, a point is reached in the procedure when it becomes necessary to select the best design concept to be presented to the administrators in the form of a proposal. In making this final selection, a more-or-less complete design evaluation is made for each of the alternative concepts under consideration. These evaluations may reveal ways that costs can be reduced and value improved; means of simplifying the design to reduce costs may also become apparent.

2.19 Design Analysis

After a design concept has been chosen as the best possible solution to the problem at hand, it must be subjected to a design analysis; that is, it must be tested against physical laws and evaluated in terms of certain design factors that are almost certain to be present (Fig. 2.22).

Total analysis of a proposed design will include a review of the engineering principles involved and a study of the materials to be used. In addition, there should also be an evaluation of such design considerations as

1. Environmental conditions under which the device will operate

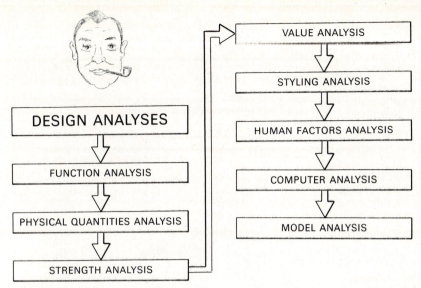

FIG. 2.22 Analysis phase of design.

2. Human factors

3. Possible production methods and production problems

4. Assembly methods

5. Maintenance requirements

6. Cost

7. Styling and market appeal

If the design is based on newly discovered scientific principles, some research may be in order before a final decision can be reached.

It is at this stage in the design procedure that physics, chemistry, and the engineering sciences are employed most fully. In making the usual design analysis, the engineers or engineering technologists must depend on the formal training that they received in school, and although considerable mathematics may be needed in making most of the necessary calculations, they will find it convenient at times to resort to graphical methods. Over the years, graphical methods have proved to be most helpful in evaluating and developing a design. For example, descriptive geometry methods can be employed for making spatial analyses, and critical information can be obtained by scaling accurate drawings.

If design analysis proves that the design as proposed is inadequate and does not meet requirements, the designer may either make certain modifications or incorporate into the designs some new concept that might well be a modification of an earlier idea that was abandoned along the way.

2.20 *Experimental Testing*

The experimental testing phase of the design process ranges from the testing of a single piece of software or hardware to verify its workability, durability, and op-

erational characteristics through the construction and testing of a full-size prototype of the complete physical system.

A component of a product should be tested in such a way that the designer can predict its durability and performance under the conditions that will be encountered in its actual use. Needed tests may be performed using standard test apparatus or with special devices that have been produced for a particular test.

There are three types of models that may be constructed for the purpose of testing and evaluating a product. These are (1) the mockup, (2) the scale model, and (3) the prototype.

2.21 *Mockups*

A mockup is a full-sized model constructed primarily to show the size, shape, component relationships, and styling of the finished design. At this point the designer's conception begins to take shape for the first time. Automobile manufacturers customarily produce mockups to evaluate proposed changes in the styling of automobile bodies for new models. Needed modifications in size and body configuration can be determined by studying the mockup and analyzing its overall appearance. Because interior styling is important also, interiors are modeled in clay to reveal the aesthetic appearance the stylist had in mind. In the automobile industry, mockups are made to secure early approval of management for model change. A mockup is more meaningful than a sketch to those whose support and approval is needed. One must realize, however, that numerous sketches and artistic renderings (Fig. 2.14) are made before any work is started on a mockup. These sketches are used as guides. Mockups may be made of clay, wood, plastic, and so forth.

2.22 Preliminary and Scale Models

Models may be made at almost any stage in the design process to assist the designer in evaluating and analyzing the design. Models are made to strengthen three-dimensional visualization, to check the motion and clearance of parts, and to make necessary tests to clear up questions that have arisen in the designer's own mind or in the mind of a colleague.

The designer may prepare a preliminary model to understand more fully what the shape of a component should be, how well it may be expected to operate, and how it might be fabricated most economically. In some cases, the model might be so simple that it could be made of paper, wood, or clay.

Scale and test models may be constructed either for analysis and evaluation, or for the purpose of presenting the design in a more or less refined stage for approval. Scale models may be made of balsa wood, plastic, aluminum, wire, steel, or any other material that can be used to a good advantage. The designer should select a scale that will make the model large enough to permit the movement of parts should the demonstration of movement be desirable.

2.23 Prototypes

A prototype is the most expensive form of model that can be constructed for experimental purposes. Yet, because it will yield valuable information that is difficult to obtain in any other way, its cost is usually justified. A prototype is a full-size working model of a physical system built in accordance with final specifications, and it represents the final step of the experimental stage (Fig. 2.23). In it the designers and stylists see their ideas come to life. From a prototype the designers can gain information needed for mass-production procedures that are to come later. Much can be learned at this point about workability, durability, production techniques, assembly procedures, and, most important of all, performance under actual operating conditions. Because prototype testing offers the last chance for modification of the design, possible changes to improve the design should not be overlooked, nor should a designer ever be reluctant to make a desirable change.

Because a prototype is a one-of-a-kind working model, it is made by hand using general-purpose machine tools. Although it might be best to use the same materials that will be used for the mass-produced product, this is not always done. Materials that are easier to fabricate by hand are often substituted for hard-to-work materials.

In the development of a design, designers deal first with the mockup; next they work out specific problems relating to single features with preliminary models; then they evaluate the design with scale

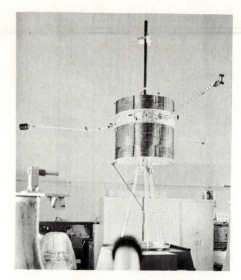

FIG. 2.23 Full-size prototype of Pioneer Satellite A-B-C-D series. A prototype provides the best means for an evaluation of a complex design. (*Courtesy Systems Group, TRW, Inc.*)

models; and, finally, they may, if desirable, test the whole concept using a prototype. This order in the use of models maintains a desirable relationship between concept and analysis, and represents a logical procedure for the total design process.

2.24 Design (Solution) Description—Final Report

In the solution description the designers describe their designs on paper to communicate their thinking to others. Although the purpose of the final report may be to sell the idea to upper management, it may also be used to instruct the production division on how to construct the product. It usually will contain specific information relating to the product or system. In some cases a process will be described in considerable detail.

A complete design description (Fig. 2.24), prepared as the main part of a formal report, should include

1. Detailed description of device or system
2. Statement of how device or system satisfies need
3. Explanation of how device operates
4. Full set of layout drawings, sketches, and graphs
5. Pictorial renderings, if needed
6. List of parts
7. Breakdown of costs
8. Special instructions to ensure that intent of designer is followed in production stage.

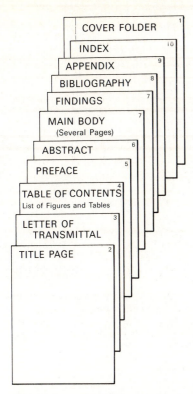

FIG. 2.24 Contents of design (final) report.

After the design description is accepted and approved, there remain only the commercial stages of the total design process, namely, implementation, manufacture, distribution (sales), and consumption.

2.25 Implementation—Design for Production

Implementation is that phase of the total design process when working drawings are prepared for those who must fabricate the nonstandard parts and assemble the product. A complete set of working drawings, both detail and assembly, are needed to permit the manufacture of a product.

Even though in theory the production design phase directly follows the preliminary design phase and the acceptance of the design recommended in the final report, in actual practice there is often no clear dividing line between these two phases. This is because detailed drawings of some components may have been started and to some extent completed back in the preliminary design stage, along with one or more design layout assemblies (see Fig. 2.25). Furthermore, it is not unusual for detail design drawings to be made for two or more likely solutions in the design-for-production stage, and the final selection of the one best solution delayed until the information derived from these detail design drawings and related assemblies can be used in making the final decision. Such a delay in deci-

sion making tends to cause the preliminary design and the production design phases to appear to melt into one another. There is still a division line, however, even though the designers themselves may not recognize this fact.

2.26 Manufacture

From the time the task specifications are written and through all the stages up to the manufacture (Fig. 2.26), the designer works closely with a production engineer who is familiar with the available shop facilities, production methods, inspection procedures, quality control, and the assembly line. If this is done, the problems encountered in the manufacturing stage will be few in number.

2.27 Distribution

Because a designer usually has little expertise in the area, task problems relating to distribution are passed along to *marketing specialists*. These specialists have the knowledge and the supporting staff required to decide on the proper release date and to set a competitive price based on market testing, and cost and profit studies. Included among these specialists will be experienced advertising personnel who prepare the needed advertising and promotional literature. These specialists, however, do consult the designer frequently during this stage because no one else knows more about the product. The designer is the one person who can be depended on to supply needed technical data and information concerning the capabilities and limitations of the product. Furthermore, the sales promotion people expect ideas from the designer that will lead to a wide and favorable distribution.

2.28 Consumption

There should, it is hoped, be *consumer feedback* from this last stage of the design process that will prove useful to the designer when it becomes necessary to alter and improve the product at the time of the next model change. Most of this feedback information will come from the sales force, from distributors, and from service departments. Some of this information will be in the form of complaints made by irate users, but much of it will be received as constructive suggestions. These constructive suggestions take the designer back to the need stage for the next model, and a new design cycle starts.

The consumption stage represents the goal sought by the designer, and this is where the design has its ultimate test. At this stage the design will be pronounced a success or a failure by the users and consumers who are and always will be the final judges.

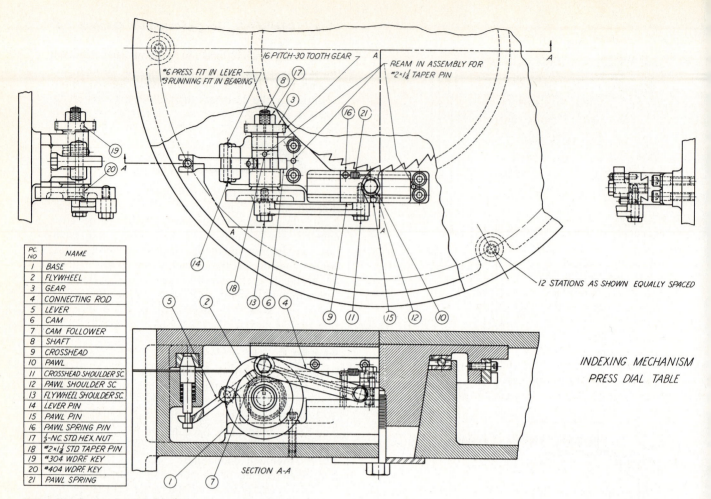

PC. NO	NAME
1	BASE
2	FLYWHEEL
3	GEAR
4	CONNECTING ROD
5	LEVER
6	CAM
7	CAM FOLLOWER
8	SHAFT
9	CROSSHEAD
10	PAWL
11	CROSSHEAD SHOULDER SC.
12	PAWL SHOULDER SC.
13	FLYWHEEL SHOULDER SC.
14	LEVER PIN
15	PAWL PIN
16	PAWL SPRING PIN
17	½-NC. STD. HEX. NUT
18	#2×1¼ STD. TAPER PIN
19	#304 WDRF. KEY
20	#404 WDRF. KEY
21	PAWL SPRING

16 PITCH-30 TOOTH GEAR

REAM IN ASSEMBLY FOR #2×1¼ TAPER PIN

#6 PRESS FIT IN LEVER
#3 RUNNING FIT IN BEARING

12 STATIONS AS SHOWN EQUALLY SPACED

SECTION A-A

INDEXING MECHANISM
PRESS DIAL TABLE

FIG. 2.25 Design layout drawing.

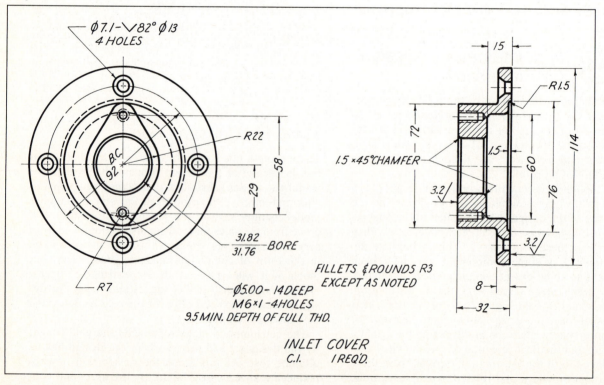

Ø7.1-⌵82° Ø13
4 HOLES

R22

B.C.
92

R1.5

1.5 ×45°CHAMFER

31.82 / 31.76 BORE

R7

Ø5.00-14DEEP
M6×1-4HOLES
9.5 MIN. DEPTH OF FULL THD.

FILLETS & ROUNDS R3
EXCEPT AS NOTED

58

29

15

72

1.5

3.2

60

76

114

8

32

3.2

INLET COVER
C.I.   1 REQ'D.

FIG. 2.26 Detail drawing.

B IMPLICATIONS OF COMPUTER IN DESIGN AND PRODUCTION PROCESSES

2.29 CAD/CAM

The progressive steps of CAD/CAM fit well into the general areas of design: design drafting, production planning, and fabrication (machining) (Fig. 2.27). In following the steps and activities, we find that CAD/CAM tends to integrate subsystems and erase the distinction that has existed in the past between engineering and the production department. With CAD/CAM, marketing may be closely linked to design and production through the sharing of a common data base. The ultimate goal of CAD/CAM is complete integration of the design and manufacturing processes such that an entire firm acts and reacts as a single entity controlled by a network of computers.

2.30 The Computer and the Design Process

In CAD, the engineer and the computer work together to form a problem-solving team. The combination of human being and machine produces better results in much less time than if a person performed alone. The human being and the electronic machine complement one another, with each having characteristics superior to the other. In comparing the capabilities of people and computers, it will be found that people can think and make decisions using intuitive and analytical thought. The computer has speed, works accurately, and has almost unlimited storage and rapid-recall capabilities.

As a part of the CAD team, the functions of the computer are to provide an extension of the designer's memory, enhance the analytical powers of the designer, and perform the repetitious tasks of design to free its human partner for other work. With the computer performing its functions, the designer will be left free to control the design process; apply powers of intuition, creativity, imagination and judgment to the development of the design; and, finally, apply experience to the analysis of significant information.

2.31 CAD

Computers are used by architects, design and production engineers, and drafting technicians in nearly all of the basic phases of total design from the identification of need through the production stages (Fig. 2.28). A CAD system provides the designer with a calculator of exceptional capabilities, a storage bank for design data, and a drafting aid for the development of a final design from the designer's (or designers') preliminary rough sketches. Furthermore, because a considerable portion of design work involves changes to an existing design, a designer can recall and reuse data from the earlier design, modifying it as needed and adding any new parts as may be required. The computer's memory capabilities may be relied on in the first stages of design when a data bank is needed for the collection and storage of raw data for quick recall. Graphical data together with alphanumeric data can provide a data bank from which information can be quickly retrieved by the designer. The computer's use continues through the ideation and conceptualization stages. Concepts and brainstorming ideas are recorded to be recalled at a later time to stimulate new ideas or for reevaluation of past thoughts. With a graphics display

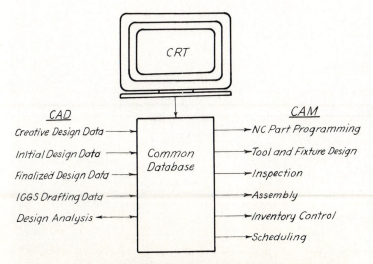

FIG. 2.27   CAD/CAM flowchart—from design through production.

FIG. 2.28 Designer at workstation of CADD system. (*Courtesy ComputerVision Corporation*)

in use, large amounts of information can be presented quickly for review in decision making (Fig. 2.29). The computer is needed early in the design process for making calculations relating to the design specifications and again at the point of selecting the optimum concept that will give maximum performance at minimum cost.

It is in the final experimental phases, where the workability, durability, and operational characteristics are tested with expensive scale models and working prototypes that the computer proves its worth in the design process by eliminating the need for expensive physical models and testing facilities. This has all been made possible by CAD/CAM computer programs that

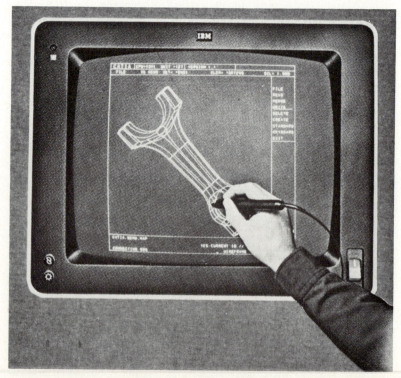

FIG. 2.29 Design displayed on CRT screen. (*Courtesy IBM Corporation*)

simulate these models under operating conditions. Programs are available or may be prepared that simulate the effects of structural, thermal, and kinematic conditions. When necessary a designer can evaluate the electrical properties of a circuit quickly and easily.

Through simulation a new design may be displayed on a CRT screen to be evaluated under operating conditions. The model, as displayed, under program control, is continually updated to simulate dynamic motion under load conditions. Different designs can be tested without the expense of constructing models.

2.32 *Computer-aided Drafting*

In a plant where numerically controlled machines are widely employed, it is possible to fabricate parts without any hard-copy drawings being made for the shop. This direct pass through arrangement from design to fabrication without shop drawings is true CAD/CAM, the ultimate goal of high-technology industry. Many companies, however, still hold to their old practice of using hard-copy drawings in the production shops (Fig. 2.30). This may be due either to the nature of their products or to the fact that they have too few NC machines. In any case, drawings for fabrication no longer need be made at the drafting board using drafting instruments to convert the engineer's preliminary sketches into useful plans. Now, a computer-aided drafting system can be called on to take over this tedious and time-consuming hand-drawing work. The drawing shown in Fig. 2.30 was prepared at the Ross Gear Division of TRW, Inc., using an IBM Graphics System.

Finally, as has already been pointed out, much drafting work involves only the modification of an existing design. Should this be the case and graphical data for the original design have been stored in the computer, the design can be modified as required, parts can be added, and new drawings produced using computer-aided drafting. CAD and computer-aided drafting systems have found wide acceptance for this purpose, and the future appears bright.

C PATENTS AND DESIGN RECORDS

2.33 *Patent*

A patent, when granted to an inventor, excludes others from manufacturing, using, or selling the device or system covered by the patent anywhere in the country for a period of seventeen years. In the patent document, in which the invention is fully described, the rights and privileges of the inventor are set forth and defined. On the issuance of the patent, the inventor has the right either to manufacture and sell the product with a protected market, or assign rights to others and collect fees for the manufacture and sale or use of the invention. After the seventeen-year period has expired, the inventor no longer has any protection, and the invention becomes public property and may be produced, sold, and used by anyone for the good of all.

To ensure full protection of the patent laws, patented products must be marked *Patent* with the patent number following. Even though an invention is not legally protected until a patent actually has been issued, a product often bears a statement that reads *Patent Pending*.

In accordance with patent law "any person who has invented any new and useful process, machine, manufacturer or composition of matter, or any new and useful improvement thereof, may obtain a patent," subject to restrictions, conditions, and requirements imposed by patent law. To be patentable an invention must be new, original, and uniquely different; it must perform a useful function; and the invention must not have been previously described in any publication anywhere nor have been sold or in general use in the United States before the applicant made the invention. It should be noted that an idea in itself is not patentable, because it is a requirement that a specific design and design description of a device accompany an application for a patent.

2.34 *Patent Attorney*

When an inventor has a patentable device, a patent attorney should be engaged to help prepare the necessary application for a patent. The inventor should depend on the attorney for advice concerning whether or not the product or process may infringe on the rights of others. Because many patent attorneys are also graduate engineers, the inventor will find the attorney to be a person who can guide the application through the searching, investigating, and processing that occurs before a patent is granted. Generally, an application remains pending for as long as four years or more before a patent is finally granted. In this period the pending patent application may well be amended to include engineering changes that have been made in the device or system.

If, after some investigation, the attorney-engineer thinks that the device is novel and therefore patentable, an application for a patent should be prepared and filed. A patent application includes a formal portion consisting of the petition, a power of attorney, and an oath or declaration. This is followed by a description of the invention, called the specifications, and a list of claims relating to it. If the device can be illustrated, one or more drawings should be included (Fig. 2.31).

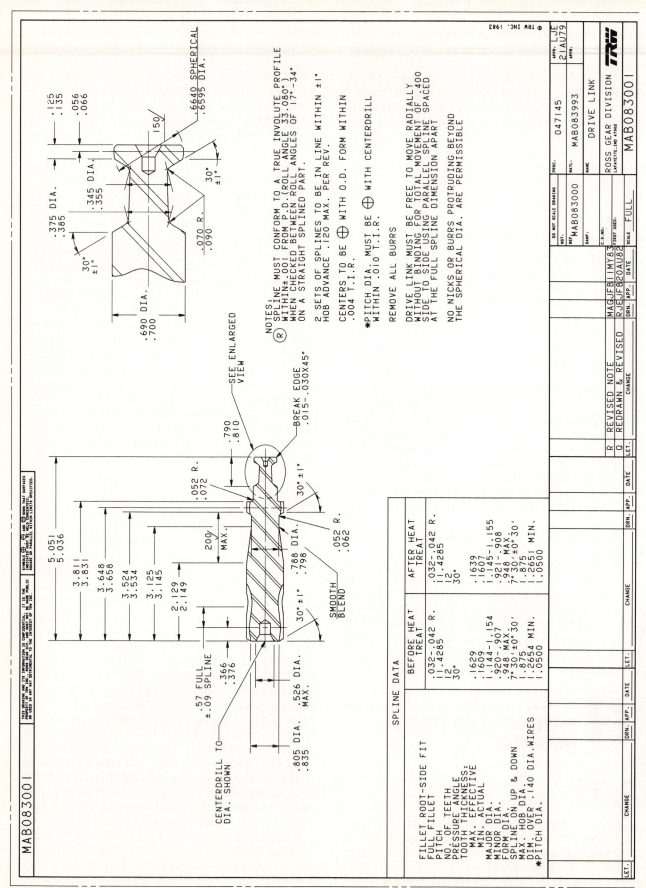

FIG. 2.30 Computer-plotterprepared drawing. (*Courtesy Ross Gear Division, TRW, Inc.*)

34

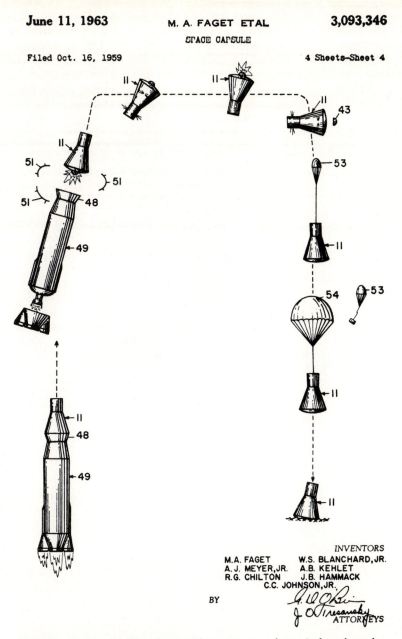

June 11, 1963   M. A. FAGET ETAL   3,093,346
SPACE CAPSULE

Filed Oct. 16, 1959   4 Sheets—Sheet 4

INVENTORS
M.A. FAGET   W.S. BLANCHARD, JR.
A. J. MEYER, JR.   A.B. KEHLET
R.G. CHILTON   J.B. HAMMACK
C.C. JOHNSON, JR.
BY

ATTORNEYS

FIG. 2.31 Patent drawing showing the sequence of events from launch to landing.

In selecting a patent attorney, the inventor should remember that this professional can be of service for many years, going well beyond the time when the patent is issued. The attorney or legal firm may be retained to prepare all agreements covering the sale and leasing of patent rights, to assist in negotiations relating to these rights, and if the need should arise, to handle charges of alleged infringements.

Many large corporations have patent divisions that operate as a section of the home office legal staff. An additional office to deal with patent matters may also be maintained in Washington, D.C. In this case, both offices, staffed with patent attorneys, will have all activities coordinated by a director of patents.

2.35 Role of Inventor in Obtaining Patent

Even though an inventor must rely almost entirely on a patent attorney to take the final steps to secure a patent, the inventor plays a vital role up to the time of filing the application. Very often what the inventor has or has not done determines whether rights to the invention can be safeguarded by the attorney.

Because court decisions in patent suits usually depend on the inventor's ability to prove that certain design events happened on a specific date, it is always advisable to keep the design records in a hardcover, permanently bound notebook so that there will be no question about whether or not pages have been added (as could be charged if a loose leaf notebook were used). A well-kept patent notebook is a complete file of information covering a design. It can serve as the basis of project reports; it can spare the designer the unnecessary expense of repeating portions of the experimental work; and it furnishes indisputable proof of dates of conception and development.

To prepare a legally effective patent notebook the designer should

1. Use a bound notebook having printed page numbers.

2. Make entries directly using either a black ink pen or an indelible pencil.

3. Keep entries in a chronological order. Do not add retroactive entries.

4. Add references to sources of information.

5. Describe all procedures, equipment, and instruments used for developmental work.

6. Insert photos of instrument and equipment set-ups. Add other photos showing models, mockups, and so forth.

7. Sign and date all photographs.

8. Have a qualified witness sign and date each completed page. The witness cannot be a coinventor and cannot have a financial interest in the development of the device. The witness must be a person who is capable of understanding the construction and operation of the device or system, who is also experienced in reading drawings and understanding the specifications.

9. Have the witness write the words "Witnessed and Understood," sign it, and date the signature.

10. Have two or more witnesses sign and date every page after reading it.

11. Avoid having blank spaces on any page.

12. Have all new entries witnessed at least once a week.

13. Have the notebook evaluated periodically by a patent attorney.

It takes a considerable time and effort to adhere to these thirteen recommendations for the preparation of an effective patent notebook. An inventor entangled in an infringement lawsuit realizes, however, that a little extra effort pays off.

Computer-Aided Design and Drafting

3.1 Introduction

This edition of *Fundamentals of Engineering Drawing* presents the fundamentals of drawing, manual or CADD, that can be applied in any engineering environment. The authors acknowledge that there are differences in CADD systems, especially in terminology. Luckily, these differences are generally superficial. If the general concepts of CADD are understood, they can be applied to any system. For example, one system may *insert* a line, whereas another may *create* a line and a third *model* a line. One system may use a *symbol*, whereas another may use a *template, pattern, library part,* or *cell*. It is important to understand the function of these concepts in engineering design and drawing. This chapter gives a general overview, covering why CADD drawings are created, how they are produced, what unique drawing techniques might be encountered in CADD, and how CADD drawings are stored and corrected. At the end of this chapter are presented nine tasks for completing a CADD drawing common to all systems. This is done intentionally without reference to a particular CADD system. Knowledge of a particular CADD system is not necessary to benefit from this chapter. The procedures and terms have been chosen to apply to a broad range of situations. Many of the terms used in this chapter are included in the glossary of CADD terms in Appendix

A. It might be helpful for readers who are totally unfamiliar with the subject to read these terms before continuing with this chapter.

3.2 Function of CADD Drawing

In most ways the functions of CADD drawings are much the same as for traditional engineering drawings. All engineering drawings are used to communicate among engineers and technologists, and between technical and nontechnical workers. CADD drawings are the way designers communicate with one another and form the basis for the historical documentation of a design. CADD drawings are used extensively in construction, manufacturing, and service industries.

CADD drawings, however, differ from traditional manually produced engineering drawings in a fundamental way. A traditional engineering drawing is the entire description of the design, based on the conception of the design in the engineer's head. Lose the drawing and you may have essentially lost the design, since the engineer responsible for the design may not be close at hand. Because traditional engineering drawings are often directly scaled or measured and the measurements are transferred to a pattern, mold, or machine tool, the engineering drawing *is* the data base.

In contrast, the CADD drawing is only the visual

representation of an underlying numeric data base, rather than actually *being* the data base. The CADD drawing is made only to display the data base to humans who have difficulty interpreting a set of numbers. The design exists independently from the drawing. The data base itself may be directly transmitted to machines that make the patterns, molds, or final parts. This is the power of CADD.

3.3 Components of CADD Drawing

A CADD engineering drawing consists of two parts: the numeric data base and supporting annotation in the form of dimensions, notes, labels and text. This supporting text is necessary for the drawing to function as a document. As a source of information for machine tools, this textual information is unnecessary because the mathematical description of a part sent directly to a numerical machine tool controlled by a computer provides the machine tool with the complete description of the part, including necessary tolerances. When engineers and drafters look at a drawing of that data base and interpret it, conventional practices must be used to further describe the design in terms understood by a particular audience.

The form of the numeric data base is unique to each CADD system but generally follows a format like that shown in Fig. 3.1. The data base in Fig. 3.1 is organized so that each entry is separated by a space or comma and records an important parameter of the geometry. To get parts designed on different CADD systems to be compatible with one another, data bases may be filtered or translated into an accepted exchange format such as the Drawing Exchange Format (DXF) or the Initial Graphics Exchange Standard (IGES).

The annotation of a drawing is part of the total data base, but not part of the numeric data base, since notes and dimensions are not part of the object's form. CADD drawings should have a border and title block showing the drawing title, drawing number, bill of materials, and history of changes, just as is done on traditional, manually prepared engineering drawings. (See Fig. 3.2.)

A FUNDAMENTAL PRACTICES OF CADD DRAWING

3.4 A Drawing that Already Exists

When preparing a CADD engineering drawing some investigation needs to be done. And as happens in manual drawing, a designer using CADD must determine if the object has already been designed by his company or by another company from which it could be purchased as a vendor-supplied item. This requires that vendor catalogs be studied, and with CADD, it requires that the operator search directories of existing drawings, looking for key words that match those for the drawing to be made. The success of this computerized search depends on several factors.

• Does the CADD system enter the drawings into an intelligent data base, where for example, all drawings having a gear of a certain diameter and number of teeth can be quickly identified?

• If not, does the CADD system have a method of naming and numbering drawings in a way that the contents of each drawing is easily identified?

• Are all of the drawings on the system in a central storage location and available to the designer?

```
406,1,3HTOP,0,0;                                                      1P      1
410,1,1.000000,0,0,0,0,0,0,0,1,1;                                     3P      2
116,2.000000,1.500000,0.0,0,0;                                        5P      3
100,0.0,2.000000,1.500000,2.200000,1.500000,2.200000,1.500000,        7P      4
0,0;                                                                  7P      5
106,1,3,0.0,1.000000,2.000000,1.000000,2.000000,1.000000,             9P      6
2.874256,0,0;                                                         9P      7
106,1,3,0.0,3.000000,2.000000,3.000000,2.000000,3.000000,            11P      8
2.874256,0,0;                                                        11P      9
214,1,0.156000,0.062061,0.0,3.000000,2.724256,2.307130,             13P     10
2.724256,0,0;                                                        13P     11
214,1,0.156000,0.062061,0.0,1.000000,2.724256,1.568844,             15P     12
2.724256,0,0;                                                        15P     13
212,1,4,0.582286,0.156000,1,1.570796,0.0,0,0,1.646844,2.646256,     17P     14
.0.0,4H2.00,0,0;                                                     17P     15
216,17,15,13,11,9,0,0;                                               19P     16
116,3.000000,1.000000,0.0,0,0;                                       21P     17
116,3.000000,2.000000,0.0,0,0;                                       23P     18
116,1.000000,2.000000,0.0,0,0;                                       25P     19
116,1.000000,1.000000,0.0,0,0;                                       27P     20
110,3.000000,2.000000,0.0,3.000000,1.000000,0.0,0,0;                 29P     21
110,1.000000,2.000000,0.0,3.000000,2.000000,0.0,0,0;                 31P     22
110,1.000000,1.000000,0.0,1.000000,2.000000,0.0,0,0;                 33P     23
110,1.000000,1.000000,0.0,3.000000,1.000000,0.0,0,0;                 35P     24
406,1,7HDRAWING,0,0;                                                 37P     25
406,2,5.000000,5.000000,0.0,0;                                       39P     26
404,1,3,0.0,0.0,0,0,0,2,37,39;                                       41P     27
S        2G       4D       42P      27                                T       1
```

FIG. 3.1 Example of geometric data base. This is a portion of a part file in Initial Graphics Exchange Standard (IHES) format.

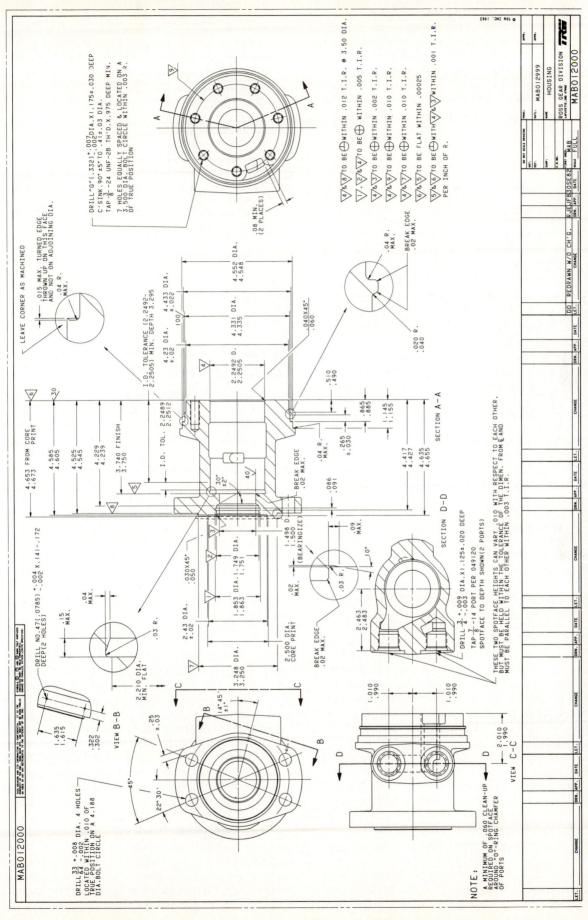

FIG. 3.2 Detail drawing of housing for hydraulic motor represented by data shown in Fig. 3.1. *(Courtesy Ross Gear Division, TRW, Inc.)*

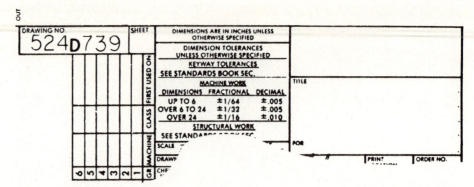

FIG. 3.3 Title block with provisions for making new drawing application from existing drawing.

If an existing drawing is found, it may not need to be changed beyond adding a new entry in the title block (Fig. 3.3). One drawing can be used for a number of applications by making the appropriate entries in the title block. If, however, a name or number change is advisable, it is important to remember that in CADD one always works on a *copy* of the original drawing. The new drawing can be renamed, renumbered, and saved as a drawing separate from the original.

3.5 *Editing of Existing Drawing*

If you find a drawing that is very similar to the one you need to make, or a part design exists that can be turned into the drawing you need, you must make several changes to both the numeric data base and the annotations.

A drawing is stored by a name, called its *file name*. The file name should be descriptive of the drawing. The exact procedure for naming files varies from company to company. As an example, the file name 120AXBRKT4HD might be interpreted as a *heavy duty*(HD)*four inch*(4) *axle*(AX)*bracket*(BRKT) for *machine number 120*(120). To turn this into a new drawing, say a 3-in heavy duty axle bracket used on machine 110, you would save the old drawing with a new name. Then you would have the start of a new drawing, 110AXBRKT3HD. Using the CADD procedures available on your system, you would delete, create, and edit the drawing as necessary. As you work, you would save your new drawing every 30 min or so, to protect against accidental drawing loss. This is called *backing up* you drawing. Some CADD systems automatically make a backup copy of the drawing each time you delete something from the data base, whereas other systems require that the operator periodically save the drawing.

When the new drawing is completed, save it with similar drawings to make finding it easier in the future. For instance, the bracket may be saved with all other drawings for machine 110 or with all other bracket drawings or with all other axle drawings.

3.6 *Need for New Drawing to Be Created*

A new drawing is made *only* after you are convinced that the object has not already been designed and that no similar design exists on which the new drawing could quickly and efficiently be based.

If no drawing exists that can be used as the basis for the new drawing, the part must be defined starting with the very first line. This is an expensive and time-consuming task and only marginally more cost effective than using manual methods. Remember, however, when you are finished you will have more than just a drawing. You will have the data base of the design from which any number of subsequent drawings can be made and by which instructions to machine tools can be given.

3.7 *Input Methods*

Several methods are commonly used to input data and instructions into a CADD system, the most effective of which is the digitizing process. For example, a drafter might digitize a sketch provided by a designer. To do this, the CADD operator would tape the sketch to a digitizing tablet and trace it using either a stylus or a puck (Fig. 3.4). In this way lines, arcs, circles, and other geometric shapes are converted into digital data. If desired, these data may be called up and displayed on the terminal where any necessary adjustments can be made. CADD operators are able to mirror views, rotate the geometry into pictorial representations for visual checking, and "zoom in" to see the smallest detail. An automated method of digitizing is called scanning (Fig. 3.5) and is appropriate for digitizing existing engineering drawings. The scanning process uses an optical device that is programmed to recognize geometric primitives and text characters.

FIG. 3.4 A puck is used as the input device for identifying geometry on an engineering drawing. The display in the background records the progress of the digitizing process. (*Courtesy Computervision Corp.*)

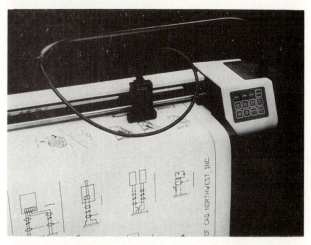

FIG. 3.5 A digital plotter can be converted into an automatic digitizer. (*Courtesy Houston Instruments*)

When digitizing, a cursor symbol (a point, intersecting lines, blinking arrow, etc.) corresponding to the digitizing position appears on the screen. The stylus need not actually touch the surface of the tablet to produce this symbol, but it is by this process of digitizing that drawing coordinates are entered into the CADD computer (Fig. 3.6).

Some CADD systems have unique menus for the input of operator commands as shown in Fig. 3.7. Commands are entered either by making choices from menus or by typing the commands from the keyboard. Use of keyboard commands requires knowing the appropriate rules of syntax, and such commands are susceptible to typing mistakes. A system using menu-driven commands is generally easier to learn and more efficient to use than one requiring the entering of commands.

FIG. 3.6 Performing drawing manipulations using a menu-driven program. At the work station are Professor Jerry Smith and Systems Manager Dennis Short. (*Courtesy Department of Technical Graphics, School of Technology, Purdue University*)

3.8 *CADD Menus*

An *application program* accomplishes a specific task and each application program has its own menu. A mechanical CADD program would have a mechanical menu while an architectural CADD program would use an architectural menu. Commercial applications use grid menus to convey instructions to the computer (Fig. 3.7). Commands are activated by contacting the touch-sensitive tablet like that shown in Fig. 3.8. Note that the processes of entering data and entering commands from a tablet are essentially the same, but commands have reserved locations on the digitizing tablet. Examples of special-purpose menus include

- Mechanical design and drafting
- Printed circuit broad design
- Electrical schematics
- Hydraulic schematics
- Plant and piping design
- Structural design
- Architectural design

Two methods exist for organizing CADD menus: *flat* and *hierarchial*. A flat menu requires the operator to reenter an almost identical string of commands as the first part of each command. A hierarchical menu works within a level of the command (creating a line parallel to another line for example) without the need to reenter that part of the command. Consider these two commands to be made one after the other in a flat menu system.

```
CREATE LINE PARALLEL LENGTH 4.345
CREATE LINE PARALLEL LENGTH 3.879.
```

The second command would have to be entered from the beginning even though only the length of the paral-

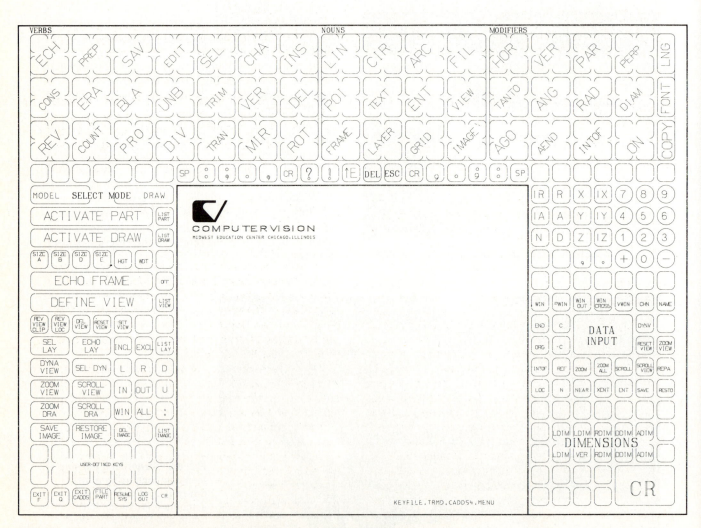

FIG. 3.7   Menu form used in conjunction with a digitizing board as an input device. The boxes around the outside activate specific commands or functions while the open area in the middle is used for inputting geometric position. (*Courtesy Computervision Corporation*)

FIG. 3.8 Entering computer commands. (*Courtesy Computervision Corporation*)

lel line changed. Using a hierarchial menu the commands would appear

```
CREATE LINE PARALLEL LENGTH 4.345
3.879.
```

Note that the CADD system assumes that the operator wishes to continue making parallel lines until instructed otherwise. It is easy to see that when making complex CADD drawings, the use of hierarchial menus can shorten the drawing time considerably.

3.9 Use of Tablet

A tablet used with a stylus or puck controls the cursor on the computer terminal so that the operator can point to and create elements like lines, circles, arcs, and other geometric forms in combinations as needed. The menu part of the tablet is divided into a matrix of squares with each square assigned a specific function (Fig. 3.8). Thus, when a selected square is touched, a programmed message is sent to the computer. The tablet and stylus or puck provide the instructions necessary for all drawing tasks and may be thought of as the paper and pencil of the CADD operator.

All CADD systems use instructions to tell the computer what to do. These instructions comprise the CADD system's *command language.* All CADD systems have subtle differences among the commands; however in general they take the form verb, noun, modifier, mask.

An example of this would be INSERT LINE HORI-ZONTAL END OF ENTITY. INSERT is the verb, LINE is the noun, HORIZONTAL is the modifier, and END OF ENTITY is the mask that allows the CADD operator to start the horizontal line at the exact end of another line.

3.10 Selection of Grid or Scale

One may think of the grid used in creating a CADD drawing as being equivalent to a piece of grid paper on a drawing board since it is used in essentially the same manner. The grid paper in traditional drafting is slipped under the drawing paper so that when finished, the grid does not appear on the drawing. A CADD grid can be turned on or off and will not show up on prints or plots of the final drawing.

On the grid, one unit of spacing may represent a value as small as 0.005 mm or as large as 500 m (.0001 in to 1000 ft). When necessary, the scale ratio of the X axis to Y or Z axes may be different. The CADD operator may change the grid scale (the world increment assigned to each grid unit) and the computer will automatically scale the graphic data to fit the display size. Therefore, the operator can think in terms of full size or world dimensions. Even though the dimensions are full size, however, the computer is scaling the data to fit a specific drawing area and working in device units (see Sec. 6.11). Note the use of a reduced scale in the designing of a highway route in Fig. 3.9.

In summary, when graphical data is input in world units, the computer makes the necessary calculations

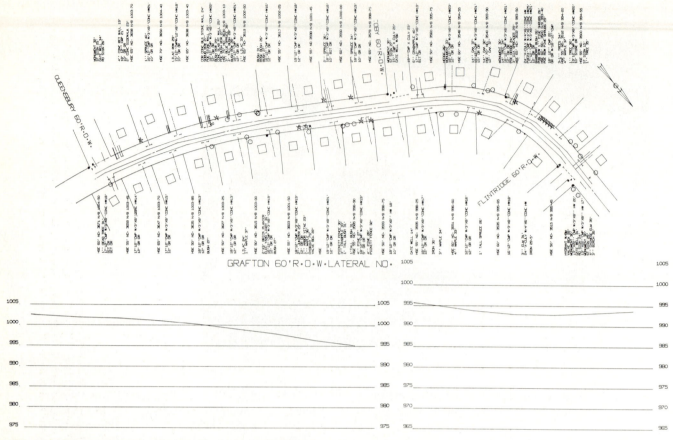

FIG. 3.9 Highway route plan and profile. Program systems have been developed to produce civil engineering plans for highway, sewer, and drainage construction. (*Courtesy Johnson & Anderson, Inc., Consulting Engineers, Pontiac, Michigan*)

to scale the data to fit a specific drawing area. The output will be accurately scaled and if dimensions are added, they will be in world units.

3.11 Drawing Activities Unique to CADD

Because the computer is such a powerful tool in engineering design and drawing, many methods used to draw manually have been replaced by new methods unique to CADD. The following sections introduce CADD operations called functions, which are used extensively in all CADD systems. The CADD functions in the following sections are universal and not representative of a particular piece of software. In examples that contain commands, the actual commands appear in capital letters, whereas other information supplied by the operator is enclosed in brackets.

3.12 Layers

CADD systems have overlaying capabilities similar to the use of translucent paper overlays. Overlays on different layers are generally used when making CADD drawings but not when building the part description. Layers are used to group related graphic elements or text and to separate groups to make work on both detail and assembly drawings easier. A complete assembly drawing may be prepared first and details drawn on successive overlays; or, individual details can be built up, each on a different layer, until an assembly results from the combined overlays. Layers are particularly important in facility engineering or architectural design. By using layers, a building designer can place the foundation, floor plan, heating plan, and electrical plans on separate layers where they can be selectively displayed, aligned, and edited. An overlay is the drawing made on a separate layer. See Fig. 3.10 in which the drawing of a subdivision was done on one

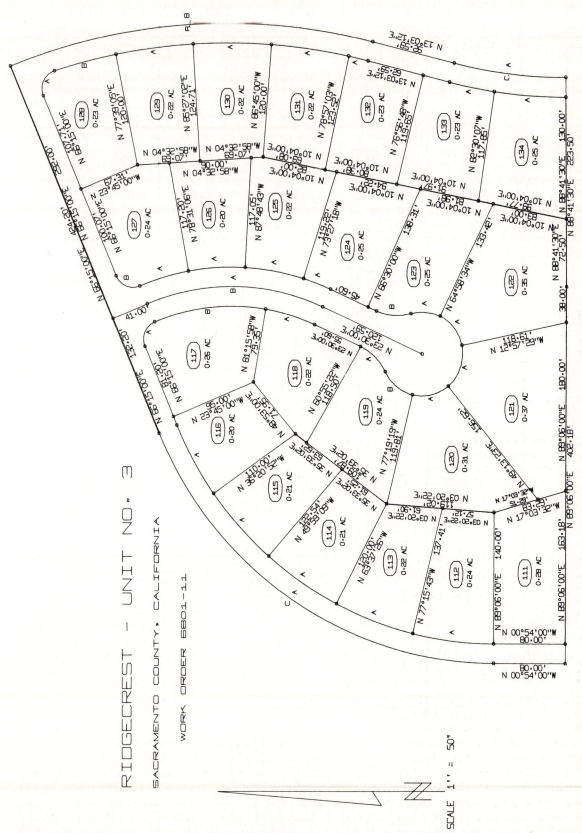

FIG. 3.10 Plot of subdivision. The computer program designated SAMPS (Subdivision and Mapping System) plots a complete subdivision map with bearings, distances, and other information ordinarily given on a map of this type. As developed by PMT Associates of Sacramento, California, the program can also be used for plotting control networks, for surveying jobs, and for primary control of aerial photographs. The program provides for choice of plotting scale, rotation of plotting axes, plotting of lines and points, plotting of a north arrow, and annotation of distances and bearings. (*Courtesy PMT Associates—Engineers, Land Surveyors, Planners*)

45

layer, and the extensive dimensions and notes on another.

A layer is the logical grouping of geometry and notation that is referenced by an index number, called the layer number. All geometry belonging to a layer can be independently displayed, deleted, plotted, scaled, rotated, or otherwise manipulated. If we assign the border and title block to layer 1, four additional layers might suffice for the detail drawing of a single part that was not too complex. The second and third overlays, arbitrarily assigned to layers 21 and 22, might show front and side views of the part, while all dimensions might be assigned to layer 121. When layers 1, 21, 22, and 121 are displayed together, a complete drawing results. Most companies have strict guidelines for what information is assigned to which layer.

To prepare a set of drawings for a product such as an air cylinder, the CADD operator would first draw each part on a separate layer. Then the overlays needed for the assembly drawing would be combined. This method of constructing an assembly drawing requires that each view be on a separate layer so that selected views may be used in preparing the assembly. For the entire assembly to appear on the screen, the operator would enter a command like DISPLAY LAYERS followed by a list of the necessary layer numbers. The final assembly drawing would include the desired layers plus a layer for the border and title block.

3.13 View Manipulation

The drawing manipulation functions of a CADD system include zoom, rotate, pan, and scroll. A view manipulation changes the manner in which the operator sees the data base. It does not alter the data base itself nor does it change the relationship of the geometry to the world axis system. Each function will be discussed briefly.

Zoom is the capability of a CADD system to either enlarge or reduce the drawing or a portion of the drawing. Zoom is required because a drawing may be so large that small detail cannot be distinguished. By creating a window, a rectangular area on the screen enclosing specific entities needing attention and using the zoom-in capabilities of the system, the operator can obtain an enlarged view of a specific portion of the drawing for close-up work (Fig. 3.11). This is done with the command ZOOM WINDOW [first corner] [opposite diagonal corner]. Zoom out is the opposite of zoom in. ZOOM OUT 2 displays twice as much of the object as can currently be seen. ZOOM ALL displays the entire object.

Rotate command enables a CADD operator to turn the world axis system and all geometry in the workplace through a selected angle about one or more device axes (Fig. 3.12). The geometry itself does not move in relation to the world axes. This rotation is accomplished by identifying the axis of rotation and by

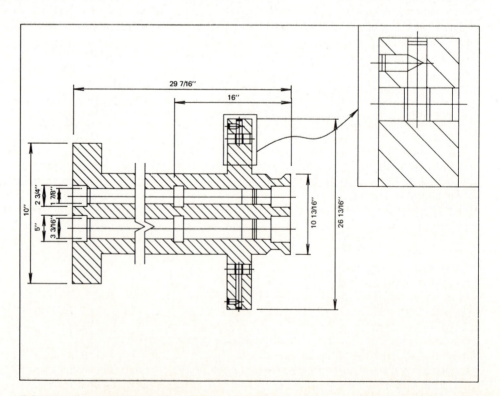

FIG. 3.11 Zoom-in function. The zoom-in view appears at the upper right. (*Courtesy Cadapple, T & W Systems, Inc.*)

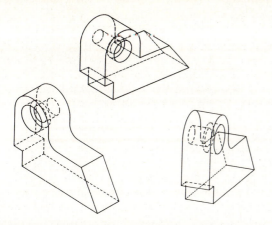

FIG. 3.12 View manipulation-rotation. (*Prepared by Dennis Short, Interactive Computer Graphics Systems, Technical Graphics Department, Purdue University*)

entering the required angle. If desired, a printer or plotter can be activated to draw several three-dimensional views of the object showing it at different angles. This function is activated by a command like RO-TATE [axis] [angle].

Commands to *scroll* and *pan* allow the operator to move smoothly from one place on the drawing to another. Scroll usually is limited to vertical movement while pan is used to describe a left-right change in viewing position, although pan may also be used to designate diagonal change. A command to move a point on the drawing from one spot to another might be PAN [point] [new position of point]. Figure 3.13 shows the image of the computer terminal superimposed on a drawing and the directions of movement that would constitute scroll and pan.

3.14 Transformation

A transformation, unlike a viewing manipulation, actually alters the data base in some way, usually by an addition; and during a transformation the operator's viewing position remains constant. The transformation functions to be discussed are translate, mirror, copy, rotate, and rotate copy.

A *translate* command causes identified geometry to be moved relative to the X, Y, or Z axis. The spatial relationship of the geometry does not change, but the entire group is moved to another location. Translation may be initiated by a command like TRANSLATE [geometry] [reference point] [new position of reference point].

Objects that are symmetrical about an axis may be *mirrored* (Fig. 3.14); that is, the operator may create one half of an object and then automatically produce the second half by mirroring. If a modifier like COPY is used, the two halves of the object will be completed; otherwise the first half will be moved to the second

half. This is accomplished by specifying what forms are to be mirrored and about which axis the mirroring is to take place. This function is activated by the command like MIRROR COPY [geometry] [axis].

A *rotate transformation* command moves geometry in a circular path about a stable axis system and differs from the rotate-viewing manipulation discussed in the previous section. Remember that a viewing manipulation does not change the geometry-to-axis relationship. A rotation transformation is accomplished by a command like ROTATE [geometry] [axis] [angle].

A *rotate copy* or *translate copy* command allows a CADD operator to efficiently display chosen forms around a circular arc or along a line. These commands might take the form ROTATE COPY [geometry] [axis] [angle] [number of copies] or TRANSLATE COPY [geometry] [X-offset] [Y-offset] [Z-offset] [number of copies]. An example of rotating and copying circles is shown in Fig. 3.15.

3.15 Filleting

A fillet is a tangent arc between two intersecting lines (see Sec. 5.22) or, in a three-dimensional sense, a partial cylinder, sphere, or torus between two surfaces. CADD systems often provide a function to create a fillet semi-automatically, allowing the operator either to trim or not to trim the lines (Fig. 3.16). This is accomplished by a command like CREATE FILLET [radius] [line 1] [line 2] or CREATE FILLET [radius] [surface 1] [surface 2]. A three-dimensional computer model is shown in Fig. 3.17 containing several filleted surfaces.

3.16 Crosshatching

In producing sectional views, areas cut by a cutting plane are shown crosshatched. CADD systems may vary slightly in how they handle this. Some systems require that the area be completely bounded by closed lines. Other systems will automatically close an area if an opening is left. The general form of the command is CROSSHATCH [pattern number] [line 1] [line 2] [line 3] . . . [line n]. An example of an assembly drawing including areas of crosshatching is shown in Fig. 3.18.

3.17 Automatic and Semiautomatic Dimensioning

Dimensioning involves the selection and placement of dimensional values for size and location. Fully automatic dimensioning requires minimal input from the operator and will create dimensions on a drawing based on an internal set of rules conforming to ANSI

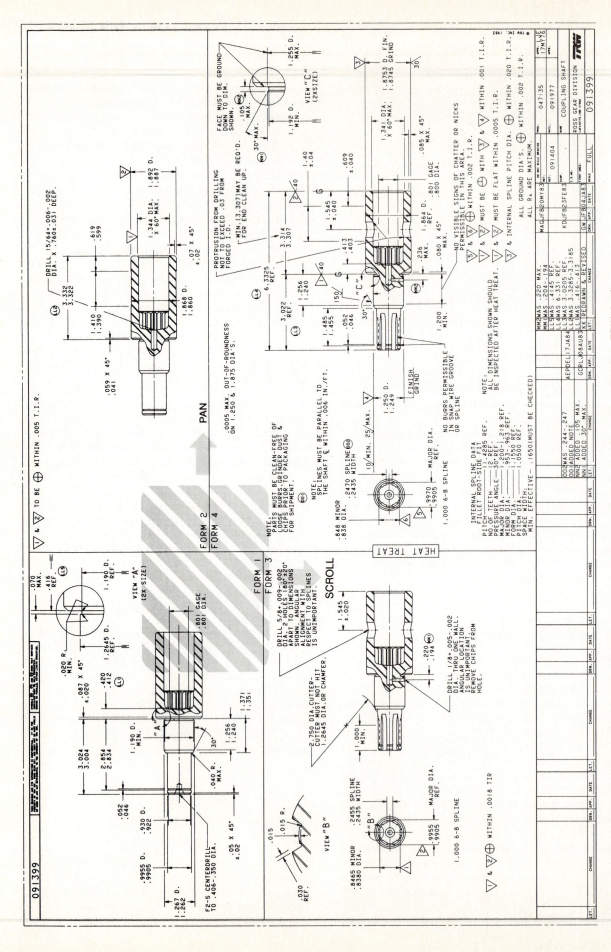

FIG. 3.13 Detail drawing of coupling shaft for hydraulic motor shown in Fig. 3.15. *(Courtesy Ross Gear Division, TRW, Inc.)*

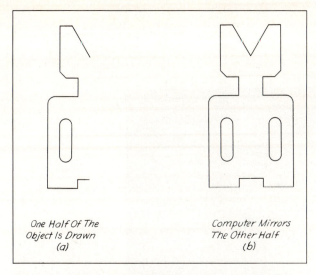

One Half Of The
Object Is Drawn
(a)

Computer Mirrors
The Other Half
(b)

FIG. 3.14   Mirrored and copied view. (*This drawing was prepared by Dennis Short, Interactive Computer Graphics Systems, Technical Graphics Department, Purdue University*)

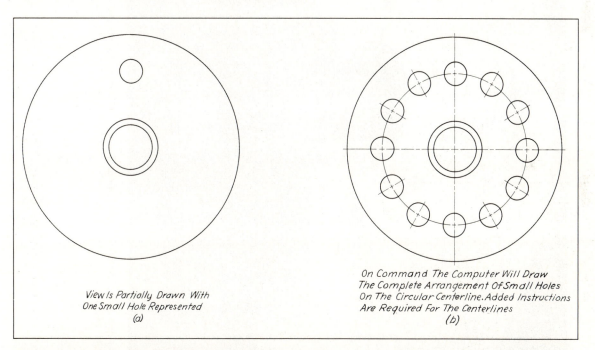

View Is Partially Drawn With
One Small Hole Represented
(a)

On Command The Computer Will Draw
The Complete Arrangement Of Small Holes
On The Circular Centerline. Added Instructions
Are Required For The Centerlines
(b)

FIG. 3.15   Move and duplicate function. The first hole was positioned at the radius at 90°. The remaining eleven holes were produced in one command, ROTATE COPY (30°, eleven copies). (*Prepared by Dennis Short, Technical Graphics Department, Purdue University*)

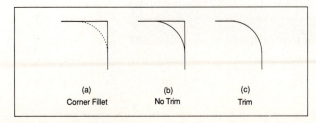

(a)
Corner Fillet

(b)
No Trim

(c)
Trim

FIG. 3.16   Fillet function.

FIG. 3.17 A computer-generated pictorial illustration of the drum shown at the start of Chapter 7. Note the fillet inside and relief slots on the top surface. *(Courtesy Computervision Corporation)*

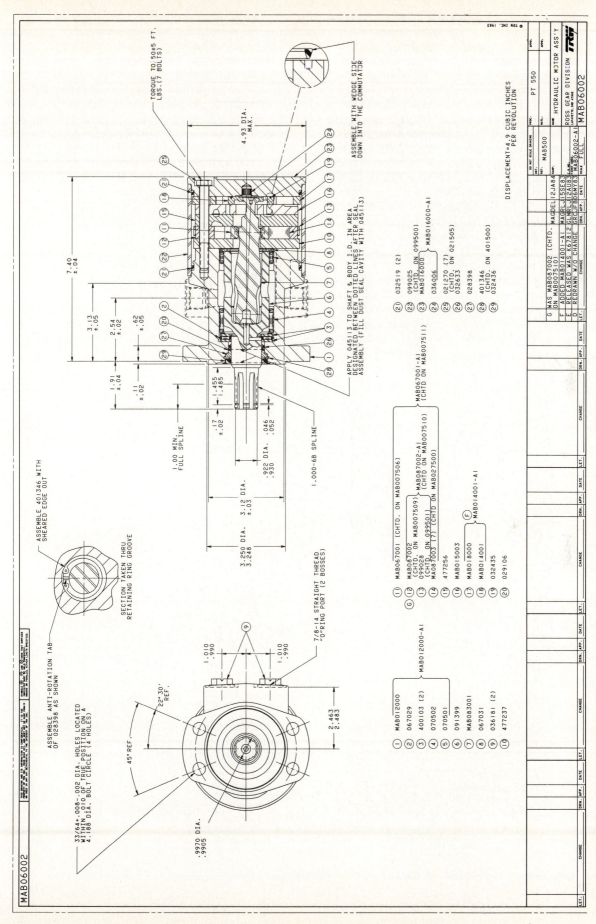

FIG. 3.18 Hydraulic motor assembly. A drawing generated by an IBM Graphics System. (*Courtesy Ross Gear Division, TRW, Inc.*)

Y14.5 standards. The operator may decide afterward to remove one or more of these automatic dimensions or to add a dimension or note that the system did not include. Semiautomatic dimensioning requires that the operator identify the type of dimension desired (horizontal, vertical, inclined, radial, or diametrial), the feature to be dimensioned, and the position of the dimension value on the drawing. The CADD system would then supply the dimension number, witness lines, dimension lines, and line terminators (arrow heads) based on the operator-specified position. A typical dimensioning command might be CREATE DIMENSION HORIZONTAL [point 1] [point 2] [text position]. In Fig. 3.19 horizontal, vertical, angular, inclined, radial, and diameter dimensions are shown along with several notes.

To supplement dimensions, a CADD operator can create a notation, note, or number value needed at a particular location on a drawing. The operator will have a choice of fonts and can select text height, aspect ratio, justification, angle, and slant. These parameters, once set, affect all subsequent text in dimensions and notes and do not have to be respecified each time a dimension or note is created. The placement of text is accomplished by digitizing the proper location. As an example, to place a note stating "REMOVE ALL BURRS AND POLISH" would require the command CREATE NOTE/REMOVE ALL BURRS AND POLISH/[text position]. The slashes (/) that set off the text string are called *delimiters*. Delimiters define for the computer the text that is to be put in the note.

3.18 Storing Drawings in Digital Form

As a CADD operator works on a drawing, the drawing is held in the temporary memory of the computer. When instructed, the computer will record the draw-

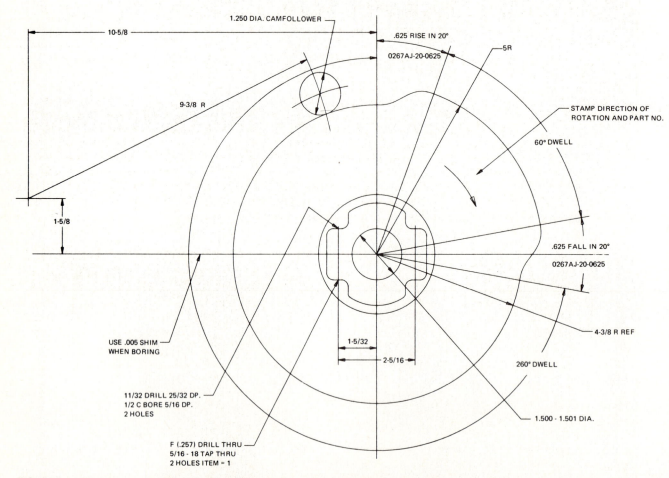

FIG. 3.19 Dimensioning techniques with CADD. (*Courtesy Westinghouse Electric Corporation*)

ing on a permanent storage medium, such as disk or tape. Unlike manually prepared designs, drawings made on a CADD system and stored on tape or disks are not generally stored on paper as well. Prints of CADD drawings are made so that they may be checked or distributed. The original CADD drawing is stored in electronic form at the manufacturing site where it can easily be recalled for use. Additional electronic copies of the CADD drawings, called backup copies, can be stored in remote locations—underground in fireproof bank vaults for instance—for safekeeping.

Both the filing and retrieving of CADD drawings are quick and easy operations. To file a drawing, a simple command to the computer is required. A typical filing command might be FILE [drawing name] [file type], where the file type could be PART, SYMBOL, or DRAWING.

Retrieving a drawing from storage is called *loading a drawing*. The CADD computer checks to see if the operator has made any additions to the drawing currently on the screen. If there have been, the operator is given the opportunity to save this altered drawing before returning it to storage and loading another. A typical command for retrieving a drawing would be: LOAD DRAWING [drawing name] [file type].

3.19 Checking and Correcting CADD Drawings

When the initial work has been completed on a set of working drawings for a project, the CADD operator may wish to submit the drawings for checking. This can be done by producing hard copies on paper or by placing copies of the drawings in a location in the computer where they can be reviewed on the display terminal. As noted before, the checker should be a person familiar with the principles of the design who has not been involved in the preparation of the drawings to be checked and corrected. A checker should have production experience coupled with a broad knowledge of drawing standards, manufacturing practices, and assembly methods. The checker should study the assembly together with the detail drawings and mark all necessary changes or corrections in colored pencil. The checker should also verify all dimensions, notes, and specifications for correctness and be certain that they are in a form that can be used for manufacturing. Any omissions should be indicated. If the checking is done on the computer, changes and corrections should be placed on a layer separate from the original.

When the marked copy has been returned for changes, the CADD operator can call up the original drawing and make the needed alterations with little difficulty.

B GENERAL STEPS—NEW CADD DRAWING

3.20 CADD Drawing

There are nine general steps that must be performed with any CADD system to complete a new drawing. During the process, part, symbol, and drawing files will be created. The difference between these files are that part files contain only geometry, symbol files contain symbol geometry that can be combined with symbols and parts, and drawing files contain part geometry, symbols, and dimensions and notes. The precise commands would of course vary from one system to the next but the tasks would remain the same. When commands are given, they appear in a general form.

STEP 1. Analyze the geometry of the design. Break the object into component parts. Can the object be defined with common geometric shapes? Are there features that repeat and can be created once and copied at the appropriate position, scale, and rotation? Is the object symmetrical? Can the shape be created and then mirrored to completion? Plan an approach. For example, the gasket in Fig. 3.20 is comprised of a quadrant that can be mirrored and copied to complete one half of the design which can then be mirror copied to form the entire design.

STEP 2. Locate the origin. Choose an appropriate location in the design to coincide with X0, Y0, Z0, the world axis system origin. This accomplishes several ends. First, it reduces the magnitude of absolute coordinate values. Second, it allows you to zoom in on the form and keep the origin on the screen. Lastly, the eventual combining of the geometry with a border and title block is facilitated if the origin of the border and the part are both at their geometric centers.

STEP 3. Select a scale that is appropriate for the size of the object. If a grid is desired, specify that the grid be defined using the smallest practicable unit, such as .125 in or 1 mm.

STEP 4. Create the object full size in world units. As you work, save the geometry every few minutes to prevent loss of more than a small portion of work should there be a power failure or other unforseen accident. To save the part as you work:

```
SAVE PART (part name)
```

STEP 5. Save the completed part as a figure or symbol. Symbols can generally be merged with parts; however, parts cannot usually be merged with other parts. For example,

```
SAVE FIGURE (figure name)
```

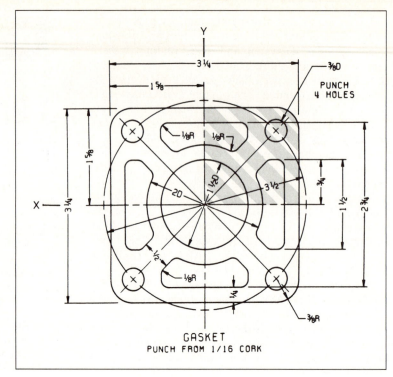

FIG. 3.20 Gasket drawing prepared using CADD drafting system and CalComp electrostatic printer-plotter. The upper right-hand quadrant can be mirror copied about the Y axis, and the top half can then be mirror copied about the X axis.

STEP 6. Turn part geometry into an engineering drawing. Locate and display a standard drawing border and title block on its own layer. For example,

```
ACTIVE LAYER (layer number)
LOAD FIGURE (border name)
```

STEP 7. Merge the part figure with the border. Merge the symbol on a layer separate from the border. Choose a scale that makes the part geometry readable. Very large objects will be reduced. Very small objects will be enlarged. Many objects will be full size. When the part and border are combined, save as a drawing. For example,

```
MERGE (symbol name) (scale)
(rotation) (position)
SAVE DRAWING (drawing name)
```

STEP 8. Dimension the drawing. On a dimensioning layer, create dimensions, notes, and title block information. For example,

```
ACTIVE LAYER (layer number)
CREATE RADIAL DIMENSION (arc) (leader
side)
CREATE VERTICAL DIMENSION (point 1)
(point 2) (text position)
CREATE NOTE/PURCHASE FROM ALLIED
FASTENER COMPANY/(text position)
```

STEP 9. Save the completed drawing.

```
SAVE DRAWING (drawing name) (file
type)
```

These steps provide for the efficient creation of a CADD drawing. The steps were organized to accomplish the following ends:

- The efficient use of terminal time by adequate pre-planning,

- Using the power of CADD (rotate, copy, mirror, merge) rather than using CADD simply as an electronic drafting board,

- Saving the geometry without border, dimensions, or notes to create a part file that is more efficient for manufacturing,

- Merging the finished part file into the border for an efficient way to make a drawing.

3.21 Examples of CADD Drawings

Figs. 3.21 to 3.23 give the reader a sense of the diversity of drawings that can be produced by CADD applications. Fig. 3.21 is a three-dimensional model of a

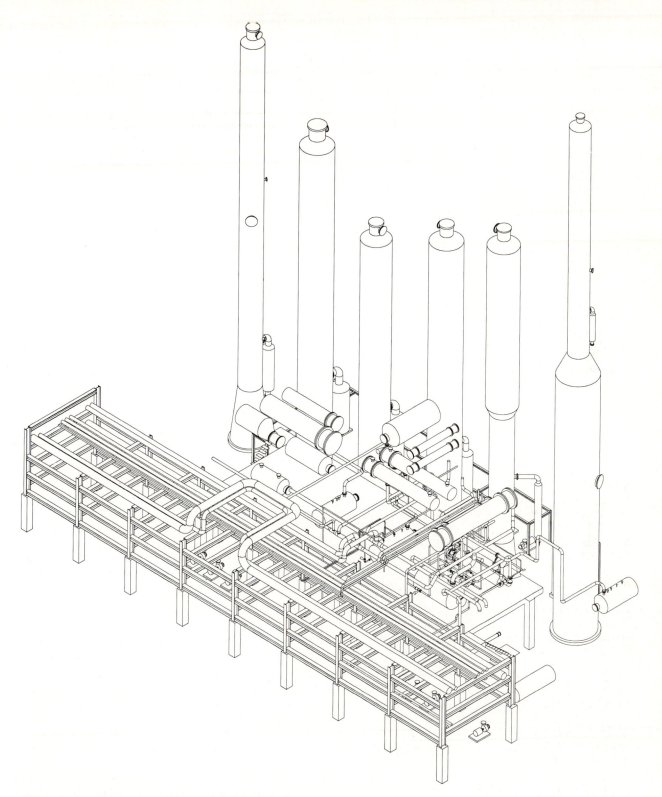

FIG. 3.21 Computer-generated piping installation drawing. The computer may check the design for inaccuracies, conflicts, or faulty representations. (*Courtesy Computervision Corporation*)

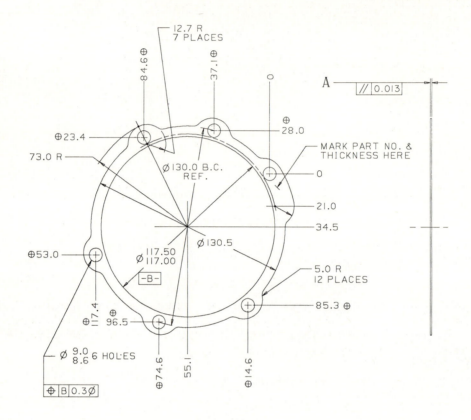

SYMBOL CODE	
PARALLELISM	//
TRUE POSITION	⊕
DENOTES BASIC DIMENSIONS	⊕

CHANGE IN DESIGN, COMPOSITION, PROCESSING OR
IN-PROCESS GAGING FROM PART PREVIOUSLY APPROVED
FOR PART PRODUCTION REQUIRES PRIOR PRODUCT
ENGINEERING APPROVAL.

ENGINEERING APPROVAL & TEST OF SAMPLES FROM
EACH SUPPLIER IS REQUIRED PRIOR TO FIRST
PRODUCTION SHIPMENT OF PARTS.

FOR ENGINEERING APPROVED SOURCE SEE
ENGINEERING NOTICE.

FIG. 3.22 Conventional drawing prepared by a plotter. (*Courtesy Ford Motor Company*)

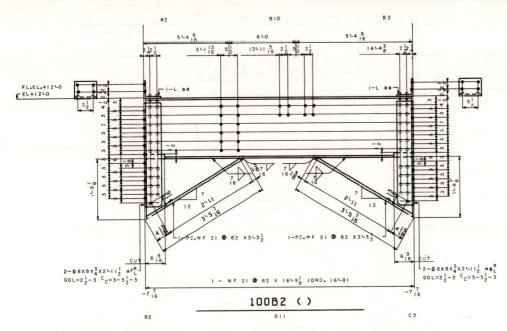

FIG. 3.23 Structural drawing prepared on plotter. Made using the CONSTRUCTS System of automated drafting. (*Courtesy Control Data Corporation*)

process plant. It functions identically with a traditional engineering model like that shown in Chapter 16. The entire plant can be designed, all clearances checked, and even the operation of the process simulated before

construction drawings are created. Fig. 3.22 is typical of CADD use in the automotive industry and Fig. 3.23 demonstrates CADD's applicability in structural design.

PART 2

ENGINEERING DRAWING FUNDAMENTALS

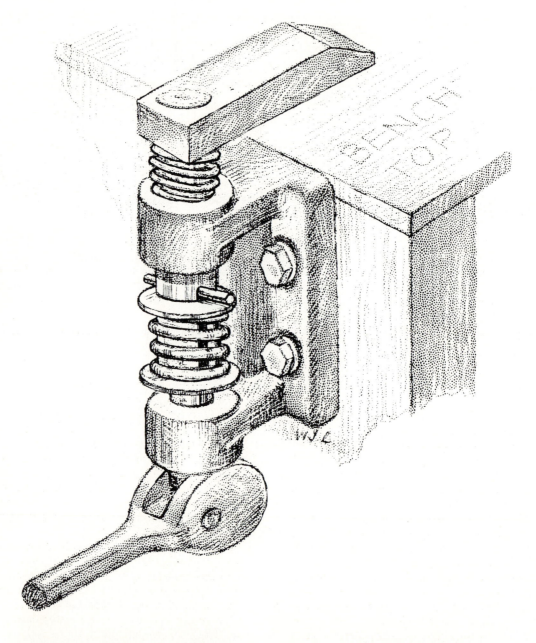

The ideas of a designer may be sketched in pictorial form as they are visualized. Later during a period of preliminary study, a combination of orthographic and pictorial sketches will be prepared as problems are recognized and possible solutions are considered. Sales engineers frequently include pictorial sketches along with orthographic sketches when preparing field reports. Sketches, when used in combination with the written and spoken language, lead to a full understanding by all persons with whom one finds it necessary to communicate.

The pictorial sketch above shows a designer's idea for a quick-acting bench clamp.

Freehand Sketching

CHAPTER 4

A *SKETCHING AND DESIGN*

4.1 Introduction

A pictorial sketch conveys a natural representation by showing the front, top, and side in the same view—much as one would see an object in the world (Fig. 4.1). This technique is especially useful when communicating the appearance of a design. Principal orthographic views (see Chapter 8) are more appropriate for communicating specific size and manufacturing data.

Differences between symbolic (language), multiview, and pictorial representation can be compared in Fig. 4.2. The symbolic representation (*a*) is restricted to those who understand the language. The multiview description (*b*) requires training in its use for full understanding though it is more generally understood than the symbolic example. The pictorial form (*c*) is generally understood independent of specific symbolic or graphical language knowledge.

An engineering technologist or designer must be able to make understandable pictorial sketches. When combined with text and multiviews, a complete description can be achieved. Use text for operational information, multiviews for geometric relationships,

and pictorials for assembly, disassembly, or identification (Figs. 4.3 and 4.4).

While sketching, designers should be able to present ideas clearly and accurately through written language; they should be familiar with the graphical method of presenting shape through the use of multiviews; finally, they should execute well-proportioned and understandable pictorial sketches. Space conditions, distances, and movement must be visualized while retaining the mental image so that it can be revised as needed.

A designer's use of sketches, both pictorial and orthographic (Fig. 4.4), continues throughout preliminary design stages, and into development and detailing stages in which CADD may be used to produce final engineering drawings. A pictorial sketch may prove to be more effective than an orthographic sketch at an early stage of design (Fig. 4.22).

The basics of both multiview and pictorial drawing are important to make effective pictorial sketches. *Just as learning the mechanics of English does not make one a creative writer, so will training in sketching not make one a creative designer.* Sketching is the means of rapidly recording your ideas.

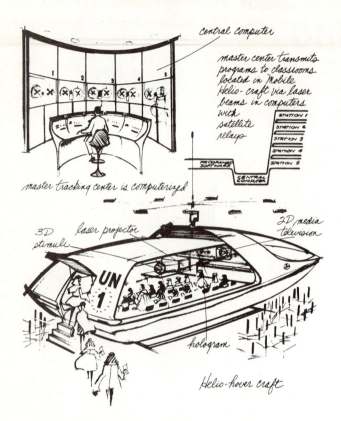

central computer

master center transmits programs to classrooms located in mobile Helio-craft via laser beams in computers with satellite relays

master tracking center is computerized

STATION 1
STATION 2
STATION 3
STATION 4
STATION 5

PROGRAMMED SOFTWARE

CENTRAL COMPUTER

3D stimuli
laser projector
2D media television
UN 1
hologram
Helio-hover craft

FIG. 4.1 Designer's idea sketch. In the future heli-lifted classrooms may be transported to every part of the earth. The lessons would be projected in 3-D. Transmittal would be carried by laser beams, relayed by satellite. (*Courtesy Raymond Loewy/William Smith, Inc., and Charles Bruning Company*)

4.2 Thinking with a Pencil

While a design is refined and different ideas develop, sketches undergo constant change. Old sketches are erased and improved, and new sketches are started. Sketching should be done as easily and as freely as writing so that you focus on the design and not on the technique of sketching. To reach a point where one can "think with a pencil" is not easy. Through continued practice and attention to detail sketching can become a valuable design tool.

4.3 Value of Freehand Drawing

Freehand technical drawing benefits the entire design process: from chief engineers to designers, drafters, technicians, and supervisors. When communicating with CADD operators, a sketch may be all that is needed to convey enough of the design that finished engineering drawings can be produced. Sketches may be *schematic*, as are those of new ideas (Fig. 4.3), or they may be *instructional*, to convey ideas to drafters or technicians. Sketches prepared for the manufacture of low-volume replacement parts may resemble complete working drawings (Fig. 4.5).

4.4 Projections

Although freehand drawback lacks the precision of instrument drawing, it is based on the same principals of projection and conventional practices that apply to

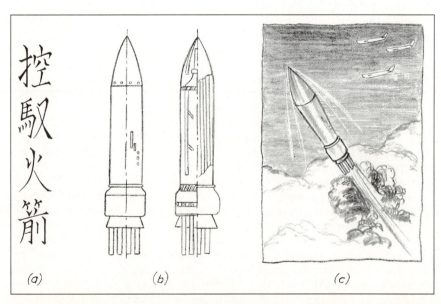

(a)

(b)

(c)

FIG. 4.2 Graphic methods for presenting ideas (symbolic, multiview, and pictorial).

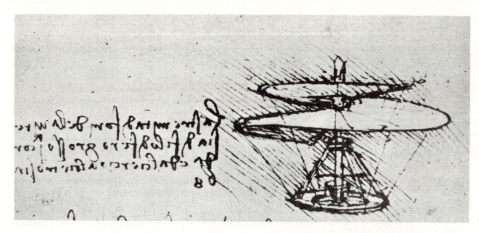

FIG. 4.3   Idea sketch of a helicopter prepared by Leonardo da Vinci (1452–1519). (*From Collections of Fine Arts Department, International Business Machines Corporation*)

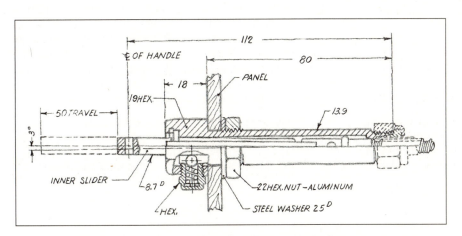

FIG. 4.4   Design sketch for a connector of a remote control unit. (*Courtesy Teleflex, Inc.*)

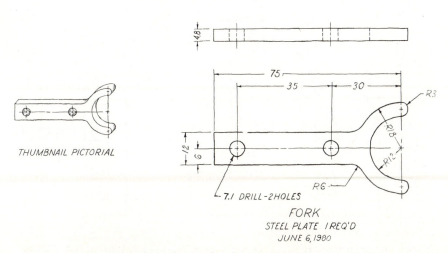

FIG. 4.5   Freehand sketch for the manufacture of a part.

multiview, pictorial, and the other divisions of mechanical drawing. The greater the familiarity with projection and the conventional practices of engineering drawing, the greater the effectiveness of the sketch.

B SKETCHING TECHNIQUES

4.5 Sketching Materials

For the type of sketching discussed in this chapter, all that is required is a pencil, a soft eraser, and some paper. In fact, many of today's most innovative designs were visualized on napkins or the back of envelopes—whatever was available! Using instruments such as a straight edge or circle template may actually slow down the sketching process. Remember: A sketch communicates information. It does not have to be an exact drawing. Use grid paper to relieve concern over straight lines (Fig. 4.6).

4.6 Technique of Lines

Freehand lines quite naturally differ in their appearance from mechanical lines. A well-executed freehand sketch will never be perfectly straight and absolutely uniform in weight, but an effort should be made to

approach exacting uniformity. Still, sketch lines resemble mechanical lines in their appearance—they should be black and clear, not broad and fuzzy (Fig. 4.7).

4.7 Straight Lines

Horizontal lines are sketched from left to right (right-handed) or from right to left (left-handed) with an easy motion that is pivoted about the muscle of the forearm. When sketching a straight line, it is advisable to first mark the end points with very light dots or small crosses (Figs. 4.8–4.11). The complete procedure for sketching a straight line is as follows:

1. Mark the end points.

2. Make a few trial motions between the marked end points.

3. Sketch a very light line between the two end points by moving the pencil in two or three sweeps. When sketching the trial line, the eye should be on the point toward which the movement is directed. The finished trial line will be relatively straight.

4. Darken the finished line in one stroke. Keep your eye again on the end point. The finished line should be distinct, black, and uniform.

It is helpful to turn the paper to a convenient angle so that all lines may be sketched naturally as horizontal lines. Short vertical lines may be sketched either downward or upward without changing the position of

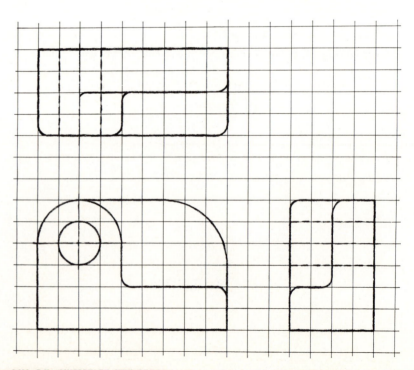

FIG. 4.6 Sketch on grid paper.

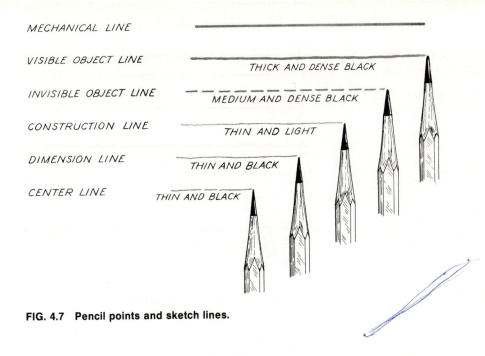

MECHANICAL LINE

VISIBLE OBJECT LINE

THICK AND DENSE BLACK

INVISIBLE OBJECT LINE

MEDIUM AND DENSE BLACK

CONSTRUCTION LINE

THIN AND LIGHT

DIMENSION LINE

THIN AND BLACK

CENTER LINE

THIN AND BLACK

FIG. 4.7 Pencil points and sketch lines.

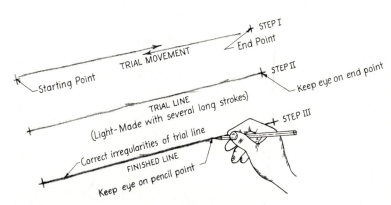

STEP I
End Point

TRIAL MOVEMENT

Starting Point

STEP II
Keep eye on end point

TRIAL LINE
(Light- Made with several long strokes)

STEP III

Correct irregularities of trial line

FINISHED LINE

Keep eye on pencil point

FIG. 4.8 Steps in sketching a straight line.

FIG. 4.9 Sketching horizontal lines.

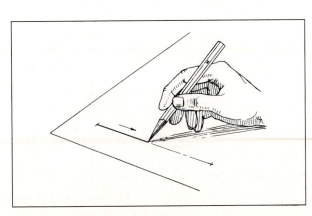

FIG. 4.10 Sketching vertical lines.

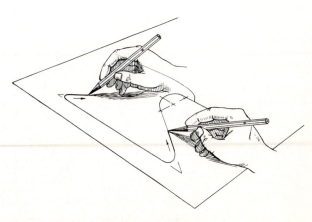

FIG. 4.11 Sketching inclined lines.

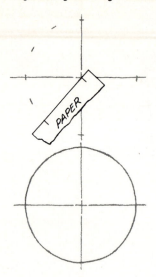

FIG. 4.12 Marking off radial distances.

the paper. A long vertical line is sketched by turning the paper so that the line assumes a horizontal position.

4.8 Circles

Small circles can be sketched in one motion by first marking radial distances on perpendicular center lines. For larger circles additional points may be needed.

Mark these off either by eye or use of a marked strip of paper for measuring (Fig. 4.12). Diagonals, in addition to the center lines, can be constructed as in Fig. 4.13.

1. Construct short perpendiculars at the end of each line the radial distance from the center.

2. Sketch short arcs tangent to these perpendiculars to approximate the circle.

3. The circle is completed in four sketched arcs. Turn the paper for convenience in sketching each quadrant.

C ■ *MULTIVIEW SKETCHES*

4.9 Creation of Multiview Sketch (Fig. 4.14)

When making orthographic working sketches a systematic order should be followed. All the rules and conventional practices used in making working drawings with instruments should be applied. The following procedure is recommended

1. Examine the object giving particular attention to detail.

2. Determine which views are necessary.

3. Block in views using light construction lines.

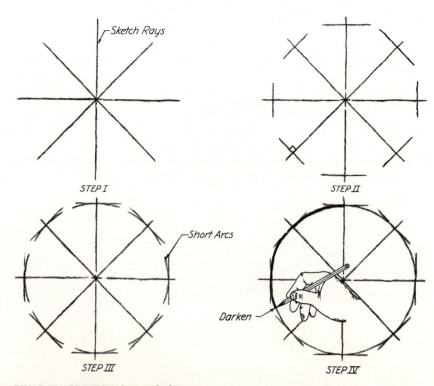

FIG. 4.13 Sketching large circles.

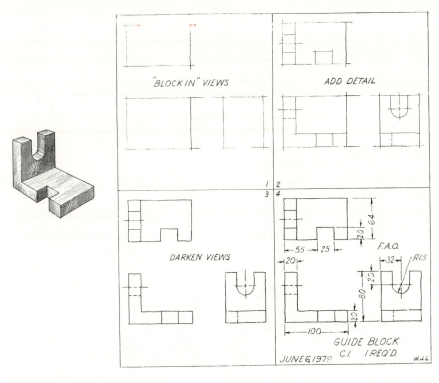

FIG. 4.14 Steps in sketching.

4. Complete the detail and darken object lines.

5. Sketch extension and dimension lines including arrowheads.

6. Complete the sketch by adding dimensions, notes, title, date, sketcher's name or initials, and any other information needed.

If you have not read Part A of Chapter 5 do so before attempting to make a multiview sketch.

4.10 *Proportions*

When planning a sketch, it is important to estimate the comparative relationships between width, height, and depth. Then, estimate the dimensions for any features—slots, holes, and projections—as percentages of the height, width, or depth. Estimate actual dimensions because sketches are not usually made to scale. For example, estimate that the width of the object is twice its height; that the width of a given slot is equal to one-half the width of the object; and that its depth is approximately one-fourth the overall height.

To become proficient in sketching, learn to recognize proportions and be able to compare dimensions by eye. This helps develop an ability to "think with a pencil." Some people can develop a keen eye for proportion after only a limited amount of practice and can maintain these estimated proportions when making views of a sketch. Others have alternately discouraging and encouraging experiences. Practice, practice, practice.

To begin a study of proportions, consider the graphical method shown in Fig. 4.15(*a–c*). In this ex-

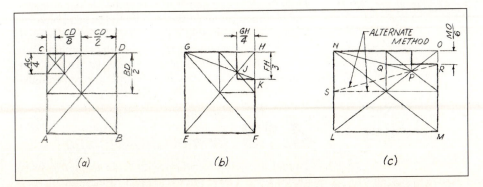

FIG. 4.15 Methods of proportioning a rectangle representing the outline of a view.

ample a square is divided and subdivided as is done in proportional sketching. To determine the midpoint of a rectangle and its sides (Fig. 4.15[*a*])

1. Sketch the diagonals of the rectangle.

2. Mark their intersection. This is the center of the rectangle.

3. A line through this point perpendicular to a side locates the center of that side.

To subdivide a rectangle into quarters or eights (Fig. 4.15[*a*])

1. Repeat midpoint construction for quadrant or octant.

To subdivide a rectangle into thirds (Fig. 4.15[*b*])

1. Sketch a line from corner *G* through the quadrant center *J* to the opposite side. Distance *H-K* is one-third the length of the side.

To subdivide a rectangle into sixths (4.15[*c*])

1. Sketch a line from corner *N* to quadrant center *P*.

2. Point *Q* is on the original rectangle's center line.

3. A line sketched from *Q* perpendicular to the side divides that side into one-sixth.

These methods can be used to proportion a view after one dimension (height, width, or depth) has been estimated (Fig. 4.16). In this method additional squares are added to the initial square whose side is the estimated dimension. As an example, suppose that you estimate that the front view should be three times as wide as it is high. In Fig. 4.17 the height of the view has been estimated as line *AB*.

To complete the front view

1. Sketch the initial square whose sides equal the estimated height.

2. Extend *AC* and *BD* to represent the top and bottom edges.

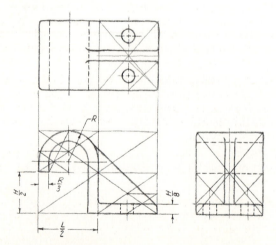

FIG. 4.16 Rectangle method applied in making an orthographic sketch.

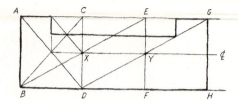

FIG. 4.17 Built-up method.

3. Locate the center of the square by the diagonal method (Fig. 4.15[*a*]).

4. Sketch center lines through the diagonals' intersection.

5. Sketch *BX* so that it intersects the top.

6. Sketch *DY* so that it intersects the top.

7. *AG* is now three times the length of *AB*.

D SKETCHING IN ISOMETRIC AND OBLIQUE

4.11 Pictorial Sketching

Pictorial sketches can be used to aid in visualizing and organizing problems. Sales engineers, for example, may use pictorial and orthographic sketches when writing field reports on client's needs and suggestions. *Artistic ability is not a requirement.* This fact is important, because many persons lack only experience to start making effective pictorial sketches.

4.12 Mechanical Methods of Sketching

Many engineers and technologists have found that they can produce satisfactory pictorial sketches by using mechanical methods (guides, straight edges, circle templates, etc.). They rely on these methods because of their familiarity with the procedures used in making pictorial drawings with instruments. The instrument procedures presented in Chapter 11 for axonometric and oblique drawing are generally followed in pictorial sketching except that angles and lengths are estimated. The greatest benefit of pictorial sketching may be to clarify certain aspects of a design. In addition, multiview drawings can often be interpreted through a pictorial sketch as shown in Fig. 4.18.

4.13 Isometric Sketching

Isometric sketching starts with three *isometric lines,* called axes. These lines represent three mutually perpendicular lines—the edges of an isometric box. One

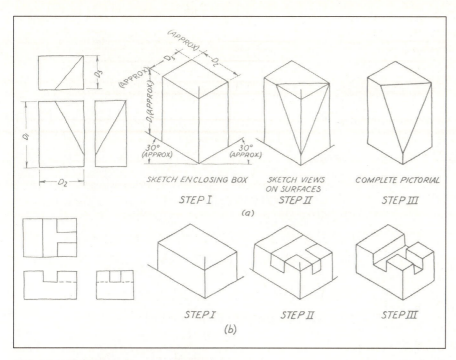

FIG. 4.18   Steps in isometric sketching.

of these lines is sketched vertically with the other two at an estimated 30° to the horizontal axis. In Fig. 4.18 (Step I), the near front corner of the enclosing box lies along the vertical axis, whereas the two receding horizontal edges of the base lie along the axes receding to the left and right.

If the object is of simple rectangular form, as in Fig. 4.18, it may be solved in the following manner

1. Sketch an enclosing isometric box (Step I).

2. On the surfaces of this box, draw the orthographic views (Step II).

3. Complete each feature by projecting it into the box (Step III).

Care must be taken in estimating lengths and distances so that the finished view will have relatively correct proportions. In constructing the enclosing

box, the vertical edges are parallel to the vertical axis, and edges receding to the right and left are parallel to the right and left horizontal axes.

Objects of more complicated construction may be "blocked in" as shown in Fig. 4.19. Note that the cylindrical features are first sketched as prisms—an application of the enclosing form method. Centers of holes are located and also blocked in. The finished part is actually enclosed in three rectangular prisms.

Sketching an ellipse in isometric requires careful layout. To produce an accurate ellipse you must pay attention to ellipse shape and tangent points. Often the ellipse is made too circular or too flat in a sketch. Follow these steps as illustrated in Fig. 4.20.

STEP 1. Sketch a isometric square (a rhombus) with sides equal to the diameter of the desired circle. Though dimensions are estimated, proportions are carefully maintained. The circle is shown for reference only and is not part of the necessary construction.

STEP 2. Sketch the diagonals and the isometric center lines. The diagonals establish the major and minor axes of the ellipse, and are helpful in keeping the ellipse symmetrical. The center lines establish points where the sketched arcs are tangent.

STEP 3. As in the four-center method (see Fig. 11.14), sketch the two larger diameter arcs. Assure that the arcs are tangent to the rhombus at the center lines.

STEP 4. Sketch the two smaller end arcs so that they are tangent to first two arcs. Assure that these arcs are tangent to the larger arcs at the center lines.

Figure 4.21 shows the three positions of an isometric circle. Note that the major axis of the ellipse (what

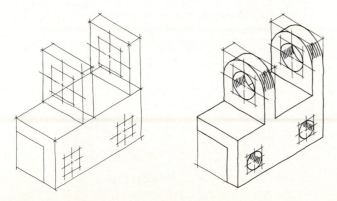

FIG. 4.19   Blocking in an isometric sketch.

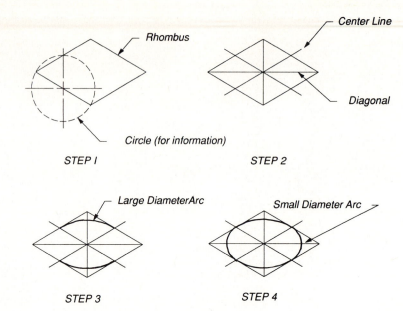

FIG. 4.20 Isometric circles by sketch method.

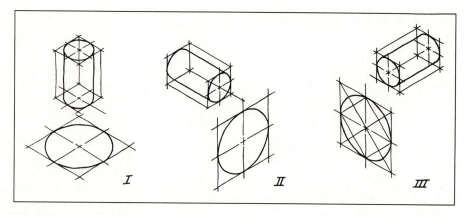

FIG. 4.21 Isometric circles.

one might call the "direction" of the ellipse) is aligned with the long diagonal in each of the three cases. An idea sketch in isometric is shown in Fig. 4.22.

4.14 *Proportioning*

To sketch rapidly, learn to judge lengths and recognize proportions. Until you are able to do this, however, the grapical method presented in Fig. 4.15 can be used in pictorial sketching. The procedures are identical to those used in orthographic only that what was rectangular in orthographic is now rhomboid in isometric. Figures 4.23 and 4.24 illustrate how this method might be applied in making a sketch of a simple object. The enclosing box was sketched first with light lines. The graphical subdivision method was then applied as shown to locate points at one-quarter, one-third, and

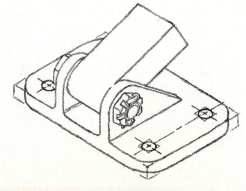

FIG. 4.22 Idea sketch in isometric.

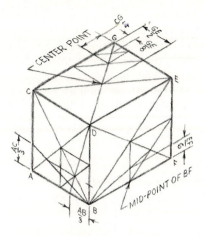

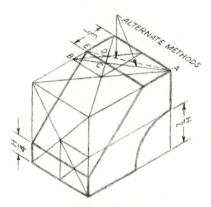

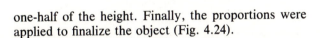

FIG. 4.23 Method for proportioning a rhomboid.

FIG. 4.24 Proportioning method applied.

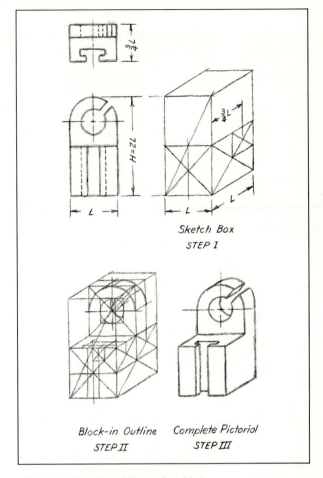

Sketch Box
STEP I

Block-in Outline
STEP II

Complete Pictorial
STEP III

FIG. 4.26 Steps in oblique sketching.

one-half of the height. Finally, the proportions were applied to finalize the object (Fig. 4.24).

4.15 *Sketches in Oblique*

A sketch in oblique shows the front face without distortion, in its true shape. It has this one advantage over an isometric, even if the final result may not be as pleasing. *It is not recommended for objects having circular or irregularly curved features on any but the front plane or a plane parallel to it.*

The methods for sketching in multiview and isometric apply to oblique as well. The principal difference between oblique and isometric is in the position of the axes. Oblique sketching is unlike isometric in that two of the axes are at right angles to each other. The third axis is at any convenient angle, as indicated in Fig. 4.25.

Figure 4.26 shows the steps in making an oblique sketch using the proportioning methods previously explained for dividing a rectangle and a rhomboid. Note that receding lines are parallel in an oblique sketch.

Objects that are deeper than they are wide or tall

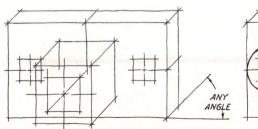

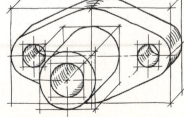

FIG. 4.25 Blocking in an oblique sketch.

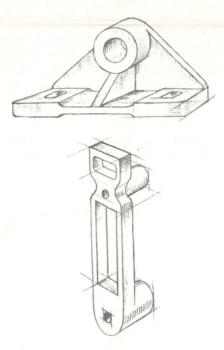

FIG. 4.27 **Sketches in parallel (*top*)
and angular (*bottom*) perspective.**

produce distortion, and may not be appropriate for oblique. This distortion and illusion of extreme elongation along the receding axis can be minimized by reducing the depth so that it appears more natural and by adding slight convergence. The resulting sketch will then be a form of pseudoperspective that resembles parallel perspective to some extent.

4.16 *Note on Perspective*

Though a perspective sketch will give a more realistic representation of an object, such drawings are not common in industry. They are commoner in architecture where the scale of a design may lend itself more to

this type of drawing. Perspective is more difficult to proportion and measure, and uses different mechanics of projection than do multiviews and isometrics. Perspectives sketches, like those shown in Fig. 4.27, accurately portray a designer's ideas but are more easily completed in isometric or oblique with almost no reduction in communication qualities.

 **SKETCHING
APPLICATIONS**

4.17 *Pencil Shading*

The addition of some shading to the surfaces of a part will force its form to stand out against the white surface of the sketching paper and increases the effect of depth in a view that might appear somewhat flat. This should be done to a sketch that is well proportioned and detailed, however. Shading should not be used to try and save a substandard sketch.

Technologists and drafters should be able to do acceptable work in technical shading. Within the scope of this chapter it is appropriate to present several simple rules as a guide for shading.

1. When shading, consider the source of light to be located to the left, above, and in front of the object (Fig. 4.28).

2. If the part actually exists and is being sketched by viewing it, duplicate the degree of shade and shadows as they are observed.

3. If the paper has a medium-rough surface, solid tone shading can be used with one shade blending into another. For best results, work from lighter to darker, with the darkest tones built up to their desired intensity. For this form of shading a flattened pencil point is used.

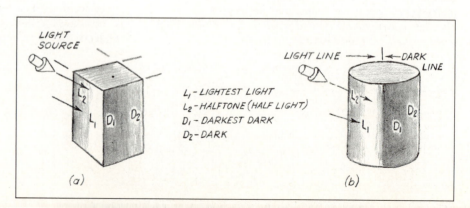

FIG. 4.28 Shading rectangular and cylindrical parts.

4.18 Conventional Treatment of Fillets, Rounds, and Screw Threads

Sketches that are not given full pencil shading may be given more realistic appearance by representing the fillets and rounds of unfinished surfaces as shown in Fig. 11.38. The conventional treatment for screw threads is shown in parts *b* and *c* of the same illustration.

4.19 Use of Overlays

Use an *overlay sheet* in making a sketch that is complicated by many details (Fig. 4.29). First, a quick sketch showing the general outline of the principal parts is made in a rather rough form. Then an overlay sheet is placed over this outline sketch, and the lines are retraced. In doing so, slight corrections can be made to the proportions of the parts or to the position of any lines of the original rough sketch. When this has been

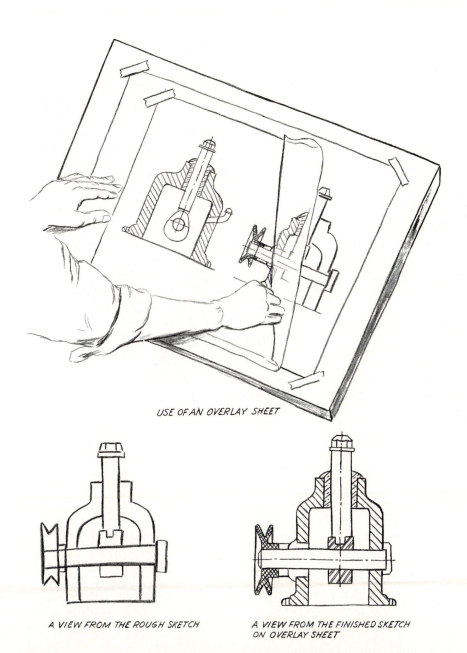

USE OF AN OVERLAY SHEET

A VIEW FROM THE ROUGH SKETCH

A VIEW FROM THE FINISHED SKETCH ON OVERLAY SHEET

FIG. 4.29 Use of overlay sheet for creating final and complete sketch of mechanism.

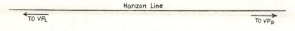

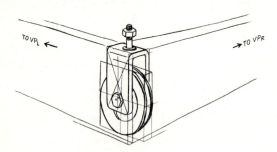

Block-in assembly in outline

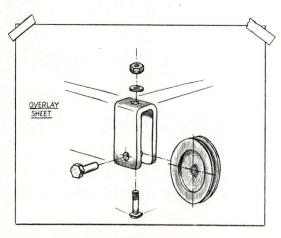

Retrace parts on overlay sheet in
exploded positions from assembly sketch

FIG. 4.30 Sketch showing the parts of a mechanism in exploded positions.

done, the representation of the related minor parts is added. When starting over, use an overlay sheet to trace parts of the original sketch that can be reused.

4.20 Illustration Sketches Showing Mechanisms Exploded

A sketch of a mechanism showing the parts in exploded positions along the principal axes is shown in Fig. 4.30. Through the use of exploded sketches it is readily understood how a mechanism should be assembled, because both the shapes of the parts and the order of assembly as denoted by their space relationship is shown in pictorial space.

4.21 Pictorial Sketches on Ruled Paper

Because ideas often come at inopportune times, you should become proficient in sketching on plain white paper. Under more controlled situations, special grid paper, as shown in Fig. 4.31, is available.

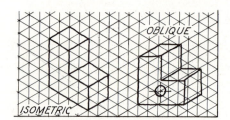

FIG. 4.31 Sketches on isometric paper.

Engineering Geometry

A PLANE GEOMETRY—ENGINEERING CONSTRUCTIONS

5.1 Introduction

The simplified geometric constructions presented in this chapter are those with which an engineer should be familiar, for they occur frequently in engineering drawing. The methods are applications of the principles found in textbooks on plane geometry. The constructions have been modified to take advantage of time-saving methods made possible by the use of drawing instruments.

Because a study of the subject of plane geometry should be a prerequisite for a course in engineering drawing, the mathematical proofs have been omitted intentionally. Geometric terms applying to lines, surfaces, and solids, are given in Figs. 5.53, 5.70 and 5.71.

5.2 To Bisect a Straight Line (Fig. 5.1)

(*a*) With *A* and *B* as centers, strike the intersecting arcs as shown using any radius greater than one-half of *AB*. A straight line through points *C* and *D* bisects *AB*.

(*b*) Draw either 60° or 45° lines through *E* and *F*. Through their intersection draw the perpendicular *GH* that will bisect *EF*.

5.3 To Trisect a Straight Line (Fig. 5.2)

Given the line *AB*. Draw the lines *AO* and *OB* making 30° with *AB*. Similarly, draw *CO* and *OD* making 60° with *AB*. *AC* equals *CD* equals *DB*.

5.4 To Bisect an Angle (Fig. 5.3)

(*a*) Given the angle *BAC*. Use any radius with the vertex *A* as a center, and strike an arc that intersects the sides of the angle at *D* and *E*. With *D* and *E* as centers and a radius larger than one-half of *DE*, draw intersecting arcs. Draw *AF*. Angle *BAF* equals angle *FAC*.

(*b*) Given an angle formed by the lines *KL* and *MN* having an inaccessible point of intersection. Draw *BA*

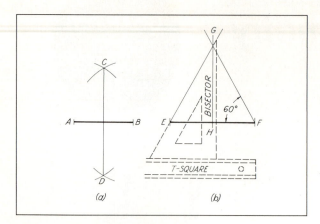

FIG. 5.1 To bisect a straight line.

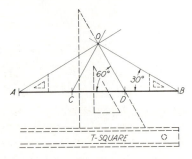

FIG. 5.2 To trisect a straight line.

parallel to *KL* and *CA* parallel to *MN* at the same distance from *MN* as *BA* is from *KL*. Bisect angle *BAC* using the method explained in part *a*. The bisector *FA* of angle *BAC* bisects the angle between the lines *KL* and *MN*.

5.5 To Draw Parallel Curved Lines about a Curved Center Line (Fig. 5.4)

Draw a series of arcs having centers located at random along the given center line *AB*. Using the French curve, draw the required curved lines tangent to these arcs.

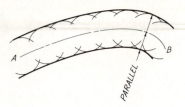

FIG. 5.4 To draw parallel curved lines.

5.6 To Trisect an Angle (Fig. 5.5)

Given the angle *BAC*. Lay off along *AB* any convenient distance *AD*. Draw *DE* perpendicular to *AC* and *DF* parallel to *AC*. Place the scale so that it passes through *A* with a distance equal to twice *AD* intercepted between the lines *DE* and *DF*. Angle *HAC* equals one-third of the angle *BAC*.

5.7 To Divide a Straight Line into a Given Number of Equal Parts (Fig. 5.6)

Given the line *LM*, which is to be divided into five equal parts.

(*a*) Step off, with the dividers, five equal divisions along a line making any convenient angle with *LM*. Connect the last point *P* and *M*, and through the remaining points draw lines parallel to *MP* intersecting

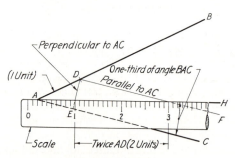

FIG. 5.5 To trisect an angle.

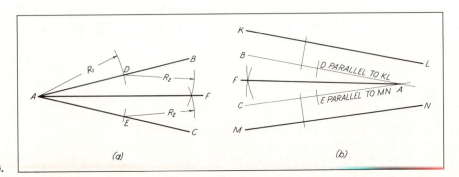

FIG. 5.3 To bisect an angle.

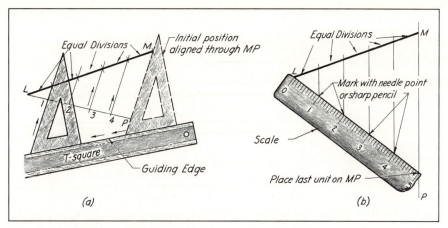

FIG. 5.6   To divide a straight line into several equal parts.

the given line. These lines divide *LM* into five equal parts.

(*b*) Some commercial draftsmen prefer a modification of this construction known as the scale method. For the first step, draw a vertical *PM* through point *M*. Place the scale so that the first mark of five equal divisions is at *L* and the last mark falls on *PM*. Locate the four intervening division points, and through these draw verticals intersecting the given line. The verticals will divide *LM* into five equal parts.

5.8 To Divide a Line Proportionally (Fig. 5.7)

Given the line *AB*. Draw *BC* perpendicular to *AB*. Place the scale across *A* and *BC* so that the number of divisions intercepted is equal to the sum of the numbers representing the proportions. Mark off these proportions and draw lines parallel to *BC* to divide *AB* as required. The proportions in Fig. 5.7 are 1 : 2 : 3.

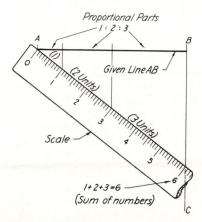

FIG. 5.7   To divide a line proportionally.

5.9 To Construct an Angle Equal to a Given Angle (Fig. 5.8)

Given the angle *BAC* and the line *A'C'* that forms one side of the transferred angle. Use any convenient radius with the vertex *A* as a center, and strike the arc that intersects the sides of the angle at *D* and *E*. With *A'* as a center, strike the arc intersecting *A'C'* at *E'*. With *E'* as a center and the chord distance *DE* as a radius, strike a short intersecting arc to locate *D'*. *A'B'* drawn through *D'* makes angle *B'A'C'* equal angle *BAC*.

5.10 To Draw a Line Through a Given Point and the Inaccessible Intersection of Two Given Lines (Fig. 5.9)

Given the lines *KL* and *MN*, and the point *P*. Construct any triangle, such as *PQR*, having its vertices falling on the given lines and the given point. At some convenient location construct triangle *STU* similar to

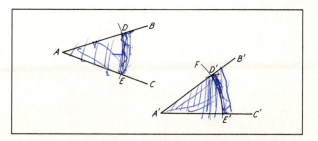

FIG. 5.8   To construct an angle equal to a given angle.

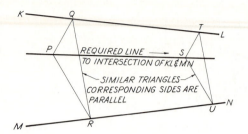

FIG. 5.9 **To draw a line through a given point and the inaccessible intersection of two given lines.**

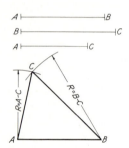

FIG. 5.10 **To construct a triangle, given its three sides.**

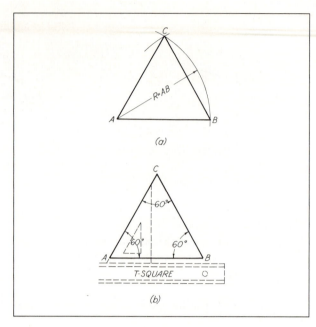

FIG. 5.11 **To construct an equilateral triangle.**

PQR, by drawing *SU* parallel to *PR*, *TU* parallel to *QR*, and *ST* parallel to *PQ*. *PS* is the required line.

5.11 To Construct a Triangle, Given Its Three Sides (Fig. 5.10)

Given the three sides *AB*, *AC*, and *BC*. Draw the side *AB* in its correct location. Using its end points *A* and *B* as centers and radii equal to *AC* and *BC*, respectively, strike the two intersecting arcs locating point *C*. *ABC* is the required triangle. This construction is particularly useful for developing the surface of a transition piece of triangulation.

5.12 To Construct an Equilateral Triangle (Fig. 5.11)

Given the side *AB*.

(*a*) Using the end points *A* and *B* as centers and a radius equal to the length of *AB*, strike two intersecting arcs to locate *C*. Draw lines from *A* to *C* and *C* to *B* to complete the required equilateral triangle.

(*b*) Using a 30° × 60° triangle, draw through *A* and *B* lines that make 60° with the given line. If the line *AB* is inclined, the 60° lines should be drawn as shown in Fig. 2.32.

5.13 To Transfer a Polygon (Fig. 5.12)

Given the polygon *ABCDE*.

(*a*) Enclose the polygon in a rectangle. Draw the "enclosing rectangle" in the new position and locate points *A*, *B*, *C*, *D*, and *E* along the sides by measuring from the corners of the rectangle. A compass may be used for transferring the necessary measurements.

(*b*) To transfer a polygon by the triangle method, divide the polygon into triangles and, using the construction explained in Sec. 5.15, reconstruct each triangle in its transferred position.

5.14 To Construct a Square (Fig. 5.13)

(*a*) Given the side *AB*. Using a T-square and a 45° triangle, draw perpendiculars to line *AB* through points *A* and *B*. Locate point *D* at the intersection of a 45° construction line through *A* and the perpendicular from *B*. Draw *CD* parallel to *AB* through *D* to complete the square. To eliminate unnecessary movements the lines should be drawn in the order indicated.

(*b*) Given the diagonal length *EF*. Using a T-square and a 45° triangle, construct the square by drawing lines through *E* and *F* at an angle of 45° with *EF* in the order indicated.

(*c*) The construction of an inscribed circle is the first step in one method for drawing a square when the location of the center and the length of one side are given.

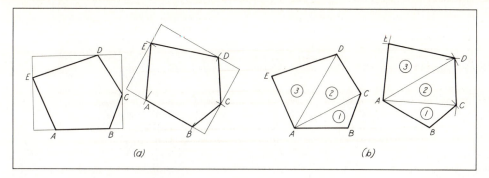

FIG. 5.12 To transfer a polygon.

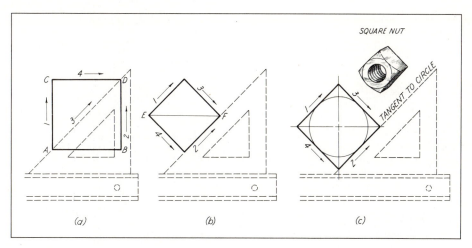

FIG. 5.13 To construct a square.

Using a T-square and a 45° triangle, draw the sides of the square tangent to the circle. This construction is used in drawing square bolt heads and nuts.

5.15 To Construct a Regular Pentagon (Fig. 5.14)

Given the circumscribing circle. Draw the perpendicular diameters *AB* and *CD*. Bisect *OB* and, with its midpoint *E* as a center and *EC* as a radius, draw the arc *CF*. Using *C* as a center and *CF* as a radius, draw

the arc *FG*. The line *CG* is one of the equal sides of the required pentagon. Locate the remaining vertices by striking off this distance around the circumference.

If the length of one side of a pentagon is given, the construction described in Sec. 3.19 should be used.

5.16 To Construct a Regular Hexagon (Fig. 5.15)

(*a*) Given the distance *AB* across corners. Draw a circle having *AB* as a diameter. Using the same radius and with points *A* and *B* as centers, strike arcs intersecting the circumference. Join these points to complete the construction.

(*b*) Given the distance *AB* across corners. Using a 30° × 60° triangle and a T-square, draw the lines in the order indicated by the numbers on the figure.

(*c*) Given the distance across flats. Draw a circle whose diameter equals the distance across flats. Using a 30° × 60° triangle and a T-square, as shown, draw the tangents that establish the sides and vertices of the required hexagon.

This construction is used in drawing hexagonal bolt heads and nuts.

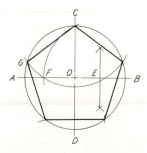

FIG. 5.14 To construct a regular pentagon.

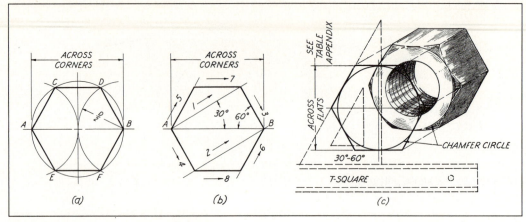

FIG. 5.15 To construct a regular hexagon.

5.17 To Construct a Regular Octagon (Fig. 5.16)

(*a*) Given the distance across flats. Draw the circumscribed square and its diagonals. Using the corners as centers and one-half the diagonal as a radius, strike arcs across the sides of the square. Join these points to complete the required octagon.

(*b*) Given the distance across flats. Draw the inscribed circle; then, using a 45° triangle and T-square, draw the tangents that establish the sides and vertices of the required octagon.

5.18 To Construct Any Regular Polygon, Given One Side (Fig. 5.17)

Given the side *LM*. With *LM* as a radius, draw a semicircle and divide it into the same number of equal parts as the number of sides needed for the polygon. Suppose the polygon is to be seven-sided. Draw radial lines through points 2, 3, and so forth. Point 2 (the second division point) is always one of the vertices of the polygon, and line *L*2 is a side. Using point *M* as a center and *LM* as a radius, strike an arc across the radial line *L*6 to locate point *N*. Using the same radius

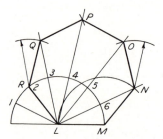

FIG. 5.17 To construct any regular polygon, given one side.

with *N* as a center, strike another arc across *L*5 to establish *O* on *L*5. Although this procedure may be continued with point *O* as the next center, more accurate results will be obtained if point *R* is used as a center for the arc to locate *Q*, and *Q* as a center for *P*.

5.19 To Divide the Area of a Triangle or Trapezoid into a Given Number of Equal Parts (Fig. 5.18)

(*a*) Given the triangle *ABC*. Divide the side *AC* into (say, five) equal parts, and draw a semicircle having *AC* the diameter. Through the division points (1, 2, 3, and 4) draw perpendicular lines to points of intersection with the semicircle (5, 6, 7, and 8). Using *C* as a center, strike arcs through these points (5, 6, 7, and 8) that will cut *AC*. To complete the construction, draw lines parallel to *AB* through the points (9, 10, 11, and 12) at which the arcs intersect the side *AC*.

(*b*) Given the trapezoid *DEBA*. Extend the sides of the trapezoid to form the triangle *ABC* and draw a semicircle on *AC* with *AC* as a diameter. Using *C* as a center and *CD* as a radius, strike an arc cutting the semicircle at point *P*. Through *P* draw a perpendicular

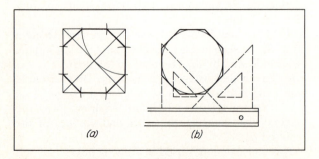

FIG. 5.16 To construct a regular octagon.

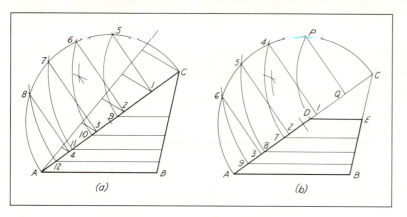

FIG. 5.18 **To divide the area of a triangle or trapezoid into a given number** of equal parts.

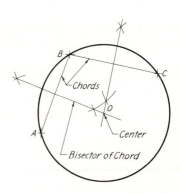

FIG. 5.19 **To find the center of** a circle through three points.

to *AC* to locate point *Q*. Divide *QA* into the same number of equal parts as the number of equal areas required (in this case, four), and proceed using the construction explained in part *a* for dividing the area of a triangle into a given number of equal parts.

5.20 To Find the Center of a Circle Through Three Given Points Not in a Straight Line (Fig. 5.19)

Given the three points *A*, *B*, and *C*. Join the points with straight lines (which will be chords of the required circle), and draw the perpendicular bisectors. The point of intersection *O* of the bisectors is the center of the required circle, and *OA*, *OB*, or *OC* is its radius.

5.21 Tangent Circles and Arcs

Figure 5.20 illustrates the geometry of tangent circles. In part *a* it can be noted that the locus of centers for circles of radius *R* tangent to *AB* is a line that is paral-

lel to *AB* at a distance *R* from *AB*. The locus of centers for circles of the same radius tangent to *CD* is a line that is parallel to *CD* at distance *R* (radius) from *CD*. Because point *O* at which these lines intersect is distance *R* from both *AB* and *CD*, a circle of radius *R* with center at *O* must be tangent to both *AB* and *CD*.

In part *b* the locus of centers for circles of radius R_3 that will be tangent to the circle with a center at *O* and having a radius R_1 is a circle that is concentric with the given circle at distance R_3. The radius of the locus of centers will be $R_1 + R_3$. In the case of the circle with center at point *P*, the radius of the locus of centers will be $R_2 + R_3$. Points *Q* and Q_1, where these arcs intersect, are points that are distance R_3 from both circles. Therefore, circles of radius R_3 that are centered at *Q* and Q_1 will be tangent to both circles with centers at *O* and *P*.

5.22 To Draw a Circular Arc of Radius R Tangent to Two Lines (Fig. 5.21)

(*a*) Given the two lines *AB* and *CD* at right angles to each other, and the radius of the required arc *R*. Using their point of intersection *X* as a center and *R* as a

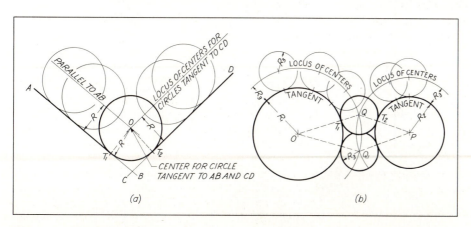

FIG. 5.20 **Tangent circles.**

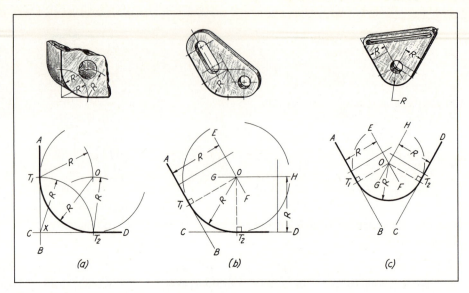

FIG. 5.21 To draw a circular arc tangent to two lines.

radius, strike an arc cutting the given lines at T_1 and T_2 (tangent points). With T_1 and T_2 as centers and the same radius, strike the intersecting arcs locating the center O of the required arc.

(b),(c) Given the two lines AB and CD, not at right angles, and the radius R. Draw lines EF and GH parallel to the given lines at a distance R. Because the point of intersection of these lines is distance R from both given lines, it will be the center O of the required arc. Mark the tangent points T_1 and T_2 that lie along perpendiculars to the given lines through O.

These constructions are useful for drawing fillets and rounds on views of machine parts.

5.23 To Draw a Circular Arc of Radius R_1 Tangent of a Given Circular Arc and a Given Straight Line (Fig. 5.22)

Given the line AB and the circular arc with center O.

(a),(b) Draw line CD parallel to AB at a distance R_1. Using the center O of a given arc and a radius equal to its radius plus or minus the required arc (R_2 plus or minus R_1), swing a parallel arc intersecting CD. Because the line CD and the intersecting arc will be the

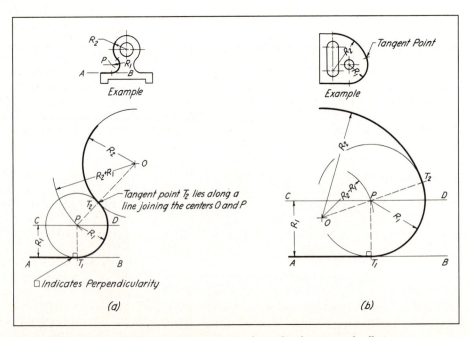

FIG. 5.22 To draw a circular arc tangent to a given circular arc and a line.

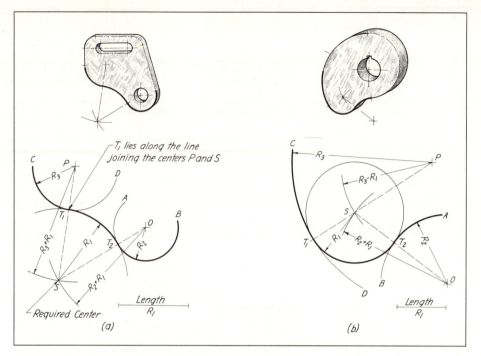

FIG. 5.23 To draw a circular arc tangent to two given arcs.

loci of centers for all circles of radius R_1, tangent, respectively, to the given line AB and the given arc, their point of intersection P will be the center of the required arc. Mark the points of tangency T_1 and T_2. T_1 lies along a perpendicular to AB through the center P, and T_2 along a line joining the centers of the two arcs.

This construction is also useful for drawing fillets and rounds on views of machine parts.

5.24 To Draw a Circular Arc of a Given Radius R_1 Tangent to Two Given Circular Arcs (Fig. 5.23)

Given the circular arcs AB and CD with centers O and $P,$ and radii R_2 and R_3, respectively.

(*a*) Using O as a center and R_2 plus R_1 as a radius, strike an arc parallel to AB. Using P as a center and R_3 plus R_1 as a radius, strike an intersecting arc parallel to CD. Because each of these intersecting arcs are distance R, away from arcs AB and CD, S will be the center for the required arc that is tangent to both. Mark the points of tangency T_1 and T_2 that lie on the lines of centers PS and OS.

(*b*) Using O as a center and R_2 and R_1 as a radius, strike an arc parallel to AB. Using P as a center and R_3 minus R_1 as a radius, strike an intersecting arc parallel to CD. The point of intersection of these arcs is the center for the required arc.

5.25 To Draw a Reverse (Ogee) Curve (Fig. 5.24)

(*a*) *Reverse (ogee) curve connecting two parallel lines.* Given the two parallel lines AB and CD. At points B and C, the termini and tangent points of the reverse curve, erect perpendiculars. Join B and C with a straight line and assume a point E as the point at which the curves will be tangent to each other. Draw the perpendicular bisectors of BE and EC. Because an arc tangent to AB at B must have its center on the perpendicular BP, the point of intersection P of the bisector and the perpendicular is the center for the required arc that is to be tangent to the line at B and the other required arc at point E. For the same reason, point Q is the center for the other required arc.

This construction is useful to engineers in laying out center lines for railroad tracks, pipelines, and so forth.

(*b*) *Reverse (ogee) curve connecting two nonparallel lines.* Given the two nonparallel lines AB and CD. At points B and C, the termini and tangent points, erect perpendiculars. Along the perpendicular at B lay off the given (or selected) radius R and draw the arc having P as its center. Then draw a construction line through point P perpendicular to CD to establish the location of point X. With the position of X known, join parts X and C with a straight line along which will lie the chords of the arcs forming the ogee curve between points X and C. The broken line XY (not a part of the construction) has been added to show that the procedure to be followed in completing the required curve will be as previously explained for drawing a reverse

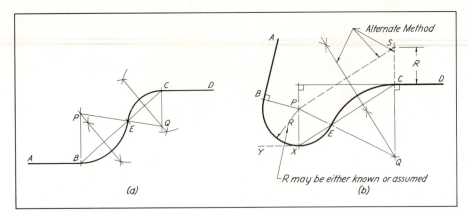

FIG. 5.24 To draw a reverse curve.

curve joining two parallel lines. In this case the parallel lines are *XY* and *CD*, instead of the lines *AB* and *CD* as in part *a*.

An alternative method for establishing the needed center for the required arc has been added to the illustration in part *b*. In this method the radius distance *R* is laid off upward along a perpendicular to *CD* through *C*. With point *S* established by this measurement, the line *PS*, as drawn, becomes the chord of an arc (not shown) that will have the same center as the required arc *EC*. The intersection of the perpendicular bisector of *PS* with the perpendicular erected downward from *C* will establish the position of point *Q*, the center of concentric arcs having chords *PS* and *EC*.

5.26 To Draw a Reverse Curve Tangent to Three Given Lines (Fig. 5.25)

Given a circle with center *O* and an external point *P*. Join the point *P* and the center *O* with a straight line, point *E* (point of tangency) along *BC* and locate the termini points T_1 and T_2 by making CT_1 equal to *CE* and BT_2 equal to *BE*. The intersections of the perpendiculars erected at points T_1, *E*, and T_2 establish the centers *P* and *Q* of the arcs that form the reversed curve.

5.27 To Draw a Line Tangent to a Circle at a Given Point on the Circumference (Fig. 5.26)

Given a circle with center *O* and point *P* on its circumference. Place a triangle supported by a T-square or another triangle in such a position that one side passes through the center *O* and point *P*. When using the method illustrated in part *a*, align the hypotenuse of one triangle on the center of the circle and the point of tangency; then, with the guiding triangle held in position, revolve the triangle about the 90° angle and slide into position for drawing the required tangent line.

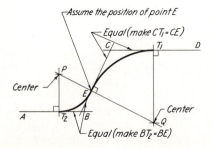

FIG. 5.25 To draw a reverse curve tangent to three lines.

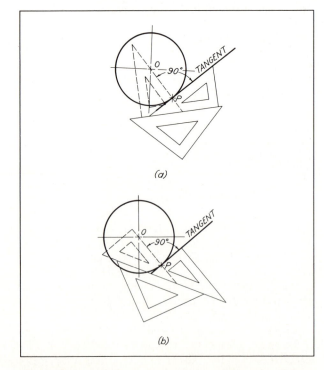

FIG. 5.26 To draw a line tangent to a circle at a point on the circumference.

Another procedure is shown in part *b*. To draw the tangent by this method, align one leg of a triangle, which is adjacent to the 90° angle, through the center of the circle and the point of tangency; then slide it along the edge of a guiding triangle into position.

This construction satisfies the geometric requirement that a tangent must be perpendicular to a radial line drawn to the point of tangency.

5.28 To Draw a Line Tangent to a Circle Through a Given Point Outside the Circle (Fig. 5.27)

Given a circle with center *O* and an external point *P*. Join the point *P* and the center *O* with a straight line, and bisect it to locate point *S*. Using *S* as a center and *SO* (one-half *PO*) as a radius, strike an arc intersecting the circle at point *T* (point of tangency). Line *PT* is the required tangent.

5.29 To Draw a Tangent Through a Point P on a Circular Arc Having an Inaccessible Center (Fig. 5.28)

Draw the chord *PB;* then erect a perpendicular bisector. With point *P* as a center swing an arc through point *C* where the perpendicular bisector cuts the given arc. With *C* as a center and a radius equal to the chord distance *CE*, draw an arc to establish the location of point *F*. A line drawn through points *P* and *F* is the required tangent.

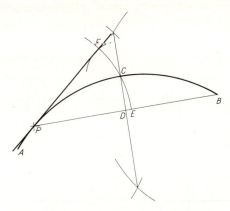

FIG. 5.28 To draw a tangent to a circular arc having an inaccessible center.

5.30 To Draw a Line Tangent to a Circle Through a Given Point Outside the Circle (Fig. 5.29)

Place a triangle supported by a T-square or another triangle in such a position that one leg passes through point *P* tangent to the circle, and draw the tangent. Slide the triangle along the guiding edge until the other leg coincides with the center *O*, and mark the point of tangency. Although this method is not as accurate as the geometric one explained in Sec. 3.30, it is frequently employed by commercial draftsmen.

5.31 To Draw a Line Tangent to Two Given Circles (Fig. 5.30)

Given two circles with centers *O* and *P* and radii *R*₁ and *R*.

(*a*) *Open belt.* Using *P* as a center and a radius equal to *R* minus *R*₁, draw an arc. Through *O* draw a tangent to this arc using the method explained in Sec. 3.30.

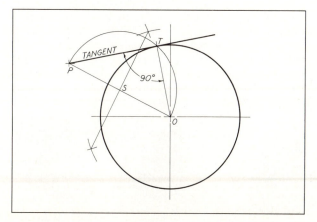

FIG. 5.27 To draw a line tangent to a circle through a given point outside.

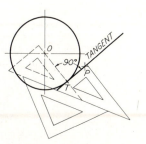

FIG. 5.29 To draw a line tangent to a circle through a given point outside.

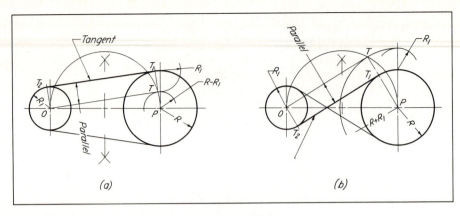

FIG. 5.30   To draw a line tangent to two given circles.

With this location of tangent point *T* established, draw line *PT* and extend it to locate T_1. Draw OT_2 parallel to PT_1. The line from T_2 to T_1 is the required tangent to the given circles.

(*b*) *Crossed belt*. Using *P* as a center and a radius equal to *R* plus R_1, draw an arc. With the location of tangent point *T* determined through use of the method shown in Fig. 3.31, locate tangent point T_1 on line *TP* and draw OT_2 parallel to *PT*. The line T_1T_2, drawn parallel to *OT,* is the required tangent.

5.32 *Conic Sections (Fig. 5.31)*

When a right circular cone of revolution is cut by planes at different angles, four curves of intersection are obtained that are called *conic sections*.

When the intersecting plane is perpendicular to the axis, the resulting curve of intersection is a *circle*.

If the plane makes a greater angle with the axis than do the elements, the intersection is an *ellipse*.

If the plane makes the same angle with the axis as the elements, the resulting curve is a *parabola*.

Finally, if the plane makes a smaller angle with the axis than do the elements or is parallel to the axis, the curve of intersection is a *hyperbola*.

The geometric methods for constructing the ellipse, parabola, and hyperbola are discussed in succeeding sections.

5.33 *Ellipse*

Mathematically the ellipse is a curve generated by a point moving so that at any position the sum of its distances from two fixed points (foci) is a constant (equal to the major diameter). It is encountered very frequently in orthographic drawing when holes and circular forms are viewed obliquely. Ordinarily, the major and minor diameters are known.

5.34 *To Construct an Ellipse, Trammel Method (Fig. 5.32)*

Given the major axis *AB* and the minor axis *CD*. Along the straight edge of a strip of paper or cardboard, locate the points *O, C,* and *A* so that the distance *OA* is equal to one-half the length of the major axis, and the distance *OC* is equal to one-half the length of the minor axis. Place the marked edge across the axes so that point *A* is on the minor axis and point *C* is on the major axis. *Point* O *will fall on the circumference of the ellipse.* Move the strip, keeping *A* on the minor axis and *C* on the major axis, and mark at least five other positions of *O* on the ellipse in each quadrant. Using a French curve, complete the ellipse by drawing a smooth curve through the points. The ellipsograph, which draws ellipses mechanically, is based on this

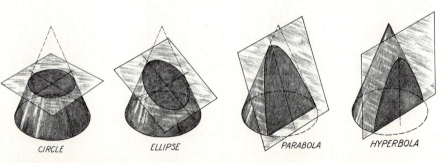

CIRCLE   ELLIPSE   PARABOLA   HYPERBOLA

FIG. 5.31   Conic sections.

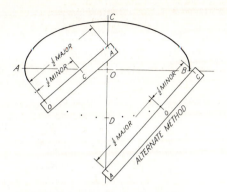

FIG. 5.32   To construct an ellipse, trammel method.

same principle. The trammel method is an accurate method.

An alternative method for marking off the location of points *A*, *O*, and *C* is given in Fig. 5.32.

5.35 *To Construct an Ellipse, Concentric Circle Method (Fig. 5.33)*

Given the major axis *AB* and the minor axis *CD*. Using the center of the ellipse (point *O*) as a center, describe circles having the major and minor axes as diameters. Divide the circles into equal central angles and draw diametrical lines such as P_1P_2. From point P_1 on the circumference of the larger circle, draw a line parallel to *CD*, the minor axis, and from point P_1' at which the diameter P_1P_2 intersects the inner circle, draw a line parallel to *AB*, the major axis. The point of intersection of these lines, point *E*, is on the required ellipse. At points P_2 and P_2' repeat the same procedure and locate point *F*. Thus, two points are established by the line P_1P_2. Locate at least five points in each of the four quadrants. The ellipse is completed by drawing a smooth curve through the points.

This is one of the most accurate methods used to form ellipses.

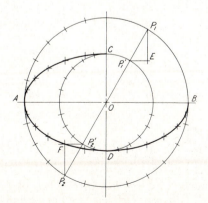

FIG. 5.33   To construct an ellipse, concentric circle method.

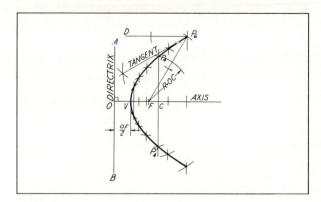

FIG. 5.34   To construct a parabola.

5.36 *Parabola (Fig. 5.34)*

Mathematically the parabola is a curve generated by a point moving so that at any position its distance from a fixed point (the focus) is always exactly equal to its distance to a fixed line (the directrix). The construction shown in Fig. 5.34 is based on this definition.

In engineering design, the parabola is used for parabolic sound and light reflectors, for vertical curves on highways, and for bridge arches.

5.37 *To Construct a Parabola, Offset Method (Fig. 5.35)*

Given the enclosing rectangle *A'ABB'*. Divide *VA'* into any number of equal parts (say, ten) and draw from the division points the perpendicular parallel to *VC*, along which offset distances are to be laid off. The offsets vary as the square of their distances from *V*.

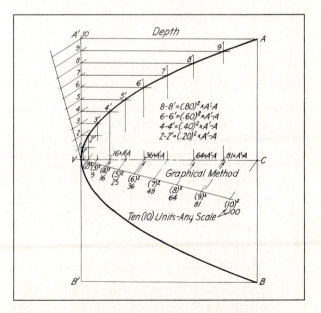

FIG. 5.35   To construct a parabola, offset method.

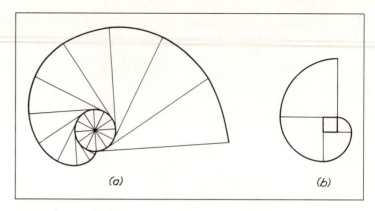

FIG. 5.36(a)   Involute.

For example, since *V* to 2 is two-tenths of the distance from *V* to *A'*, 2–2' will be (.2)² or .04 of *A'A*. Similarly, 6–6' will be (.6)² or .36 of *A'A*; and 8–8' will be .64 of *A'A*. To complete the parabola, lay off the computed offset values along the perpendiculars and form the figure with a French curve.

The offset method is preferred by civil engineers for laying out parabolic arches and computing vertical curves for highways. The parabola shown in Fig. 5.35 could represent a parabolic reflector.

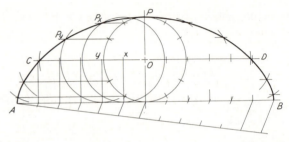

FIG. 5.37   Cycloid.

5.38 Involute

The spiral curve traced by a point on a cord as it unwinds from around a circle or a polygon is an *involute curve*. Figure 5.36(*a*) shows an involute of a circle, whereas part *b* shows that of a square. The involute of a polygon is obtained by extending the sides and drawing arcs using the corners, in order, as centers. The circle in part *a* may be considered to be a polygon having an infinite number of sides.

5.39 To Draw an Involute of a Circle (Fig. 5.36[a])

Divide the circumference into a number of equal parts. Draw tangents through the division points. Then, along each tangent, lay off the rectified length of the corresponding circular arc, from the starting point to the point of tangency. The involute curve is a smooth curve through these points. The involute of a circle is used in the development of tooth profiles in gearing.

5.40 Cycloid

A cycloid is the curve generated by a point on the circumference of a moving circle when the circle rolls in a plane along a straight line, as shown in Fig. 5.37.

5.41 To Draw a Cycloid (Fig. 5.37)

Draw the generating circle and the line *AB* tangent to it. The length *AB* should be made equal to the circumference of the circle. Divide the circle and the line *AB* into the same number of equal parts. With this much of the construction completed, the next step is to draw the line of centers *CD* through point *O* and project the division points along *AB* to *CD* by drawing perpendiculars. Using these points as centers for the various positions of the moving circle, draw circle arcs. For the purpose of illustration, assume the circle is moving to the left. When the circle has moved along *CD* to *x*, point *P* will have moved to point P_x. Similarly, when the center is at *y*, *P* will be at P_y. To locate positions at *P* along the cycloidal curve, project the division points of the divided circle in their proper order, across to the position circles. A smooth curve through these points will be the required cycloid.

5.42 Epicycloid (Fig. 5.38)

An epicycloid is the curve generated by a point on the circumference of a circle that rolls in a plane on the outside of another circle. The method used in drawing an epicycloid is similar to the one used in drawing the cycloid.

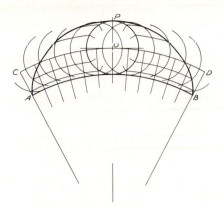

FIG. 5.38 Epicycloid.

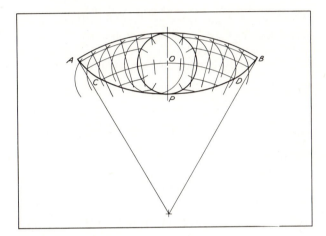

FIG. 5.39 Hypocycloid.

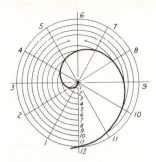

FIG. 5.40 Spiral of Archimedes.

5.43 *Hypocycloid (Fig. 5.39)*

A hypocycloid is the curve generated by a point on the circumference of a circle that rolls in a plane on the inside of another circle. The method used to draw a hypocycloid is similar to the method used to draw the cycloid.

5.44 *Spiral of Archimedes*

Archimedes' spiral is a plane curve generated by a point moving uniformly around and away from a fixed point. In order to define this curve more specifically, it can be said that it is generated by a point moving uniformly along a straight line while the line revolves with uniform angular velocity about a fixed point.

The definition of the spiral of Archimedes is applied in drawing this curve as illustrated in Fig. 5.40. To find a sufficient number of points to allow the use of an irregular curve for drawing the spiral it is the practice to divide the given circle into a number of equal parts (say, 12) and draw radial lines to the division points.

Next, divide a radial line into the same number of equal parts as the circle and number the division points on the circumference of the circle beginning with the radial line adjacent to the divided one. With the center of the circle as a center, draw concentric arcs that in each case will start at a numbered division point on the divided radial line and will end at an intersection with the radial line that is numbered correspondingly. The arc starting at point 1 gives a point on the curve at its intersection with radial line 1, the arc starting at 2 gives an intersection point on radial line 2, ect. The spiral is a smooth curve drawn through these intersection points.

5.45 *Helix (Fig. 5.41)*

The cylindrical helix is a space curve that is generated by a point moving uniformly on the surface of a cylinder. The point must travel parallel to the axis with uniform linear velocity while at the same time it is moving with uniform angular velocity around the axis. The curve can be thought of as being generated by a point moving uniformly along a straight line while the line is revolving with uniform angular velocity around the axis of the given cylinder. Study the pictorial drawing, Fig. 5.41.

The first step in drawing a cylindrical helix is to lay out the two views of the cylinder. Next, the lead should be measured along a contour element and divided into a number of equal parts (say, 12). Divide the circular view of the cylinder into the same number of parts and number the division points.

The division lines of the lead represent the various positions of the moving point as it travels in a direction parallel to the axis of the cylinder along the moving line. The division points on the circular view are the related position of the moving line. For example, when the line has moved from the 0 to 1 position, the point has traveled along the line a distance equal to one-twelfth of the lead; when the line is in the 2 position, the point has traveled one-sixth of the lead. (See pictorial drawing, Fig. 5.41.) In constructing the curve the necessary points are found by projecting from a numbered point on the circular view to the division line of the lead that is numbered similarly.

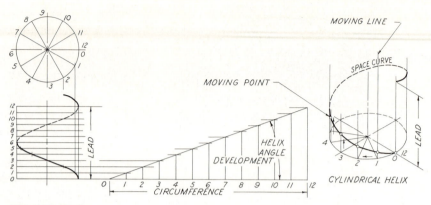

FIG. 5.41 Helix.

A helix may be either right-hand or left-hand. The one shown in Fig. 5.41 is a left-hand helix.

When the cylinder is developed, the helix becomes a straight line on the development, as shown. It is inclined to the base line at an angle known as the "helix angle." A screw thread is an example of a practical application of the cylindrical helix.

B GEOMETRY AND THE COMPUTER—PLANE AND SOLID, TWO- AND THREE-DIMENSIONAL

5.46 *Importance of Geometry*

For a designer to fully understand how a part functions in an assembly, how it operates, and how it interacts with other parts around it, the designer must visualize in three-dimensions. Before the advent of the computer, designers drew or *drafted* their ideas as two-dimensional diagrams. These geometric constructions have been covered in the first part of this chapter. If a real feeling was needed of how the design might appear, models or mock-ups were often crafted out of clay or wood. Then the designer could study the design, viewing it from different vantage points, checking how the design functioned in the space around it.

Using CADD, a three-dimensional *model* of the design is kept as a mathematical description in the memory of the computer; thus allowing the designer to see any and all views of the design and how the design operates. This is a fundamental change in the way a designer works. Previously, a designer had to translate the mental conception or mathematical model into a two-dimensional diagram before the object could be made. With CADD, it is the three-dimensional model that is translated as needed into two-dimensional diagrams for documentation and communication.

This necessitates thinking directly in three dimensions, always knowing the direction in space that you are viewing, and (the topic of this section) the characteristics of the geometry you are creating.

5.47 *Two- and Three-Dimensional Geometry*

The difference between two-dimensional and three-dimensional geometry can be seen in Fig. 5.42. A circle may be drawn on a two-dimensional surface and may represent either a circle or the two-dimensional view of a three-dimensional form such as a sphere or a cylinder. A square may exist on a two-dimensional plane and may represent a quadrilateral (four-sided form) or may be the two-dimensional view of three-dimensional geometry like cubes or cylinders.

Two-dimensional geometry may exist in three-dimensional space as shown in Fig. 5.43 where two-dimensional profiles through a car body are arranged along the depth axis. Each profile is flat, but when taken together, they create a three-dimensional design.

The difference between two- and three-dimensional geometry is evident when an image is viewed from

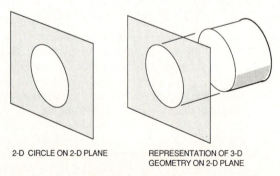

2-D CIRCLE ON 2-D PLANE   REPRESENTATION OF 3-D GEOMETRY ON 2-D PLANE

FIG. 5.42 Two-dimensional circle and representation of three-dimensional geometry.

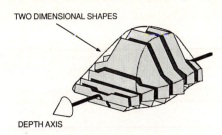

FIG. 5.43 Two-dimensional shapes arranged along depth axis to form three-dimensional shape.

different vantage points: three-dimensional geometry yields additional correct geometric views. Two-dimensional geometries are really diagrams whose three-dimensional properties are derived from the arrangement of various flat views on the page.

5.48 *Geometric Primitives (Fig. 5.44)*

The plane geometry constructions presented in the first part of this chapter required basic geometric drawing. Lines, arcs, circles, points, and curves were used to construct useful forms (see Fig. 5.44). Many of the same constructions apply to computer drawing, except that the method of supplying the needed information is changed.

All CADD computers have basic two-dimensional geometric shapes called *primitives* that are available for the operator and from which more complex shapes can be made. Most CADD systems would include the following primitives.

- *Line* may be horizontal, vertical, oblique, parallel, perpendicular, or tangent, and of specific length.
- *Point* is a dimensionless location where two lines cross.
- *Rectangle* is a four-sided figure specified by its diagonal.
- *Polygon* is a multi-sided figure defined by a contiguous set of lines.
- *Circle* is a round form specified by center and diameter or radius, or by three points.
- *Arc* is a piece of the circumference of a circle specified by radius and starting and ending angle.
- *Irregular curve* passes through three or more specific points.

5.49 *Geometric Lines*

CADD computers store lines by the coordinates of their end points (Fig. 5.45). This allows lines, which make up the majority of CADD drawings, to be stored very efficiently. The *origin* of a line is located at its

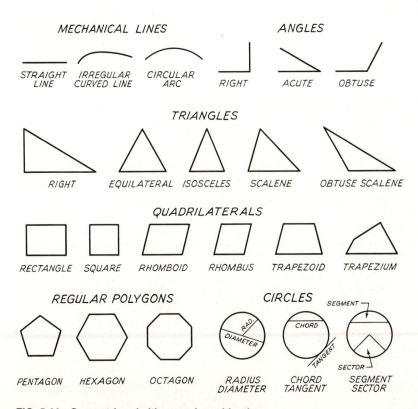

FIG. 5.44 Geometric primitives and combinations.

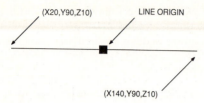

FIG. 5.45   A line with origin and end points.

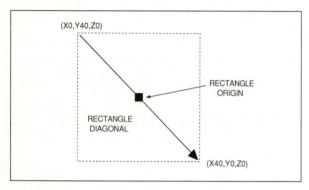

FIG. 5.46   Specification of a rectangle by its diagonal.

center, but the line may be identified at any point between its ends. A special kind of line is a *rectangle* (Fig. 5.46). By giving the computer the coordinates of the rectangle's diagonal, a box is formed. Each line segment of the box may then be treated separately.

5.50 *Circles*

To draw a circle, the CADD computer must be given the coordinates of its center and either the radius or diameter. This corresponds to the manual process of marking the center, setting the compass radius, and swinging the arc. Even when three points on the circumference of the circle are specified, the center is found in much the same way as in Fig. 5.19 where a circle was circumscribed around a triangle. *A CADD circle is drawn counterclockwise* from its origin at 0° to 360° (Fig. 5.47). A circle is identified by its origin or by any point on its circumference. The origin of a circle and its geometric center are then different points.

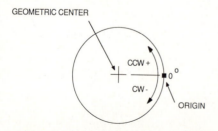

FIG. 5.47   Circle identification of clockwise (negative) and counterclockwise (positive) movement.

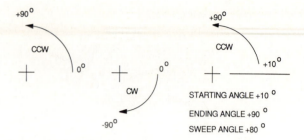

FIG. 5.48   Positive arc, negative arc, and arc by starting, ending, and sweep angles.

5.51 *Arcs*

Arcs are special cases of circles that are also drawn counterclockwise. Information necessary for drawing an arc is the beginning angle or point, the ending angle or point, and the radius. As an alternative method, an arc may be specified by the center, radius, beginning point, and sweep angle (Fig. 5.48). An arc whose beginning angle is zero degrees and whose ending angle is 360° is an *arc circle*. The origin of an arc is at the center of the arc curve and the geometric center of the arc is at its usual position, equidistant from the curve (Fig. 5.49). CADD systems do not confuse arcs and circles because they are different objects.

5.52 *Curves*

A curve may be drawn through a number of points not on the same line by circular arc approximation (Fig. 5.50) or by a number of mathematical curves. An im-

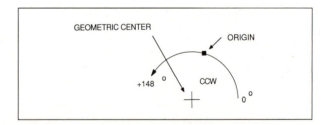

FIG. 5.49   Arc identification-positive movement.

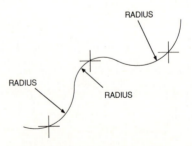

FIG. 5.50   Arc through three points—circular arc approximation

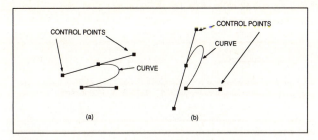

FIG. 5.51 Arc through three points—Bezier curve method.

portant curve to engineers is the *Bezier curve,* a curve that is *attracted* to points. The curve may actually touch a point and if it does it always maintains contact with the point. Or, a point may lie off the curve and attract the curve like a magnet. The closer the point is to the curve, the greater the attraction. A Bezier curve may be reshaped by moving these points called *control points or handles* and adjusting the curve as shown in Fig. 5.51. Note that the curve is not defined by circular arcs as was the case in Fig. 5.50. Rather, it behaves much like a spring, trying to connect smoothly the control points to which it is attached while also being attracted to other points.

5.53 *Figures*

A group of primitives that have been grouped together by a CADD operator is called a *figure* and may be identified and moved like one of the predefined CADD primitives. A graphic that can be identified as a unit is called an *entity.* Figures and primitives are both entities. Some CADD computers have *libraries* of figures, such as electronic, hydraulic, pneumatic, and mechanical parts, and of course these figures have been made from primitives (Fig. 5.52). The advantage of CADD is in having to create a figure only once, and then using that figure repeatedly.

5.54 *Figure Attributes*

Each figure created on a CADD computer has assigned to it certain properties or attributes. The most important of these properties is the origin of the figure. As noted earlier, the origin is the handle that is used for identification and as the reference point for placing the figure on the drawing (Fig. 5.53). Figures may also have *gravity points,* spots on the figure that will attract other figures or primitives (Fig. 5.54). Figure attributes are much like the text attributes that were discussed in Appendix D. Each figure is created in a convenient size, with its origin at the most popular position, with gravity points where the operator would expect them, and in a typical orientation (zero degrees rotation) as shown in Fig. 5.55. These attributes may be changed so that more complex drawings may be created as shown in Fig. 5.56. Note that the square fastener head has been inserted into the drawing four times, twice at

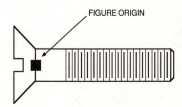

FIG. 5.53 Figure origin is located at a convenient position.

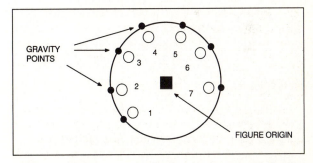

FIG. 5.54 Gravity points allow the correct attachment of lines to a figure.

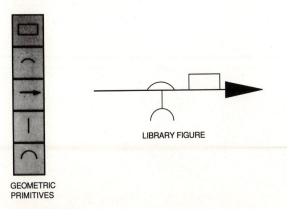

FIG. 5.52 Library figure constructed from geometric primitives.

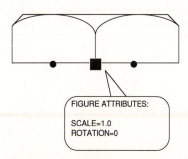

FIG. 5.55 A square fastener head as a library figure with its figure attributes.

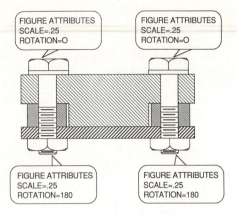

FIG. 5.56 The use of a library figure (square fastener head) in a sectional detail.

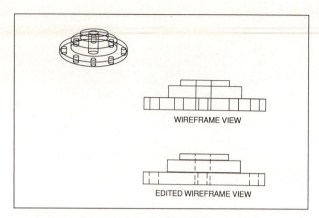

FIG. 5.58 Wire frame (edge) model, wire frame front view, and edited engineering drawing.

the default (zero degree rotation) and twice at 180° rotation.

5.55 *Geometric Modeling*

Sophisticated computer programs allow a designer to *build* the three-dimensional mathematical description of a part just as one might sculpt the part out of wood or plastic. This is a fundamental change in how designers work and requires a solid understanding of the two-dimensional geometric principles covered in the first part of this chapter as well as three-dimensional geometry. Geometric modeling combines the power of the computer with the creativity of the designer, producing solutions to engineering problems that are more accurate, more standardized, and less time-consuming. Not all computers are capable of geometric modeling and among those that are, the extent of capabilities varies.

5.56 *Wire Frame Modeling*

The most elementary modeling technique describes the object as a set of lines. Actual objects do not have lines, they have surfaces, intersections, and limits. Lines provide a technique to approximate the visual

representation of solid geometry (Fig. 5.57). Yet with *wire frame modeling,* the computer knows nothing of the material inside the object; it recognizes only the artificial lines that connect the object's corners or vertices. This modeling technique is of little benefit to designers other than for getting a quick idea of the geometry and for producing views of the design as a drawing. The views must be changed or edited to reflect standard drafting practices as in Fig. 5.58, where solid lines have been changed to dashed lines.

5.57 *Surface Modeling*

Objects defined by their surfaces yield more information than do wire frame descriptions. The *surface model* may look like a wire frame, or the planes themselves may be shaded to yield a more realistic view (Fig. 5.59). The surface model is hollow, however, and nothing is known about the material inside the object. The surface model, like the wire frame model, can be turned into standard engineering drawings.

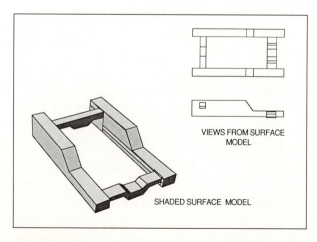

FIG. 5.59 Shaded surface model and top and front views of that model.

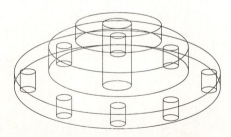

FIG. 5.57 Wire frame (edge) model.

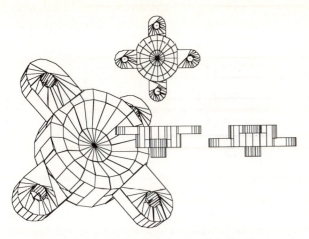

FIG. 5.60 Constructive solid model constructed using the Boolean operators difference and union.

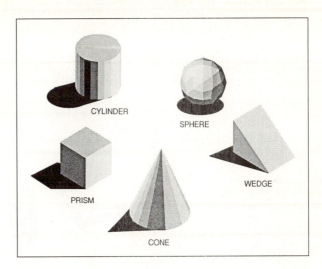

FIG. 5.61 Constructive solid geometry primitives: prism, wedge, cylinder, cone, and sphere.

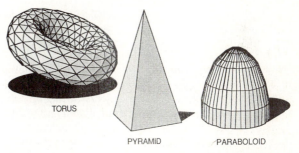

FIG. 5.62 Additional solids formed from the constructive primitives.

5.58 *Constructive Solid Geometry*

Constructive solid geometry (CSG) fully defines the object, both its planes and the material inside. This gives an engineer full freedom to carve or model the object and to combine objects into more sophisticated designs. This type of modeling is called *solid modeling* because of its similarity to traditional model making.

CSG models can be shaded or shown as wire frame representations. Because CSG models do not have the artificial outline of wire frames, these lines must be added so that an unshaded object can be seen (Fig. 5.60).

5.59 *Solid Modeling Primitives*

Solid models are constructed from three-dimensional primitive shapes (Fig. 5.61). These shapes may include

- Prism
- Cylinder
- Sphere
- Wedge
- Cone

Other basic shapes may be used to make additional primitive shapes (Fig. 5.62) such as

- Torus
- Pyramid
- Paraboloid

5.60 *Boolean Operators*

Primitive shapes are combined and changed by mathematical operators called *Boolean operators*. These operations are *union* (addition), *difference* (subtraction), and *intersection* (multiplication). Solids may be added or subtracted just as numbers are added or subtracted.

■ *UNION*

Two solid forms may be joined together by the *union operator*. The forms may occupy the same space or they may be separated (Fig. 5.63). In either case, after

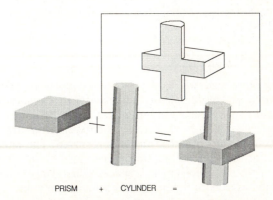

PRISM + CYLINDER =

FIG. 5.63 Union (addition) operation of prism and cylinder primitives.

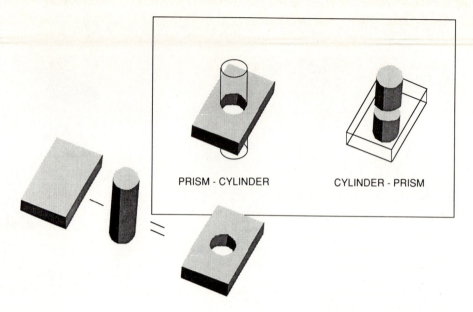

FIG. 5.64   Difference (subtraction) operation of prism and cylinder primitives: both cases.

the addition operation, the two forms are considered to be one shape. (They may just happen to be separated by empty space.) If the objects do occupy the same space, all intersections are calculated and visibility is determined. In Fig. 5.63, all points belonging to the prism are added to all points belonging to the cylinder, and the resulting shape is a new geometric form.

■ DIFFERENCE

The most common use of the *difference operation* is to subtract (or extract) a hole from solid material (Fig. 5.64). In this case the objects *must* occupy the same physical space for the subtraction operation to have any effect. In Fig. 5.64, the cylinder is subtracted from the prism, resulting in a hole in the prism. In this case, all points in the cylinder that are common with the prism are subtracted. The outcome of a subtraction operation depends on which form is being subtracted. Note the inset in Fig. 5.64 and the difference between subtracting the cylinder from the prism, and subtracting the prism from the cylinder.

■ INTERSECTION

The objects shown in the previous examples may also be intersected. In this case, all material *not common* to both shapes is removed. What remains is the intersection (Fig. 5.65). Note that this is different from union where no part of either object is removed. The intersection uses the multiplication operator (×), and it is unimportant which object is specified first. Only points common to *both* the prism and cylinder are kept.

5.61 *Other Modeling Techniques*

Once the object has been described three-dimensionally, several additional operations may be performed on that object's data base. From the mathematical description of the object, *mass properties* may be extracted. These include the *center of mass,* the *geometric centroid, moments of inertia, weight,* and *mass.* Even accounting information such as *unit cost* can be figured from the model. In each of these cases, the data base is acted on after it is created. This is called *postprocessing.* Under no circumstances do any of these postprocessing techniques alter the actual geometric description or data base of the object.

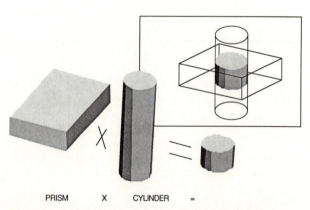

FIG. 5.65   Intersection operation of prism and cylinder primitives.

The Theory of Shape Description

6.1 Introduction

Engineers record the shapes and sizes of three-dimensional objects on a sheet of drawing paper. This drawing paper is the engineer's picture plane (Fig. 6.1) on which the geometry is projected or drawn. *Size description and shape description* are equally important, but to simplify learning to make drawings and sketches, this chapter deals only with methods used to describe shape. A later chapter will discuss size description.

Three methods for representing shape are used by engineers and technologists, and the theory governing each method should be understood thoroughly before it is used. These are

- Orthographic projection
- Axonometric projection
- Oblique projection

A ONE-PLANE PROJECTION—PICTORIAL

6.2 Perspective Projection (Convergent Projection)

Before discussing the three methods, let us analyze *perspective projection,* the view each of us is accustomed to seeing.

In perspective projection, the projecting lines or *visual rays* converge at a point, as shown in Figure 6.1. The representation on the transparent picture plane may be considered the view that would be seen by a single eye at a known point in space. The picture is formed on the picture plane by the *piercing points* of the projecting lines from the eye to the object. The size of the view depends on the distance from the observer

95

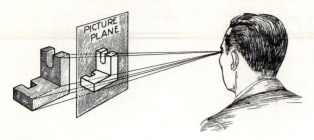

FIG. 6.1 Perspective projection.

to the plane and the distance from the plane to the object.

Perspective projections are *not* used by engineers for manufacturing and construction because the perspective view does not reveal exact size and shape. Perspectives may be used in marketing where a *natural* view of a product may be desirable.

6.3 Axonometric and Oblique Projection

If the object is turned and then tilted so that the three faces are inclined to the plane of projection, the resulting projection is a special type of *orthographic projection* (see Sec. 6.4) known as *axonometric projection*. Figure 6.2 illustrates an axonometric projection of a cube. Note that the projectors from the plane to the object are perpendicular to the plane. This axonometric or pictorial view shows three of the object's sides in one projection and therefore is called a *one-plane projection*. The three subdivisions of axonometric projection are *isometric,* where the three sides are equally inclined, *dimetric,* where two of the three sides are equally inclined, and *trimetric,* where all three sides are inclined differently.

Another form of one-plane projection is *oblique projection*. This is not an orthographic projection because, although one face is imagined to be parallel to the plane of projection, the projectors are not perpendicular to it (Fig. 6.3). Oblique projection provides an easy way of turning an existing orthographic view into a pictorial view. Oblique projection and oblique drawing are covered in detail in Chapter 11.

Perspective projection, axonometric projection, and oblique projection may be classed together as *one-plane pictorial projections*.

B COORDINATE PLANES (2-D) PROJECTION

6.4 Orthographic Projection (Parallel Projection)

The projection system that engineers use for manufacturing and construction drawings is called *orthographic projection*. If the observer in Figure 6.1 moves straight back from the picture plane an infinite distance, the projecting lines (visual rays or projectors) from the eye to the object become parallel to each other and perpendicular to the picture plane. The resulting projection (Fig. 6.4) will be an accurate representation of the object's shape parallel to the picture plane. For convenience, the projection may be formed by extending perpendicular projectors from the object to the plane. This view is the orthographic projection.

Because the view shown in Fig. 6.4 does not reveal the thickness of the object or the shape on planes perpendicular to the first picture plane, one or more addi-

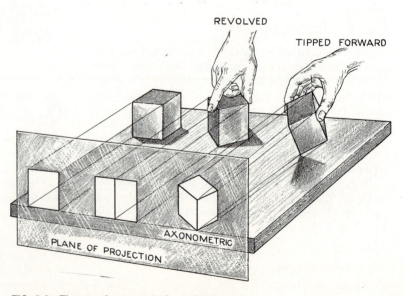

FIG. 6.2 Theory of axonometric projection.

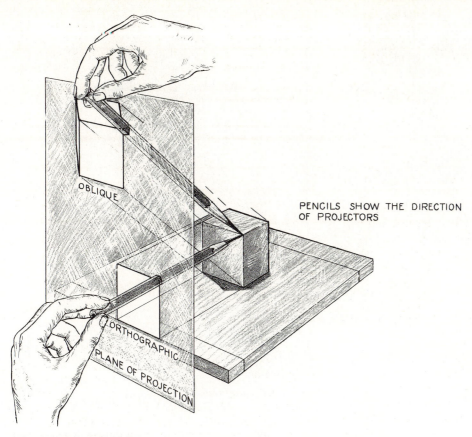

PENCILS SHOW THE DIRECTION
OF PROJECTORS

FIG. 6.3 Oblique projection.

tional picture planes may be established (Fig. 6.5). Two projections are usually sufficient to describe most simple objects, but three or more may be needed for complicated geometry.

The picture planes are customarily called the *principal* or *coordinate* planes of projection and the perpendiculars, *projectors*. There are three principal coordinate planes of projection: the *frontal* plane, the

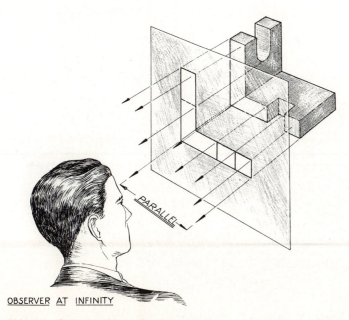

OBSERVER AT INFINITY

FIG. 6.4 Orthographic projection.

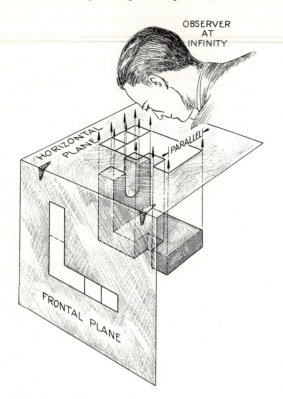

FIG. 6.5   Planes of projection.

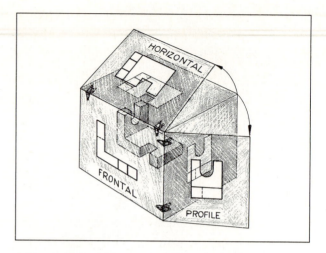

FIG. 6.7   Revolution of the planes of projection.

- Front view ⎤
- Rear view ⎦ Frontal projections
- Top view ⎤
- Bottom view ⎦ Horizontal projections
- Right-side view ⎤
- Left-side view ⎦ Profile projections

To maintain this mutual relationship when laying out the views, the frontal plane is usually considered to coincide with the plane of the paper and the horizontal (top) and profile (side) planes as revolving 90° into the position shown in Figs. 6.7 and 6.8. Note in Fig. 6.7 the manner in which the planes are revolved.

horizontal plane, and the *profile* plane. In engineering drawing the planes are usually arranged as shown in Fig. 6.6. All three are *mutually perpendicular*. Were all views perpendicular to the three coordinate planes drawn, a total of six views would be formed.

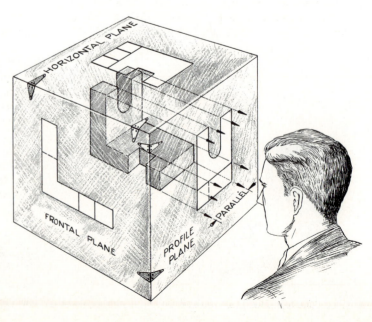

FIG. 6.6   Planes of projection.

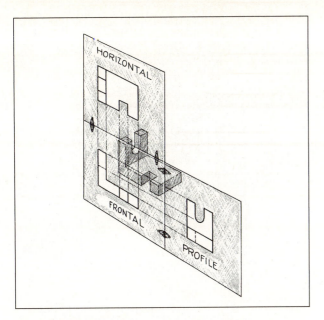

FIG. 6.8 **Planes revolved into the plane of the paper.**

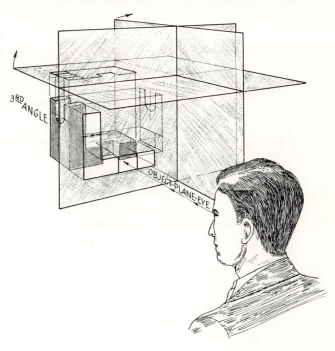

FIG. 6.10 **Third-angle projection.**

This theoretical treatment of the coordinate planes establishes an absolute relationship between the views. Visualizing an object would be considerably more difficult than it is were it not for this fixed relationship, because it would be impossible to determine quickly the direction of sight for a particular view.

6.5 *First- and Third-Angle Projection*

If the frontal and horizontal projection planes are assumed to extend infinitely in space on one side of the profile plane, four *dihedral angles* (90°) are formed and are designated as the first, second, third, and fourth angles (Fig. 6.9). The lines of intersection between

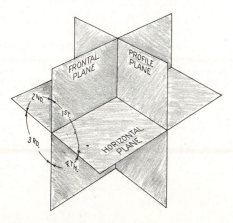

FIG. 6.9 **Planes of projection.**

these planes are called *coordinate axes* and their point of intersection is called the *origin*.

Assume an object is placed so that its main faces are parallel to the frontal, horizontal, and profile planes (Fig. 6.10). The respective projections will show the true size and shape of all surfaces that are parallel to the planes. Theoretically, the object could be placed in any of the four quadrants. It has been placed in the third quadrant because engineering custom in the United States dictates the use of the third angle. This quadrant is used because the views, when revolved 90° into the plane of the front view, are in their natural positions. That is, the top view appears above the front view. The profile view showing the right side falls to the right of the front view, and so on.

In some countries, the first-angle projection is used for engineering drawings. Study the differences between Fig. 6.10 and Fig. 6.11. Observe that, when the planes are revolved, the top view will be below the front view and that the left side view will be to the right of the front view. Two views of a truncated cone (Fig. 6.12) are used to identify which angle of projection was used in a drawing.

6.6 *Systems of Projection*

As a review, the different systems of projection are shown diagramatically in Fig. 6.13.

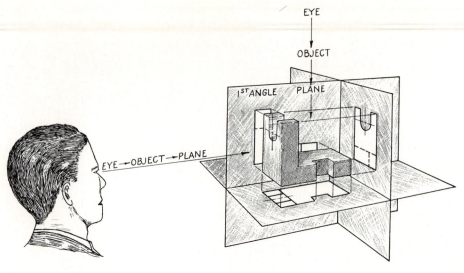

FIG. 6.11 **First-angle projection.**

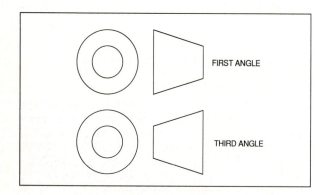

FIRST ANGLE

THIRD ANGLE

FIG. 6.12 **Identifying the angle of projection.**

C CADD CONSTRUCTION PLANES

6.7 Construction Planes Used in CADD

Construction planes are used in CADD to create three-dimensional geometry on two-dimensional surfaces that are parallel to coordinate planes. Construction planes are perpendicular or *normal* to the direction of sight for that view. For example, the front and

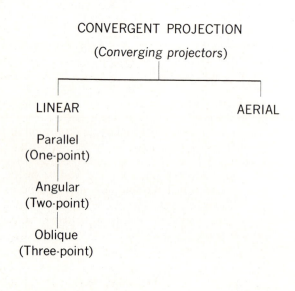

CONVERGENT PROJECTION

(Converging projectors)

LINEAR

Parallel
(One-point)

Angular
(Two-point)

Oblique
(Three-point)

AERIAL

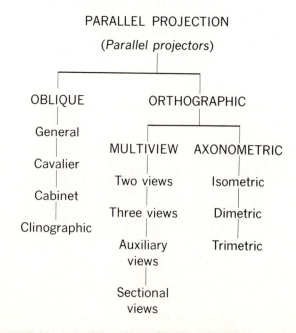

PARALLEL PROJECTION

(Parallel projectors)

OBLIQUE

General

Cavalier

Cabinet

Clinographic

ORTHOGRAPHIC

MULTIVIEW

Two views

Three views

Auxiliary
views

Sectional
views

AXONOMETRIC

Isometric

Dimetric

Trimetric

FIG. 6.13 **Systems of projection**

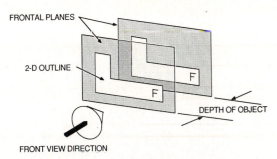

FIG. 6.14 Frontal construction planes separated by the depth of the object.

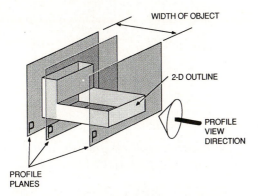

FIG. 6.15 Profile construction planes separated by the width of the object.

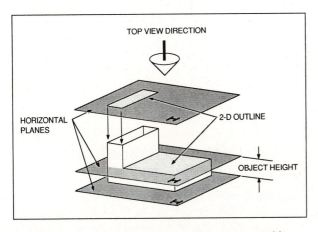

FIG. 6.16 Horizontal construction planes separated by the height of the object.

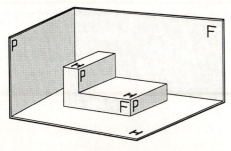

FIG. 6.17 Completed object and its relationship to principal construction planes.

rear of an object can be drawn on *frontal construction planes*, separated by the depth or thickness of the object (Fig. 6.14). Right- and left-side geometry can be drawn on *profile construction planes*, separated by the width of the object (Fig. 6.15) with the front and rear geometry placed in the proper relationship. Horizontal construction planes, positioned perpendicular to the frontal and profile planes, are used for required top or plan views (Fig. 6.16). The views made on these construction planes will define a three-dimensional object that is not too complex. The result is the representation of the object defined on construction planes set in three dimensions (Fig. 6.17). Angular and oblique construction planes are used for features not in horizontal, frontal, or profile position.

D COORDINATE AXES

6.8 Creating a Three-Dimensional Data Base

The fundamental difference between projection onto coordinate planes and the use of coordinate axes is that with the axes, a three-dimensional numerical description of the object must be created first. This description or data base may be created by a variety of methods including two- and three-dimensional digitizing, and may be a full solid geometric model or a simple wire frame description. For example, an object may be manually digitized as a wire frame where the object is represented by vertices and boundary edges. The geometry is transparent and points that would normally be obscured can be seen. This description is the most elemental form of modeling. The student should realize, however, that no matter what modeling technique is used, the process is the same—describing the coordinates of the object in X-Y-Z space.

To demonstrate this process of building a data base, we will manually digitize a familiar object—the angle block (Fig. 6.18). The first step in manually digitizing an object is to describe the object as a picture (Fig. 6.19[a]). All vertices and connections should be shown whether or not they can actually be seen. Next, locate the object in space relative to the origin. Placing the origin at the lower left rear of the object results in positive values along the X, Y, and Z axes (Fig. 6.19[b]). Note that in Fig. 6.20 all vertices lying in the Z = 0 plane have been identified. Only their X and Y values change. Finally, assign values for the rest of the vertices relative to the origin as shown in Fig. 6.21. With this done the numeric data base can be built.

When the object is being drawn, the computer must know whether to "move" the pen without drawing a line or put the pen down and connect the two points.

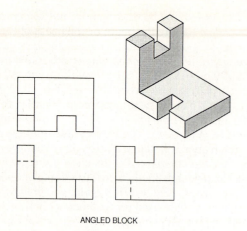

FIG. 6.18 **Angle block to be digitized.**

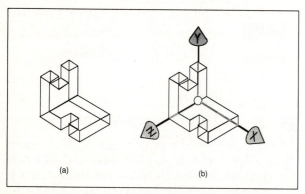

FIG. 6.19 **Wire frame of angle block (a) and Cartesian axis system with origin installed at left, rear, and bottom corner.**

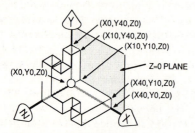

FIG. 6.20 **Geometry on Z = 0 plane digitized relative to origin.**

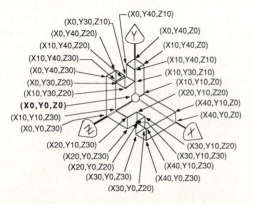

FIG. 6.21 **Object completely digitized.**

NUMERIC DATA BASE

Data Set	X	Y	Z	Pen	Data Set	X	Y	Z	Pen
01	00	00	00	1	29	20	00	30	2
02	00	40	00	2	30	20	00	20	2
03	10	40	00	2	31	30	00	20	2
04	10	10	00	2	32	30	.00	30	2
05	40	10	00	2	33	40	00	30	2
06	40	00	00	2	34	40	00	00	2
07	00	00	00	2	35	40	00	30	1
08	00	00	30	2	36	40	10	30	2
09	00	40	30	2	37	30	10	30	1
10	00	40	20	2	38	30	10	30	2
11	00	30	20	2	39	30	00	20	1
12	00	30	10	2	40	30	10	20	2
13	00	40	10	2	41	20	00	30	1
14	00	40	00	2	42	20	10	20	2
15	10	40	00	1	43	20	00	30	1
16	10	40	10	2	44	20	10	30	2
17	10	30	10	2	45	00	40	30	2
18	10	30	20	2	46	10	40	30	1
19	10	40	20	2	47	10	40	20	1
20	10	40	30	2	48	00	40	20	2
21	10	10	30	2	49	10	30	20	1
22	10	10	30	2	50	00	30	20	2
23	20	10	20	2	51	10	30	10	1
24	30	10	30	2	52	00	30	10	2
25	30	10	30	2	53	10	40	10	1
26	40	10	30	2	54	00	40	10	2
27	40	10	00	2					
28	00	00	30	1					

FIG. 6.22 **Numeric data base for angle block.**

This is called *pen control*. A pen control value of 0 may result in a move, a pen control value of 1 in a line being drawn.

The data base is built by writing down the X, Y, and Z values in order as one moves from vertex to vertex, starting by moving to the origin without drawing a line (Fig. 6.22). An attempt should be made to complete the object without redrawing a line and with the fewest number of pen = 0 moves. If it appears necessary to redraw a line, the pen should be picked up and moved to another vertex. This is repeated until all edge boundaries are drawn.

A CADD computer program can use this data to display the wire frame from any orientation.

6.9 Cartesian (World) Axis System

Once the object is described any and all views may be found by either of two methods. The axes and all space geometry may be revolved, or the object may be left alone and the viewing direction changed. Although this may seem to be a fine distinction, the distinction is important in determining one's position in relation to the object and from what direction the object is being viewed.

Figure 6.9 shows the coordinate planes and their intersection in space to form the angles of projection. Consider Fig. 6.23 where these planes are shown to form coordinate or Cartesian axes, also called *world axes*. The engineer designs in world units and in relation to the world axis system.

The horizontal plane is used to define all points of height in space where Y = 0 at the origin. The frontal plane defines all points of depth where Z = 0 at the origin. The profile plane defines all points of width

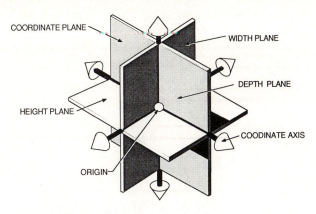

FIG. 6.23 Cartesian axes.

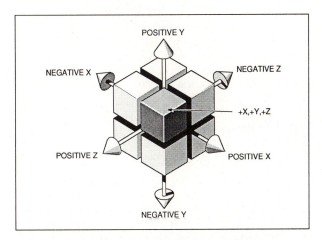

FIG. 6.24 Axes positive and negative values.

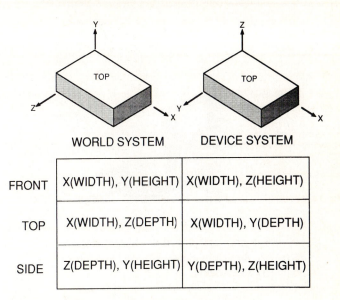

	WORLD SYSTEM	DEVICE SYSTEM
FRONT	X(WIDTH), Y(HEIGHT)	X(WIDTH), Z(HEIGHT)
TOP	X(WIDTH), Z(DEPTH)	X(WIDTH), Y(DEPTH)
SIDE	Z(DEPTH), Y(HEIGHT)	Y(DEPTH), Z(HEIGHT)

FIG. 6.25 Right- and left-hand axes systems.

where X = 0 at the origin. The intersection of these three planes is the location in space where X = 0, Y = 0, and Z = 0, the point known as the origin. The intersection of any two of the coordinate planes forms an axis. An object may have positive and negative values in its data base, depending on how it is positioned in relation to the origin (Fig. 6.24). At times, it may be convenient to position the object in the +X, +Y, +Z octant.

6.10 *Right-Hand Axes*

The description in the previous section is of a *right-hand axes system*. In a right-hand system, the system generally used in drawing, the front view contains normal width (X) and height (Y) dimensions. The fields of mathematics and physics, as well as the machining and aircraft industries, have adopted a modified right-handed system, however. Figure 6.25 shows the difference between these two methods of specifying directions in space. If the representation of the axes is included with the drawing, an engineer can always relate the object to special directions.

6.11 *Device Axes*

The world axes system establishes height (Y), width (X), and depth (Z) dimensions in space. A CADD system, however, may choose to define space relative to a device, such as a milling machine or the terminal used by the designer. In general, it is best to keep device axes and world axes aligned. The more powerful the CADD computer, the greater the chance that device and world axes systems may be manipulated independent of one another. To be able to predict how a view will be altered by a rotate command, for example, this difference must be understood. In the case of device axes, the Z axis is considered to always come directly toward the operator.

Note, in Fig. 6.26, the axis markers attached to the terminal. These represent device axes and do not change. The world axes system that the operator sees inside the computer has not been rotated and is in

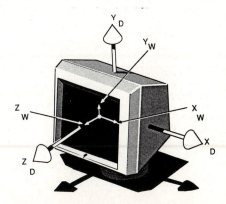

FIG. 6.26 Normally aligned world (W) and device (D) axes.

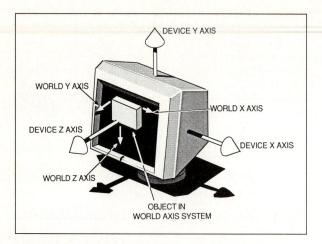

FIG. 6.27 **Stationary device (D) axes and top view of world (W) axis system.**

alignment with the device axis system. CADD operators are advised to establish world axes in the workspace so that world and device axes may be aligned when needed.

Figure 6.27 shows the relationship between device and world axes systems. The operator is looking down the device Z axis but is seeing what is generally called the top view. Only the device and world X axes are aligned. This means that rotation or translation relative to the Y or Z axes must be done by specifying world or device axes. Otherwise, a completely different result than had been intended may result.

6.12 Rotation About Cartesian Axes

To change the orientation of the object relative to a stationary viewer, the object may be rotated about the Cartesian axes as shown in Fig. 6.28. Rotating the shape relative to stationary axes assumes a constant viewing direction. *The device and world axes remain aligned.* Rotation is positive in a counterclockwise direction when the axis is viewed as a point (Fig. 6.29).

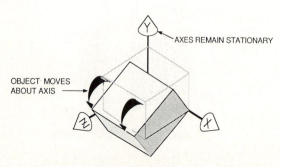

FIG. 6.28 **Rotation about stationary Cartesian axes.**

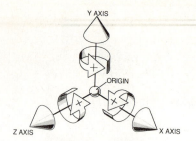

FIG. 6.29 **Positive rotation.**

6.13 Rotation of Geometry by Direction of Sight Vector

Another way of specifying axis orientation is through a *direction of sight vector* (Fig. 6.30). In this case, world and device axes become misaligned. In Fig. 6.30 this vector is normal to surface A, and when the vector is viewed as a point, a view *in the direction of the vector* results. This causes the direction of sight vector and the device Z axis to coincide (Fig. 6.31). Note that two of the three world axes are out of alignment with the matching device axes. Were the object to be subsequently rotated about the device Y axis, all three sets of axes would be misaligned.

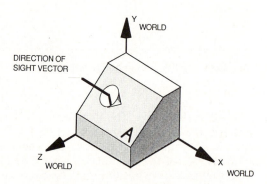

FIG. 6.30 **Specifying new view by a direction of sight vector.**

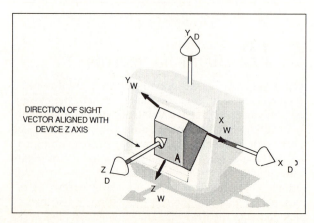

FIG. 6.31 **View in direction of sight vector.**

6.14 *2-D CADD Rotation*

CADD computers that maintain a 2-D data base can only perform 2-D rotations. A command like RO-TATE ALL 45 tells the computer to rotate the X-Y plane of the figure 45° counterclockwise around a point to be specified. Consider the shaded object shown in Fig. 6.32 to be the front view of the L-shaped bracket used to illustrate concepts throughout this chapter. The command ROTATE ALL 45 has been entered and a Z axis of rotation identified. The rotation, counterclockwise from zero, is generally from the right horizontal (Fig. 6.33). Note that the computer understands about which axis the rotation will occur because, as was stated previously, a 2-D CADD computer can only rotate geometry about the device Z axis.

6.15 *3-D CADD Rotation*

Rotation of 3-D geometry is predicated on a computer's ability to manipulate 3-D data. This is definitely the future for all engineering drawing and de-

sign, because with 3-D capabilities any and all views of an object are available by either altering the orientation of the object relative to the Cartesian axes, or by taking an auxiliary viewing position (direction of sight vector). Also, designers work more effectively when they "model" in 3-D than when they draw on paper. To model in 3-D may require retraining and the acquisition of new design skills, but the benefits are well worth the effort.

To be able to use 3-D rotations a CADD operator must

- Know whether the computer rotates geometry relative to world or device axis systems

- Know the orientation of the object relative to that axis system

- Be able to specify axis direction (X-Y-Z, or user defined; positive or negative), and the angle in degrees through which the object will be revolved

Figure 6.34 demonstrates 3-D rotation. The object appears normal to the axis system, not unlike the object in the 2-D CADD example in the previous section. In both cases the operator sees at first a negative Z or front view. The instructions to the computer, RO-TATE ALL X90, has caused all geometry to be revolved +90° about the X axis, resulting in a top view (Fig. 6.35). In Fig. 6.36, the original front view has

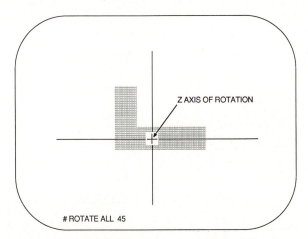

FIG. 6.32   2-D rotation front view of L-shaped bracket.

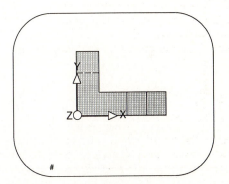

FIG. 6.34   3-D rotation; object is normal to the axis system.

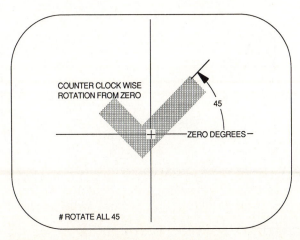

FIG. 6.33   2-D counterclockwise revolution.

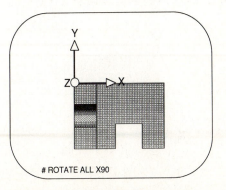

FIG. 6.35   Revolved 90° about the X axis to produce a top view.

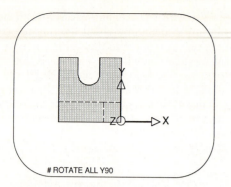

FIG. 6.36   Front view revolved to produce a left-side view.

been revolved with the command ROTATE ALL Y90. This results in a left-side view. These separate objects, when assembled together as shown in Fig. 6.37, form a three-view orthographic drawing.

Two successive rotations of a single object, one about the Y axis and one about the X axis, can be used

to illustrate further this concept of how rotation changes views. With the command ROTATE ALL Y45 the geometry has been rotated around the vertical Y axis (Fig. 6.38[*a*]). Note in Fig. 6.38(*b*) how the front and profile views have been changed by this command. Next, in Fig. 6.39, the command ROTATE ALL X35 has further changed the object relative to the axes. The top and left-side views are strange, but the front view should look pleasing and even a bit familiar. This front view is an *isometric view*. See Chapter 11 for an in-depth discussion of isometric presentation.

6.16 CADD Approach to Orthographic Views

In the previous sections the manner in which CADD computers manipulate geometry through rotation has been discussed. We now know the difference between a device axis system and the world axis system, and

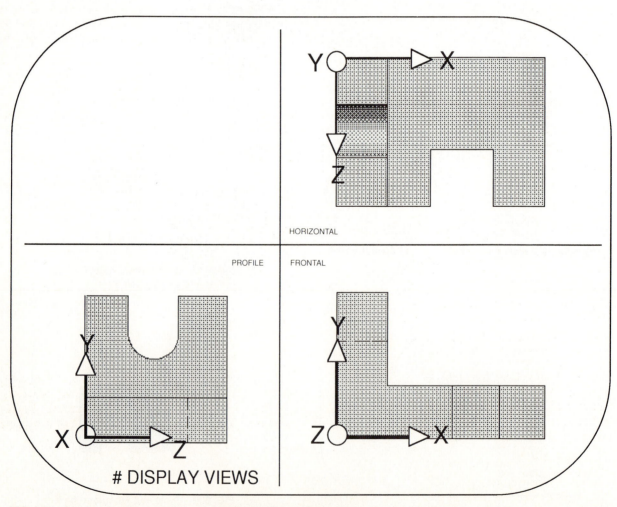

FIG. 6.37   Previously given rotation commands result in a three-view orthographic drawing.

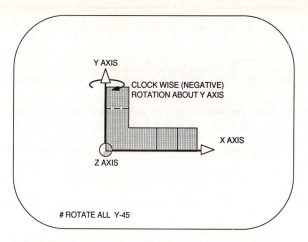

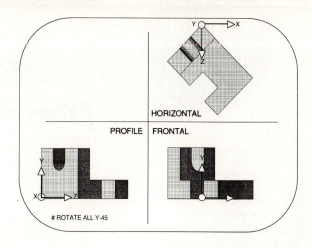

FIG. 6.38 Rotation about Y axis (ROTATE ALL Y45).

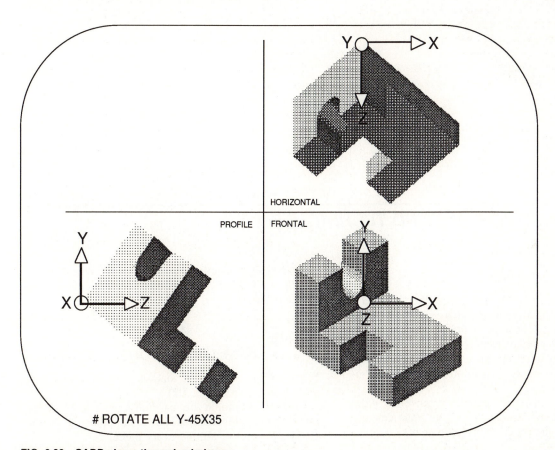

FIG. 6.39 CADD views through windows.

between 2-D and 3-D data. To complete this discussion, various strategies for displaying multiple views will be presented in Chapter 8.

CADD computers offer a view of the world's geometry through windows. These windows may correspond to top, front, side, and axonometric views as shown in Fig. 6.39. Though the screen may be flat, the display of views is far from a flat drawing. Rather, each window provides the CADD operator a means of viewing and manipulating the geometric model.

CHAPTER 7

The Theory of Size Description— Dimensions and Notes

7.1 Introduction

A detail drawing, in addition to giving the shape of a part, must furnish information such as the distances between surfaces, locations of holes, kind of finish, type of material, number required, and so forth. The expression of this information on a drawing by the use of lines, symbols, figures, and notes is known as *dimensioning*.

Intelligent dimensioning requires engineering judgment and a thorough knowledge of the practices and requirements of the production departments.

7.2 Theory of Dimensioning

Any part may be dimensioned easily and systematically by dividing it into simple geometric solids. Even complicated parts, when analyzed, are usually found to be composed principally of cylinders and prisms and, frequently, frustums of pyramids and cones (Fig. 7.1). The dimensioning of an object may be accomplished by dimensioning each elemental form to indicate its size and relative location from a center line, base line, or finished surface. A machine drawing requires two types of dimensions: *size dimensions and location dimensions*.

7.3 Size Dimensions

Size dimensions give the size of a piece, component part, hole, or slot (Fig. 7.2).

Figure 7.1 should be carefully analyzed, as the placement of dimensions shown is applicable to the elemental parts of almost every piece.

The rule for placing the three principal dimensions (width, height, and depth) on the drawing of a prism or modification of a prism is as follows: *Give two dimensions on the principal view and one dimension on one of the other views.*

The circular cylinder, which appears as a boss or shaft, requires only *the diameter and length, both of which are shown preferably on the rectangular view*. It is better practice to dimension a hole (negative cylinder) by giving the diameter and operation as a note on the contour view with a leader to the circle (Figs. 7.1 and 7.59).

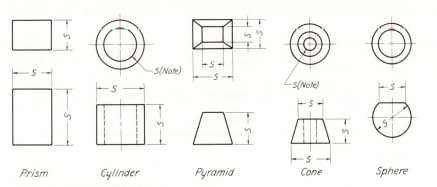

Prism Cylinder Pyramid Cone Sphere

FIG. 7.1 Dimensioning geometric shapes.

FIG. 7.2 Size dimensions.

Cones are dimensioned by giving *the diameter of the base and the altitude on the same view.* A taper is one example of a conical shape found on machine parts (Figs. 7.51 and 7.52).

Pyramids, which frequently form a part of a structure, are dimensioned by giving *two dimensions on the view showing the shape of the base.*

A sphere requires only the diameter.

7.4 Location Dimensions

Location dimensions fix the relationship of the component parts (projections, holes, slots, and other significant forms) of a piece or structure (Fig. 7.3). Particular care must be exercised in the selection and placing of location dimensions because on them depends the accuracy of the operations in making a piece and the proper mating of the piece with other parts. To select location dimensions intelligently, one must first determine the contact surfaces, finished surfaces, and center lines of the elementary geometric forms and, with the accuracy demanded and the method of production in mind, decide from what other surface or center line each should be located. Mating locating dimensions must be given from the same center line or finished surface on both pieces.

Location dimensions may be from center to center, surface to center, or surface to surface (Fig. 7.4).

7.5 Procedure in Dimensioning

The theory of dimensioning may be applied using the following six steps:

1. Mentally divide the object into its component geometric shapes.

2. Place the size dimensions on each form.

3. Select the locating center lines and surfaces after giving careful consideration to mating parts and to the processes of manufacture.

4. Place the location dimensions so that each geometric form is located from a center line or finished surface.

5. Add the overall dimensions.

6. Complete the dimensioning by adding the necessary notes.

7.6 Placing Dimensions

Dimensions must be placed where they will be most easily understood—in the locations where the reader will expect to find them. They generally are attached to the view that shows the contour of the features to which they apply, and most of them usually will appear on the principal view (Fig. 7.14). Except in cases

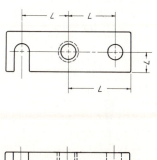

FIG. 7.3 Location dimensions.

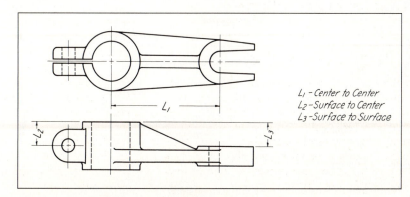

L_1 – Center to Center
L_2 – Surface to Center
L_3 – Surface to Surface

FIG. 7.4 Types of location dimensions.

in which special convenience and ease in reading are desired, or when a dimension would be so far from the form to which it referred that it might be misinterpreted, dimensions should be placed outside a view. They should appear directly on a view only when clarity demands.

All extension and dimension lines should be drawn before the arrowheads have been filled in or the dimensions, notes, and titles have been lettered. Placing dimension lines not less than 15 mm (.62 in) from the view and at least 10 mm (.38 in) from each other will provide spacing ample to satisfy the one rule to which there is no exception: *Never crowd dimensions*. If the location of a dimension forces a poor location on other dimensions, its shifting may allow all to be placed more advantageously without sacrificing clarity. Important location dimensions should be given where they will be conspicuous, even if a size dimension must be moved.

The person dimensioning a drawing must make certain that every feature has been completely dimensioned and that no dimension has been repeated in a second view.

7.7 *Dimensioning Practices*

A generally recognized system of lines, symbols, figures, and notes is used to indicate size and location. Fig. 7.5 illustrates dimensioning terms and notation.

A *dimension line* is a lightweight line that is terminated at each end by an arrowhead. A numerical value, given along the dimension line, specifies the number of units for the measurement that is indicated (Fig. 7.6). When the numerals are in a single line, the dimension line is broken near the center, as shown in

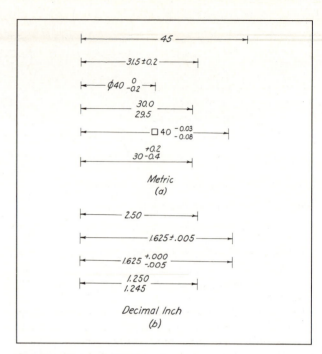

FIG. 7.6   Dimension line.

parts *a* and *b*. Under no circumstances should the line pass through the numerals.

Extension lines are light, continuous lines extending from a view to indicate the extent of a measurement given by a dimension line that is located outside a view. They start 1.5 mm (.06 in) from the view and extend 3 mm (.12 in) beyond the dimension line (Fig. 7.5).

Arrowheads are drawn from each dimension line, before the figures are lettered. They are made with the same pen or pencil used for the lettering. The size of an arrowhead, although it may vary with the size of a drawing, should be uniform on any one drawing. To have the proper proportions, the length of an arrowhead must be approximately three times its spread. This length for average work is usually 3 mm (.12 in). Figure 7.7 shows enlarged drawings of arrowheads of correct proportions. Although many drafters draw an arrowhead with one stroke, the beginner will get better

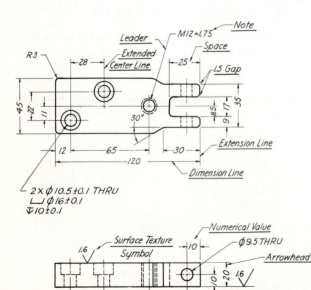

FIG. 7.5   Terms and dimensioning notation. (Dimensions are in millimeters.)

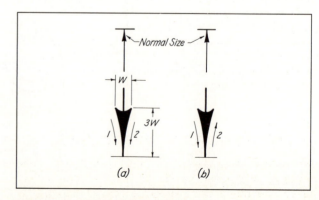

FIG. 7.7   Formation of arrowheads.

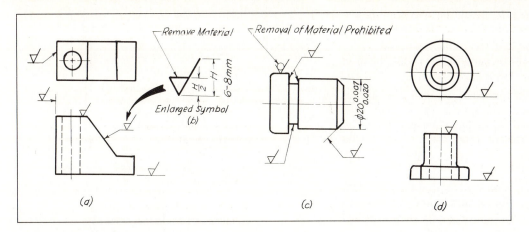

FIG. 7.8 Material removal symbol (finish mark).

results by using two slightly concave strokes drawn toward the point (*a*), or one stroke drawn to the point and one away from it (*b*).

A *leader* or *pointer* is a light, continuous line (terminated by an arrowhead) that extends from a note to the feature of a piece to which the note applies (Fig. 7.5). It should be made with a straightedge, and should not be curved or made freehand.

A leader pointing to a curve should be radial, and the first 3 mm (.12 in) of it should be in line with the note (Fig. 7.5).

Finish marks indicate the particular surfaces of a rough casting or forging that are to be machined or "finished." They are placed in all views, touching the visible or invisible lines that are the edge views of surfaces to be machined (Fig. 7.8). When a surface is to be finished by the removal of material and it is not necessary to indicate surface quality, a bar is added to the check mark (✔) portion of the texture symbol at the top of the short leg. When material removal is prohibited, a small circle is added to the "vee" in place of the horizontal bar. See Sec. 7.38.

It is not necessary to show finish marks on holes. they are also omitted, and a title note, "finish all over," is substituted, if the piece is to be completely machined. Finish marks are not required when limit dimensions are used.

Dimension figures should be lettered either horizontally or vertically with the whole numbers equal in height to the capital letters in the notes, and guidelines and slope lines must be used. The numerals must be legible; otherwise, they might be misinterpreted in the shop and cause errors.

7.8 *Fractional Dimensioning*

For ordinary work, where accuracy is relatively unimportant, technicians work to nominal dimensions given as common fractions of an inch, such as $\frac{1}{2}$, $\frac{1}{4}$, $\frac{1}{8}$, $\frac{1}{16}$, $\frac{1}{32}$, and $\frac{1}{64}$. When dimensions are given in this way,

many large corporations specify the required accuracy through a note on the drawing that reads as follows: *Permissible variations on common fraction dimensions to machined surfaces to be ± .010 unless otherwise specified.* It should be understood that the allowable variations will differ among manufacturing concerns because of the varying degree of accuracy required for different types of work.

7.9 *Decimal System*

A student should first be interested in selecting and placing dimensions. Later it will become easy to use fractional or decimal inch or the metric system as required by the needs of the design. To assist you in using any standard system, a standard conversion table has been provided in the Appendix.

In Fig. 7.9 a drawing is shown that illustrates decimal-inch dimensioning.

The following practices are recommended for decimal-inch dimensioning.

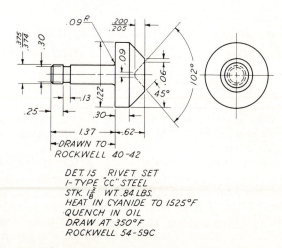

FIG. 7.9 Decimal-inch dimensioning. (*Courtesy Ford Motor Company*)

1. Two-place decimals should be used for dimensions where tolerance limits of $\pm$ .01 or more can be allowed (Fig. 7.9).

2. Decimals to three or more places should be used for tolerance limits less than $\pm$ .010 (Fig. 7.6[*b*]).

3. In the case of a two-place decimal, the second decimal place should preferably be an even digit such as .02, .04, and .06 so that when it is divided by 2, the result will remain a two-place decimal. Odd two-place decimals may be used where necessary for design reasons.

4. Common fractions may be used to indicate standard nominal sizes for materials and for features produced by standard tools as in the case of drilled holes, threads, keyways, and so forth.

5. When desired, decimal equivalents of nominal commercial sizes may be used for materials and for features such as drilled holes, threads, and so forth that are produced by standard tools.

7.10 Use of the Metric System

Under the metric system (Fig. 7.10), drawings are prepared to scales based on divisions of 10, such as 1 to 2, 1 to 5, 1 to 10, and so forth. A millimeter is one-thousandth part of a meter, which was established as being 39.37 inches in length.

Most of the illustrations in this chapter have been dimensioned using millimeters.

B GENERAL DIMENSIONING PRACTICES

7.11 Selection and Placement of Dimensions and Notes

The reasonable application of the selected dimensioning practices that follow should enable a student to dimension acceptably. The practices in **boldface** type should never be violated. In fact, these have been so definitely established by practice that they might be called rules.

When applying the dimensioning practices that follow, the student should realize that each company has its own drafting standards, and thus the practices set forth in this chapter may not be exactly the same as the practices followed in all corporations throughout the United States. The practices given are in general agreement with recommendations set forth in ANSI standards, however.

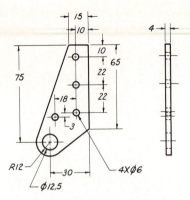

FIG. 7.10 Metric dimensioning.
(Dimensions are in millimeters.)

1. Place dimensions using either of two recognized methods—aligned or unidirectional.
(a) *Aligned method.* Place the numerals for the dimension values so that they are readable from the bottom and right side of the drawing. An aligned expression is placed along and in the direction of the dimension line (Fig. 7.11). Make the values for oblique dimensions readable from the directions shown in Fig. 7.32.
(b) *Unidirectional method.* Place the numerals for the dimension values so that they can be read from the bottom of the drawing (Fig. 7.12). The fraction bar for a common fraction should be parallel to the bottom of the drawing.

2. Place dimensions outside a view, unless they will be more easily and quickly understood if shown on the view (Figs. 7.12 and 7.13).

3. Place dimensions between views unless the rules, such as the contour rule, the rule against crowding, and so forth, prevent their being so placed.

4. Do not use an object line or a center line as a dimension line.

5. Locate dimension lines so that they will not cross extension lines.

6. If possible, avoid crossing two dimension lines.

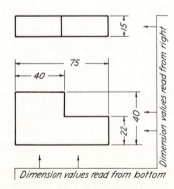

FIG. 7.11 Reading dimensions—aligned method.

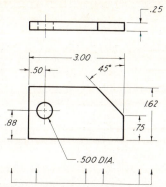

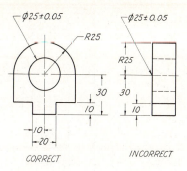

All dimension values read from the bottom

FIG. 7.12 Reading dimensions— unidirectional method.

FIG. 7.14 Contour principle of dimensioning.

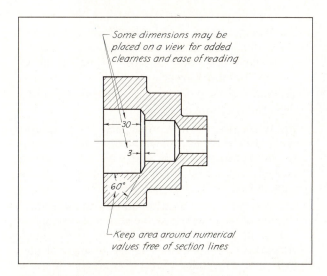

FIG. 7.13 Dimensions on the view.

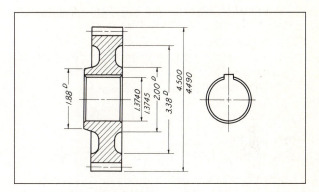

FIG. 7.15 Parallel dimensions.

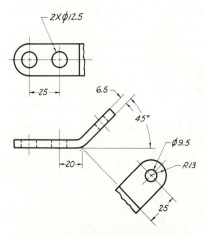

FIG. 7.16 Dimensioning angle bracket. (Dimensions are in millimeters.)

7. A center line may be extended to serve as an extension line (Fig. 7.14).

8. Keep parallel dimensions equally spaced [usually 10 mm [.38 in] apart] and the figures staggered (Fig. 7.15).

9. Always give locating dimensions to the centers of circles that represent holes, cylindrical projections, or bosses (Figs. 7.5 and 7.14).

10. If possible, attach the location dimensions for holes to the view on which they appear as circles (Fig. 7.16).

11. Group related dimensions on the view showing the contour of a feature (Fig. 7.14).

12. Arrange a series of dimensions in a continuous line (Fig. 7.17).

13. Dimension from a finished surface, center line, or base line that can be readily established (Figs. 7.40 and 7.54).

14. Stagger the figures in a series of parallel dimension lines to allow sufficient space for the figures and to prevent confusion (Fig. 7.15).

15. Place longer dimensions outside shorter ones so that extension lines will not cross dimension lines.

16. Give three overall dimensions located outside any other dimensions (unless the piece has cylindrical ends—see practice 43 and Fig. 7.44).

17. When an overall is given, one intermediate distance should be omitted unless given for reference. Reference dimensions are to be identified by enclosure within parentheses (Figs. 7.18 and 7.19).

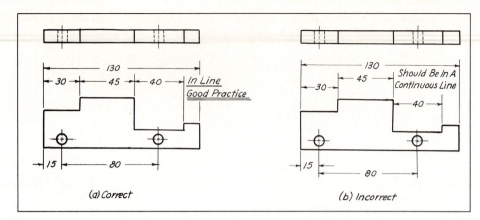

FIG. 7.17 Consecutive dimensions.

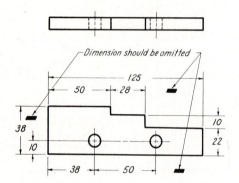

FIG. 7.18 Omit unnecessary dimensions.

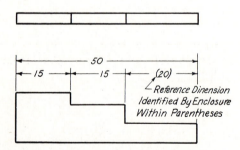

FIG. 7.19 Place reference dimensions in parentheses.

18. Do not repeat a dimension. One of the duplicated dimensions may be missed if a change is made. Give only those dimensions that are necessary to produce or inspect the part.

19. Make decimal points of a sufficient size so that dimensions cannot be misread.

20. When dimension figures appear on a sectional view, show them in a small uncrosshatched portion so that they may be easily read. This may be accomplished by doing the section lining after the dimensioning has been completed (Fig. 7.20).

21. When an arc is used as a dimension line for an angular measurement, use the vertex of the angle as the center (Fig. 7.21[a]). It is usually undesirable to terminate the dimension line for an angle at lines that represent surfaces. It is better practice to use an extension line (Fig. 7.21[b]).

22. Place the figures of angular dimensions so they will read from the bottom of a drawing, except in the case of large angles (Fig. 7.22).

23. Dimension an arc by giving its radius preceded by the abbreviation R, and indicate the center with a small cross. (Locate the center by dimensions [Fig. 7.23]).

24. TRUE R precedes the radius value, where the radius is dimensioned in a view that does not show the true shape of the arc (Fig. 7.24).

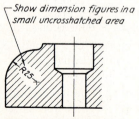

FIG. 7.20 Dimension figures on section view.

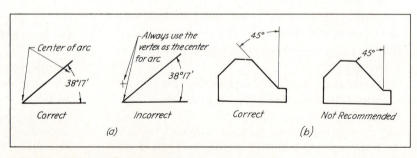

FIG. 7.21 Dimensioning an angle.

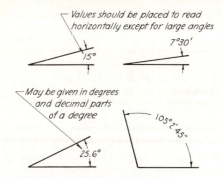

FIG. 7.22   Angular dimensions.

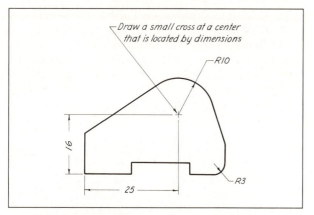

FIG. 7.23   Dimensioning a circular arc. (Dimensions are in millimeters.)

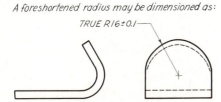

FIG. 7.24   Dimensioning a circular arc—true R.

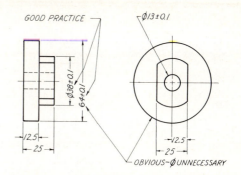

FIG. 7.25   Dimensioning a cylindrical piece.

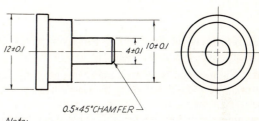

Note:
Although it is better practice to use a minimum of two views, a cylindrical part may be completely described in one view (no end view) by using the ∅ symbol with the value of the diameter.

FIG. 7.26   Dimensioning machined cylinders.

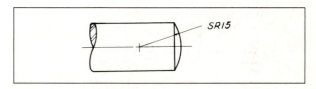

FIG. 7.27   Dimensioning a piece with a spherical end.

25. Show the diameter of a circle, never the radius. If it is not clear that the dimension is a diameter, the figures should be preceded by the diameter symbol φ (Figs. 7.25 and 7.26). Often this will allow the elimination of one view.

26. When dimensioning a portion of a sphere with a radius the term SPHER R or SR is added (Fig. 7.27).

27. Letter all notes horizontally (Fig. 7.54).

28. Make dimensioning complete, so that it will not be necessary for a worker to add or subtract to obtain a desired dimension or to scale the drawing.

29. Give the diameter of a circular hole, never the radius, because all hole-forming tools are specified by diameter. If the hole does not go through the piece, the depth may be given as a note (Fig. 7.28).

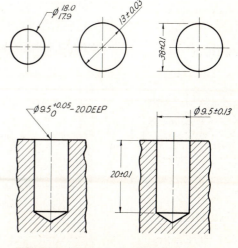

FIG. 7.28   Dimensioning holes.

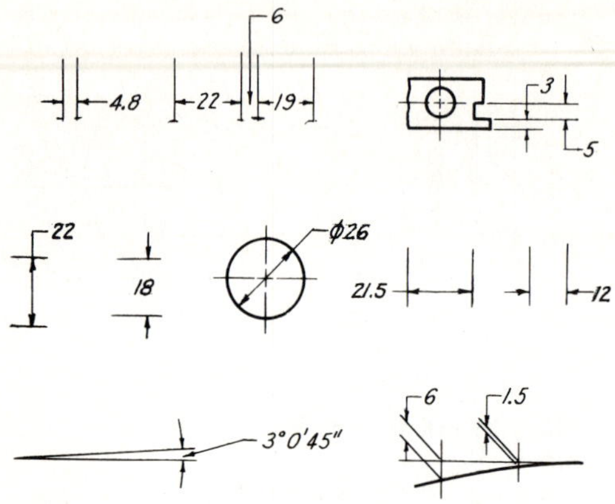

FIG. 7.29 Dimensioning in limited spaces.

30. Never crowd dimensions into small spaces. Use the practical methods suggested in Fig. 7.29.

31. When space is limited and a radius dimension cannot be placed between the arrowhead and the center as shown in Fig. 7.43, the radius line can be extended and the dimensional value placed outside the arc with a leader as shown in Fig. 7.30(a). Two other methods of dimensioning small arcs are shown in parts b and c. Where the center of a radius is not dimensionally located, the center should not be indicated.

32. Avoid placing inclined dimensions in the shaded areas shown in Fig. 7.31. Place them so that they may be conveniently read from the right side of the drawing. If this is not desirable, make the figures read from the left in the direction of the dimension line (Fig. 7.32[b]). The unidirectional method is shown in part a.

33. Omit superfluous dimensions. Do not supply dimensional information for the same feature in two different ways.

34. Give dimensions up to 72 in, except on structural and architectural drawings (Fig. 7.33). Omit the inch marks when all dimensions are in inches.

35. Show dimensions in feet and inches as illustrated in Fig. 7.34. Note that the use of the hyphen in parts a and b and the cipher in part b eliminates any chance of uncertainty and misinterpretation.

36. If feasible, design a piece and its elemental parts to such dimensions as .10, .40 and .50 in or 4, 10, 15, and 20 mm. Except for critical dimensions and hole sizes, dimension values in millimeters should be given in a full number of millimeters, preferably to an even number (12, 16, 20, 40, etc.) so that, when divided by 2, they will remain a full number.

37. Chamfers may be dimensioned either by an angle and a linear dimension or by two linear dimensions (Fig. 7.35). When an angle and a linear dimension are given, the dimension specifies the distance from the indicated surface to the start of the chamfer. A note may be used for 45° chamfers. Where the edge of a rounded hole is to be chamfered, the practices shown in Fig. 7.36 are followed.

38. Equally spaced holes in a circular flange may be dimensioned by giving the diameter of the bolt circle, across the circular center line, and the size and number of holes, in a note (Fig. 7.37).

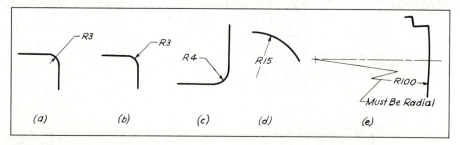

FIG. 7.30 Dimensioning radii.

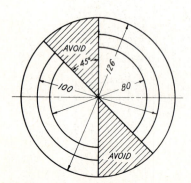

FIG. 7.31 Areas to avoid

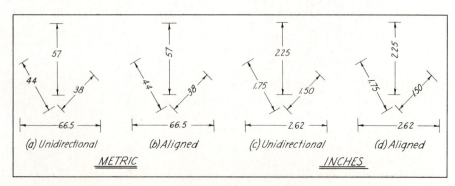

FIG. 7.32 Reading horizontal, vertical, and oblique dimensions.

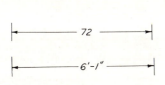

FIG. 7.33 Dimension values.

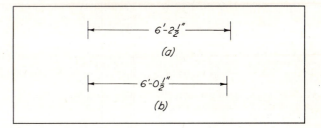

FIG. 7.34 Feet and inches.

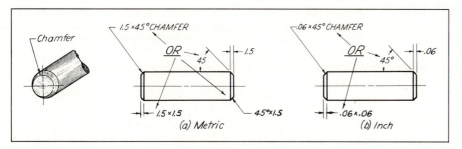

FIG. 7.35 Dimensioning an external chamfer.

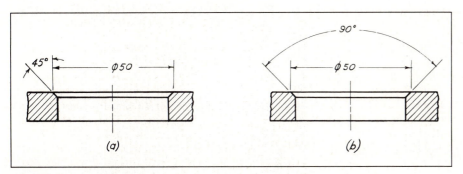

FIG. 7.36 Internal chambers.

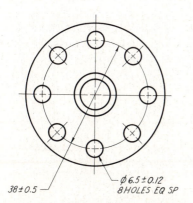

FIG. 7.37 Equally spaced holes.

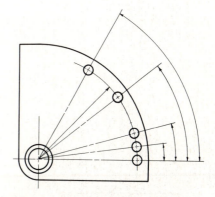

**FIG. 7.38 Locating holes on circle
by polar coordinates.**

39. When holes are unequally spaced on a circular center line, give the angles as illustrated in Fig. 7.38.

40. Holes that must be accurately located should have their location established by the coordinate method. Holes arranged in a circle may be located as shown in Fig. 7.39 rather than through the use of angular measurements. Figure 7.40 shows the application of the coordinate method to the location of holes arranged in a general rectangular form. The method with all dimensions referred to datum lines is sometimes called *base-line dimensioning*.

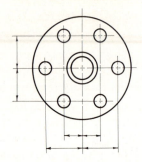

FIG. 7.39 Accurate location dimensioning of holes.

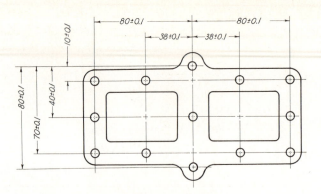

FIG. 7.40 Location dimensioning of holes.

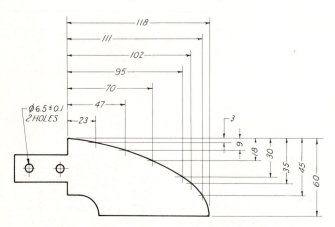

FIG. 7.41 Dimensioning curves by offsets.

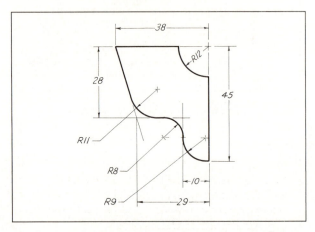

FIG. 7.42 Dimensioning curves consisting of circular arcs.

41. Dimension a curved line by giving offsets or radii.

(a) A noncircular curve may be dimensioned by the coordinate method illustrated in Fig. 7.41. Offset measurements are given from datum lines.

(b) A curved line, which is composed of circular arcs, should be dimensioned by giving the radii and locations of either the centers or points of tangency (Figs. 7.42 and 7.43).

42. Show an offset dimension line for an arc having an inaccessible center (Fig. 7.43). Locate with true dimensions the point placed in a convenient location that represents the true center.

43. Dimension, as required by the method of production, a piece with cylindrical ends. Give the diameters and center-to-center distance (Fig. 7.44). No overall is required.

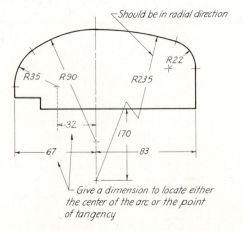

FIG. 7.43 Dimensioning curves by radii.

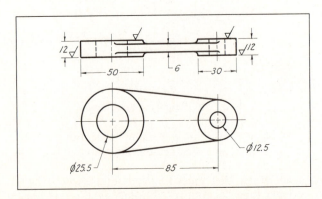

FIG. 7.44 Dimensioning a part with cylindrical ends—link.

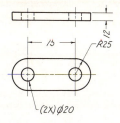

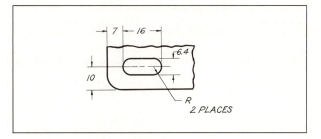

FIG. 7.45 Link with rounded ends.

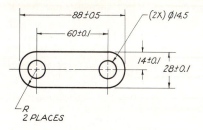

FIG. 7.46 Dimensioning a part with rounded ends.

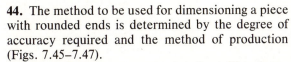

FIG. 7.47 Dimensioning a slot.

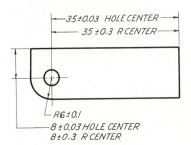

FIG. 7.48 Dimensioning a piece with a hole and rounded end.

44. The method to be used for dimensioning a piece with rounded ends is determined by the degree of accuracy required and the method of production (Figs. 7.45–7.47).

(a) It has been customary to give the radii and center-to-center distance for parts and contours that would be laid out or machined using centers and radii. A link (Fig. 7.45) or a pad with a slot is dimensioned in this manner to satisfy the requirements of the patternmaker and machinist. An overall dimension is not needed.

(b) Overall dimensions are recommended for parts having rounded ends when considerable accuracy is required. The radius is indicated but is not dimensioned when the ends are fully rounded. In Fig. 7.46, the center-to-center hole distance has been given because the hole location is critical.

(c) Slots are dimensioned by giving length and width dimensions. They are located by dimensions given to their longitudinal center line and to either one end or a center line (Fig. 7.47).

(d) When the location of a hole is more critical than the location of a radius from the same center, the radius and the hole should be dimensioned separately (Fig. 7.48).

45. A keyway on a shaft or hub should be dimensioned as shown in Fig. 7.49.

46. When knurls are to provide a rough surface and control is not important, it is necessary to specify only the pitch and kind of knurl, as shown in Fig. 7.50(*a* and *c*). When specifying knurling for a press fit, it is best practice to give the diameter before knurling with a tolerance and include the minimum diameter after knurling in the note that gives the pitch and type of knurl (*b*).

47. Conical tapers can be specified in one of the following ways.

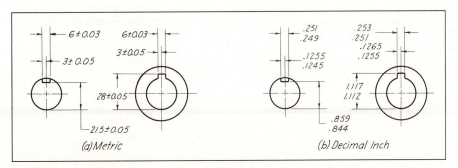

FIG. 7.49 Dimensioning keyways and keyslots.

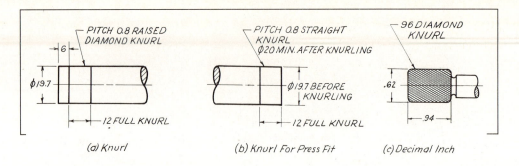

FIG. 7.50   Dimensioning knurls.

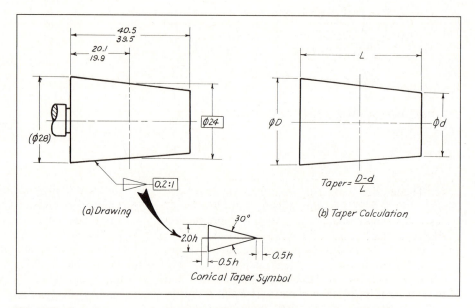

FIG. 7.51   Specifying a conical taper using a basic taper and a basic diameter.

(a) Basic taper and basic diameter (Fig. 7.51).
(b) A toleranced diameter at each end and a toleranced length (Fig. 7.52). This method is used mainly for noncritical tapers such as a transition taper between the diameters of a shaft.

Flat tapers may be specified by a tolerance slope and a toleranced height at one end as shown in Fig. 7.53.

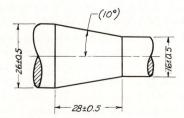

FIG. 7.52   Specifying a noncritical taper.

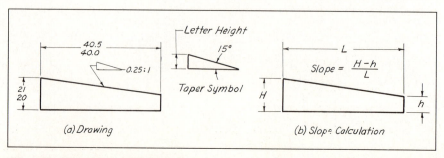

FIG. 7.53   Specifying a flat taper.

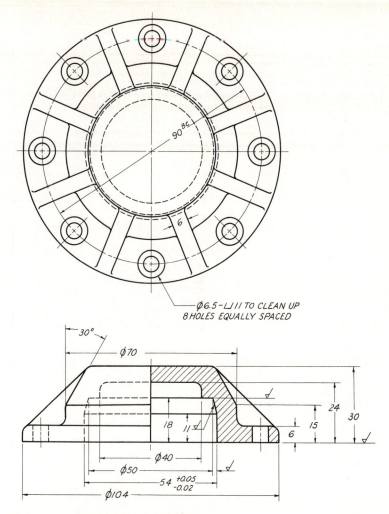

∅6.5-⌴11 TO CLEAN UP
8 HOLES EQUALLY SPACED

FIG. 7.54   Dimensioning a half section.

48. A half section may be dimensioned through the use of hidden lines on the external portion of the view (Fig. 7.54).

49. The fact that a dimension is out of scale may be indicated by a straight line placed underneath the dimension value (Fig. 7.55).

50. In sheet-metal work, mold lines are used in dimensioning instead of the centers of the arcs (see Fig. 7.56). A mold line (construction line) is the line at the intersection of the plane surfaces adjoining a bend.

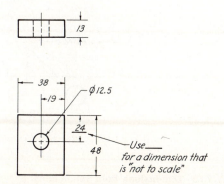

FIG. 7.55   Dimension out of scale.

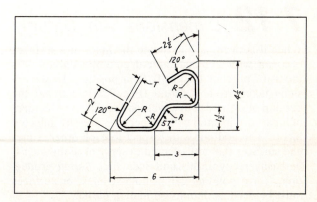

FIG. 7.56   Profile dimensioning.

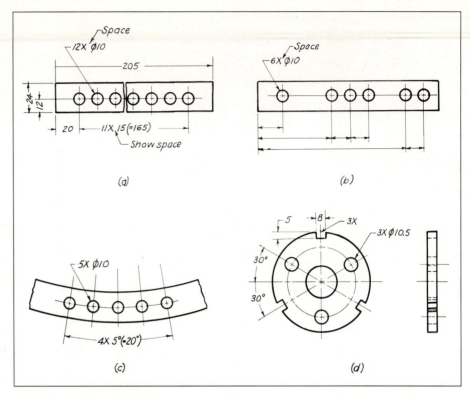

FIG. 7.57 Dimensioning repetitive features.

51. Features such as holes and slots that may be repeated in a series or in the form of a pattern may be specified by indicating the number of the like features followed by an X and the size dimension of the feature. As indicated in Fig. 7.57, a space is shown between the X and the size dimension of the feature.

7.12 *Dimensions from Datum*

When it is necessary to locate the holes and surfaces of a part with a considerable degree of accuracy, it is the usual practice to specify their positions by dimensions taken from a datum (Fig. 7.58) to avoid the buildup of error. By this method the different features of a part are located with respect to carefully selected bits of data and not with respect to each other. Lines and surfaces that are selected to serve as datums must be easily recognizable and accessible during production. Corresponding datum points, lines, or surfaces must be used as datums on mating parts.

7.13 *Notes*

The use of properly composed notes often adds clarity to the presentation of dimensional information involving specific operations (Fig. 7.59). Notes also are used

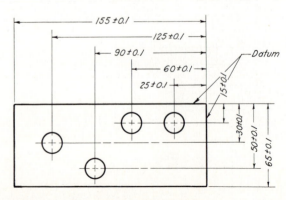

FIG. 7.58 Dimensions from datum lines.

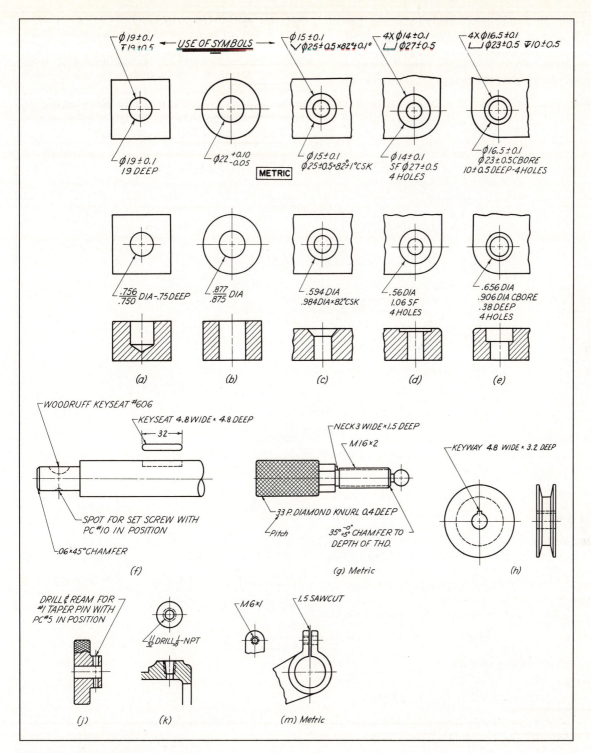

FIG. 7.59   Shop notes.

to convey supplementary instructions about the kind of material, kind of fit, degree of finish, and so forth. Brevity in form is desirable for notes of general information or specific instruction. In the case of threaded parts one should use the terminology recommended in Chapter 14.

7.14 Drawing Symbols

The symbols shown in Fig. 7.60 are used with dimensions and notes. A symbol must be shown before its associated linear dimension value in a dimension line or in place with a note as shown by the examples. The symbols have been shown at the left in the illustration and their interpretations directly follow.

ANSI Y14.5M-1982 AND ISO			
SYMBOL FOR	ANSI	ISO	EXAMPLES
Radius	R	R	R100
Spherical Radius	SR	None	SR 24 Space
Diameter	ϕ	ϕ	$\phi 10 \pm 0.1$
Spherical Diameter	Sϕ	None	$S\phi 36 \,_{-0.4}^{0}$
Arc Length	⌒	None	40
Square (Shape)	□	□	$\phi 24 \pm 0.1$ □10
Dimension Origin	⊕→	None	26 ± 0.4
Dimension Not To Scale	18	18	95
Number Of Times/Places	X	X	5X ϕ8 Space
Reference Dimension	( )	None	(50)
Counterbore/Spotface	⊔	None	$\phi 6 \pm 0.1$ THRU ⊔ $\phi 10 \pm 0.1$ ⊤3 ± 0.1
Countersink	∨	None	$\phi 6 \pm 0.1$ THRU ∨ $\phi 10 \pm 0.1 \times 82°$
Depth/Deep	⊤	None	⊤3 ± 0.1
Slope	◺	◺	◺ 0.25:1
Conical Taper	▷	▷	▷ 0.25:1

FIG. 7.60 General drawing symbols.

7.15 Limit Dimensions

Present-day competitive manufacturing requires quantity production and interchangeability for many parts. The production of each of these parts to an exact decimal dimension, although theoretically possible, is economically unfeasible, because the cost of a part rapidly increases as an absolute correct size is approached.

For this reason, the commercial drafter specifies an allowable error (tolerance) between decimal limits (Fig. 7.61).

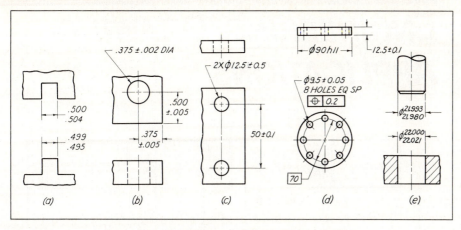

FIG. 7.61   Limit dimensioning for production of interchangeable parts.

PART 3 — ENGINEERING DRAWING APPLICATIONS

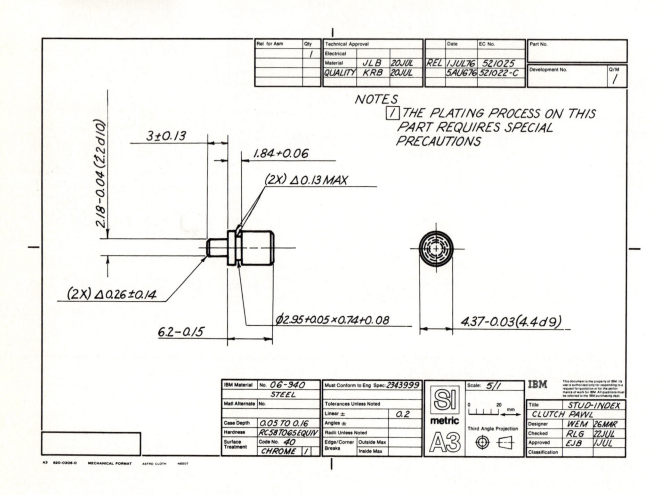

Multiview drawing. (*Courtesy IBM Corporation*)

Multiviews

A *MULTIVIEW PROJECTION—COORDINATE PLANES METHOD*

8.1 Introduction

Engineers use the orthographic system of projection for describing the shape of machine parts and structures (see facing page). Practical application of this method of describing an object results in a drawing consisting of a number of systematically arranged views that reproduce the object's exact shape. It was explained in Chapter 6, Sec. 6.4, that a set of views, showing the object from different positions, is always taken. These views, positioned in strict accordance with the universally recognized arrangement, must show the three dimensions, width, height, and depth. Although three views (Fig. 8.1) are usually required to describe an ordinary object, only two may be needed for a particularly simple one. A very complicated object may require four or more views. A view projected on an auxiliary plane also may be desirable (Fig. 9.3). Such a view often makes possible the elimination of one of the principal views. Therefore, it is up to the individual to determine the number and type of views needed to produce a satisfactory drawing. You will soon develop a knack for this, if you remember that the number of views required depends entirely on the complexity of the shape to be described.

8.2 Definition

Multiview (multiplanar) projection is a method by which the exact shape of an object can be represented by two or more separate views produced on projection planes that are at right angles to each other.

8.3 Methods of Obtaining the Views

The views of an object may be obtained by either of two methods:

1. *Natural* method
2. *Glass box* method.

Because the resulting views will be the same in either case, the beginner should adopt the method that is

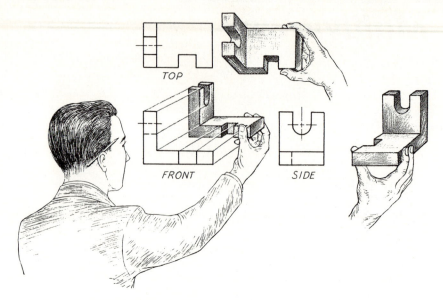

FIG. 8.1 Obtaining three views of an object.

the easiest to understand. Both methods are explained here in detail.

8.4 *Natural Method*

In using this method, each of the necessary views is obtained by looking directly at the particular side of the object the view is to represent. This method is often called the "direct view" method and more directly relates to the ways models are displayed in views of CADD computers.

Figure 8.1 shows three of the principal views of an object: the front, top, and side views. They were obtained by looking directly at the front, top, and right side, respectively. In the application of this method, some consider the position of the object as fixed and the position of the observer as shifted for each view; others find it easier to consider the observer's position

as fixed and the position of the object as changed for each view (Fig. 8.1). Regardless of which procedure is followed, the top and side views must be arranged in their natural positions relative to the front view.

Figure 8.2 illustrates the natural relationship of views. Note that the top view is *vertically above* the front view, and the side view is *horizontally in line with* the front view. In both of these *views the front of the block is toward the front view.*

8.5 *"Glass Box" Method*

An imaginary glass box is used widely by instructors to explain the arrangement of orthographic views. An explanation of this scheme can best be made by reviewing the use of planes of projection (Chapter 6). It may be considered that planes of projection placed parallel to the six faces of an object form an enclosing glass box (Fig. 8.3). The observer views the enclosed object from the outside. The views are obtained by running projectors from points on the object to the planes. This procedure is in accordance with the theory of orthographic projection explained in Sec. 6.3, as well as the definition in Sec. 8.2. The top, front, and right side of the box represent the H (horizontal), F (frontal), and P (profile) projection planes.

Because the projections on the sides of the three-dimensional transparent box are to appear on a sheet of drawing paper, it must be assumed that the box is hinged (Fig. 8.4) so that, when it is opened outward into the plane of the paper, the planes assume the positions illustrated in Figs. 8.4 and 8.5. Note that all of the planes, except the back one, are hinged to the frontal plane. In accordance with this universally recognized assumption, the top projection must take a

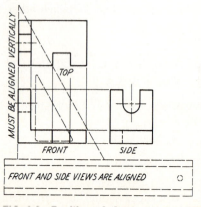

FIG. 8.2 Position of views.

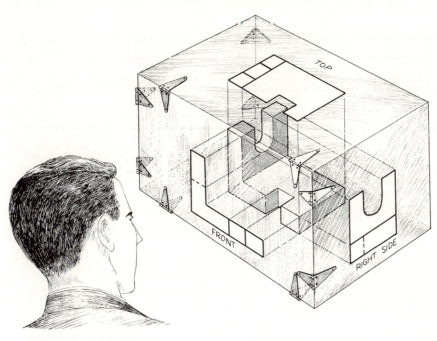

FIG. 8.3 "Glass box."

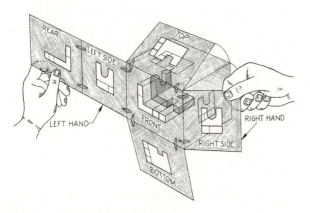

FIG. 8.4 Opening the glass box.

position directly above the front projection, and the right-side projection must lie horizontally to the right of the front projection. To identify the separate projections, engineers call the one on the frontal plane the *front view* or *front elevation,* the one on the horizontal plane the *top view* or *plan,* and the one on the side or profile plane the *side view, side elevation,* or *end view.* Figure 8.5 shows the six views of the same object as they would appear on a sheet of drawing paper. Ordinarily, only three of these views are necessary (front, top, and right side). A bottom or rear view will be required in comparatively few cases.

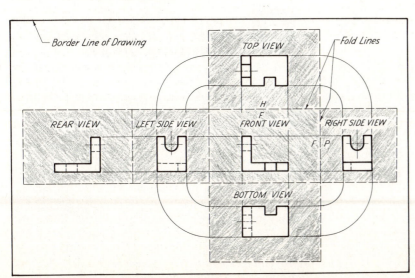

FIG. 8.5 Six views of an object on a sheet of drawing paper.

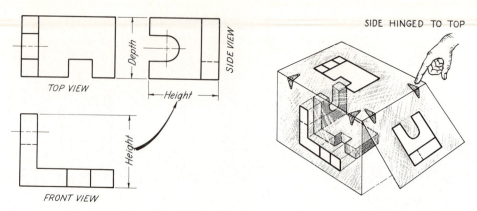

FIG. 8.6 "Second position" for the side view.

8.6 "Second Position"

Sometimes, especially in the case of a broad, flat object, it is desirable to hinge the sides of the box to the horizontal plane so that the side view will fall to the right of the top view, as illustrated in Fig. 8.6. This arrangement conserves space on the paper and gives the views better balance.

8.7 Principles of Multiview Drawing

The following principles should be studied carefully and understood thoroughly before any attempt is made to prepare an orthographic drawing:

1. The front and top views are *always* in line vertically (Fig. 8.2).

2. The front and side views are in line horizontally, except when the second position is used (Fig. 8.2).

3. The front of the object in the top view faces the front view (Fig. 8.4).

4. The front of the object in the side view faces the front view (Fig. 8.4).

5. The depth of the top view is the same as the depth of the side view (or views) (see Fig. 8.7).

6. The width of the top view is the same as the width of the front view (Fig. 8.7).

7. The height of the side view is the same as the height of the front view (Fig. 8.7).

8. A view taken from above is a top view and *must* be placed above the front view (Fig. 8.5).

9. A view taken from the right, in relation to the selected front, is a right-side view and *must* be placed to the right of the front view (Fig. 8.5).

10. A view taken from the left is a left-side view and *must* be placed to the left of the front view (Fig. 8.5).

11. A view taken from below is a bottom view and *must* be placed below the front view (Fig. 8.5).

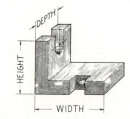
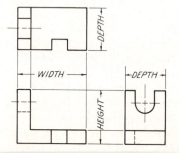

FIG. 8.7 View terminology.

B CADD STRATEGIES FOR PRINCIPAL VIEWS

8.8 CADD Strategies for Displaying Multiple Views

CADD computers are capable of displaying multiple views of complex geometry by any of several methods. First, and most powerful, is the display of multiple views from a single data base (Fig. 8.8). This method's results are similar to those obtained by placing video cameras in specific positions relative to the object and projecting the image captured by each camera onto the appropriate location of the CADD screen. Here, *changes made to the object in one view alter the data base from which all other views are made.* This means that a change made in one view will automati-

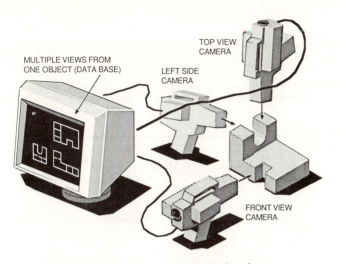

FIG. 8.8   Multiple views from a single data base.

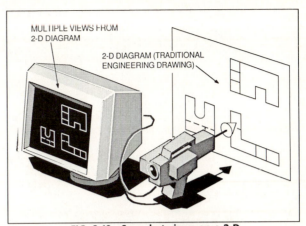

FIG. 8.10   Snapshot views on a 2-D

FIG. 8.10   Snapshot views on a two-dimensional
construction plane.

cally be made in the other views. The three-dimensional model can be finished as an engineering drawing by the operator, adding two-dimensional notes, symbols, and dimensions to the plane of the drawing (usually the X-Y plane).

Next in terms of power is the use of a single camera to view *duplicate geometry* rotated into positions of principal views (Fig. 8.9). For three views, you have three identical objects, each in its unique orientation. Changes made to one view are not recorded in the other views because each view has its own data base. As with a single data base, a multiple data base can be finished as an engineering drawing.

Least powerful are *snapshots* of two-dimensional views placed in proper orientation on a two-dimensional construction plane (Fig. 8.10). This is very much like traditional paper and pencil drafting. Not only are the views not a display of the same data base where changes in one view will correctly change all views, but all three-dimensionality has been lost, and the views are literally graphic diagrams. The two-dimensional diagram of views, with the addition of di-

mensions, notes, and symbols, becomes an engineering drawing.

C   PROJECTION OF POINTS, LINES, AND PLANES

8.9   *Projection of Lines*

A line may project either in *true length, foreshortened,* or as a *point* in a view depending on its relationship to the projection plane on which the view is projected (see Fig. 8.11). In the top view, the line projection $a^H b^H$ shows the true length of the edge *AB* (see pictorial) because *AB* is parallel to the horizontal plane of projection. Looking directly at the frontal plane, along the line, *AB* projects as a point ($a^F b^F$). Lines, such as *CD,* that are inclined to one of the planes of projection, will show a foreshortened projection in the view on the projection plane to which the line is inclined and true length in the view on the plane of projection to which the line is parallel. The curved line projection $e^F f^F$ shows the true length of the curved edge.

The student should study Fig. 8.12 and attempt to visualize the space position of each of the given lines. It is necessary both in preparing and reading graphical representations to recognize the position of a point, line, or plane and to know whether the projection of a line is true length or foreshortened, and whether the projection of a plane shows the true size and shape. The indicated reference lines may be thought of as representing the edges of the glass boxes shown. The projections of a line are identified as being on either a frontal, horizontal, or profile plane by the use of the letters *F, H,* or *P* with the lowercase letters that identify the end points of the line. For example, in Fig. 8.12(a), $a^H b^H$ is the horizontal projection of line *AB,*

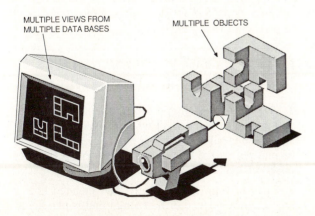

FIG. 8.9   Single camera to view duplicate geometry rotated into positions of principle views.

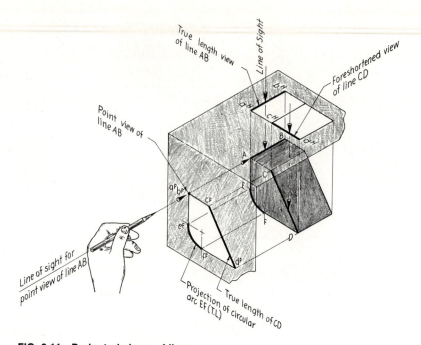

FIG. 8.11 Projected views of lines.

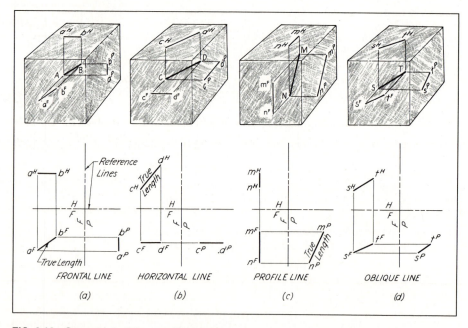

FIG. 8.12 Some typical line positions.

$a^F b^F$ is the frontal projection, and $a^P b^P$ is the profile projection.

It is suggested that the student hold a pencil and move it into the following typical line positions to observe the conditions under which the pencil representing a line, appears in true length.

1. *Vertical line.* The vertical line is perpendicular to the horizontal and will therefore appear as a point in the *H* (top) view. It will appear in true length in the *F* (frontal) view and in the *P* (profile) view.

2. *Horizontal line* (Fig. 8.12[*b*]). The horizontal line will appear in true length when viewed from above because it is parallel to the *H* plane of projection and its end points are theoretically equidistant from an observer looking downward.

3. *Inclined line* (Fig. 8.12[*c*]). The inclined line is any line not vertical or horizontal that is parallel to either the frontal plane of the profile plane of projection. An inclined line will show true length in the *F* (frontal) view or *P* (profile) view.

4. *Oblique line* (Fig. 8.12[*d*]). The oblique line will not appear in true length in any of the principal views because it is inclined to all of the principal planes of projection. It should be apparent in viewing the pencil alternately from the directions used to obtain the principal views, namely, from the front, above, and side, that one end of the pencil is always farther away from the observer than the other. Only when looking directly at the pencil from such a position that the end points are equidistant from the observer can the true length be seen. On a drawing, the true length projection of an oblique line will appear in a supplementary *A* (auxiliary) view projected on a plane that is parallel to the line (Chapter 9).

8.10 Meaning of Lines

On a multiview drawing a visible or invisible line may represent the following:

1. *Intersection* of two surfaces

2. *Edge view* of a surface

3. *Limiting element* of a surface.

These three different meanings of a line are illustrated in Fig. 8.13. In the top view, the curved line is an edge view of surface *C*, while a straight line is the edge view of surface *A*. The full circle in the front view may be considered as the edge view of the cylindrical surface of the hole. In the side view, the top line, representing the limiting element of the cylindrical surface, indicates the limits for the surface and therefore can be thought of as being a surface limit line. The short vertical line in this same view represents the intersection of two surfaces. In reading a drawing, one can be sure of the meaning of a line on a view only after an analysis of the related view or views. All views must be studied carefully.

8.11 Projection of Surfaces

The components of most machine parts are bounded by either plane or single-curved surfaces. *Plane surfaces* bound cubes, prisms, and pyramids, while *single-curved surfaces,* ruled by a moving straight line, bound cylinders and cones. The projected representations (lines or areas) of both plane and single-curved surfaces are shown in Fig. 8.14. From this illustration the student should note that

1. When a surface is *parallel to a plane* of projection, it will appear in true size in the view on the plane of projection to which it is parallel.

2. When it is *perpendicular to the plane* of projection, it will project as a line in the view.

3. When it is positioned at an *angle,* it will appear foreshortened.

A surface will always project either as a line or an area on a view. The area representing the surface may be either a full-size or foreshortened representation.

In Fig. 8.14 the cylindrical surface *A* appears as a line in the side (profile) view and as an area in the top and front views. Surface *B* shows true size in top view and as a line in both the front and side views. Surface *C*, a vertical surface, will appear as a line when observed from above.

8.12 Analysis of Surfaces, Lines, and Points in Three Principal Views

An analysis of the representation of the surfaces of a mutilated block is given pictorially in Fig. 8.15. It can be noted that each of the surfaces *A*, *B*, and *C* appears in true size and shape in one view and as a line in each

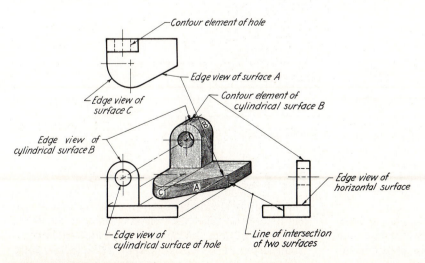

FIG. 8.13 Meaning of lines.

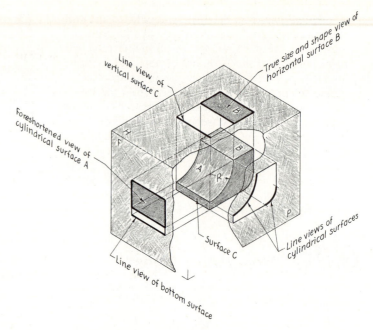

FIG. 8.14 Projected views of surfaces.

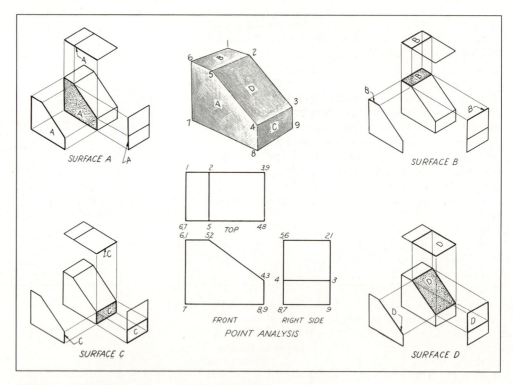

FIG. 8.15 Analysis of surfaces, lines, and points.

of the other two related views. Surface *D,* which is inclined, appears with foreshortened length in the top and side views and as an inclined line in the front view.

Three views of each of the visible points are shown on the multiview drawing. At the very beginning of an elementary course in drawing, a student will often find it helpful to number the corners of an object in all views.

8.13 *Selection of Views*

Careful study should be given to the outline of an object before the views are selected; otherwise there is no assurance that the object will be described completely from the reader's viewpoint (Fig. 8.16). Only those views that are necessary for a clear and com-

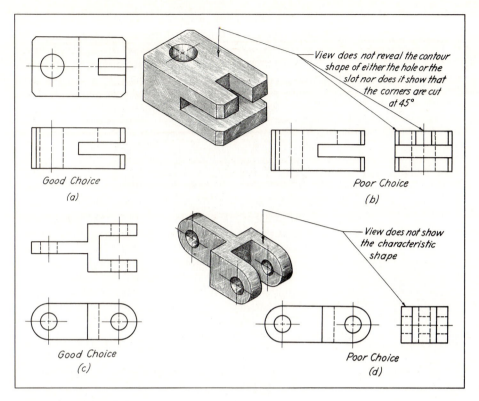

View does not reveal the contour shape of either the hole or the slot nor does it show that the corners are cut at 45°

Good Choice
(a)

Poor Choice
(b)

View does not show the characteristic shape

Good Choice
(c)

Poor Choice
(d)

FIG. 8.16 Choice of views.

plete description should be selected. Because the repetition of information only tends to confuse the reader, superfluous views should be avoided.

Although some objects, such as cylinders, bushings, bolts, and so forth, require only two views (front and side), more complicated pieces may require an auxiliary or sectional view in addition to the ordinary three views.

The space available for arranging the views often governs the choice between the use of a top or side view. The difference between the descriptive values of the two frequently is not great. For example, a draftsman often finds that the views of a long object will have better balance if a top view is used (Fig. 8.17[a]), whereas in the case of a short object (see [b]), the use of a side view may make possible a more pleasing arrangement. It should be remembered that the choice of views for many objects is definitely fixed by the contour alone, and no choice is offered as far as spacing is concerned. It is more important to have a set of views that describes an object clearly than one that is artistically balanced.

Often there is a choice between two equally important views, such as between a right-side and left-side view or between a top and bottom view (Fig. 8.5). In such cases, one should adhere to the following rule. *A right-side view should be used in preference to a left-side view and a top view in preference to a bottom view.* When this rule is applied to irregular objects, the

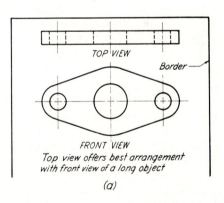

TOP VIEW

Border

FRONT VIEW
Top view offers best arrangement with front view of a long object
(a)

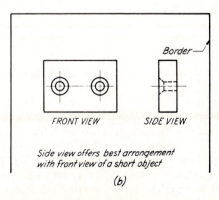

Border

FRONT VIEW   SIDE VIEW

Side view offers best arrangement with front view of a short object
(b)

FIG. 8.17 Choice of views.

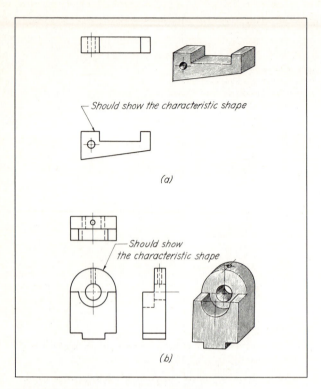

FIG. 8.18 Principal view of an object.

front (contour) view should be drawn so that the most irregular outline is toward the top and right side.

Another rule, one that must be considered in selecting the front or profile view is as follows. *Place the object to obtain the smallest number of hidden lines.*

8.14 Principal (Front) View

The principal view is the one that shows the characteristic contour of the object (Fig. 8.18[*a*] and [*b*]). Good practice dictates that this be used as the front view on a drawing. It should be clearly understood that the view of the natural front of an object is not always the principal view, because frequently it fails to show the object's characteristic shape. Therefore, another rule

to be followed is *ordinarily, select the view showing the characteristic contour shape as the front view, regardless of the normal or natural front of the object.*

When an object does have a definite normal position, however, the front view should be in agreement with it. In the case of most machine parts, the front view can assume any convenient position that is consistent with good balance.

8.15 Invisible Lines

Dashed lines are used on an external view of an object to represent surfaces, intersections, and limits invisible at the point from which the view is taken. In Fig. 8.19(*a*), one invisible line represents a line of intersection or edge line, whereas the other invisible line may be considered to represent either the surface or lines of intersection. On the side view in (*b*) there are invisible lines, which represent the contour elements of the cylindrical holes.

8.16 Treatment of Invisible Lines

The short dashes that form an invisible line should be drawn carefully in accordance with the recommendations in Sec. 8.25. An invisible line always starts with a dash in contact with the object line from which it starts, unless it forms a continuation of a visible line. In the latter case, it should start with a space, to establish at a glance the exact location of the end point of the visible line (see Fig. 8.20[c]). Note that the effect of definite corners is secured at points *A*, *B*, *E*, and *F*, where, in each case, the end dash touches the intersecting line. When the point of intersection of an invisible line and another object line does not represent an actual intersection on the object, the intersection should be open as at points *C* and *D*. An open intersection tends to make the lines appear to be at different distances from the observer.

Parallel invisible lines should have the breaks staggered.

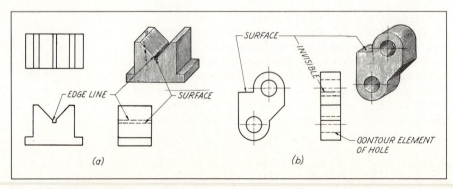

FIG. 8.19 Invisible lines.

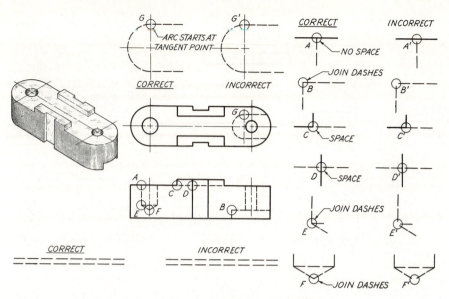

FIG. 8.20 Correct and incorrect junctures of invisible outlines.

The correct and incorrect treatment for starting invisible arcs is illustrated at *G* and *G'*. Note that an arc should start with a dash at the point of tangency. This treatment enables the reader to determine the exact end points of the curvature.

8.17 Omission of Invisible Lines

It is common practice for commercial drafters to omit hidden lines when their use tends to further confuse an already overburdened view or when the shape description of a feature is sufficiently clear in another view. It is not advisable for a beginning student to do so. It would be wise, until experience is gained, that *all* hidden lines be shown.

8.18 Precedence of Lines

When one discovers in making a multiview drawing that two lines coincide, the question arises, which line should be shown or, in other words, which line will have precedence. For example, as revealed in Fig. 8.21, a solid line may have the same position as an invisible line representing the contour element of a hole, or an invisible line may occur at the same place as a center line for a hole. In these cases the decision rests on the relative importance of each of the two lines that can be shown. The precedence of lines is as follows:

1. *Solid lines* (visible object lines) take precedence over all other lines.

2. *Dashed lines* (invisible object lines) take precedence over center lines, although evidence of center

lines may be indicated as shown in both the top and side views of Fig. 8.21.

3. A *cutting-plane line* takes precedence over a center line where it is necessary to indicate the position of a cutting plane.

8.19 Projection of Angles

When an angle lies in a plane that is parallel to one of the planes of projection the angle will show in true size in the normal view of that particular plane. In Fig. 8.22 those angles indicated as actual show in their true size. The 60° angle, which lies in a surface that is not parallel to the *H* plane, appears at less than 60° in the top view. The 30° angle for the sloping line on the compo-

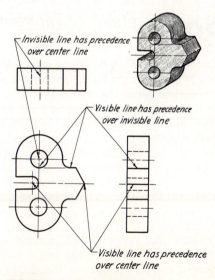

FIG. 8.21 Precedence of lines.

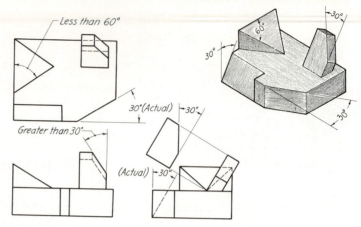

FIG. 8.22 Projection of angles.

nent portion that is inclined backward projects at greater than 30° in the front view. It may be said that, except for a 90° angle having one leg as a normal line, angles lying on inclined planes will project either larger or smaller than true size, depending on the position of the plane in which the angle lies. A 90° angle always projects in true size, even on an inclined plane, if the line forming one side of the angle is parallel to the plane of projection and a normal view of the line results. The normal view of a line is any view of a line that is obtained with the direction of sight perpendicular to the line.

What has been stated concerning angles on inclined surfaces can be easily verified by the student when observing what happens to the angles of a 30° × 60° triangle resting on the long leg, as it is revolved from a vertical position downward onto the surface of his desk top.

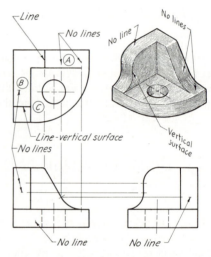

FIG. 8.23 Treatment of tangent surfaces.

8.20 Treatment of Tangent Surfaces

When a curved surface is tangent to a plane surface, as illustrated in several ways on the pictorial drawing in Fig. 8.23, no line should be shown as indicated at A and B in the top view and as noted for the front and side views. At C in the top view the line represents a small vertical surface that must be shown even though the upper and lower lines for this surface may be omitted in the front view, depending on the decision of the drafter. In the top view a line has been drawn to represent the intersection of the inclined and horizontal surfaces at the rear, even though they meet in a small round instead of a sharp edge. The presence of this line emphasizes the fact that there are two surfaces meeting here that are at a definite angle, one to the other. Several typical examples of tangencies and intersections have been illustrated in Fig. 8.24.

8.21 Parallel Lines

When parallel surfaces are cut by a plane, the resulting lines of intersection will be parallel. This is shown by the pictorial drawing in Fig. 8.25(b), where the near corner of the object has been removed by the oblique plane ABC. It can be observed from the multiview drawing in part c that *when two lines are parallel in space, their projections will be parallel in all of the views,* even though at times both lines may appear as points on one view.

In Fig. 8.25, three views are to be drawn that show the block after the near front corner has been removed (see [b]). Several of the required lines of intersection can be readily established through the given points A, B, and C that define the oblique plane. For example, $c^F b^F$ can be drawn in the front view and the line

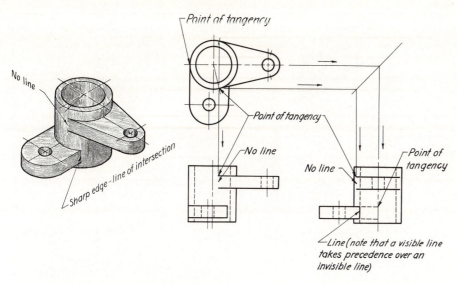

FIG. 8.24 Treatment of tangent surfaces.

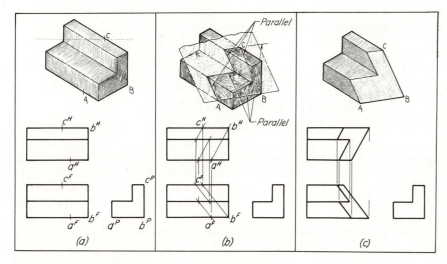

FIG. 8.25 Parallel lines.

through a^F can be drawn parallel to it. In the top view, $a^H b^H$ should be drawn first and the intersection line through c^H should then be drawn parallel to this H view of AB. The drawing can now be completed by working back and forth from view to view while applying the rule that a plane intersects parallel planes along lines of intersection that are parallel. The remaining lines are thus drawn parallel to either AB or CB (see the pictorial in [*b*]).

8.22 Plotting an Elliptical Boundary

The actual intersection of a circular cylinder or cylindrical hole with a slanting surface (inclined plane) is an *ellipse* (Fig. 8.26). The elliptical boundary in part *a*

appears as an ellipse in the top view, as a line in the front view, and as a semicircle in the side view. The ellipse is plotted in the top view by projecting selected points (such as points *A* and *B*) from the circle arc in the side view, as shown. For example, point *A* was projected first to the inclined line in the front view and then to the top view. The mitre line shown was used to project the depth distance for *A* in the top view for illustrative purposes only. Ordinarily, dividers should be used to transfer measurements to secure great accuracy.

In part *b* the intersection of the hole with the sloping surface is represented by an ellipse in the side view. Points selected around the circle in the top view (such as points *C* and *D*) projected to the side view as shown permit the draftsman to form the elliptical outline. It is recommended that a smooth curve be sketched free-

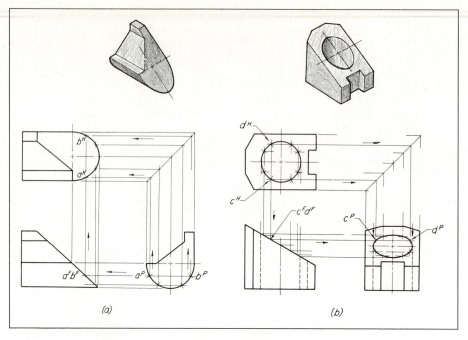

FIG. 8.26   Representation of an elliptical boundary.

hand through the projected points before a French curve or ellipse guide is applied to draw the finished ellipse, because it is easier to fit a curved ruling edge to a line than to scattered points.

8.23 Projecting a Curved Outline (Space Curve)

When a boundary curve lies in an inclined plane, the projection of the curve may be found in another view by projecting points along the curve, as illustrated in Fig. 8.27. In the example, points selected along the arcs forming the curve in the top view were first located in the side view, using distances taken from the top view, as shown by the X and Y measurements. Then the front view positions of these points, through which the front view of the curve must pass, were established by projecting horizontally from the side view and downward from the top view.

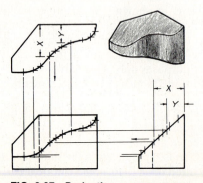

FIG. 8.27   Projecting a space curve.

8.24 Treatment of Intersecting Finished and Unfinished Surfaces

Figure 8.28 illustrates the removal of material when machining surfaces, cutting a slot, and drilling a hole in a small part. The italic f on a surface of a pictorial drawing in this text indicates that the surface has been machined. The location of sharp and rounded corners, as illustrated in parts *b* and *c,* are noted on the multiview drawing. A discussion covering rounded internal and external corners is given in Sec. 8.36.

8.25 To Make an Orthographic Drawing

The location of all views should be determined before a drawing is begun. This will ensure balance in the appearance of the finished drawing. The contour view is usually started first. After the initial start, the drafter should construct views simultaneously by projecting back and forth from one to the other. It is poor practice to complete one view before starting the others, as much more time will be required to complete the drawing. Figure 8.29 shows the procedure for laying out a three-view drawing. The general outline of the views first should be drawn lightly with a hard pencil and then heavied with a medium-grade pencil. Although experienced persons sometimes deviate from this procedure in drawing in the lines of known length and location in finished weight while constructing the views, it is not recommended that beginners do so (see Fig. 8.29, step III).

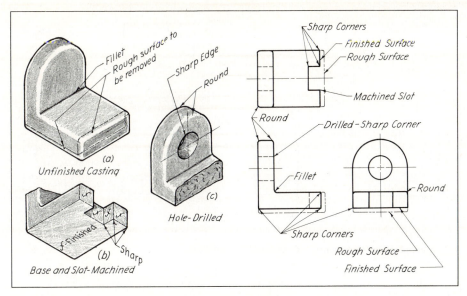

FIG. 8.28 Rough and finished surfaces on a casting.

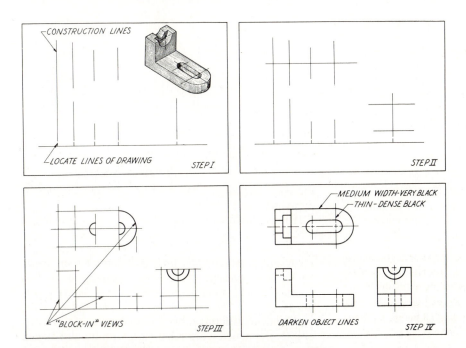

FIG. 8.29 Steps in making a three-view drawing of an object.

Although a 45° mitre line is sometimes used for transferring depth dimensions from the top view to the side view, or vice versa, as shown in Fig. 8.30(*b*), it is better practice to use dividers, as in part *a*. Continuous lines need not be drawn between the views and the mitre line, as in the illustration, for one may project from short dashes across the mitre line. The location of the mitre line may be obtained by extending the construction lines representing the front edge of the top view and the front edge of the side view to an intersection.

When making an orthographic drawing in pencil, the beginner should endeavor to use the line weights recommended in Sec. D1.17. The object lines should be made very dark and bright, to give snap to the drawing as well as to create the contrast necessary to cause the shape of the object to stand out. Special care should be taken to gauge the dashes and spaces in invisible object lines. On ordinary drawings, 3 mm (.12 in) dashes and 0.8 mm (0.3 in) spaces are recommended (Fig. 8.31).

Center lines consist of alternate long and short

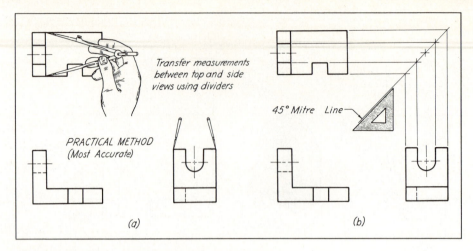

FIG. 8.30 Methods for transferring depth dimensions.

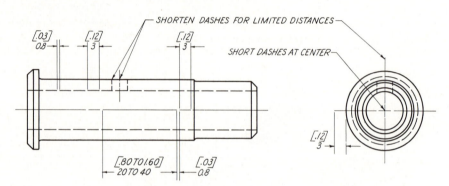

FIG. 8.31 Invisible lines and center lines.

dashes. The long dashes are from 20 to 40 mm (.80–1.60 in) long, the short dashes 3 mm (.12 in), and the spaces 0.8 mm (.03 in) (Fig. 8.31). The following technique is recommended in drawing center lines.

1. Where *center lines* cross, the short dashes should intersect symmetrically (Fig. 8.31). (In the case of very small circles the breaks may be omitted.)

2. The *breaks* should be so located that they will stand out and allow the center line to be recognized as such.

3. *Center lines* should extend approximately 3 mm (.12 in) beyond the outline of the part whose symmetry they indicate (Fig. 8.31).

4. *Center lines* should not end at object lines.

5. *Center lines* that are aligned with object lines should have not less than a 1.5 mm (.06 in) space between the end of the center line and the object line.

For a finished drawing to be pleasing in appearance, all lines of the same type must be uniform, and each type must have proper contrast with other symbolic types. The contrast between the types of pencil lines is similar to that of ink lines, except that pencil lines are never as wide as ink lines. On commercial drawings,

the usual practice is to "burn in" the object lines by applying heavy pressure.

If reasonable care is taken not to soil a drawing, it will not be necessary to clean any part of it with an eraser. Because the practice in engineering drawing is not to erase construction lines if they have been drawn lightly, the student, at the very beginning of the first course, should try to acquire habits that ensure cleanliness.

When constructing a two-view drawing of a circular object, the pencil work must start with the drawing of the center lines, as shown in Fig. 8.32. This is necessarily the first step because the construction of the circular (contour) view is based on a horizontal and a vertical center line. The horizontal object lines of the rectangular view are projected from the circles.

8.26 *Visualizing an Object from Given Views*

Most students in elementary graphics courses find it difficult to visualize an object from two or more views. This trouble is largely due to the lack of systematic procedure for analyzing complex shapes.

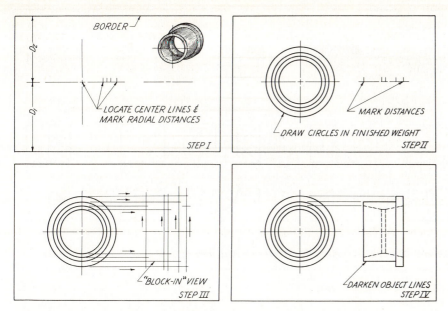

FIG. 8.32 Steps in making a two-view drawing of a circular object.

FIG. 8.33 "Breaking down" method.

The simplest method of determining shape is illustrated pictorially in Fig. 8.33. This method of "breaking down" may be applied to any object, because all objects may be thought of as consisting of elemental geometric forms, such as prisms, cylinders, cones, and so on. This is consistent with computer-aided geometric modeling. These imaginary component parts may be additions in the form of projections or subtractions in the form of cavities. Following such a detailed geometric analysis, a clear picture of an entire object can be obtained by mentally assembling a few easily visualized forms.

It should be realized, when analyzing component parts, that it is usually impossible to determine whether a form is an addition or a subtraction by looking at one view. For example, the small circles in the top view in Fig. 8.33 indicate a cylindrical form, but they do not reveal whether the form is a hole or a projection. By consulting the front view, however, the form is shown to be a hole (subtracted cylinder).

The graphic language is similar to the written language in that neither can be read at a glance. A drawing must be read patiently by referring systematically back and forth from one view to another. At the same time the reader must imagine a three-dimensional object and not a two-dimensional flat projection.

A student usually will find that a pictorial sketch will clarify the shape of a part that is difficult to visualize. The method for preparing quick sketches in isometric projection is explained in Secs. 4.12 through 4.16.

8.27 *Interpretation of Adjacent Areas of a View*

To obtain a full understanding of the true geometric shape of a part, all the areas on a given view must be carefully analyzed, because each area represents a surface on the part. For example, in reading a drawing it must be determined whether a particular area in a top view represents a surface that is inclined or horizontal and whether the surface is higher or lower than adjacent ones. Five distinctly different objects are shown in Fig. 8.34, all having the same top view. In

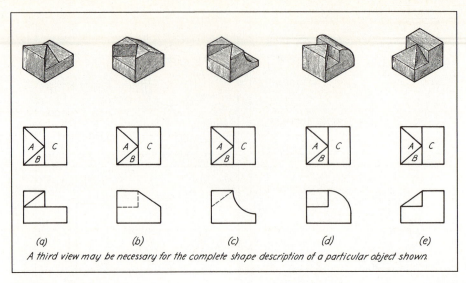

A third view may be necessary for the complete shape description of a particular object shown.

FIG. 8.34 Meaning of areas.

determining the actual shape of these objects, memory and previous experience can be a help, but one can easily be misled if the analysis is not approached with an open mind, for it is only by trial-and-error effort and by referring back and forth from view to view that a drawing can be read. In considering area *A* in part *a* it might be thought that the triangular surface could be high and horizontal, which would be correct because of the arrangement of lines in the front view. In considering the top view alone, however, *A* could be either sloping, as in parts *c* and *e,* or low and horizontal, as in part *b.* An analysis of the five parts reveals that the surface represented by area *B* can also be either sloping, high and horizontal, or low and horizontal. Area *C* offers even a wider variety of possibilities in that it may be either low and horizontal (*a*), sloping (*b*), cylindrical ([*c*] and [*d*]), or high and horizontal (*e*).

The student must realize at this point that because there are infinite possibilities for the shape, position, and arrangement of surfaces that form objects, one must learn to study tediously the views of any unfamiliar object until sure of the exact shape. Multiview drawings cannot be read with the ease of our written language, which lists all the components in a dictionary.

8.28 *True-length Lines*

Students who, lacking a thorough understanding of the principles of projection (Sec. 8.9), find it difficult to determine whether or not a projection of a line in one of the principal views shows the true length of the line should study carefully the following facts:

1. If the principal projection of a line shows the true length of the line, one of the other projections must appear as a horizontal line, a vertical line, or a point, on one of the other views of the drawing.

2. If the front view of the line is horizontal, and the top view of the line is parallel to the frontal plane, both views show true length.

3. If the top view of a line is a point, the front and side views show the true length.

4. If the front view of a line is a point, the top and side views show the true length.

5. If the top and front views of a line are parallel to the profile plane, the side view shows true length.

6. If the side projection of a line is a point, the top and front views show the true length.

7. If the front view of a line is horizontal and the top view is inclined to the frontal plane, the top inclined view shows the true length.

8. If the top view of a line is horizontal and the front view is inclined to the horizontal plane, the front inclined view shows the true length.

8.29 *Representation of Holes*

In preparing drawings of parts of mechanisms, a drafter finds it necessary to represent machined holes, which most often are drilled, drilled and reamed, drilled and countersunk, drilled and counterbored, or drilled and spotfaced. Graphically, a hole is represented to conform with the finished form. The form may be completely specified by a note attached to the view showing the circular contour (Fig. 8.35). The shop note, as prepared by the drafter, usually specifies the several shop operations in the order that they are to be performed. For example, in part *d* the hole, as specified, is drilled before it is counterbored. When depth has not been given in the note for a hole, it is understood to be a through hole; that is, the holes goes entirely through the piece ([*a*], [*c*], [*d*], and [*e*]). A hole

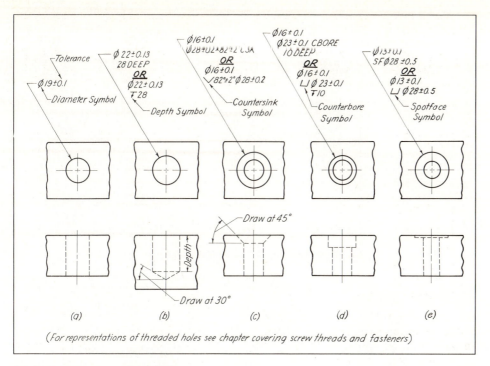

FIG. 8.35 Representation of holes.

that does not go through is known as a *blind hole* (*b*). For such holes, depth is the length of the cylindrical portion. Drilled, bored, reamed, cored, or punched holes are always specified by giving their diameters, never their radii.

In drawing the hole shown in part *a*, which must be drilled before it is reamed, the limits are ignored and the diameter is scaled to the nearest regular inch or millimeter size. In part *b* the 30° × 60° triangle is used to draw the approximate representation of the conical hole formed by the drill point. In part *c* a 45° triangle has been used to draw an approximate representation of the outline of the conical enlargement. The actual angle of 82° is ignored in order to save time in drawing. The spotface in part *e* is most often cut to a depth of 1.5 mm (.06 in); however, the depth is usually not specified.

The beginner should now scan the several sections in the chapter on shop processes to obtain some general information on the production of holes.

CONVENTIONAL PRACTICES

8.30 *Practices Defined*

To reduce the high cost of preparing engineering drawings and at the same time to convey specific and concise information without a great expenditure of effort,

some generally recognized systems of symbolic representation and conventional practices have been adopted by American industry.

A *standard symbol* or conventional representation can express information that might not be understood from a true-line representation unless accompanied by a lettered statement. In many cases, even though a true-line representation would convey exact information, very little more would be gained from the standpoint of better interpretation. Some conventional practices have been adopted for added clarity. For instance, they can eliminate awkward conditions that arise from strict adherence to the rules of projection.

These methods of drawing have slowly developed with the graphic language until at the present time they are universally recognized and observed and appear in the various standards of the American National Standards Institute.

Skilled professionals have learned to accept and respect the use of the symbols and conventional practices, for they can interpret these representations accurately and realize that their use saves valuable time in both the drawing room and the shop.

8.31 *Half Views and Partial Views*

When the available space is insufficient to allow a satisfactory scale to be used for the representation of a *symmetrical piece,* it is considered good practice to make one view either a half view or a partial view, as shown in Fig. 8.36. The half view, however, must be

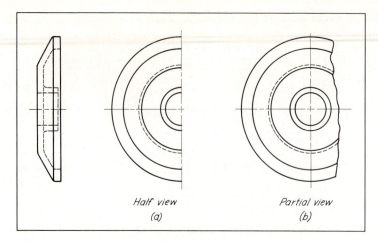

FIG. 8.36   Half views and partial views.

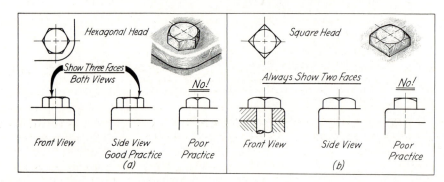

FIG. 8.37   Treatment of bolt heads.

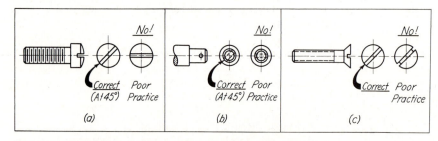

FIG. 8.38   Treatment of slots and holes in fasteners and pins.

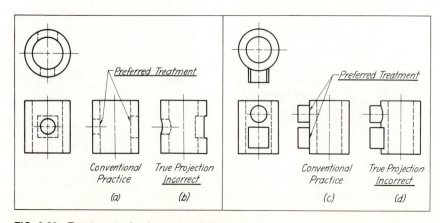

FIG. 8.39   Treatment of unimportant intersections.

the top or side view and not the front view, which shows the characteristic contour. The half view should be the front half of the top or side view. In the case of the partial view shown in part *b,* a break line is used to limit the view.

Accepted Violations of True Projection in the Representation of Boltheads, Slots, and Holes for Pins

8.32

A departure from true projection is encountered in representing a *bolthead.* For example, on a working drawing, it is considered the best practice to show the head *across corners* in both views, regardless of the fact that in true projection one view would show *across flats.* This method of treatment eliminates the possibility of a reader's interpreting a hexagonal head to be a square head (Fig. 8.37). Furthermore, the showing of a head across corners in both views clearly reveals the space needed for proper clearance.

In the case of the slotted head fasteners, the slots are shown at 45° in the end views to avoid placing a slot on a center line, where it is usually difficult to draw so that the center line passes accurately through the center (Fig. 8.38). This practice does not affect the descriptive value of the drawing, because the true size and shape of the slot is shown in the front view. The hole for a pin is shown at 45° for the same

reason. In such a position it may be more quickly observed.

8.33 *Treatment of Unimportant Intersections*

The conventional methods of treating various unimportant intersections are shown in Fig. 8.39. To show the true line of intersection in each case would add little to the value of the drawing. Therefore, in the views designated as preferred, true projection has been ignored in the interest of simplicity. On the side views, in parts *a* and *b,* for example, there is so little difference between the descriptive values of the true and approximate representations of the holes that the extra labor necessary to draw the true representation is unwarranted.

8.34 *Aligned Views*

Pieces that have arms, ribs, lugs, or other features at an angle are shown aligned or *straightened out* in one view, as illustrated in Fig. 8.40. By this method, it is possible to show the true shape as well as the true position of such features. In Fig. 8.41, the front view has been drawn as though the slotted arm had been revolved into alignment with the element projecting outward to the left. This practice is followed to avoid drawing an element—that is at an angle—in a foreshortened position.

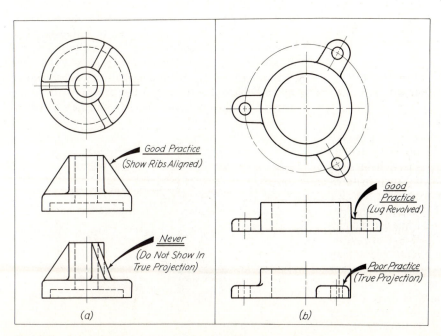

FIG. 8.40 Conventional practice of representing ribs and lugs.

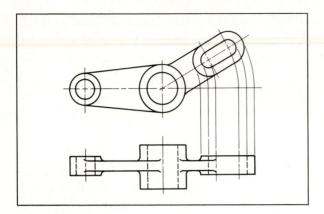

FIG. 8.41 Aligned views.

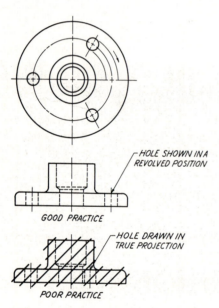

HOLE SHOWN IN A REVOLVED POSITION

GOOD PRACTICE

HOLE DRAWN IN TRUE PROJECTION

POOR PRACTICE

FIG. 8.42 Radially arranged holes.

8.35 Conventional Treatment of Radially Arranged Features

Many objects that have radially arranged features may be shown more clearly if true projection is violated, as in Fig. 8.40(*b*). Violation of true projection in such cases consists of intentionally showing such features swung out of position in one view to present the idea of symmetry and show the true relationship of the features at the same time. For example, while the radially arranged holes in a flange (Fig. 8.42) should always be shown in their true position in the circular view, they should be shown in a revolved position in the other view to show their true relationship with the rim.

Radial ribs and radial spokes are similarly treated [Fig. 8.40(*a*)]. The true projection of such features may create representations that are unsymmetrical and misleading. The preferred conventional method of

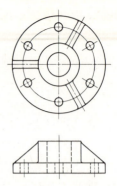

FIG. 8.43 Conventional treatment of radially arranged ribs.

treatment, by preserving symmetry, produces representations that are more easily understood and that at the same time are much simpler to draw. Figure 8.43 illustrates the preferred treatment for radial ribs and holes.

8.36 Representations of Fillets and Rounds

Interior corners, which are formed on a casting by unfinished surfaces, are always *filleted* at the intersection in order to avoid possible fracture at that point. Sharp corners are also difficult to obtain and are avoided for this reason as well. Exterior corners are *rounded* for appearance and for the comfort of persons who must handle the part when assembling or repairing the machine on which the part is used. A rounded internal corner is known as a *fillet;* a rounded external corner is known as a *round* (Fig. 8.44).

When two intersecting surfaces are machined, however, their intersection will become a sharp corner. For this reason, all corners formed by unfinished surfaces should be shown "broken" by small rounds, and all corners formed by two finished surfaces, or one finished surface and one unfinished surface, should be shown "sharp." Although in the past it has been the practice to allow patternmakers to use their judgment

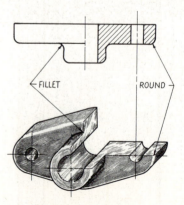

FILLET   ROUND

FIG. 8.44 Fillets and rounds.

about the size of fillets and rounds, many present-day companies require their designers and draftsmen to specify their size even though their exact size may not be important.

Because fillets and rounds eliminate the intersection lines of intersecting surfaces, they create a special problem in orthographic representation. To treat them in the same manner as they would be treated if they had large radii results in views that are misleading. For example, the true-projection view in Fig. 8.45(c) confuses the reader, because at first glance it does not convey the idea that there are abrupt changes in direction. To prevent such a probable first impression and to improve the descriptive value of the view, it is necessary to represent these theoretically nonexisting lines. These characteristic lines are projected from the approximate intersections of the surfaces, with the fillets disregarded.

Figure 8.46 illustrates the accepted conventional method of representing the *run-out* intersection of a fillet in cases where a plane surface is tangent to a cylindrical surface. Although run-out arcs such as these are usually drawn freehand, a French curve or a bow instrument may be used. If they are drawn with the bow instrument, a radius should be used that is equal to the radius of the fillet, and the completed arc should form approximately one-eighth of a circle.

The generally accepted methods of representing intersecting fillets and rounds are illustrated in Fig. 8.47. The treatment, in each of these cases shown, is determined by the relationship existing between the sizes of the intersecting fillets and rounds.

8.37 *Conventional Breaks*

A relatively long piece of uniform section may be shown to a larger scale, if a portion is broken out so that the ends can be drawn closer together (Fig. 8.48). When such a scheme is employed, a conventional break is used to indicate that the length of the representation is not to scale. The American National Standard conventional breaks, shown in Fig. 8.49, are used on either detail or assembly drawings. The break representations for indicating the broken ends of rods, shafts, tubes, and so forth, are designed to reveal the characteristic shape of the cross section in each case. Although break lines for round sections may be drawn freehand, particularly on small views, it is better to draw them with either an irregular curve or a bow instrument. The breaks for wood sections, however, always should be drawn freehand.

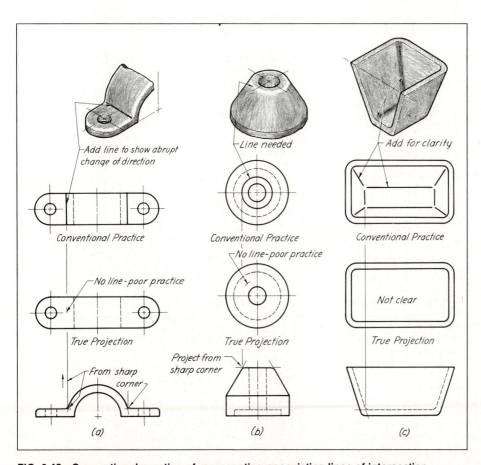

FIG. 8.45 Conventional practice of representing nonexisting lines of intersection.

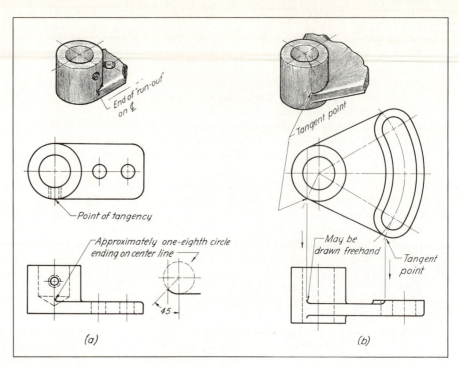

FIG. 8.46 Conventional treatment for fillets.

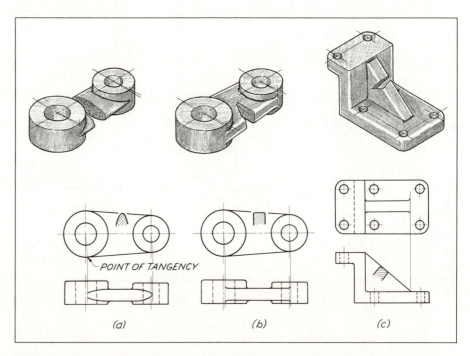

FIG. 8.47 Approximate methods of representing run-outs for intersecting fillets and rounds.

8.38 *Ditto Lines*

When it is desirable to minimize labor to save time, *ditto lines* may be used to indicate a series of identical features. For example, the threads on the shaft shown in Fig. 8.50 are just as effectively indicated by ditto lines as by a completed profile representation. When ditto lines are used, a long shaft of this type may be shortened without actually showing a conventional break.

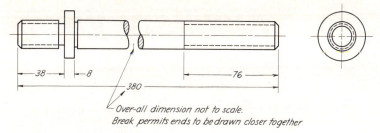

FIG. 8.48   **Broken-out view.**

Over-all dimension not to scale.
Break permits ends to be drawn closer together

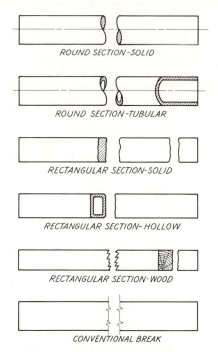

ROUND SECTION-SOLID

ROUND SECTION-TUBULAR

RECTANGULAR SECTION-SOLID

RECTANGULAR SECTION-HOLLOW

RECTANGULAR SECTION-WOOD

CONVENTIONAL BREAK

FIG. 8.49   **Conventional breaks.**

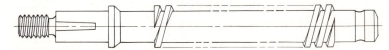

FIG. 8.50   **Ditto lines.**

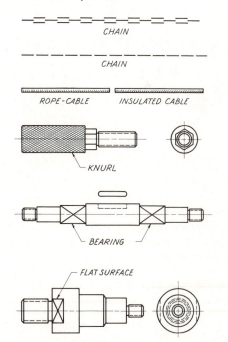

FIG. 8.51   **Alternative positions.**

CHAIN

CHAIN

ROPE-CABLE   INSULATED CABLE

KNURL

BEARING

FLAT SURFACE

FIG. 8.52   **Conventional symbols.**

8.39   *Conventional Method for Showing Part in Alternative Positions*

A method frequently used for indicating an alternative position of a part or a limiting position of a moving part is shown in Fig. 8.51. The dashes forming the object lines of the view showing the alternative position should be of medium weight. The *phantom line* shown in Fig. 8.51 is recommended for representing an alternative position.

8.40   *Conventional Representation*

Symbols are used on topographical drawings, architectural drawings, electrical drawings, and machine drawings. No engineer serving in a professional capacity can very well escape their use.

Most of the illustrations that are shown in Fig. 8.52 should be easily understood. The *crossed-lines* (diago-

nals) symbol, however, has two distinct and different meanings. First, this symbol may be used on a drawing of a shaft to indicate the position of a surface for a bearing or, second, it may indicate that a surface perpendicular to the line of sight is flat. These usages are illustrated with separate examples.

CHAPTER 9

Auxiliary Views

A PRIMARY AUXILIARY VIEWS

9.1 Introduction

When it is desirable to show the true size and shape of a surface that is not parallel to one of the principal planes of projection, an *auxiliary line of vision* must be taken. This line of vision is perpendicular to the surface and therefore perpendicular to the *auxiliary plane of projection* on which the surface is drawn (Fig. 9.1).

The theories underlying principal views apply to auxiliary views as well. In other words, an auxiliary view shows the object as it would appear to an observer stationed an infinite distance away and viewing the plane of projection perpendicularily. An auxiliary plane is referred to as a *supplementary* plane and is always perpendicular to a principal plane (Fig. 9.2).

9.2 Use of Auxiliary Views

In commercial drafting, an auxiliary view is usually a *partial view* showing only the desired informtion. The reason for this is that a projection showing the entire object adds very little to the description of the shape. Showing all of the object in the auxiliary view is likely to defeat the intended purpose of the view. For example, a complete drawing of the casting in Fig. 9.3 must include an auxiliary view of the inclined surface to show the true shape of the surface and the location of the holes. Compare the views in parts *a* and *b*, and note that the addition of foreshortened information actually makes the view more difficult to read. Some teachers may require that an auxiliary view show the entire object—including all hidden features. Though impractical commercially, this requirement is justified in the classroom as practice in projection.

A *partial auxiliary view* is often needed to complete the description of a foreshortened feature in a principal view. Another important auxiliary view function is to complete a principal view. This is illustrated in Fig. 9.16 and explained in Sec. 9.13.

9.3 Types of Auxiliary Views

Auxiliary views may have an infinite number of positions in relation to the three principal planes of projection. *Primary auxiliary views* may be classified into three general types by their position relative to the principal views.

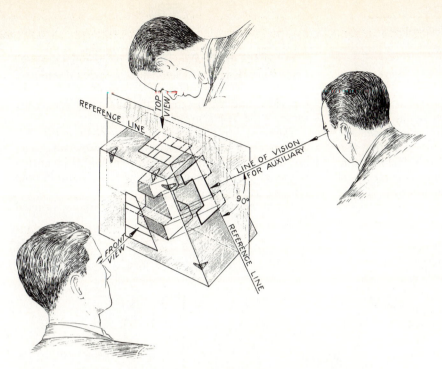

FIG. 9.1 Theory of projecting an auxiliary view.

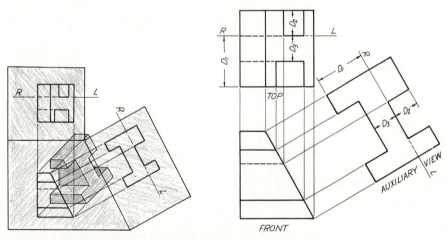

FIG. 9.2 Auxiliary view.

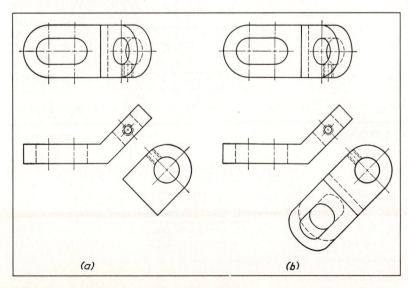

FIG. 9.3 Partial and complete auxiliary views.

1. Adjacent to front view
2. Adjacent to top view
3. Adjacent to side view.

Fig. 9.4 shows the first type, where the auxiliary plane is *perpendicular to the frontal plane, and inclined to the horizontal and profile planes*. Here the auxiliary and top views have the depth dimension in common. Note that the auxiliary plane is adjacent to the frontal plane and that the auxiliary view is projected from the front view.

In Fig. 9.5 the auxiliary plane is *perpendicular to the horizontal plane, and inclined to the frontal and profile planes*. The auxiliary view is projected from the top view, and the height in the auxiliary view is the same as the height in the front view.

The third type of auxiliary view is shown in Fig. 9.6. The auxiliary plane is *perpendicular to the side view, and inclined to the top and front*. The width dimension in the auxiliary view is shared with the width in both top and front views.

The three types of auxiliary views are constructed

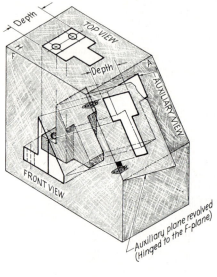

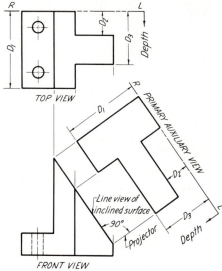

Transfer the D distances in the top, taken from R-L in the direction of the arrow, to the auxiliary view. Both of these views show related distances that are equal in the direction of depth. (See pictorial drawing)

FIG. 9.4 Auxiliary view projected from front view.

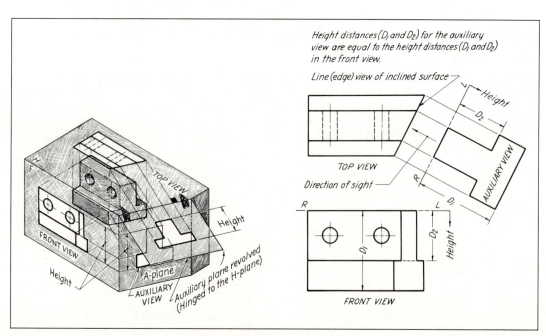

Height distances (D_1 and D_2) for the auxiliary view are equal to the height distances (D_1 and D_2) in the front view.

FIG. 9.5 Auxiliary view projected from top view.

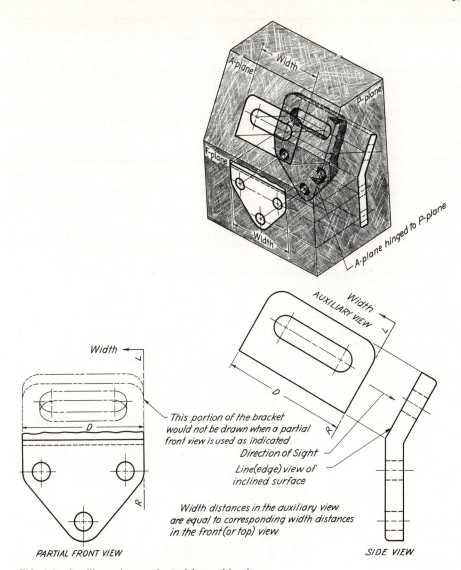

FIG. 9.6 Auxiliary view projected from side view.

similarly. Each is projected from the view that shows the inclined surface as an edge. Measurements for the auxiliary view are projected from the *adjacent view* and taken from the *related view*. For example, in Fig. 9.6 adjacent information from the side view is combined with related width information from the front view to complete the auxiliary view. A careful study of the three illustrations will reveal the fact that a primary auxiliary view is always adjacent to the principal view to which the auxiliary plane is perpendicular.

9.4 Symmetrical and Nonsymmetrical Views

Auxiliary views can be termed (1) *symmetrical*, (2) *unilateral*, or (3) *bilateral*. A symmetrical view is drawn about a reference—usually a center line. A unilateral view may be either symmetrical or nonsymmet-

rical, but is entirely on one side of a reference. A bilateral view may also be either symmetrical or nonsymmetrical. It differs from the first two examples in that the reference is placed at a convenient location—usually not in the center or on one side.

9.5 Method to Draw Symmetrical Auxiliary View

When an inclined surface is symmetrical, the auxiliary view is constructed from a center line representing the axis of symmetry (Fig. 9.7). The following steps describe the construction of a symmetrical auxiliary view.

1. Draw a center line parallel to the line that represents the edge of view of the surface. This center line may be considered the intersection of the auxil-

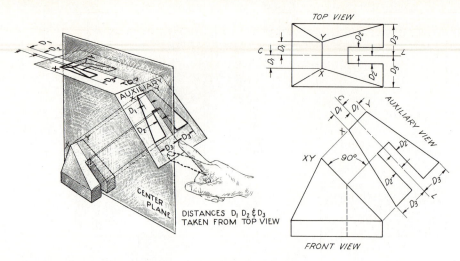

FIG. 9.7 Symmetrical auxiliary view of an inclined surface.

iary plane and a center reference plane. Although this center line can be drawn at any distance from the principal view, it should be located so that the principal and auxiliary views can be read together. In the top view the center plane is shown in the same position, providing a reference for depth to be transferred to the auxiliary view.

2. Draw projectors at 90° to the edge line from points on the inclined surface. With the projectors drawn, the location of each point in the auxiliary can be established by *setting your dividers to each point's depth distance relative to the reference line in the top view and transferring that distance to the auxiliary view.* For example,

(a) Point X is found in the auxiliary by drawing a projector from point X in the front view perpendicular to the edge.

(b) The distance from the reference to X is measured in the top view.

(c) The same distance is set off along the ''X projector'' in the auxiliary view.

3. A careful study of Fig. 9.7 shows that if a point lies to the front of the reference in the top view it will lie to the front of the reference in the auxiliary view. Conversely, if a point lies to the rear of the reference in the top view it will lie the same distance to the rear of the reference in the auxiliary view.

9.6 Unilateral Auxiliary Views

A *unilateral auxiliary view* is constructed so that all points fall either on the near or far side of the reference. The construction procedure is identical to that used in a symmetrical auxiliary view. The unilateral reference line represents the line of intersection of a reference plane, coinciding with an outer face, and the auxiliary plane (Fig. 9.8). The position of the reference in the top view is identical to its position in the auxil-

iary view. That is, if the reference is at the rear (Fig. 9.8) in the top view, it must be at the rear in the auxiliary view. All points are projected from the edge view of the surface and in setting them off, all fall on the same side of the reference.

Figure 9.9 shows an auxiliary view of an entire object. Note that the projectors from all points of the object are perpendicular to the auxiliary plane. This is true because the observer views the entire object by looking directly at (perpendicular to) the inclined surface. Height distances perpendicular to the reference were measured in the front view and transferred to the auxiliary view.

9.7 Bilateral Auxiliary Views

The method of drawing a *bilateral auxiliary view* is identical to that used in drawing either a symmetrical or unilateral view. The exception is that the bilateral reference lies simply at a convenient location and not at the outside or symmetrical center of the object (Fig. 9.10).

9.8 Curved Lines in Auxiliary Views

To draw a *curve* in an auxiliary view, a sufficient number of points must be plotted to ensure the curve is smooth (Fig. 9.11).

1. Establish an auxiliary line of vision perpendicular to the surface and a center line representing the symmetrical reference.

2. Locate a sufficient number of points on the curve in the right side view to describe the curve adequately. In addition to random points, you will want points at corners, tangents, and limits.

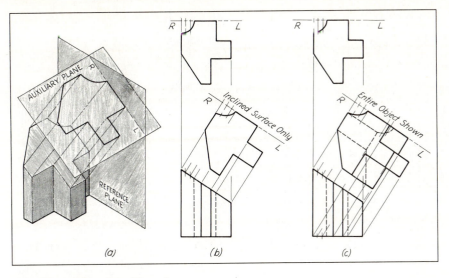

FIG. 9.8   Unilateral auxiliary view.

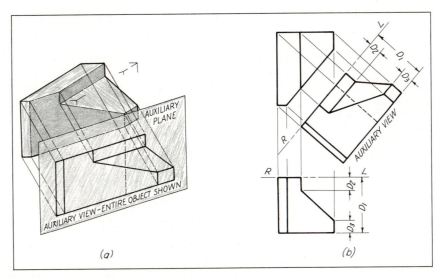

FIG. 9.9   Auxiliary view of an object.

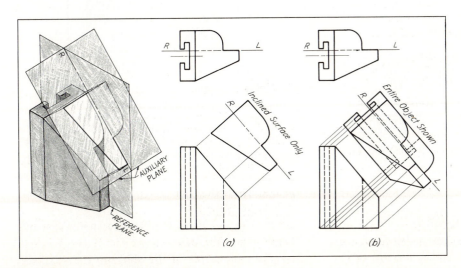

FIG. 9.10   Bilateral auxiliary view.

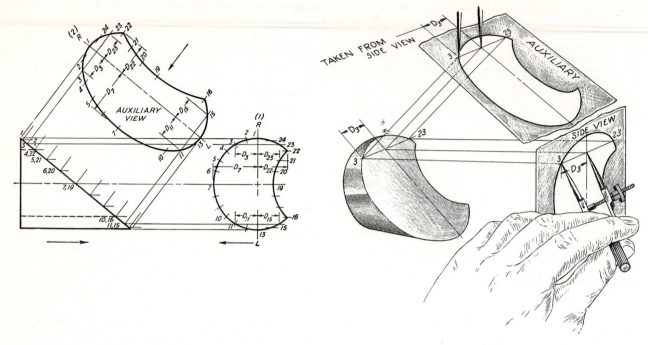

FIG. 9.11 Curved-line auxiliary view.

3. Project these points from the curve in the right side view to the edge of the plane in the front view.

4. Project these points into the auxiliary view.

5. The distance from the center line in the auxiliary view is the same as the distance from the center line in the side view for every point found on the curve.

9.9 *Projection of Curved Boundary*

In Fig. 9.11, the procedure is illustrated for plotting the true size and shape of an inclined surface bounded by a *curved outline*. A similar procedure can be followed to plot a curve not on the inclined surface as is shown on the left side of the object in Fig. 9.12.

1. Establish elements of the cylindrical surface so that *A* and *B* are on the incline, and *A'* and *B'* are on the left end of the cylinder.

2. A reference is established at a convenient location in the right-side view and in the auxiliary.

3. Distances from the reference for *A* and *A'*, and all other sets of points, are identical in the side and in auxiliary views.

9.10 *Dihedral Angles*

Frequently an auxiliary view may be needed to show the true size of a *dihedral angle*—that is, the true size of the angle between two planes. In Fig. 9.13, the true

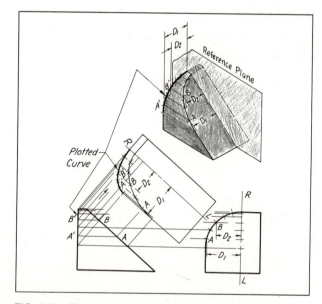

FIG. 9.12 Plotted boundary curves.

angle between the planes forming the V slot is shown by means of a partial auxiliary view. Refer to Fig. 9.13 during the following discussion.

1. Take a direction of view parallel to the edges of the slot. This establishes the projectors between the top and auxiliary views.

2. Establish a convenient reference, in this case the top surface of the base.

3. Project the edges of the slot into the auxiliary view.

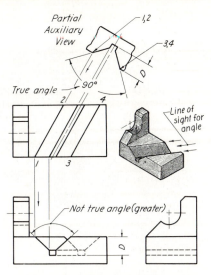

FIG. 9.13 To determine the true dihedral angle between inclined surfaces.

4. Transfer the height dimensions from the reference in the front view to the auxiliary view.

5. The angle between the planes where they both appear as edges is the dihedral angle.

9.11 Construction of Auxiliary View—Practical Method

The usual steps in constructing an auxiliary view are shown in Fig. 9.14. Study the illustration carefully and note the position of the reference.

9.12 Partial Views in Auxiliary

Often the use of an auxiliary view allows the elimination of one of the principal views or makes possible the use of a partial principal view. The shape description furnished by the partial views shown in Fig. 9.15 is sufficient for a complete understanding of the shape of the part. The use of partial views simplifies the drawing, saves valuable drafting time, and tends to make the drawing easier to read.

A break line is used at a convenient location to indicate the imaginary break for the partial view.

9.13 Use of Auxiliary View to Complete Principal View

To draw a foreshortened feature in a principal view it may be necessary to project the feature from an auxiliary view where it appears true shape. In the case of the object shown in Fig. 9.16, the foreshortened projection of the inclined face in the top view can be constructed by first drawing the true shape of the face in an auxiliary view. Refer to Fig. 9.16 during the following discussion.

1. Construct a true-shape auxiliary view of the face.

2. Locate several points (D_1 and D_2, for example) on the curve of the face. Project these points to the edge view of the surface and into the top view.

3. Using the center line of the face as a reference, locate these points in the top view.

The steps in preparing an auxiliary view and using it to complete a principal view are shown in Fig. 9.17.

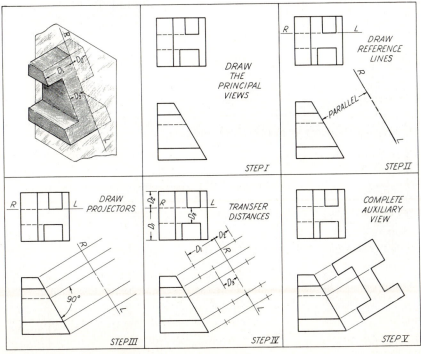

FIG. 9.14 Steps in constructing an auxiliary view.

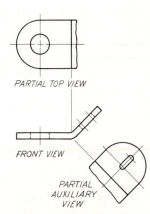

FIG. 9.15 Partial views.

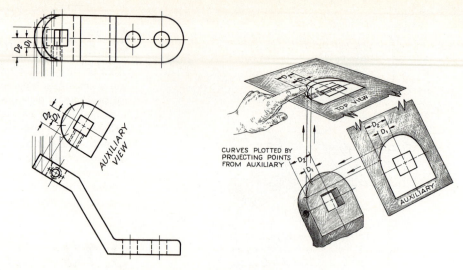

FIG. 9.16 Use of auxiliary to complete a principal view.

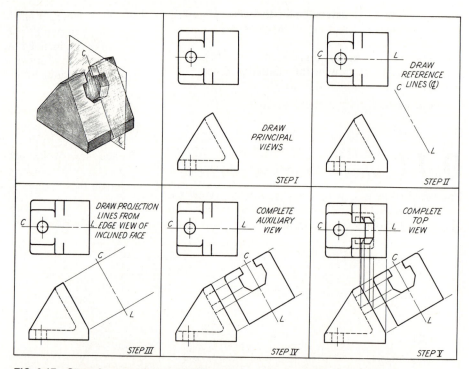

STEP I — DRAW PRINCIPAL VIEWS

STEP II — DRAW REFERENCE LINES (₵)

STEP III — DRAW PROJECTION LINES FROM EDGE VIEW OF INCLINED FACE

STEP IV — COMPLETE AUXILIARY VIEW

STEP V — COMPLETE TOP VIEW

FIG. 9.17 Steps is preparing an auxiliary view and completing a principal view.

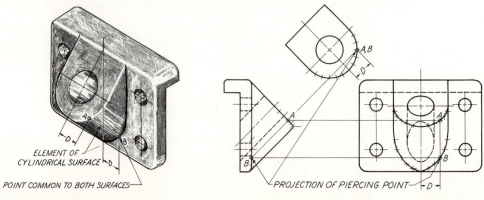

ELEMENT OF CYLINDRICAL SURFACE

POINT COMMON TO BOTH SURFACES

PROJECTION OF PIERCING POINT

FIG. 9.18 Line of intersection.

160

9.14 *Line of Intersection*

It is frequently necessary to represent a *line of intersection* between two surfaces when making a multiview drawing involving an auxiliary view. Fig. 9.18 shows a method for drawing the line of intersection on a principal view. Assume that you have a front, left side, and auxiliary view.

1. Draw elements on the surface of the cylindrical portion of the part in the three views. Element *AB* is one of those elements.

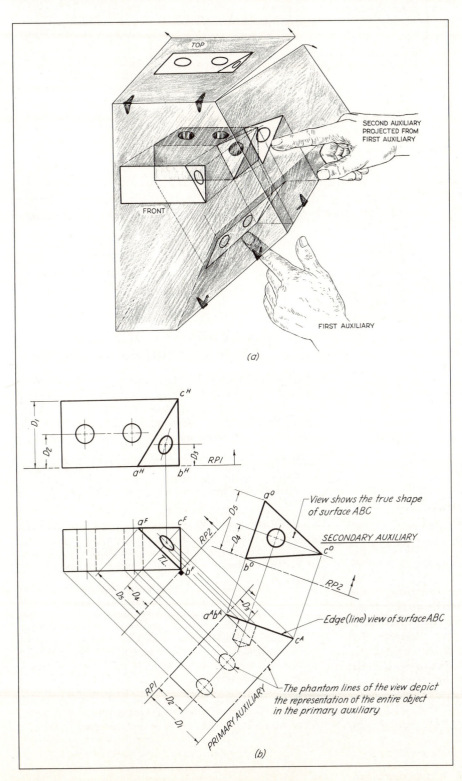

(a)

(b)

FIG. 9.19 Secondary auxiliary view of an oblique face.

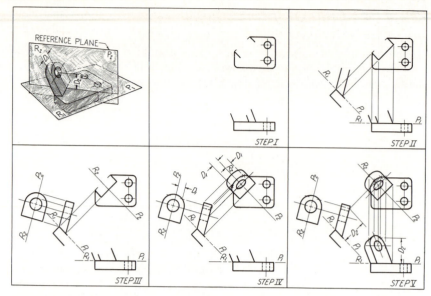

FIG. 9.20 Steps in drawing a secondary auxiliary view and using it to complete a principal view.

2. The intersection of the element and the vertical surface at *B* is evident by inspection in the left-side view.

3. Points *A* and *B* are found in the front view by setting off the distance *D* from the auxiliary view.

![B] **SECONDARY AUXILIARY VIEWS**

9.15 Secondary Auxiliary Views Explained

Frequently an object will have a face that is not perpendicular to any one of the principal planes of projection. In such cases it is necessary to draw an additional supplementary view after the primary auxiliary. This view is called an *oblique* or *secondary* auxiliary view.

The primary (inclined) auxiliary view is constructed in the manner described in Fig. 9.14. The secondary (oblique) auxiliary is then projected onto a plane perpendicular to the plane of the first auxiliary. Figure 9.19 shows a practical application of the theoretical principals shown pictorially in part *a*.

It is suggested that the student read Sec. 9.16 in which the procedure for drawing the normal (true shape) view of an oblique surface is presented step by step.

9.16 Summary of Steps in Secondary Auxiliaries

Figure 9.20 shows the progressive steps in preparing and using a secondary auxiliary view of an oblique face to complete a principal view. Reference planes have been used as datum planes from which to take the necessary measurements.

STEP I. Draw partial front and top views.

STEP II. Show the partial construction of the primary auxiliary view in which the inclined surface appears as a line.

STEP III. Show the secondary auxiliary view projected and completed from the primary auxiliary view using known dimensions. The primary auxiliary view is completed by projecting from the secondary auxiliary view.

STEP IV. Project the top view from the secondary auxiliary view through the primary auxiliary view. This completes the foreshortened top view. It should be noted that distance D_1 taken from reference R_2P_2 in the secondary auxiliary is transferred to the top view because both views show width dimensions in true length. A sufficient number of points should be obtained to allow the use of an irregular curve to draw the outline.

STEP V. Project the points found in the top view to the front view. Set off height measurements from R_1P_1 in the primary auxiliary from R_1P_1 in the front view.

Sectional Views

10.1 Introduction

Although the interior features of a simple object can usually be described by the use of hidden lines in an exterior view, it is often confusing to describe the interior of a complicated object or an assembled mechanism using only hidden lines. Whenever a representation becomes so complicated that is is difficult to read, it is customary to make one or more of the views "in section" (Fig. 10.1). A view "in section" is one obtained by imagining the object to have been cut by a plane, the front portion being removed to reveal the interior features. It should be understood that the portion is removed in the sectional view only and not in any of the other views.

When the cutting plane cuts an object lengthwise, the section obtained is commonly called a *longitudinal section;* when crosswise, it is called a *cross section.* The section is designated by name as being a *full section,* a *half section,* a *broken section,* or the like. If the plane cuts entirely across the object, the section represented is called a full section. If it cuts halfway across a symmetrical object, the section is a half section. A broken section is a partial one, used when less than a full or half section is needed (Fig. 10.3).

On a completed sectional view, fine *section lines* are drawn across the surface cut by the imaginary plane to emphasize the contour of the interior (see Sec. 10.8).

10.2 Full Section

Because a cutting plane that cuts a *full section* passes entirely through an object, the resulting view will appear as illustrated in Fig. 10.2. Although the plane usually passes along the main axis, it may be offset (Fig. 10.3) to reveal important features. See Sec. 7.12 for techniques for representing the cutting plane.

A full section showing the object's characteristic shape usually replaces an exterior front view. One of the other principal views—side or top—may be converted to a sectional view, however, if some interior feature can be shown to better advantage, or if the view is needed in addition to a sectioned front view.

The procedure in making a full section is simplified because it is an orthogonal view. The imaginary cut face is shown as it would appear to an observer looking directly at it an infinite distance away. In any sectional view, *it is considered good practice to omit all hidden lines unless such lines are necessary to clarify the representation.* Even then they should be used sparingly.

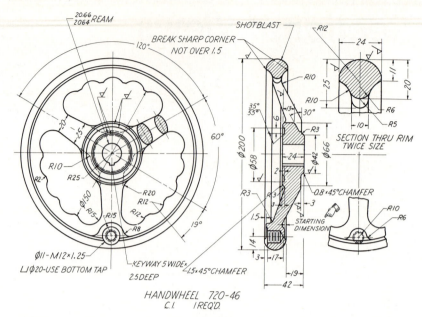

FIG. 10.1 Working drawing with sectional views. (*Courtesy Warner and Swasey Co.*)

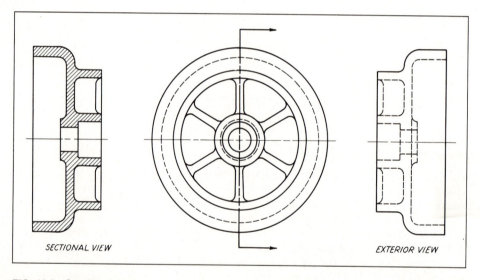

FIG. 10.2 Sectional view.

10.3 *Half Section*

The cutting plane for a half section removes one-quarter of an object. The plane cuts halfway through to the axis of the center line so that *half the finished sectional view appears in section and half appears as an external view* (Fig. 10.4). This technique is used when a view is needed showing both the exterior and interior construction of a symmetrical object. Good practice dictates that hidden lines be omitted from both halves of the view unless they are absolutely necessary to explain the object.

The preferred method of representing the edge of the cutting plane in the sectional view is shown in Fig.

10.5(*b*) where the plane, being imaginary, is represented by the center line of the object. An alternative method (Fig. 10.5[*a*]) is to show the edge as a solid line.

10.4 *Broken Section*

A *broken section* is used mainly to expose the interior of objects where less than a half section is required for a satisfactory description (Fig. 10.6). The object is theoretically cut, the front portion then removed by breaking material away. The "breaking away" gives an irregular boundary to the section. No cutting plane

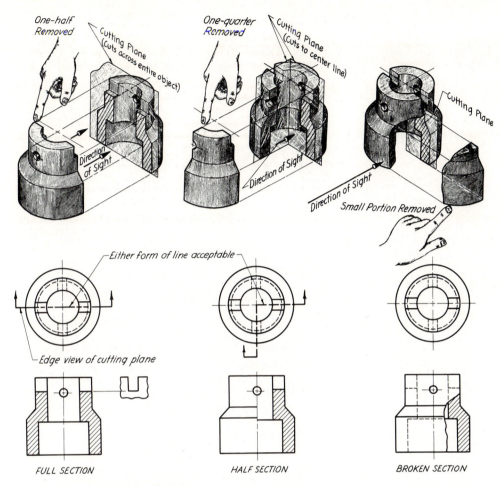

FIG. 10.3 **Types of sectional views.**

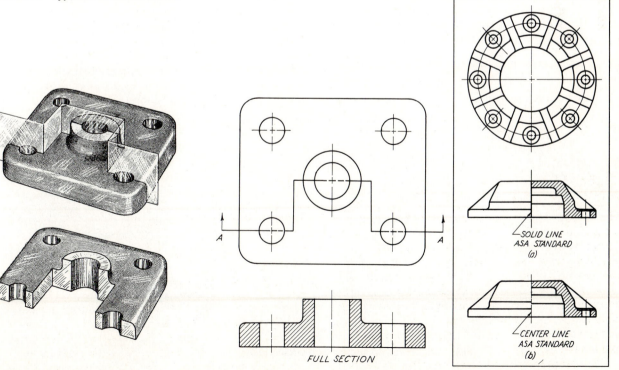

FIG. 10.4 **Offset cutting plane.**

FIG. 10.5 **Half section.**

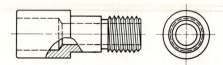

FIG. 10.6   Broken section.

edge is shown because the section is shown where it is taken.

10.5 Revolved Section

A revolved section is useful for showing the true shape of the *cross section* of an object like a bar, arm, spoke, or rib (Figs. 10.1 and 10.7). This removes the need to draw a separate complete view.

To obtain a revolved section, pass an imaginary cutting plane through the arm, spoke, or rib perpendicular to the longitudinal axis. Revolve the shape revealed by the cutting plane 90° into the plane of the paper (Fig.

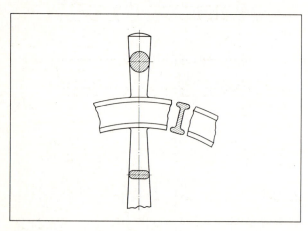

FIG. 10.7 Revolved section.*

10.8). When revolved, the section should appear true shape and in its true revolved position. If any lines in the exterior view interfere with the revolved section they may be omitted (Fig. 10.9). For better understanding, it may be necessary to break the object to provide an open space for the revolved section.

10.6 Removed (Detail) Section

A *removed section* is similar to a revolved section except that it does not appear where it was revolved but instead is drawn "out of place." A removed section appears adjacent to the view in which the section was taken (Fig. 10.10). There are two reasons why removed sections are frequently desirable. First, their use may prevent a principal view with nonuniform cross section from being cluttered with numerous revolved sections (Fig. 10.11). Second, a section when removed may be drawn to an enlarged scale to emphasize detail and allow adequate dimensioning.

Whenever a removed section is used there must be some means of identifying it. Usually this is accomplished by showing the cutting plane on the principal view, and by labeling both the plane and the resulting view as shown in Fig. 10.11.

10.7 Phantom Section

A *phantom section* is a regular exterior view on which the interior construction is emphasized by crosshatching an imaginary cut surface with dashed section lines (Fig. 10.12). This type of section is only used when a regular or broken section would remove some important detail, or in some instances, to show an accompanying part in relative position (Fig. 10.13).

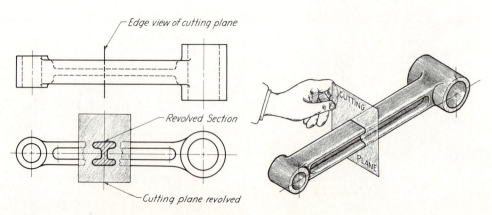

FIG. 10.8   Revolved section and cutting plane.

* ANSI Y14.2.

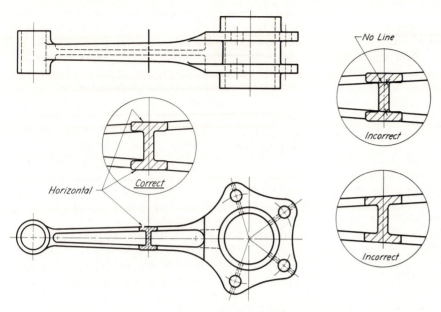

FIG. 10.9 Correct and incorrect treatment of a revolved section.

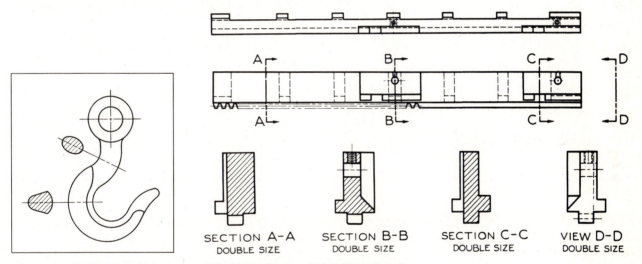

SECTION A-A
DOUBLE SIZE

SECTION B-B
DOUBLE SIZE

SECTION C-C
DOUBLE SIZE

VIEW D-D
DOUBLE SIZE

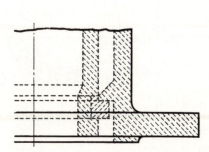

FIG. 10.10 Removed sections.*

FIG. 10.11 Removed (detail) sections.*

FIG. 10.12 Phantom section.

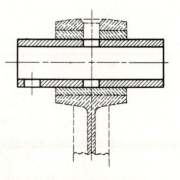

FIG. 10.13 Phantom section-ing—adjacent parts.

10.8 *Section Lining*

Section lines are *light* parallel lines drawn across the imaginary cut surface for the purpose of emphasizing its contour. The lines continue across sectioned areas though they may be broken by unsectioned areas. Usually the lines are drawn at 45° except in cases in which several adjacent parts are shown assembled (Fig. 10.17).

On ordinary work the lines are spaced about 2 mm (.09 in) apart. *There is no set rule governing their spacing, however.* They should be spaced to suit the drawing and the areas to be crosshatched. For example, on small views having small areas, the section lines may be as close as 0.8 mm (.03 in), whereas on large views having large areas they may be as far apart as practicable. In the case of thin material such as gaskets, shims,

or sheet metal, the cross section should be shown solid black (Fig. 10.14).

A typical mistake is to draw the lines too close together. This, plus unavoidable slight variations, causes cross-hatching to appear streaked. Several mechanical aids are available to space and incline section lines. Assure that the initial pitch as set by the first few lines is maintained across the area. To accomplish this, check back from time to time to make sure that there has been no slight increase or decrease in the spacing. An example of correct spacing is shown in Fig. 10.15(*a*), and, for comparison, examples of faulty practice may be seen in Fig. 10.15(*b–d*). Nothing will do more to ruin the appearance of a drawing than carelessly executed section lines.

As shown in Fig. 10.16, the section lines of two adjacent pieces should slope at 45° in the opposite direction. If a third piece adjoins the first two as in

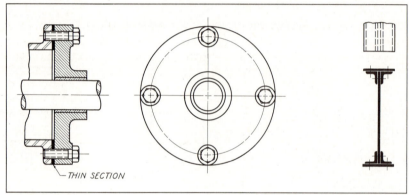

*THIN SECTION

*ANSI Y14.2-1957.

FIG. 10.14   Thin sections.

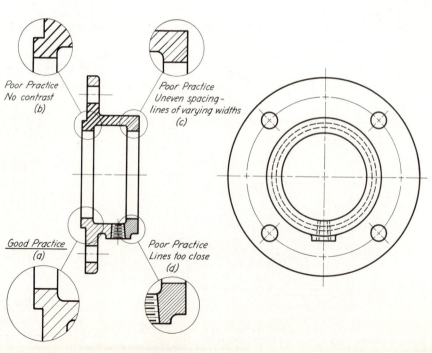

Poor Practice
No contrast
(b)

Poor Practice
Uneven spacing-
lines of varying widths
(c)

Good Practice
(a)

Poor Practice
Lines too close
(d)

FIG. 10.15   Faults in section lining.

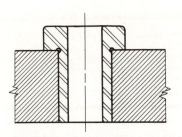

FIG. 10.16   Two adjacent pieces.

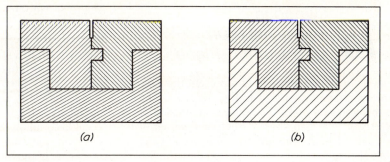

FIG. 10.17   Three adjacent pieces.

Fig. 10.17(*a*), it is usually sectioned lined at 30°. An alternative treatment that might be used would be to vary the spacing without changing the angle. On a sectional view showing an assembly of related parts, *all portions of the cut surface of any part must be section lined the same because a change in direction or spacing would lead the reader to consider the portions to belong to different parts. Furthermore,*

*to allow quick identification, each piece (and all identical pieces) in **every view** of the assembly drawing should be sectioned in the same direction and at the same spacing.*

Shafts, bolts, screws, rivets—parts whose axes lie in the plane of the section and that have no interior detail—are not treated the same as ordinary parts. They are drawn full and unsectioned, and thus tended to make the adjacent sectioned parts stand out to better advantage (Fig. 10.18).

Whenever section lines drawn at 45° with the horizontal are parallel to the outline of the section (Fig. 10.19), it is advisable to draw them at some other angle (say, 30° or 60°). Those drawn as in parts *a* and *c* produce an unusual appearance that is contrary to what is expected. Note the more natural effect obtained in parts *b* and *d* by setting the section lines at 30° and 60°.

10.9 *Outline Sectioning*

Very large surfaces may be sectioned lined around the bounding outline, as illustrated in Fig. 10.20.

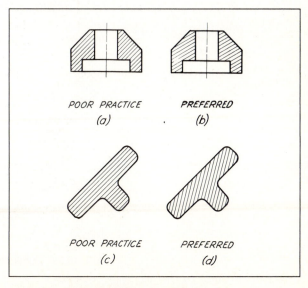

POOR PRACTICE
(a)

PREFERRED
(b)

POOR PRACTICE
(c)

PREFERRED
(d)

FIG. 10.19   Section lining at 30°, 60°, or 75°.

FIG. 10.18   Treatment of shafts, fasteners, ball bearings, and other parts. (*Courtesy New Departure Division, General Motors Corporation*)

10.10 Symbolic Representation for a Cutting Plane

The symbolic lines that are used to represent the edge of the *cutting plane* are shown in Fig. 10.21(*a*). The line is as heavy as an object line, and is composed of either alternate long and short dashes or a series of dashes of equal length. The latter form is used in the automobile industry and has been approved by the Society of Automobile Engineers (SAE) and ANSI (the

American National Standards Institute). On drawings of ordinary size, when alternate long and short dashes are used for the edge of the cutting plane, the sizes are those shown in Fig. 10.21(*b*).

Arrowheads are used to show the direction in which the imaginary plane is viewed. Referrence letters are added to identify the section (Fig. 10.22).

Whenever the location of the cutting plane is obvious, it is common practice to omit the edge view representation, particularly in the case of symmetrical objects. If it *is* shown, however, and coincides with the center line, it takes precedence over the center line.

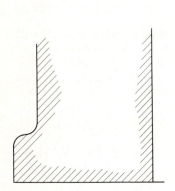

FIG. 10.20   Outline sectioning.

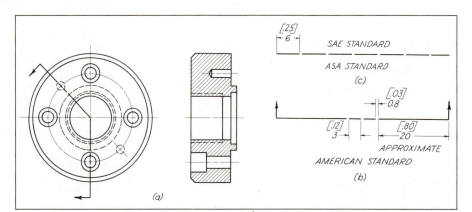

FIG. 10.21   Cutting plane lines.

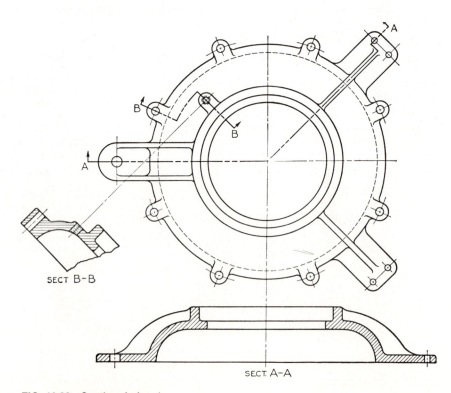

SECT B-B

SECT. A-A

FIG. 10.22   Sectional view.*

* ANSI Y14.2.

10.11 Summary of Sectioning Practices

1. A cutting plane may be offset to reveal an important detail that would not be shown if the cutting plane were continuous (Fig. 10.4).

2. All visible (solid) lines beyond the cutting plane in full and half sections are usually shown.

3. Hidden lines beyond the cutting plane are usually not shown unless they are absolutely necessary to clarify the construction of the piece. In a half section, hidden lines are omitted in the unsectioned half. Either the center line or a solid line is used to separate the two halves of the view (Figs. 10.4 and 10.5).

4. On a view showing assembled parts, section lines on adjacent pieces are drawn in opposite directions—usually at an angle of 45°.

5. On an assembly drawing, the portions of the cut surface of a single piece in the same view or different views should always be section-lined in the same direction with the same spacing (Fig. 10.18).

6. The symbolic line indicating the location of the cutting plane may be omitted if the location of the plane is obvious (Fig. 10.1).

7. On a sectional assembly, an exterior view is preferred for shafts, rods, bolts, nuts, and any parts that have no interior detail (Fig. 10.18).

10.12 Conventional Sectioning Techniques

Sometimes a less confusing sectioned representation is obtained if certain of the strict rules of projection as explained in Chapter 5 are disregarded. For example, an unbalanced and misleading view results when the sectioned view of the pulley shown in Fig. 10.23 is drawn in true projection as in part *a*. It is better practice to preserve symmetry by showing the spokes as if

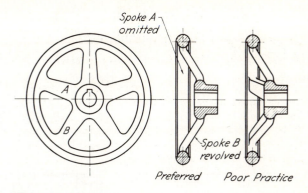

FIG. 10.24   Spokes in section.*

they were aligned into one plane as shown in part *c*. Such treatment of unsymmetrical features is not misleading because their actual arrangement is revealed in the circular view. The spokes are not sectioned in the preferred view. If they were, the first impression would be that the wheel had a solid web, as shown in part *b*. See also Fig. 10.24.

When there are an odd number of holes in a flange as is the case with the part in Fig. 10.25, two holes should be aligned in the section view to reveal their true location with reference to the rim and the axis of the piece. To draw a section with aligned features follow these steps:

1. Pass the cutting plane so that it is bent to include the radial hole. This is shown in the pictorial drawing in Fig. 10.25.

2. Revolve the bent portion of the plane until it lies in the same plane as the unbent portion.

3. The hole is represented its true distance from the center and the rim.

Figure 10.26 shows another example of conventional representation. The sectioned view is drawn as though the rear projecting lug had been swung forward until the portion of the cutting plane through it forms a continuous plane with the other lug (Sec. 8.34). It

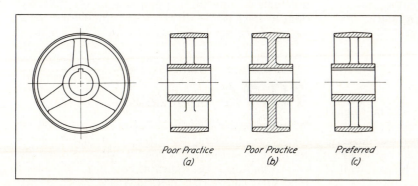

FIG. 10.23   Conventional treatment of spokes in section.

* ANSI Y14.2.

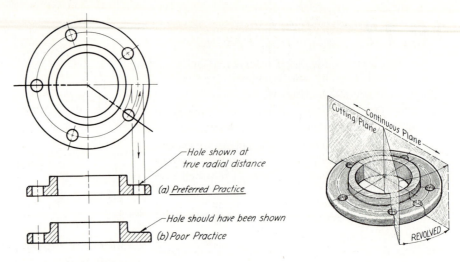

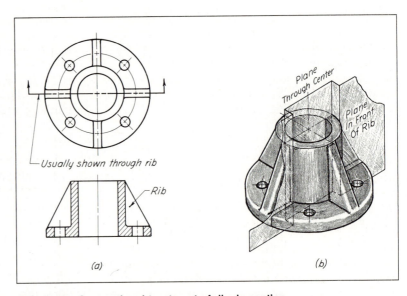

FIG. 10.25 Drilled flanges.

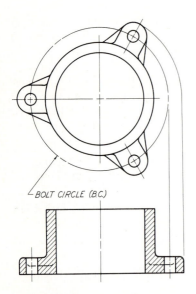

FIG. 10.26 Revolution of a portion of an object.

FIG. 10.27 Conventional treatment of ribs in section.

should be noted that the hidden lines in the section view are necessary for a complete description of the construction of the lugs.

10.13 *Ribs in Section*

When a part has a rib cut by a plane of section (Fig. 10.27), a "true" sectional view taken through the rib would be false and misleading because the cross-hatching of the rib would cause the object to appear "solid." The correct sectional view is obtained with the cutting plane offset just in front of the rib (*b*).

An alternative method of showing ribs in section is illustrated in Fig. 10.28. This omitting of alternate sec-

tion lines is sometimes appropriate in assembly sections to emphasize a rib that might otherwise be overlooked. Note the use of hidden lines in Fig. 10.28.

10.14 *Half Views*

When the space available on a drawing is insufficient to allow a satisfactory scale to be used for a symmetrical piece in section, it is good practice to make one view a *half view,* as shown in Fig. 10.29. Because a front view shows characteristic shape, the half view should be the top or side view. The half view should be the rear half.

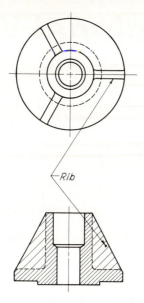

FIG. 10.28 Alternative treatment of ribs in section.

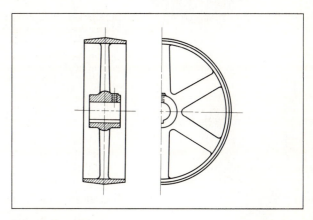

FIG. 10.29 Half view.

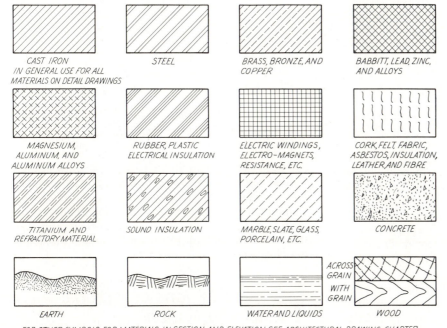

FOR OTHER SYMBOLS FOR MATERIALS IN SECTION AND ELEVATION SEE ARCHITECTURAL DRAWING CHAPTER

FIG. 10.30 Material symbols (ANSI Standard).

10.15 *Material Symbols*

The *section line symbols* recommended by ANSI for indicating various materials are shown in Fig. 10.30. Symbolic section lining is not usually used on a detail drawing of a single part. It is unnecessary to indicate a material symbolically when its exact specification is given as a note. For this reason, and to save time in manual drawing, the easily drawn symbol for cast iron is commonly used to represent all materials.

Use symbolic section lining on an assembly section showing various parts in position. This change in section lining causes the parts to "stand out" to better advantage. In addition, a knowledge of a part's material may help the reader to identify it more quickly and better understand its function.

CHAPTER 11

Pictorial Views

11.1 Introduction

An orthographic drawing of two or more views describes an object accurately in form and size. Because each of the views shows only two dimensions, however, such a drawing can convey information only to those who are trained in reading engineering multiview drawings. For this reason, multiview drawings are used mainly by engineers, designers, and technologists.

Engineers and technologists often find that they must use pictorial drawings to convey technical information to persons who do not possess the training necessary to construct an object mentally from multiviews. To make such drawings, several specific schemes of pictorial drawing have been devised that combine the pictorial effect of perspective with the advantage of having the principal dimensions to scale. Pictorial drawings, despite certain advantages, have disadvantages that limit their use, however. A few of these are as follows:

1. Some pictorial drawings frequently have a distorted, unreal appearance that is disagreeable.

2. The time required for execution is, in many cases, greater than for multiview drawings.

3. Pictorial drawings are difficult to dimension.

4. Some lines on a pictorial drawing cannot be directly measured.

Even with these limitations, pictorial drawings are used extensively for technical publications, Patent Office records, piping diagrams, and furniture design. Occasionally they are used, in one form or another, to supplement and clarify machine and structural details that would be difficult to visualize through multiview drawing (Fig. 11.1)

11.2 Divisions of Pictorial Projection

Pictorial projection is classified in the following three general divisions (Fig. 11.2):

1. Axonometric projection

2. Oblique projection

3. Perspective projection.

Perspective methods produce the most realistic drawings, but the necessary construction is more difficult and tedious than are oblique or axonometric. For this reason, engineers customarily use some form of axonometric or oblique projection. Modified axonometric or oblique methods are often used to produce the desired effects.

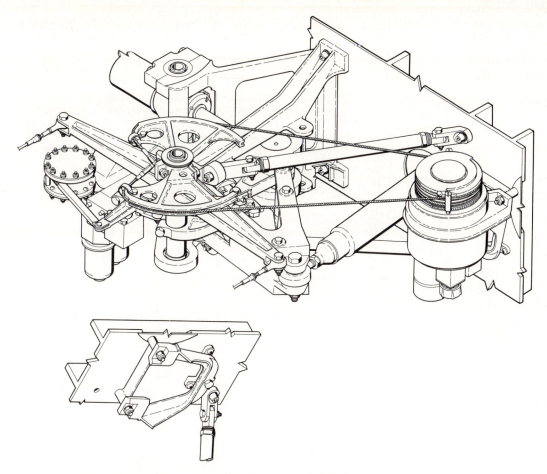

FIG. 11.1   Pictorial illustration. (*Courtesy Lockheed Aircraft Corp.*)

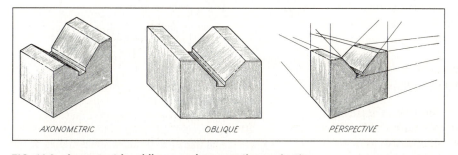

AXONOMETRIC   OBLIQUE   PERSPECTIVE

FIG. 11.2   Axonometric, oblique, and perspective projection.

A   AXONOMETRIC PROJECTION

11.3   *Divisions of Axonometric Projection*

Axonometric projection is a form of orthographic projection. The distinguishing difference is that only one plane (the axonometric plane) is used to display the drawing. In multiview drawing, horizontal, frontal, and profile planes are used. The object is turned from its customary position so that three faces are displayed (Fig. 11.3). Because an object can be placed in an unlimited number of positions relative to the axonometric plane of projection, *an infinite number of axonometric views may be drawn*. These views will vary in general proportions, lengths, and sizes of angles. For practical reasons, a few of these positions have been classified into the following recognized divisions or axonometric projection:

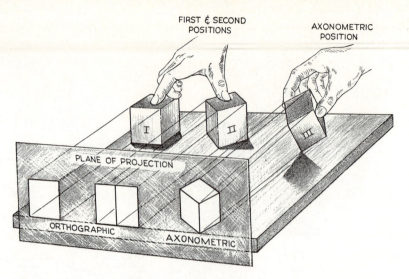

FIG. 11.3 Theory of axonometric projection.

1. Isometric
2. Dimetric
3. Trimetric.

Isometric projection is the simplest of these because the principal axes make equal angles with the plane of projection and are therefore foreshortened equally. In isomeric projection, all lines parallel to these axes are foreshortened equally and are called *isometric lines.* Isometric projection is widely used in industry because of its ease of construction, the ability to measure and compare dimensions parallel to the isometric axes directly, and the ability to combine isometrics from different sources into composite projections. Dimetric and trimetric projection, which are often topics for separate technical illustration courses, are not covered in this chapter.

11.4 *Isometric Projection*

If the cube in Fig. 11.3 is revolved through an angle of 45° about the vertical axis, as shown in position II, and then tilted forward until the body diagonal is perpendicular to the vertical plane, its edges will be foreshortened equally, and the cube will be in the correct position to produce an isometric projection.

The three front edges, called *isometric axes,* make angles of approximately 35° 16′ with the vertical plane of projection. In this form of pictorial, the visual angle between pairs of axes at the front corner of the cube is 120°. The projected lengths of the edges along or parallel to these axes are approximately 81% of their true lengths. It should be observed that the 90° angles of the cube appear in the isometric projection as either 120° or 60°.

As an alternative, instead of turning and tilting the object in relation to a principal plane of projection, an auxiliary plane can be used that will be perpendicular

to the body diagonal. The *O* view or secondary auxiliary view will be an axonometric projection and will be identical to the view achieved by rotating the object in relation to a principal plane. Because the auxiliary plane will be inclined to the principal planes, the isometric projection will be a secondary auxiliary view, as shown in Fig. 11.4.

11.5 *Isometric Drawing*

Objects are seldom drawn in true isometric projection, because the use of an isometric scale (81%) is inconvenient and impractical. Instead, a conventional method is used in which all foreshortening is ignored, and actual true lengths are laid off along isometric axes and isometric lines. To avoid confusion and to set this method apart from true isometric projection, it is called *isometric drawing.*

The isometric drawing is slightly larger (approximately 22.5%) than the isometric projection. Because the proportions are the same, however, increased size does not affect the pictorial value of the representation (Fig. 11.4[b]). The use of a standard scale makes possible a satisfactory drawing with a minimum expenditure of time and effort.

Isometric lines that are parallel to the isometric axes can be directly measured. Lines that are not parallel to the axes cannot be directly measured.

11.6 *Making an Isometric Drawing of a Rectangular Object*

The procedure followed in making an isometric drawing of a rectangular block is illustrated in Fig. 11.5. Follow these steps to complete the construction.

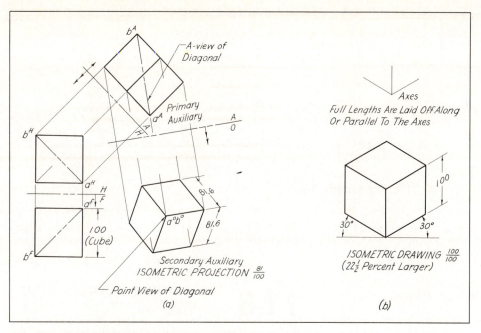

FIG. 11.4. Comparison of isometric projection and isometric drawing.

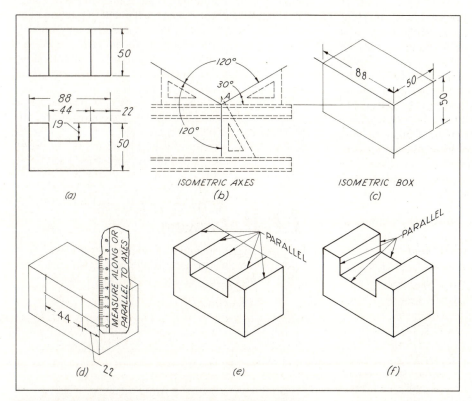

FIG. 11.5 Procedure for constructing isometric drawing.

1. Draw the isometric axes through a convenient point *A*. One axis extends vertically downward, and the other two upward to the right and left at an angle of 30° to the horizontal (*b*).

2. Set off actual edge lengths along each axis (*c* and *d*).

3. The remainder of the view is completed by drawing lines parallel to the axes (*e* and *f*). *Hidden lines,*

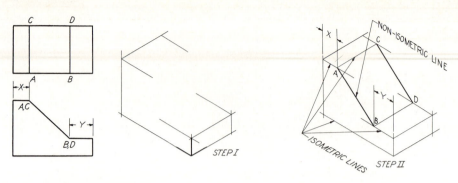

FIG. 11.6 Nonisometric lines.

unless absolutely necessary for clarity should always be omitted in a pictorial drawing.

11.7 Nonisometric Lines

Those lines that are inclined and not parallel to the isometric axes are called *nonisometric lines*. A line of this type cannot be measured directly. Its position and projected length must be established by locating its end points. In Fig. 11.6, *AB* and *CD*, which represent the edges of the block, are nonisometric lines. The location of *AB* is established in the pictorial view by locating points *A* and *B*. Point *A* is on the top edge, distance *X* from the left-side surface. Point *B* is on the upper edge of the base, distance *Y* from the right-hand surface. All other lines coincide with or are parallel to the axes and may be measured directly with a scale.

The pictorial drawing of an irregular solid containing several nonisometric lines may be conveniently constructed by the *box method*. The object is enclosed in a rectangular box so that both isometric and nonisometric lines are located by points of contact with the box's surfaces and edges (Fig. 11.7).

A study of Figs. 11.6 and 11.7 reveals the important fact that *lines that are parallel on an object are parallel in the pictorial view*. Conversely, *lines that are not parallel on the object are not parallel in the pictorial view*. It is often possible to eliminate much tedious construction by the practical application of the principle of parallel lines.

11.8 Coordinate Construction Method

When an object contains several inclined surfaces, such as that shown in Fig. 11.8, the use of the coordinate construction method is advisable. In this method, the end points of the edges are located in relation to an assumed isometric base line located on an *isometric reference plane*. For example, the line *RL* is used as a base line from which measurements are made along isometric lines. The distances required to locate point *A* are taken directly from the orthographic views.

Irregular curved edges are easily drawn in isometric by the *offset method,* which is a modification of the coordinate construction method (Fig. 11.9). The position of the curve is established by sampling the curve and locating these points along isometric lines.

11.9 Angles in Isometric Drawing

Because angles specified in degrees do not appear in true size on an isometric drawing, angular measurements must be converted in some way to linear mea-

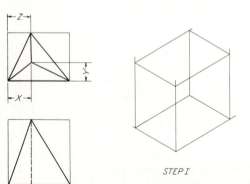
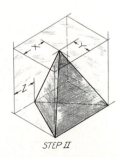

FIG. 11.7 Box construction.

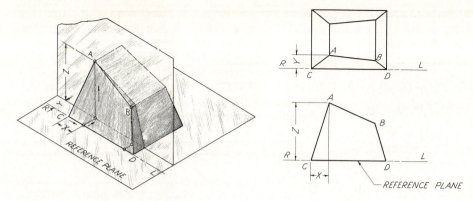

FIG. 11.8   Coordinate construction.

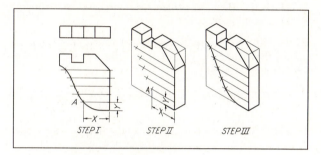

FIG. 11.9   Offset construction.

surements that can be laid off along isometric lines. Usually, one or two measurements taken from an orthographic view may be laid off along isometric lines on the pictorial drawing to locate an inclined edge that has been specified by an angular dimension.

In Fig. 11.10(*a*), the position of the inclined line *AB* was established on the isometric drawing by using distance *X* taken from the front view of the orthographic drawing. When an orthographic drawing is available, but has been drawn to a scale other than the one used for the isometric drawing, a *partial* orthographic view

with the needed dimensions is drawn. A practical application of this, finding an angle of 60°, is shown (*b*).

1. Using point *B*, construct a true 60° angle.

2. Project the true height from the top corner to intersect the 60° angle at a^F.

3. Swing radius R from a^F into the isometric, locating point *A*. The desired 60° angle in isometric is drawn from *A* to *B*.

By making the construction of the partial view at a place where the angle is to appear in the isometric drawing, the position of the required line can be obtained graphically.

1. Lay off a length equal to 10 units at any scale along an isometric line that is to form the side adjacent to the angle.

2. Set off a distance at the same scale equal to 10 times the tangent of the angle along a second isometric line that represents the side opposite the desired angle.

3. Draw a line through the end points of these lines, making the required line at the specified angle. Note

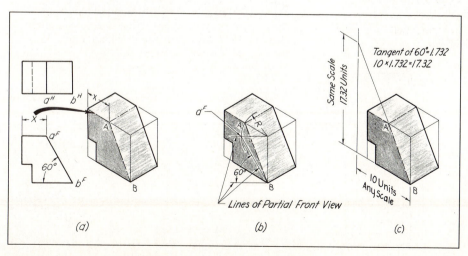

FIG. 11.10   Angles in isometric.

that in the example only a portion of the angled line is used. It may also be necessary at times to extend the angled line until it is the desired length.

11.10 Circle and Circle Arcs in Isometric Drawing

In isometric drawing, a circle appears as an ellipse. The tedious construction required for plotting an ellipse (Figs. 11.11 and 11.12) can be avoided by using an approximate method. This is accurate enough for most work, although the true ellipse, which is slightly

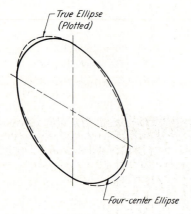

FIG. 11.11 Pictorial ellipses.

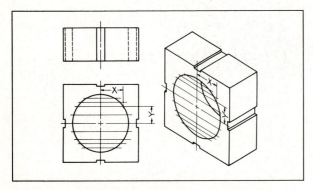

FIG. 11.12 To plot an isometric circle.

narrower and longer, is more pleasing in shape (Fig. 11.11). For an approximate construction, the four-center method is generally used.

To draw a circle in isometric, a square is drawn about the circle in the orthographic projection. When transferred to the isometric plane, the square becomes a rhombus (isometric square), and the circle becomes an ellipse tangent to the rhombus at the midpoints of its sides (Fig. 11.13). To find the four centers of circular arcs used to approximate an ellipse using an enclosing rhombus, the steps are as follows:

STEP I. Construct a rhombus inclined at 30°, the sides of which are equal in measure to the diameter of the circle.

STEP II. Locate the four centers by constructing a perpendicular bisector of each side.

STEP III. Using these centers, swing arcs that connect the tangent points.

If the ellipse is to be drawn by the four-center method using the isometric center lines, the steps are as follows (Fig. 11.14):

STEP I. Draw the isometric center lines of the required circle.

STEP II. Using a radius equal to the radius of the circle, strike arcs across the isometric center lines.

STEPS III and IV. Through each of these points of intersection erect a perpendicular to the other isometric center line.

STEPS V and VI. Using the intersection points of the perpendiculars as centers and lengths along the perpendiculars as radii, draw the four arcs that form the ellipse (Fig. 11.15).

A circle arc will appear in isometric drawing as a segment of an ellipse. Therefore, it may be drawn using as much of the four-center method as is required to locate the needed centers (Fig. 11.16).

To draw isometric concentric circles by the four-center method, a set of centers must be located for each circle as shown in Fig. 11.17.

When several circles of the same diameter occur in parallel planes, the construction may be simplified. Figure 11.18 shows two views of an object and its

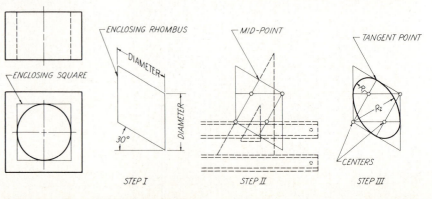

FIG. 11.13 Four-center approximation.

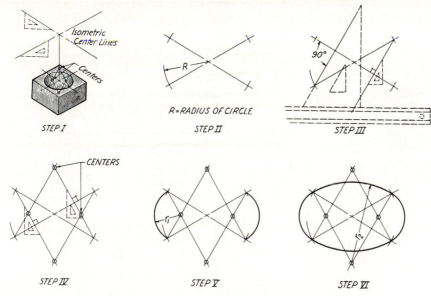

FIG. 11.14   Steps in drawing a four-center isometric circle (ellipse).

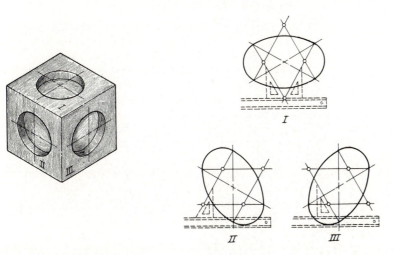

FIG. 11.15   Isometric circles.

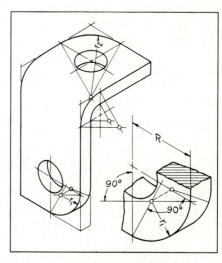

FIG. 11.16   Isometric circle arcs.

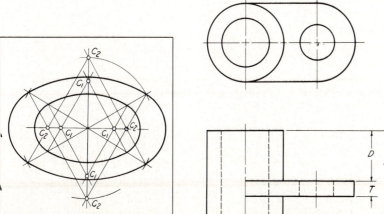

FIG. 11.17   Isometric concentric circles.

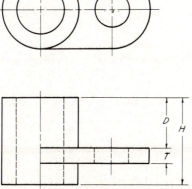

FIG. 11.18   isometric parallel circles.

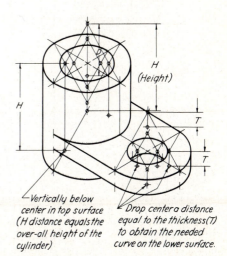

Vertically below center in top surface (H distance equals the over-all height of the cylinder)

Drop center a distance equal to the thickness(T) to obtain the needed curve on the lower surface.

corresponding isometric drawing. In Fig. 11.18, the centers for the ellipse representing the upper base of the large cylinder are found in the usual way, whereas the centers for the lower base are located by moving the centers of the upper base downward a distance equal to the height of the cylinder. By observing that portion of the object projecting to the right, it can be noted that corresponding centers lie along an isometric line parallel to the axis of the cylinder.

Circles and circle arcs in nonisometric planes can be plotted by using the offset or coordinate method. Sufficient points for establishing a curve must be located by transferring measurements from the orthographic views to isometric lines in the pictorial view. There is a rapid and easy way for drawing the cylindrical portion of the object shown in Fig. 11.19.

1. The semicircular arc is plotted on the rear surface. This becomes the reference shape and surface.

2. Each point is projected forward toward the inclined face.

3. The depth distances D_1, D_2, D_3, and so on from the orthographic side view are transferred into the isometric and onto the corresponding lines.

4. The shape of the hole as it intersects the inclined surface is completed by transferring depth measurements from the hole on the back surface forward. A smooth curve through these points defines the hole on the inclined surface.

The isometric drawing of a sphere is the envelope of all the great circles that could be drawn on its surface. In isometric drawing, the great circles appear as ellipses, and a circle is their envelope. In practice, it is necessary to draw only one ellipse, using the true radius of the sphere and the four-center method of construction. The diameter of the sphere is the major axis of the ellipse (Fig. 11.20).

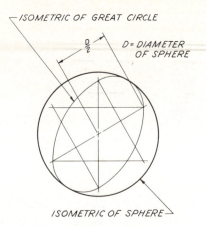

FIG. 11.20 Isometric drawing of sphere.

11.11 Positions of Isometric Axes

It is sometimes desirable to place the principal isometric axes so that an object will be in position to reveal certain faces to a better advantage (Fig. 11.21).

The difference in direction should cause no confusion because the angle between the axes and the procedure followed in constructing the view are the same for any position. The choice of isometric direction may depend on the design of the object. The normal position shows an object from the direction ordinarily viewed.

Reversed axes (*b*) are used in architectural work to show a feature for a natural position below. Sometimes long objects are drawn with the long axis horizontal, as shown in Fig. 11.22.

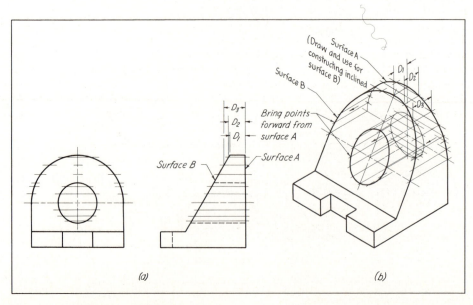

FIG. 11.19 Circles in nonisometric planes.

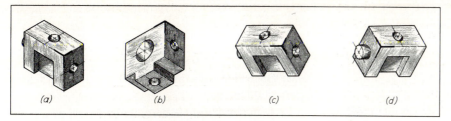

FIG. 11.21 Convenient positions of axes.

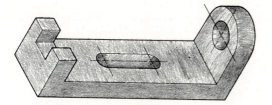

FIG. 11.22 Main axis horizontal—long objects.

11.12 *Isometric Section Views*

Generally, an isometric sectional view is used for showing the inner construction of an object when there is a complicated interior to be explained or when it is desirable to emphasize features that would not appear in a usual outside view. The use of an isometric section is preferable to using hidden lines to show interior detail. Sectioning in isometric drawing is based on the same principles as sectioning in multiview drawing. Isometric planes are used for cutting the object, and the general procedure followed in constructing the isometric view is the same as for an exterior view.

Figure 11.23 shows an isometric half section. It is easier, in this case, to outline the outside view of the object in full and then remove a front quarter with isometric cutting planes.

Figure 11.24 illustrates a full section in isometric. The accepted procedure for constructing this form of sectional view is to first draw the cut face and then add the portion that lies behind.

Section lines should be sloped at an angle that produces the best effect, but they should never be drawn parallel to object lines. In Fig. 11.25(a) illustrates the

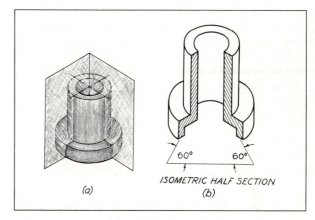

FIG. 11.23 Isometric half section.

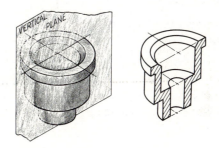

FIG. 11.24 Isometric full section.

slope that is correct for most isometric drawings, whereas parts *b* to *d* show the poor effect produced when this consideration in section lining is ignored. Ordinarily, isometric section lines are drawn at 60°.

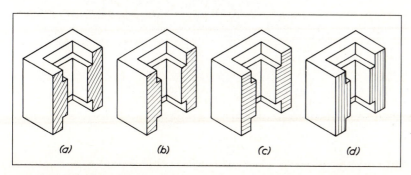

FIG. 11.25 Section lining.

B OBLIQUE PROJECTION

11.13 Oblique Projection

An oblique projection is produced by parallel projectors that make some angle other than 90° with the plane of projection. In doing so, an oblique projection is *not* an orthographic view. Rather, it is a contrived view without orthogonal basis. Generally, one face is placed parallel to the plane of projection, and projection lines are taken at 45°. This gives a view that is pictorial in appearance by showing the front, and one or more additional faces of an object. In Fig. 11.26, the orthographic and oblique projections of a cube are shown. When the angle is 45° as in the illustration, the pictorial is sometimes called a *cavalier projection*.

11.14 Oblique Drawing

When measurements are laid off directly along oblique pictorial axes, rather than projected onto a plane, the pictorial is referred to as an *oblique drawing*. This form of drawing is based on three mutually perpendicular axes along which, or parallel to which, necessary measurements are made for constructing the pictorial. Oblique drawing differs from isometric drawing in that two of the axes are always visually perpendicular to each other, whereas the third (receding axis) is at some convenient angle with the horizontal, such as 30°, 45°, or 60°. Oblique drawing is often more flexible

and has the following advantages over isometric drawing:

1. Circular or irregular outlines on the front face show in their true shape.

2. Distortion can be reduced by foreshortening measurements along the receding axis.

3. A greater choice is permitted in selecting the position of the axes.

A view of the various views that can be obtained by varying the inclination of the receding axis are illustrated in Fig. 11.27. Usually, the selection of the position is governed by the characteristic features of the object.

Oblique drawings can be made with ease in two-dimensional CADD. The same construction outlined in Fig. 11.28 can be followed in CADD, quickly producing an oblique drawing. Special CADD functions such as grouping and copying allow principal views to be used as the basis for an oblique drawing. Depth distances from the orthographic side view can be copied, rotated, and moved to the oblique drawing.

11.15 To Make an Oblique Drawing

The procedure to follow in constructing an oblique drawing is illustrated in Fig. 11.28. To complete an oblique drawing

1. Draw the three axes that form the perpendicular edges through a point representing the front corner (*b*). Point *O* has been used for this purpose.

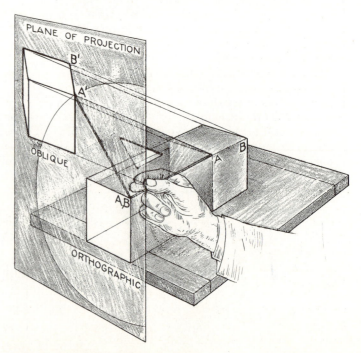

FIG. 11.26 Theory of oblique projection.

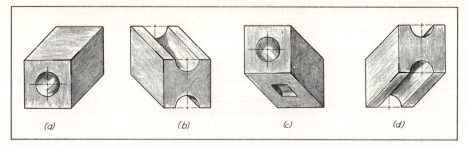

FIG. 11.27 Various positions of the receding axis.

2. Set off width and height to construct the front face in true size and shape. This is identical to the orthographic front view (*c*).

3. Draw depth lines parallel to the receding axis from corners and centers of the front face (*d*). Use depth distances from the orthographic top view (*a*) to determine the position of the back face.

4. The center of the hole and radius arc is found in the same manner. Note that a small portion of the 12.5 radius arc is needed to complete the drawing (*e*).

The circle and semicircle are shown parallel to the picture plane to avoid distortion and to make their construction as easy as possible. The actual mechanics

of oblique construction—laying out distances, finding corners, using reference planes—is the same as for an isometric drawing.

11.16 *Use of Basic Plane*

If the front face of an object is in one plane, it will appear in the oblique drawing exactly the same as in the orthographic drawing. Note this face in Fig. 11.28. The front may be composed of two or more parallel planes whose relationship must be carefully established, however. The convenient way to assure this is to use one of the planes as a basic (starting or reference) plane. Starting the construction at the basic

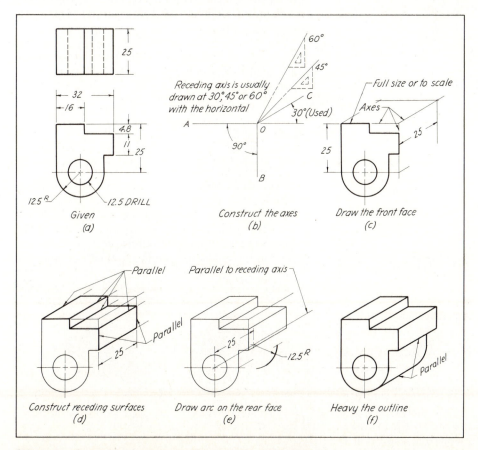

FIG. 11.28 Procedure for constructing an oblique drawing.

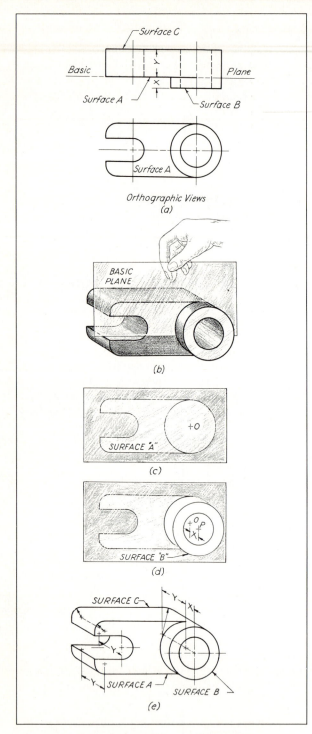

FIG. 11.29 Basic plane theory of construction.

plane and then working to the rear or front as necessary is illustrated in Fig. 11.29. Because surface *A* presents the object's contour shape, it should be selected as the basic plane and drawn first (*c*). The center of the circles on surface *B* (forward along the axis) is located distance *X* forward of point *O*. The measurement must be taken forward along the axis from *O* because surface *B* is in front of surface *A*. The centers

of the arcs on surface *C* are located in a similar manner, except that the direction of making the measurements is from the basic plane toward the back, distance *Y*.

When an object has one or more inclined surfaces with a curved outline, construct a right section, as shown in Fig. 11.33. Offset measurements can then be made along receding lines.

11.17 Rules for Placing Object in Oblique

Generally, the most irregular face, or the one with the most circular outlines, should be drawn true shape as the front face. By following this practice, all or most of the circles and circle arcs can be drawn with a compass when using manual methods, or with the CIRCLE and ARC commands when using CADD. The tedious construction that would be required to complete their elliptical representations on receding planes is eliminated.

In selecting the position of an object, two rules should be followed. First, draw the face having the most irregular contour or the most circular outlines in true shape on the front face. Note in Fig. 11.30 the advantage of this rule. Second, choose the longest face to be the front face. When the longest face of an object is used as the front face, the pictorial view will appear less distorted. Compare the views shown in Fig. 11.31, and note the greater distortion in part *a* over part *b*.

If these two rules clash, the first should govern. It is more desirable to have an irregular face show in true shape than to lessen the distortion in the direction of the receding axis.

11.18 Angles, Circles, and Circle Arcs in Oblique

As previously stated, angles, circles, and irregular outlines on front surfaces show in true size and shape. When located on receding faces, the construction methods used in isometric drawing may usually be applied. Figure 11.32 shows the method of drawing the elliptical representation of a circle on an oblique face. Note that the method is identical to that used for con-

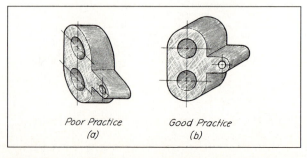

Poor Practice
(a)

Good Practice
(b)

FIG. 11.30 Irregular contour parallel to picture plane.

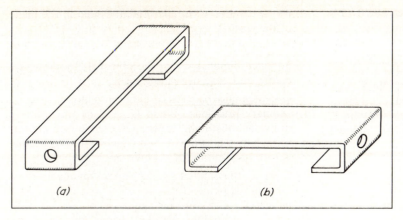

FIG. 11.31   Long axis parallel to picture plane.

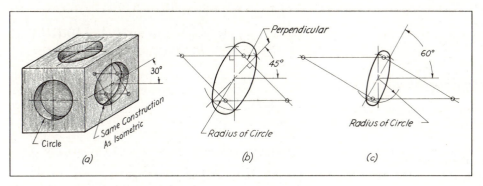

FIG. 11.32   Oblique circles.

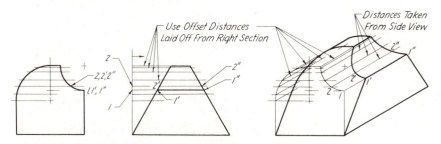

FIG. 11.33   Curved outlines on inclined plane.

structing isometric circles, except in the slight change in the position of the axes.

Circle arcs and circles on inclined planes must be plotted by using the offset or coordinate method as is shown in Fig. 11.33 (also see Fig. 11.19).

11.19 Reduction of Measurements in the Direction of the Receding Axis

An oblique drawing often presents a distorted appearance that is unnatural or disagreeable to the eye. In some cases an oblique view is so misleading in appearance that it is unsatisfactory for any practical purpose.

As a matter of interest, the effect of distortion is due to the fact that the receding lines are parallel and do not appear to converge as the eye is accustomed to anticipating (Fig. 11.34).

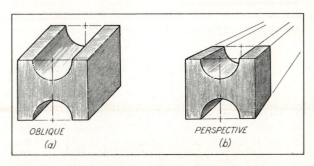

FIG. 11.34   Comparison of oblique and perspective.

The appearance of excessive thickness can be overcome by reducing the length of the receding lines. In practice, receding measurements are usually reduced one-half, but any scale of reduction may be arbitrarily adopted if the resulting view is more realistic in appearance (Fig. 11.35[*b*]). When receding lines are drawn one-half their actual length, the oblique drawing is called a *cabinet drawing*. For comparison, Fig. 11.35 shows an oblique drawing (*a*) and a cabinet drawing (*c*) of the same object.

11.20 Oblique Sectional Views

Oblique sectional views are drawn to show the interior construction of objects. The construction procedure is the same as for an isometric sectional view, except that oblique planes are used for cutting the object. An oblique half section is illustrated in Fig. 11.36.

11.21 Pictorial Dimensioning

The dimensioning of isometric and oblique working drawings is done in accordance with the following rules:

1. Draw extension and dimension lines (except those dimension lines applying to cylindrical features) parallel to the pictorial axes and in the plane of the surface to which they apply (Fig. 11.37).

2. If possible, apply dimensions to visible surfaces.

3. Place dimensions on the object if, by doing so, clarity and ease of reading result.

4. Notes may be lettered either in pictorial or as on ordinary drawings. When lettered as on ordinary drawings the difficulties encountered in forming pictorial letters is avoided. Some feeling of the pictorial is lost when doing this, however.

5. Make the characters of a dimension appear to be lying in the plane of the surface whose dimension it indicates. Use vertical guide lines for vertical strokes and guides parallel to horizontal axes for horizontal strokes.

11.22 Conventional Treatment in Pictorial Drawings

When it is desirable for an isometric or oblique drawing of a casting to be more realistic, use conventional treatment of fillets and rounds on unfinished surfaces (Fig. 11.38). In part *a*, one method of representing fillets and rounds is shown. Compare this to part *b*, where all of the edges have been treated as if they were sharp. The conventional treatment for threads in pictorial is illustrated in parts *b* and *c*.

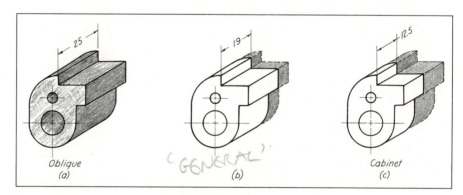

FIG. 11.35 Foreshortening in direction of receding axis.

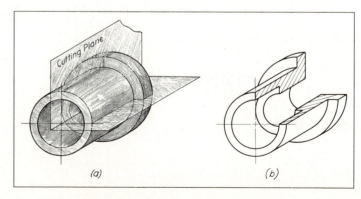

FIG. 11.36 Oblique half section.

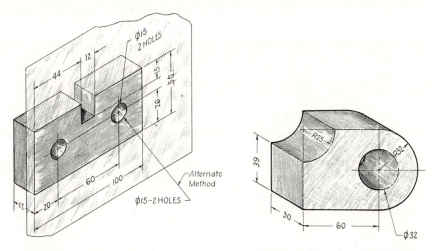

FIG. 11.37 **Extension and dimension lines in isometric (*left*); numerals, fractions, and notes in oblique (*right*).**

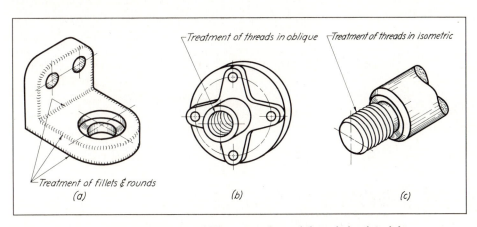

FIG. 11.38 **Conventional treatment of fillets, rounds, and threads in pictorial.**

Appendix

A Glossary of Terms
B Abbreviations
C Millimeters/Inch Tables
**D Engineering Drawings—
Instruments,
Equipment, and
Lettering**

Shop Terms

Anneal (*v*) To heat a piece of metal to a particular temperature and then allow it to cool slowly for the purpose of removing internal stresses.

Bore (*v*) To enlarge a hole using a boring bar to make it smooth, round, and coaxial. Boring is usually done on a lathe or boring mill.

Boss (*n*) A circular projection, which is raised above a principal surface of a casting or forging.

Braze (*v*) To join two pieces of metal by the use of hard solder. The solder is usually a copper-zinc alloy.

Broach (*v*) To machine a hole to a desired shape, usually other than round. The cutting tool, known as a broach, is pushed or pulled through the rough-finished hole. It has transverse cutting edges.

Burnish (*v*) To smooth or apply a brilliant finish.

Bushing (*n*) A removable cylindrical sleeve, which is used to provide a bearing surface.

Carburize (*v*) To harden the surface of a piece of low-grade steel by heating in a carbonizing material to increase the carbon content and then quenching.

Case-harden (*v*) To harden a surface as described above or through the use of potassium cyanide.

Chamfer (*v*) To bevel an external edge or corner.

Chase (*v*) To cut screw threads on a lathe using a chaser, a tool shaped to the profile of a thread.

Chill (*v*) To cool the surface of a casting suddenly so that the surface will be white and hard.

Chip (*v*) To cut away or remove surface defects with a chisel.

Collar (*n*) A cylindrical part fitted on a shaft to prevent a sliding movement.

Color-harden (*v*) A piece is color-hardened mainly for the sake of appearance. (*See* Case-harden).

Core (*v*) To form a hole or hollow cavity in a casting through the use of a core.

Counterbore (*v*) To enlarge the end of a cylindrical hole to a certain depth, as is often done to accommodate the head of a fillister-head screw. (*n*) The name of the tool used to produce the enlargement.

Countersink (*v*) To form a conical enlargement at the end of a cylindrical hole to accommodate the head of a screw or rivet. (*n*) The name of the tool used to form a conical shaped enlargement.

Crown (*n*) The angular or curved contour of the outer surface of a part, such as on a pulley.

Die (*n*) A metal block used for forming or stamping operations. A thread-cutting tool for producing external threads.

Die casting (*n*) A casting that has been produced by forcing a molten alloy having an aluminum, copper, zinc, tin, or lead base into a metal mold composed of two halves.

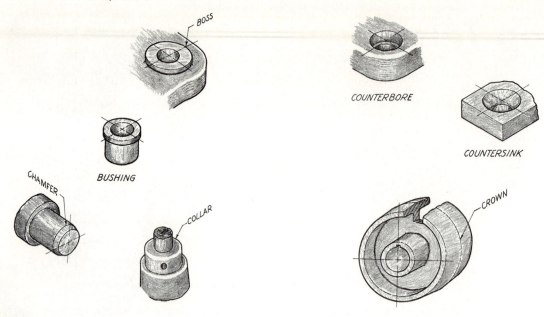

Die stamping (*n*) A piece that has been cut or formed from sheet metal through the use of a die.

Draw (*v*) To form metal, which may be either cold or hot, by a distorting or stretching process. To temper steel by gradual or intermittent quenching.

Drill (*v*) To form a cylindrical hole in metal. (*n*) A revolving cutting tool designed for cutting at the point.

Drop forging (*n*) A piece formed while hot between two dies under a drop hammer.

Face (*v*) To machine on a lathe a flat face, which is perpendicular to the axis of rotation of the piece.

Feather (*n*) A rectangular sliding key, which permits a pulley to move along the shaft parallel to its axis.

File (*v*) To shape, finish, or trim with a fine-toothed metal cutting tool, which is used with the hands.

Fillet (*n*) A rounded filling, which increases the strength at the junction of two surfaces that form an internal angle.

Fit (*n*) The tightness of adjustment between the contacting surfaces of mating parts.

Flange (*n*) The top and bottom member of a beam. A projecting rim added on the end of a pipe or fitting for making a connection.

Forge (*v*) To shape hot metals by hammering, using a hand-hammer or machine.

Galvanize (*v*) To coat steel or iron by immersion in a bath of zinc.

Graduate (*v*) To mark off or divide a scale into intervals.

Grind (*v*) To finish a surface through the action of a revolving abrasive wheel.

Kerf (*n*) A groove or channel cut by a saw or some other tool.

Key (*n*) A piece used between a shaft and a hub to prevent the movement of one relative to the other.

Keyway or Keyseat (*n*) A longitudinal groove cut in a shaft or a hub to receive a key. A key rests in a keyseat and slides in a keyway.

Knurl (*v*) To roughen a cylindrical surface to produce a better grip for the fingers.

Lap (*v*) To finish or polish with a piece of soft metal, wood, or leather impregnated with an abrasive.

Lug (*n*) A projection or ear, which has been cast or forged as a portion of a piece to provide a support or to allow the attachment of another part.

Malleable casting (*n*) A casting that has been annealed to toughen it.

Mill (*v*) To machine a piece on a milling machine by means of a rotating toothed cutter.

Neck (*v*) To cut a circumferential groove around a shaft.

Pack-harden (*v*) To case-carburize and harden.

Pad (*n*) A low, projecting surface, usually rectangular.

Peen (*v*) To stretch or bend over metal using the peen end (ball end) of a hammer.

Pickel (*v*) To remove scale and rust from a casting or forging by immersing it in an acid bath.

Plane (*v*) To machine a flat surface on a planer, a machine having a fixed tool and a reciprocating bed.

Polish (*v*) To make a surface smooth and lustrous through the use of a fine abrasive.

Punch (*v*) To perforate a thin piece of metal by shearing out a circular wad with a nonrotating tool under pressure.

Ream (*v*) To finish a hole to an exact size using a rotating fluted cutting tool known as a reamer.

Rib (*n*) A thin component of a part that acts as a brace or support.

Rivet (*n*) A headed shank, which more or less permanently unites two pieces. (*v*) To fasten steel plates with rivets.

Round (*n*) A rounded external corner on a casting.

Sandblast (*v*) To clean the surface of castings or forgings by means of sand forced from a nozzle at a high velocity.

Shear (*v*) To cut off sheet or bar metal through the shearing action of two blades.

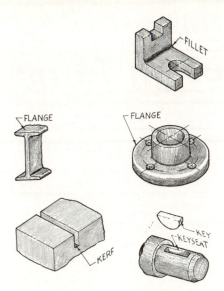

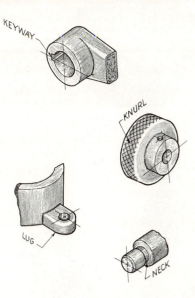

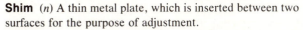

Shim (*n*) A thin metal plate, which is inserted between two surfaces for the purpose of adjustment.

Spline (*n*) A keyway, usually for a feather key. (*See* Feather.)

Spotface (*v*) To finish a round spot on the rough surface of a casting at a drilled hole for the purpose of providing a smooth seat for a bolt or screw head.

Spot weld (*v*) To weld two overlapping metal sheets in spots by means of the heat of resistance to an electric current between a pair of electrodes.

Steel casting (*n*) A casting made of cast iron to which scrap steel has been added.

Swage (*v*) To form metal with a swag block, a tool so constructed that through hammering or pressure the work may be made to take a desired shape.

Sweat (*v*) To solder together by clamping the pieces in contact with soft solder between and then heating.

Tack weld (*n*) A weld of short intermittent sections.

Tap (*v*) To cut an internal thread, by hand or with power, by screwing into the hole a fluted tapered tool having thread-cutting edges.

Taper (*v*) To make gradually smaller toward one end. (*n*) Gradual diminution of diameter or thickness of an elongated object.

Taper pin (*n*) A tapered pin used for fastening hubs or collars to shafts.

Temper (*v*) To reduce the hardness of a piece of hardened steel through reheating and sudden quenching.

Template (*n*) A pattern cut to a desired shape, which is used in layout work to establish shearing lines, to locate holes, and so on.

Tumble (*v*) To clean and smooth castings and forgings through contact in a revolving barrel. To further the results, small pieces of scrap are added.

Turn (*v*) To turn-down or machine a cylindrical surface on a lathe.

Undercut (*n*) A recessed cut.

Upset (*v*) To increase the diameter or form a shoulder on a piece during forging.

Weld (*v*) To join two pieces of metal by pressure or hammering after heating to the fusion point.

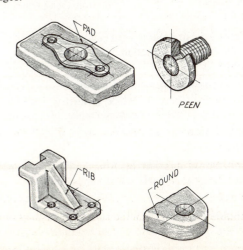

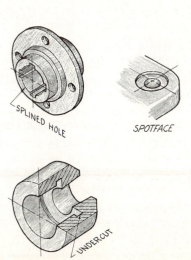

Computer-Aided Design Terms

The following terms are those most commonly encountered when operating a CADD computer. The list is by no means exhaustive. Rather, these terms will provide the student with a working vocabulary to better understand CADD applications of engineering drawing.

Attribute (*n*) The characteristic of a single drawing component such as text *height* or line *thickness;* a specific example of a drawing parameter.

Axis (*n*) A direction in space; one of the principal axes of Y (height), X (width), and Z (depth).

Back up (*v*) To make a copy of a file separate from the original.

Bit map graphics (*n*) A method of organizing graphics into a grid of dots or bits and characterized by a lack of changeable entity attributes such as line width or circle diameter; raster graphics.

CAD (*n*) Computer-aided design; the use of computers to model and test the performance of a design while providing visual feedback to the designer.

CADD (*n*) Computer-aided design and drafting; the use of computers to assist in the description of engineering designs in terms of engineering drawings.

CAM (*n*) Computer-aided manufacturing; the use of computers to assist in the planning, execution, monitoring, and necessary adjustment of the manufacturing process.

Cartesian coordinates (*n*) A position in space relative to the intersection of the X, Y, and Z axes (the origin); absolute coordinates relative to XO, YO, ZO; relative or delta coordinates from a temporary origin.

Character string (*n*) A pattern of alphabetic, numeric, or punctuation characters used to annotate the geometric data base.

CIM (*n*) Computer-integrated manufacturing; the overall term used for the systems integration of all manufacturing activities.

Command (*n*) An instruction from the operator to the computer.

Computer graphics (*n*) The use of computing machinery to assist in the creation, storage, and display of visual imagery.

Construction plane (*n*) A two-dimensional plane in three-dimensional space on which geometry is constructed; the method by which a wire frame model is constructed.

Coordinate (*n*) A location in space specified by X, Y, and Z positions.

Coordinate system (*n*) A method of specifying exact locations in space such as the cartesian or polar coordinate systems.

Cross-hatch or Hatch (*n*) The filling of an area with a pattern of parallel lines or similar symbols.

Cursor (*n*) The graphic symbol on a display screen corresponding to the current position in either world or device coordinates.

Data base (*n*) The organized description of data; in *geometric* data base, the organized description of a part's geometry.

Default (*n*) A predefined setting within a CADD program established when the program was created; a setting that an operator may change during a work session that reverts to the predefined setting when the session is ended; a setting that an operator may permanently change.

Delete (*v*) To remove information from the data base.

Device coordinate (*n*) The coordinate location on the screen of a point in space.

Digitizer (*n*) An input device which translates an X-Y or X-Y-Z position into digital information understood by a CADD program; a tablet.

Digitizing (*n*) The identification of coordinate points by using a digitizer; the assigning of coordinate values by keyboard entry.

Display (*n*) An output device which accurately presents the image of a geometric data base; a display terminal such as a video terminal (VT), a cathode ray tube (CRT), or a direct view storage tube (DVST).

Edit (*v*) To change the parameters or attributes of drawing components; to change a text string.

Engineering workstation (*n*) An easily networked computer able to fit on an engineer's desk capable of rapid, accurate creation and display of engineering drawings and designs.

Entity (*n*) A drawing component that cannot be readily broken apart; a basic drawing shape or object resident with the CADD program such as a line, arc, circle, or point; a symbol that is stored as a single grouped graphic.

File (*n*) The CADD drawing as stored in the computer; any information stored as a unit in the computer such as a font file, a pattern file, or plot file; when used as a verb, the act of saving a file.

Fill (*n*) Crosshatching of an area with a fill or crosshatch pattern.

Firmware (*n*) Program instructions that are permanently built into electronic circuitry.

Font (*n*) In *text font,* all of the characters of a particular type style and size; as in *line font,* all available line styles (solid, dashed, center, phantom, user defined).

Geometric data base (*n*) The organization of information in the computer that describes the physical nature of an object.

Graphic application (*n*) A program intended to perform a specific task such as a piping application, an electronic circuit board application, or a bridge beam analysis application.

Grid (*n*) A matrix or pattern of dots displayed on the terminal used to facilitate drawing and design; the spacing of the pattern of dots set to coincide with major features of the design.

Hard copy (*n*) A print or plot of a drawing on paper or film.

Hardware (*n*) The physical equipment necessary for computer drawing; the computer, terminal, keyboard, tablet, plotter and storage disks or tapes.

Hidden line editing (*n*) The automatic changing of line type parameter from solid to hidden to correctly show visibility; the manual changing of such lines.

Input device (*n*) A device that facilitates entering data or instructions into the computer; the keyboard, mouse, joy stick, or tablet with puck or stylus.

Interactive computer graphics (*n*) Computer drawing that shows the operator's actions and the response of the computer to such actions in graphical form.

Layer (*n*) The organization of associated geometry, dimensions, or notes by an index number known as the layer number; (*v*) to organize a drawing into groups that can be displayed, edited, or plotted individually.

Load (*v*) To bring a file from storage to current memory to be worked on.

Mask (*n*) An instruction that limits the possible responses to an operator command such as a position mask.

Menu (*n*) A list of possible commands from which the operator selects.

Mirror (*v*) To revolve selected geometry 180° about the normal view of an axis as differentiated from revolution which is done about the point view of an axis.

Modifier (*n*) An instruction that limits the possible responses to an operator's command.

Mouse (*n*) A hand-held input device used for entering X-Y data or instructions.

Network (*n*) A group of computers linked together for the purpose of sharing information (data bases or drawings) or resources (printers or plotters).

Object graphics (*n*) The method of organizing graphics into objects or entities.

Origin (*n*) The position XO, YO, ZO in Cartesian space; the position radius O, Angle O in polar space; the insertion point of a symbol.

Output device (*n*) A device like a terminal, plotter, or printer used for viewing a data base.

Pan (*v*) To move the drawing left, right, up or down without altering the object's relationship to the world coordinate system (no translation or rotation) or the object-viewer distance (no zoom).

Parameter (*n*) A setting used in making a drawing such as a scale, line type, or text font that is applied to the drawing globally.

Part (*n*) The completed description of an object.

Part file (*n*) The saved description of an object.

Pattern (*n*) A grouping of graphics used as a symbol; the design of lines used to fill an area.

Plotter (*n*) An output device that represents the data base as drawn lines. In a drum plotter, paper is fed around a cylindrical drum and both paper and pens move. In a flat bed plotter, sheet paper is held stationary on a large table and only the pens move. In a belt bed plotter, the paper is held against a moving flat belt with moving pens. A photo plotter uses a light beam to draw on light sensitive film.

Polar coordinates (*n*) Designate a position in space at a specific angle and at a specific radius from an origin.

Primitives (*n*) The lowest level graphic shapes available to construct more complex shapes; entities that cannot be ungrouped into more simplistic parts.

Printer (*n*) An output device that changes object graphic files into raster images. Examples are the dot matrix printer, an electrostatic printer, and a laser printer.

Prompt (*n*) An instruction from the computer to the operator.

Puck (*n*) A hand-held input device used in conjunction with a tablet for recording X and Y coordinates.

Raster graphics (*n*) Drawings comprised of a grid of dots; a bit map; the opposite of object graphics.

Rotate (*v*) To move circularly in a plane perpendicular to an axis; positive rotation is counterclockwise. (See mirror.)

Snap (*n*) An invisible grid that acts like a magnet to attract the cursor to grid intersection points.

Software (*n*) Instructions written in a language understood by computing machinery.

Solid model (*n*) The complete description of an object in the computer consistent with its three-dimensional properties (material, mass, weight, surface finish, and so on.)

Storage media (*n*) The disks or tapes used for the permanent storage of data and drawings.

Surface model (*n*) A hollow three-dimensional model comprised only of surfaces with no solid material inside.

Surface shading (*n*) The assigning of values to the surfaces of a three-dimensional computer model consistent with light source position and material characteristics.

Stylus (*n*) An electronic input device held like a pencil.

Symbol (*n*) A graphic created and stored for subsequent use; a library part or figure such as a cell, a pattern, or a template.

Tablet (*n*) A device used to record X and Y positions. Tablets are used either to digitize geometry or input operator's commands from a menu on the tablet.

Three-dimensional (*a*) Having dimensional characteristics in X, Y, and Z directions.

Translate (*v*) To move in a linear fashion in relation to the X, Y, and Z axes.

Two-dimensional (*a*) Having dimensional characteristics in X and Y directions.

Two-and-one-half dimensional (*a*) Having the appearance of three-dimensionality but with only X and Y information in the geometric data base; a two-dimensional pictorial representation.

Workspace (*n*) The world coordinate space in which a CADD operator works.

World coordinate (*n*) The position of a point given in the same units that is used to create the actual object; the design in full scale.

Window (*n*) A section of the computer terminal set aside for displaying information independently of information shown in other windows.

Wire frame model (*n*) A transparent three-dimensional model comprised of vertices, connecting lines, or surface elements but having no solid planes or mass.

Zoom (*v*) To change the apparent size by getting closer to or farther from the object; *zoom in* increases the apparent size and *zoom out* reduces the apparent size.

ANSI Abbreviations

alternating current	AC	cubic foot	CU FT
aluminum	AL	cubic inch	CU IN
American Standard	AMER STD	cubic yard	CU YD
approved	APPD	cylinder	CYL
average	AVG	degree	DEG or °
Babbitt	BAB	detail drawing	DET DWG
ball bearing	BB	diagonal	DIAG
brass	BRS	diameter	DIA
Brinell hardness number	BHN	diametral pitch	DP
bronze	BRZ	direct current	DC
Brown & Sharpe	B & S	drawing	DWG
cast iron	CI	drawn	DR
center line	CL or ℄	effective	EFF
center to center	C to C	electric	ELEC
centimeter	CM	engineer	ENGR
chemical	CHEM	external	EXT
circular	CIR	fabricate	FAB
circular pitch	CP	fillister	FIL
cold-rolled steel	CRS	finish	FIN.
copper	COP	foot	' or FT
counterbore	CBORE	gallon	GAL
countersink	CSK	galvanized iron	GI
cubic	CU	grind	GRD

harden	HDN	pounds per square foot	PSF
hexagon	HEX	pounds per square inch	PSI
horsepower	HP	Pratt & Whitney	P & W
hour	HR	quantity	QTY
impregnate	IMPREG	radius	R or RAD
inch	″ or IN.	required	REQD
inside diameter	ID	revolution per minute	RPM
internal	INT	right hand	RH
lateral	LAT	round	RD
left hand	LH	round bar	ϕ
linear	LIN	screw	SCR
long	LG	second (angular measure)	″
longitude	LONG.	second (time)	SEC
machine	MACH	section	SECT
malleable iron	MI	Society of Automotive Engineers	SAE
material	MATL	square	SQ
maximum	MAX	square foot	SQ FT
meter	M	square inch	SQ IN
miles	MI	standard	STD
miles per hour	MPH	steel	STL
millimeter	MM	steel casting	STL CSTG
minimum	MIN	thousand	M
minute (angular measure)	′ or MIN	thread	THD
minute (time)	MIN	ton	TON
outside diameter	OD	traced	TR
pattern	PATT	volt	V
phosphor bronze	PH BRZ	watt	W
piece	PC	weight	WT
pitch	P	Woodruff	WDF
pitch diameter	PD	wrought iron	WI
plate	PL	yard	YD
pound	# or LB	year	YR

Inch-Millimeter Table

Table 3 Inch–millimeter equivalents

4ths	8ths	16ths	32nds	64ths	To 4 places	To 3 places	To 2 places	To 4 places
				1/64	.0156	.016	.02	0.3969
			1/32		.0312	.031	.03	0.7938
				3/64	.0469	.047	.05	1.1906
		1/16			.0625	.062	.06	1.5875
				5/64	.0781	.078	.08	1.9844
			3/32		.0938	.094	.09	2.3813
				7/64	.1094	.109	.11	2.7781
	1/8				.1250	.125	.12	3.1750
				9/64	.1406	.141	.14	3.5719
			5/32		.1562	.156	.16	3.9688
				11/64	.1719	.172	.17	4.3656
		3/16			.1875	.188	.19	4.7625
				13/64	.2031	.203	.20	5.1594
			7/32		.2188	.219	.22	5.5563
				15/64	.2344	.234	.23	5.9531
1/4					.2500	.250	.25	6.3500
				17/64	.2656	.266	.27	6.7469
			9/32		.2812	.281	.28	7.1438
				19/64	.2969	.297	.30	7.5406
		5/16			.3125	.312	.31	7.9375
				21/64	.3281	.328	.33	8.3344
			11/32		.3438	.344	.34	8.7313
				23/64	.3594	.359	.36	9.1281
	3/8				.3750	.375	.38	9.5250
				25/64	.3906	.391	.39	9.9219
			13/32		.4062	.406	.41	10.3188
				27/64	.4219	.422	.42	10.7156
		7/16			.4375	.438	.44	11.1125
				29/64	.4531	.453	.45	11.5094
			15/32		.4688	.469	.47	11.9063
				31/64	.4844	.484	.48	12.3031
					.5000	.500	.50	12.7000
				33/64	.5156	.516	.52	13.0969
			17/32		.5312	.531	.53	13.4938
				35/64	.5469	.547	.55	13.8906
		9/16			.5625	.562	.56	14.2875
				37/64	.5781	.578	.58	14.6844
			19/32		.5938	.594	.59	15.0813
				39/64	.6094	.609	.61	15.4781
	5/8				.6250	.625	.62	15.8750
				41/64	.6406	.641	.64	16.2719
			21/32		.6562	.656	.66	16.6688
				43/64	.6719	.672	.67	17.0656
		11/16			.6875	.688	.69	17.4625
				45/64	.7031	.703	.70	17.8594
			23/32		.7188	.719	.72	18.2563
				47/64	.7344	.734	.73	18.6531
3/4					.7500	.750	.75	19.0500
				49/64	.7656	.766	.77	19.4469
			25/32		.7812	.781	.78	19.8438
				51/64	.7969	.797	.80	20.2406
		13/16			.8125	.812	.81	20.6375
				53/64	.8281	.828	.83	21.0344
			27/32		.8438	.844	.84	21.4313
				55/64	.8594	.859	.86	21.8281
	7/8				.8750	.875	.88	22.2250
				57/64	.8906	.891	.89	22.6219
			29/32		.9062	.906	.91	23.0188
				59/64	.9219	.922	.92	23.4156
		15/16			.9375	.938	.94	23.8125
				61/64	.9531	.953	.95	24.2094
			31/32		.9688	.969	.97	24.6063
				63/64	.9844	.984	.98	25.0031
					1.0000	1.000	1.00	25.4000

Inch-Millimeter Table*

Inches	Inches									
	0	1	2	3	4	5	6	7	8	9
0–9	0	25.4	50.8	76.2	101.6	127.0	152.4	177.8	203.2	228.6
10–19	254.0	279.4	304.8	330.2	355.6	381.0	406.4	431.8	457.2	482.6
20–29	508.0	533.4	558.8	584.2	609.6	635.0	660.4	685.8	711.2	736.6
30–39	762.0	787.4	812.8	838.2	863.6	889.0	914.4	939.8	965.2	990.6
40–49	1016.0	1041.4	1066.8	1092.2	1117.6	1143.0	1168.4	1193.8	1219.2	1244.6
50–59	1270.0	1295.4	1320.8	1346.2	1371.6	1397.0	1422.4	1447.8	1473.2	1498.6
60–69	1524.0	1549.4	1574.8	1600.2	1625.6	1651.0	1676.4	1701.8	1727.2	1752.6
70–79	1778.0	1803.4	1828.8	1854.2	1879.6	1905.0	1930.4	1955.8	1981.2	2006.6
80–89	2032.0	2057.4	2082.8	2108.2	2133.6	2159.0	2184.4	2209.8	2235.2	2260.6
90–99	2286.0	2311.4	2336.8	2362.2	2387.6	2413.0	2438.4	2463.8	2489.2	2514.6

* Based on 1 in. = 25.4 mm.
Examples: To obtain the millimeter equivalent of 14 in., read the value below 4 in. in the horizontal line of values for 10–19 in. (355.6). The equivalent value of 52.4 in. is: 1320.8 *plus* 10.16 = 330.96, the 10.16 value being obtained by moving the decimal point left in the equivalent value for 4 in.

APPENDIX C-3

Decimal Inch-Millimeter Table*

mm = in.	mm = in.	mm = in.	mm = in.	mm = in.
1 = 0.0394	21 = 0.8268	41 = 1.6142	61 = 2.4016	81 = 3.1890
2 = 0.0787	22 = 0.8661	42 = 1.6535	62 = 2.4409	82 = 3.2283
3 = 0.1181	23 = 0.9055	43 = 1.6929	63 = 2.4803	83 = 3.2677
4 = 0.1575	24 = 0.9449	44 = 1.7323	64 = 2.5197	84 = 3.3071
5 = 0.1969	25 = 0.9843	45 = 1.7717	65 = 2.5591	85 = 3.3465
6 = 0.2362	26 = 1.0236	46 = 1.8110	66 = 2.5984	86 = 3.3858
7 = 0.2756	27 = 1.0630	47 = 1.8504	67 = 2.6378	87 = 3.4252
8 = 0.3150	28 = 1.1024	48 = 1.8898	68 = 2.6772	88 = 3.4646
9 = 0.3543	29 = 1.1417	49 = 1.9291	69 = 2.7165	89 = 3.5039
10 = 0.3937	30 = 1.1811	50 = 1.9685	70 = 2.7559	90 = 3.5433
11 = 0.4331	31 = 1.2205	51 = 2.0079	71 = 2.7953	91 = 3.5827
12 = 0.4724	32 = 1.2598	52 = 2.0472	72 = 2.8346	92 = 3.6220
13 = 0.5118	33 = 1.2992	53 = 2.0866	73 = 2.8740	93 = 3.6614
14 = 0.5512	34 = 1.3386	54 = 2.1260	74 = 2.9134	94 = 3.7008
15 = 0.5906	35 = 1.3780	55 = 2.1654	75 = 2.9528	95 = 3.7402
16 = 0.6299	36 = 1.4173	56 = 2.2047	76 = 2.9921	96 = 3.7795
17 = 0.6693	37 = 1.4567	57 = 2.2441	77 = 3.0315	97 = 3.8189
18 = 0.7087	38 = 1.4961	58 = 2.2835	78 = 3.0709	98 = 3.8583
19 = 0.7480	39 = 1.5354	59 = 2.3228	79 = 3.1102	99 = 3.8976
20 = 0.7874	40 = 1.5748	60 = 2.3622	80 = 3.1496	100 = 3.9370

*To nearest fourth decimal place.

Engineering Drawing—Instruments, Equipment and Lettering

D1 MANUAL DRAWING EQUIPMENT AND ITS USE

D1.1 Introduction

The instruments and materials needed for making engineering drawings are shown in Fig. D.1. There will be individual differences among brands, but functionally the equipment will be the same. Drawing instruments should be well made. Inferior equipment often makes it difficult to produce drawings of professional quality and often costs more in the long run.

D1.2 Basic List of Equipment and Materials

The following list contains the selection of equipment necessary for making instrument drawings:

1. Case of drawing instruments
2. Drawing surface (board or table)
3. Drafting edge (T-square, parallel edge, drafting machine)
4. Triangles (30°, 45°, or adjustable)
5. French curve

6. Scales (see Secs. D.24 and D.25)
7. Drawing pencils
8. Lead pointer
9. Drafting tape
10. Eraser
11. Dry cleaning pad
12. Erasing shield
13. Dusting brush
14. Drawing paper
15. Tracing paper or drafting film.

D1.3 Set of Drawing Instruments

The minimum contents of a drawing instrument set should include a large bow compass, small bow compass, and set of frictional dividers (Fig. D.2). Sets which contain the large bow are preferred by many persons, especially in the aircraft and automotive fields. The set often comes in a velvet-lined case, designed to protect the instruments. Some sets also con-

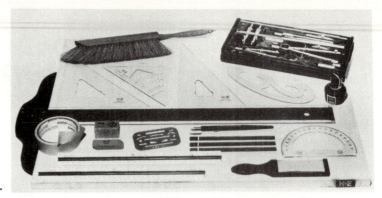

FIG. D.1　Manual drafting equipment.

FIG. D.2　A drawing instrument set.

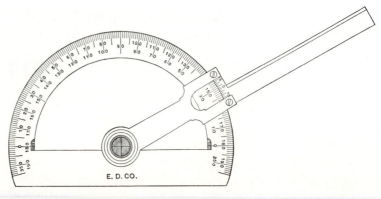

FIG. D.3　Protractor.

tain a "beam compass" for constructing large arcs. The bow compass has a center wheel for adjustment and will hold its setting as the draftsman applies pressure to draw a line. Modern bow compasses often have a "quick bow" feature which allows rapid adjustment.

D1.4 Protractor

The protractor (Fig. D.3) is used for measuring and laying off angles. An alternative to this device is the protractor head of a drafting machine (Fig. D.9).

D1.5 Special Instruments and Templates

A few of the many special instruments available are shown in Figs. D4 to D8. *Drafting templates* are by far the most important special equipment. The use of templates (Fig. D.4) can save valuable time in the drawing of standard figures and symbols. Electrical, hydraulic, and pneumatic equipment, springs, fasteners, gears, circles, ellipses, curves, boxes, and architectural symbols are all available on templates. Template manufacturers will make custom templates for specialized applications on request.

To supplement standard plastic curves, *flexible curves* (Fig. D.5) provide limitless variations and are very convenient. The type shown in (a) is a lead bar enclosed in rubber. The more desirable one shown in

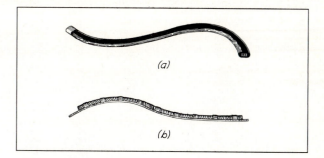

FIG. D.5   Flexible curves.

(b) has a steel ruling edge attached to a spring with a lead core. Flexible curves are limited to gentle curves and are unsuitable for small radius arcs.

The *electric erasing machine* (Fig. D.6) saves valuable drafting time for those persons who correct and update engineering drawings. An assortment of eraser stock is available for different papers and films.

When an ink drawing is required, the *technical pen* shown in Fig. D.7 is available in the thirteen metric line widths shown. These pens are suitable for instrument linework and for lettering using plastic lettering guides. For proper use, these pens should be held perpendicular to the drawing surface and moved with light downward pressure. Different inks and tips are available for different papers and films. These pens require occasional cleaning. These are precision drawing instruments and users are advised to follow the manufacturer's recommendations for filling, cleaning, and storing.

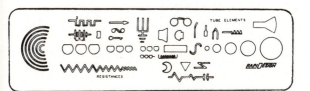

ELECTRO SYMBOL TEMPLATE

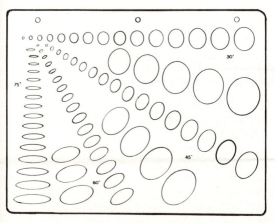

ELLIPSES

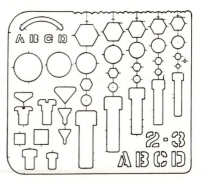

TOOLING TEMPLATE

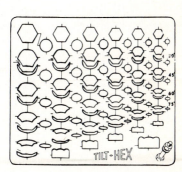

TILT-HEX DRAFTING TEMPLATE

FIG. D.4   Special templates. (*Courtesy Frederick Post Co.*)

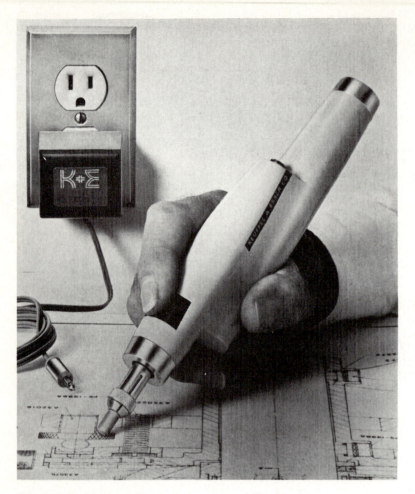

FIG. D.6 Erasing machine.

6x0	4x0	3x0	00	0	1	2	2½	3	3½	4	6	7
.13	.18	.25	.30	.35	.50	.60	.70	.80	1.00	1.20	1.40	2.00
.005 in	.007 in	.010 in	.012 in	.014 in	.020 in	.024 in	.028 in	.031 in	.039 in	.047 in	.055 in	.079 in
.13mm	.18mm	.25mm	.30mm	.35mm	.50mm	.60mm	.70mm	.80mm	1.00mm	1.20mm	1.40mm	2.00mm

FIG. D.7 Technical fountain pen.
(*Courtesy Koh-I-Noor, Inc.*)

FIG. D.8 Proportional dividers.

Proportional dividers (Fig. D.8) supplement the dividers found in drawing instrument sets. They are used for reducing or enlarging drawings without converting numerical values.

D1.6 *T-Square, Parallel Edge, and Drafting Machine*

The *T-square* and *parallel edge* are used to draw horizontal lines and as a guide for triangles when drawing vertical and inclined lines (Figs. D25 and D26). Lines are drawn along the top of the straight edge.

The *drafting machine* (Fig. D.9) combines straight edge, protractor, scale, and triangles. It is estimated that drafting machines lead to a 25% to 50% savings in time in commercial drafting rooms. Drafting machines may be of the parallel arm type or the more modern "track" design. Some include a digital electronic readout of protractor angles, much like a calculator. Many

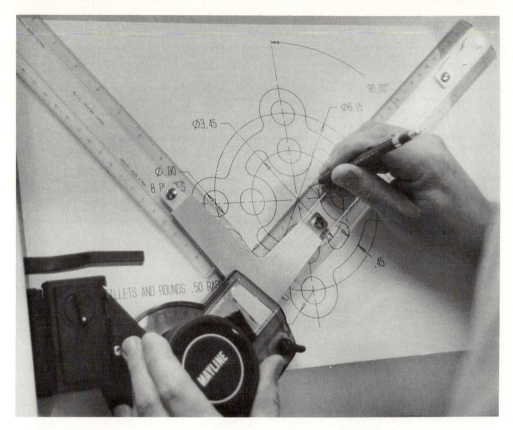

FIG. D.9 Drafting machine. Blades are in position for drawing inclined lines.

optional devices may be attached to the head of a drafting machine including electronic lettering machines and computer-interfaced digitizers (see Sec. D3.10).

D1.7 *Tracing Paper and Drafting Film*

White lightweight tracing paper called *drafting vellum,* on which pencil drawings can be made and from which prints can be produced, is used in most commercial drafting rooms. Drafting vellum is not a permanent medium for drawings, however. Over time it will swell with humidity, crack with dryness, or yellow with age. It also does not keep its "dimensional stability," that is, exacting distances will change over time as vellum shrinks. Drawings done on vellum must be reduced and stored on microfilm for permanence.

A more expensive solution is polyester *drafting film*. This film is transluscent (frosted on one or both sides) and exhibits excellent dimensional stability and printing qualities. Drawings are made on drafting film either in ink or polymer (plastic) lead. Erasures can be made without leaving "ghost marks" that might show when making a print.

D1.8 *Pencils*

Both the student and the professional should be equipped with a selection of pencils with leads of various degrees of hardness (Fig. D.10). Examples of these leads are

FOR VELLUM		FOR FILM	
9H	Very hard		
6H	Hard	6P	Hard plastic
2H	Medium	2P	Medium plastic
H	Medium soft	P	Soft plastic
F	Soft		

The grade of pencil chosen depends on the type of line desired, the kind of paper used, and humidity which affects the surface of the paper. *Hard leads* produce sharp but grey lines. *Soft leads* produce black but sometimes fuzzy lines. Standards for line quality will govern selection of lead (see Fig. D.22). As a minimum, however, the student should have available a 6H pencil for light layout work where accuracy is required, a 4H for reproducing light finished lines (dimension lines, center lines, and dashed lines), a 2H for visible object lines, and an F or H for all lettering and freehand work.

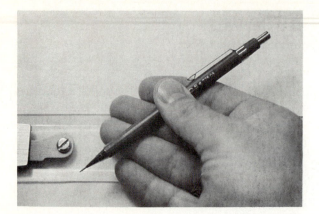

FIG. D.10 Drafting pencil.

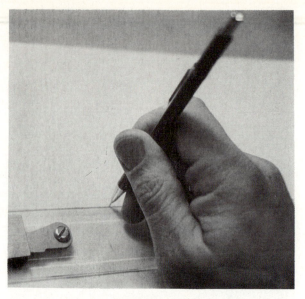

FIG. D.12 Using the mechanical pencil.

The most popular pencils use .7-, .5-, and .3-mm leads. These mechanical pencils are filled with lead stock of the desired hardness and should be held perpendicular to the drawing surface much like a technical ink pen. Graphite lead for vellum and polymer lead for drafting film are available. These leads do not need to be sharpened but may be "burnished" to a sharp point for particularly precise work.

When sharpening a wood-encased graphite pencil, the wood should be cut away (on the unlettered end) with a knife or a pencil sharpener equipped with draftsman's cutters. About 10 mm (.38 in) of the lead should be exposed and should form a cut, including the wood, about 40 mm (1.5 in) long. The lead then should be shaped to a conical point on a pointer or burnished on a piece of rough paper (see Fig. D.11).

D1.9 *Drawing Pencil Lines*

Pencil lines should be sharp and uniform along their entire length as well as uniform with similar lines elsewhere on the drawing. *Construction lines* (preliminary or layout lines) should be drawn *very* lightly so that they will not reproduce when copied. *Finished lines* should be made boldly and distinctly so that a distinction will be evident between solid and dashed object lines and *auxiliary lines* (dimension, center, and section lines). To give this contrast, necessary for clearness and ease in reading the drawing, object lines

should be of medium width and very black; dashed lines, black and less wide; and auxiliary lines, dark and thin.

When drawing a line, a .3-, .5-, or .7-mm mechanical pencil should be held perpendicular to the drawing surface (Fig D12). This type of pencil will produce a line consistent with the diameter of the lead. Traditional wooden drawing pencils or lead holders like those in Fig. D.13 should be inclined slightly (about 60°) in the direction that the line is being drawn. The pencil should be "pulled" (never pushed) at the same inclination for the full length of the line. If the pencil is rotated slowly between the fingers as the line is drawn, a symmetrical point will be maintained and a straight uniform line will be ensured.

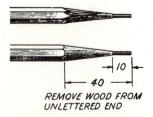

REMOVE WOOD FROM UNLETTERED END

FIG. D.11 Sharpening a wood-encased pencil.

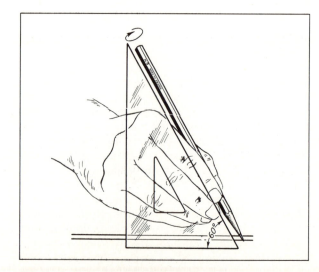

FIG. D.13 Using the wooden pencil.

D1.10 Placing and Fastening the Paper

The *drawing paper* should be placed on the board or table so that your drawing blade will be parallel to one edge of the paper and perpendicular to the other and so that areas at the top and bottom of the sheet can be used. Align the lower edge of the sheet (or the lower border line if the paper is preprinted) with a straight edge placed parallel to the edge of the board before securing the sheet at each corner with drafting tape. Tape opposite corners of the sheet, working the sheet flat from the center with the side of your hand.

D1.11 Large Bow Compass

The *compass* or *large bow* is used for drawing circles and circle arcs. For drawing pencil circles, the style of point illustrated in Fig. D.14 should be used because it gives more accurate results and is easier to maintain than most other styles. This style of point is formed by first sharpening the outside of the lead, as shown in Fig. D.15, to a long flat bevel approximately 6 mm long (Fig. D.14[*a*]) and then finishing it (Fig. D.14[*b*]) with a slight rocking motion to reduce the width of the point. Although a hard lead (4H–6H) will maintain a point longer without resharpening, it gives a finished object line that is too light in color. Soft lead (F or H) gives a darker line but quickly loses its edge and, on larger circles, gives a thicker line at the end than at the beginning. Some draftsmen have found that a medium-grade (2H–3H) lead is a satisfactory compromise for ordinary working drawings. For design drawings, layout work, and graphical solutions, however, a harder lead will give better results.

The needle point should have the shouldered end out and should be adjusted approximately 10 mm (.38 in) beyond the end of the split sleeve (Fig. D.14[*a*]).

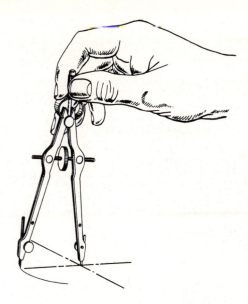

FIG. D.16 Using the large bow (Vemco).

D1.12 Using the Compass

When possible, it is preferable to use a *circle template* to draw common diameter circles. Choose a lead hardness identical to that used for straight lines of similar intensity and sharpen the lead before drawing each arc (see Sec. D1.11). To draw a circle with a compass, it is first necessary to draw two lines intersecting at right angles; along one, mark off the radius. Place the compass point carefully on the point of intersection. Adjust the lead point to the radius mark and draw the circle in a clockwise direction if you are right-handed (Fig. D.16). While drawing the circle, the instrument should be inclined slightly forward. If the line is not dark enough, draw over it again.

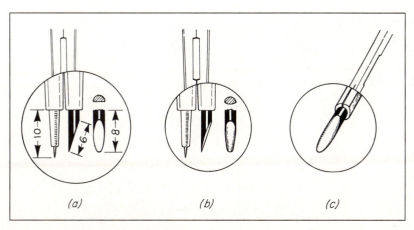

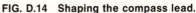

(a)   (b)   (c)

FIG. D.14 Shaping the compass lead.

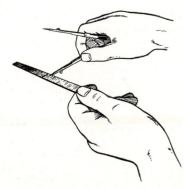

FIG. D.15 Sharpening the compass lead.

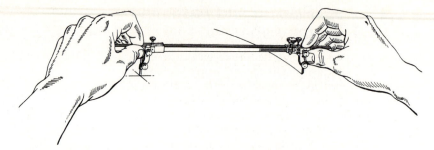

FIG. D.17   Drawing large circles (Vemco beam compass).

A beam compass is manipulated by steadying the instrument at the pivot leg with one hand while drawing the marking leg toward you with the other (Fig. D.17).

D1.13 *Dividers*

The *dividers* are used principally for dividing curved and straight lines into any number of equal parts and for transferring measurements. If the instrument is held with one leg between the forefinger and second finger, and the other leg between the thumb and third finger, as illustrated in Fig. D.18, an adjustment may be made quickly and easily with one hand. The second and third fingers are used to ''open out'' the legs, and the thumb and forefinger to close them. This method of adjusting may seem awkward to the beginner at first, but with practice absolute control can be developed.

D1.14 *Using Dividers*

The trial method is used to divide a line into a given number of equal parts (Fig. D.19). To divide a line into a desired number of equal parts, open the dividers until the distance between the points is estimated to be equal to the length of a division, and step off the line *lightly*. If the last mark misses the end point, increase or decrease the setting by an amount estimated to be equal to the error divided by the number of divisions, before lifting the dividers from the paper. Step off the line again. Repeat this procedure until the dividers are correctly set, then space the line again and indent the division points. When stepping off a line, the dividers are rotated alternately in an opposite direction on either side of the line, each half-revolution, as shown in Fig. D.19.

It is the common practice of many expert draftsmen to draw a small freehand circle around a very light indentation to establish location of the divider point.

D1.15 *Use of French and Adjustable Curves*

A *French curve* is used for drawing irregular curves that are not circle arcs. After sufficient points have been located, the French curve is applied so that a portion of its ruling edge passes through at least *three points*, as shown in Fig. D.20. It should be so placed that the increasing curvature of the section of the ruling edge being used follows the direction of that part of the curve which is changing most rapidly. To ensure that the finished curve will be free of humps and sharp

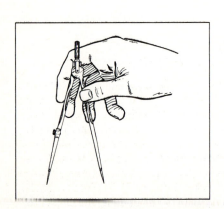

FIG. D.18   To adjust the large dividers.

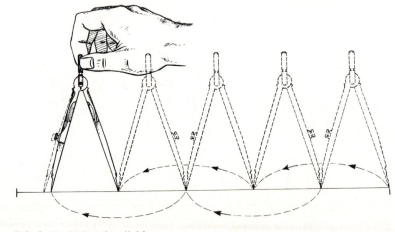

FIG. D.19   Using the dividers.

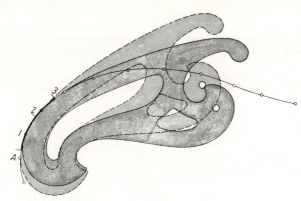

FIG. D.20   Using the irregular curve.

breaks, the first line drawn should start and stop short of the first and last points to which the French curve has been fitted. Then the curve is adjusted in a new position with the ruling edge coinciding with a section of the line previously drawn. Each successive segment should stop short of the last point matched by the curve. In Fig. D.20 the curve fits the three points, *A*, 1, and 2. A line is drawn from between point A and point 1 to between point 1 and point 2. Then the curve is shifted, as shown, to fit again points 1 and 2 with an additional point 3, and the line is extended to between point 2 and point 3.

Some people sketch a smooth continuous curve through the points in pencil before drawing the mechanical line. This procedure makes the task of drawing the curve less difficult, because it is easier to adjust the ruling edge to segments of the freehand curve than to the points.

The *adjustable curve* is laid flat on the drawing surface and gently bent until its edge follows as many points of the curve as possible (Fig. D.5). If the curve becomes tight and the adjustable curve cannot be bent into position to follow it, finish the line with a small French curve.

D1.16   Use of Erasing Shield and Eraser

An erasure is made on an engineering drawing by placing an opening in the *erasing shield* over the work to be erased and rubbing with an eraser appropriate for the medium used for the line (Fig. D.21). Excessive pressure should not be applied to the eraser because

FIG. D.21   Using the erasing shield.

the surface of the drawing is likely to be damaged. The fingers holding the erasing shield should rest partly on the drawing surface to prevent the shield from slipping.

D1.17   Conventional Line Symbols

Symbolic lines of various weights are used in making technical drawings. The recommendations of the American National Standards Institute, as given in ANSI Y14.2M–1979, are the following:

Two widths of lines—thick and thin—are recommended for use on drawings (Fig. D.22). Pencil lines in general should be in proportion to the ink lines except that the thicker pencil lines will be necessarily thinner than the corresponding ink lines but as thick as practicable for pencil work. Exact thicknesses may vary according to the size and type of drawing. For example, where lines are close together, the lines may be slightly thinner. The ratio of line thickness should be about two to one. The thin line width should be approximately 0.35 mm (.015 in) and the thick line width approximately 0.7 mm (.03 in).

Ink lines on drawings prepared for catalogs and books may be drawn using three widths—thick, medium, and thin. This provides greater contrast between types of lines and gives a better appearance.

The lines illustrated in Fig. D.22 are shown full size. When symbolic lines are used on a pencil drawing they should not vary in color. For example, center lines, extension lines, dimension lines, and section lines should differ from object lines only in width. The resulting contrast makes a drawing easier to read. All lines, except construction lines, should be very dark and bright to give the drawing the "snap" that is needed for good appearance. If the drawing is on tracing paper the lead must be "packed on" so that a satisfactory print can be obtained. Construction lines should be drawn *very* fine so as to be unnoticeable on the finished drawing. The lengths of the dashes and spaces shown in Figs. 8.20, 8.31, and 10.21 are recommended for the hidden lines, center lines, and cutting-plane lines on average-size drawings.

D1.18   Triangles

The 45° and 30° × 60° *right triangles* (Fig. D.23) are commonly used to make engineering drawings. Even with a drafting machine, triangles are used to keep drafting machine movement to a minimum. Triangles should receive special care to prevent nicks and chips. Never use a triangle with an art knife. A triangle may be checked for nicks by sliding your thumbnail along the ruling edges, as shown in Fig. D.24. Some triangles have "inking edges" to keep ink from running under the plastic.

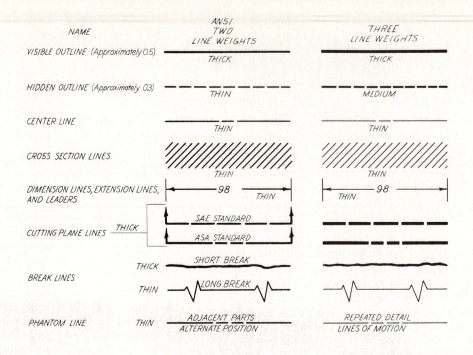

NAME	ANSI TWO LINE WEIGHTS		THREE LINE WEIGHTS	
VISIBLE OUTLINE (Approximately 0.5)	THICK		THICK	
HIDDEN OUTLINE (Approximately 0.3)	THIN		MEDIUM	
CENTER LINE	THIN		THIN	
CROSS SECTION LINES	THIN		THIN	
DIMENSION LINES, EXTENSION LINES, AND LEADERS	⟵ 98 ⟶ THIN		⟵ 98 ⟶ THIN	
CUTTING PLANE LINES — THICK	SAE STANDARD			
	ASA STANDARD			
BREAK LINES — THICK	SHORT BREAK			
— THIN	LONG BREAK			
PHANTOM LINE — THIN	ADJACENT PARTS ALTERNATE POSITION		REPEATED DETAIL LINES OF MOTION	

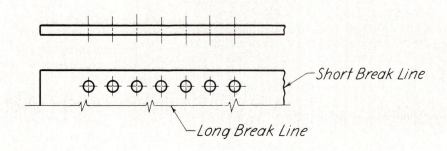

—Short Break Line

—Long Break Line

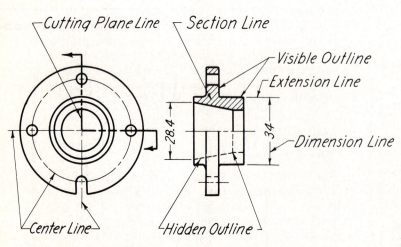

—Cutting Plane Line   — Section Line

—Visible Outline

—Extension Line

—Dimension Line

28.4   34

—Center Line   —Hidden Outline

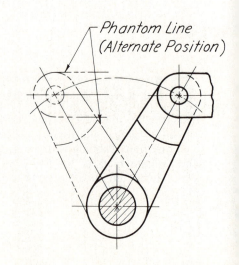

—Phantom Line (Alternate Position)

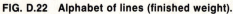

FIG. D.22   Alphabet of lines (finished weight).

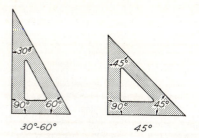

FIG. D.23   Triangles.

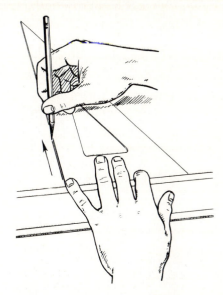

FIG. D.26   Drawing vertical lines.

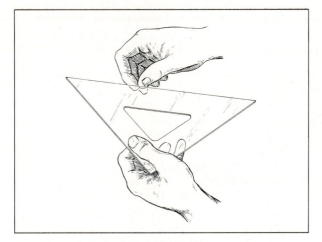

FIG. D.24   Testing a triangle for nicks.

D1.19   *Horizontal and Vertical Lines*

Horizontal lines are drawn along the top edge of the drafting straight edge, T-square, parallel bar, or drafting machine blade. A right-handed person draws horizontal lines left to right (Fig. D.25). A left-handed person draws horizontal lines right to left.

Vertical lines are drawn upward along the vertical leg of a triangle whose adjacent leg is supported by the drafting straight edge. In the case of a right-handed person, the triangle should be to the right of the line being drawn (Fig. D.26). Or, the vertical line may be drawn by setting the drafting-machine protractor head at zero degrees and bringing the vertical blade of the drafting machine into proper position (Fig. D.9). Either the 30° × 60° or the 45° triangle may be used because both have a right angle. The 30° × 60° triangle, however, is generally preferred because it usually has a longer perpendicular leg.

FIG. D.25   Drawing horizontal lines using a T-square.

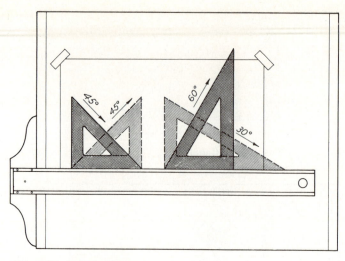

FIG. D.27 Inclined lines.

D1.20 *Inclined Lines*

Triangles are also used for drawing *inclined lines* of 30°, 60°, and 45° (Fig. D.27). Angles in multiples of 15° can be made with the two standard triangles and the drafting straight edge (Fig. D.28). Triangles, used singly or in combination, provide a useful method for dividing a circle into 4, 6, 8, 12, or 24 equal parts (Fig. D.29). These angles, as well as any others not divisible by 15, can also be drawn using the drafting machine.

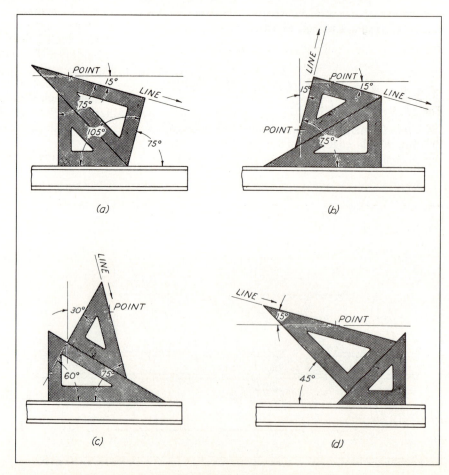

FIG. D.28 Drawing inclined lines with triangles.

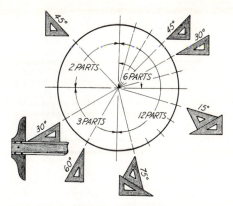

FIG. D.29   To divide a circle into 4, 6, 8, 12, or 24 equal parts.

D1.21 *Parallel Lines*

Triangles are used in combination to draw a line parallel to a given line. To draw such a line, place an edge of a triangle, supported by a straight edge or another triangle, along the given line. Then, slide the triangle as shown in Fig. D.30 to the new position and draw the parallel line along the triangle's same edge.

This process is greatly simplified by using a drafting machine. Unlock the protractor head and align the blade edge with the given line. Lock the protractor in this position. Move the drafting machine to the new position and draw the parallel line using the same edge (Fig. D.9).

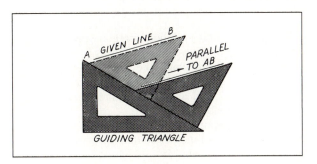

FIG. D.30   To draw a line parallel to a given line.

D1.22 *Perpendicular Lines*

Either the *sliding triangle method* (Fig. D.31[*a*]) or the *revolved triangle method* (Fig. D.31[*b*]) may be used to draw a line perpendicular to a given line. When using the sliding triangle method, adjust to the given line a side of a triangle that is adjacent to the right angle. Guide the side opposite the right angle with a second triangle, as shown in Fig. D.31(*a*); then slide the first triangle along the guiding triangle until it is in the required position for drawing the perpendicular along the other edge adjacent to the right angle.

Although the revolved triangle method (Fig. D.31[*b*]) is not so quickly done, it is widely used. To draw a perpendicular using this method, along the given line align the hypotenuse of a triangle, one leg of which is guided by a straightedge or another triangle; then hold the guiding member in position and revolve the triangle about the right angle until the other leg is against the guiding edge. The new position of the hy-

The protractor readout on the drafting machine head registers deviation from 0° (horizontal). Incremental deviation from an inclined line can be laid out by resetting zero degrees equal to the inclined line.

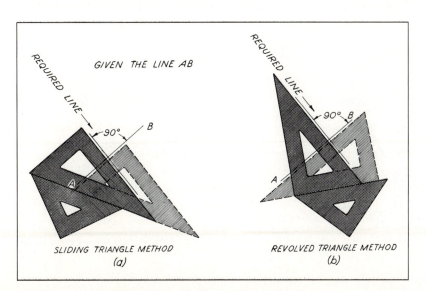

FIG. D.31   To draw a line perpendicular to another line.

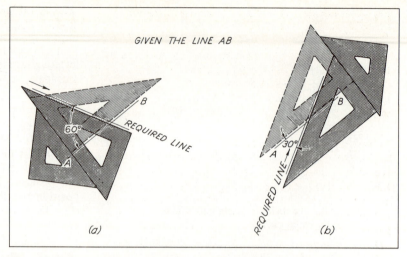

GIVEN THE LINE AB

(a)

(b)

FIG. D.32   To draw lines making 30°, 45°, or 60° with a given line.

potenuse will be perpendicular to its previous location along the given line and, when moved to the required position, may be used as a ruling edge for the desired perpendicular.

D1.23 *Inclined Lines at 15°, 30°, 45°, 60°, or 75° with an Oblique Line*

A line making an angle with an oblique line equal to any angle of a triangle may be drawn with the triangles. The two methods previously discussed for drawing perpendicular lines are applicable with slight modifications. To draw an oblique line using the revolved triangle method (Fig. D.32[a]), adjust the edge that is opposite the required angle along the given line; then revolve the triangle about the required angle, slide it into position, and draw the required line along the side opposite the required angle.

To use the sliding triangle method (Fig. D.32[b]), adjust to the given line one of the edges adjacent to the required angle, and guide the side opposite the required angle with a straight edge; then slide the triangle into position and draw the required line along the other adjacent side.

To draw a line making a 75° angle with a given line, place the triangles together so that the sum of a pair of adjacent angles equals 75°, and adjust one side of the angle thus formed to the given line; then slide the triangle, whose leg forms the other side of the angle, across the given line into position, and draw the required line, as shown in Fig. D.33(a).

To draw a line at 15° to a given line, select any two angles whose difference is 15°. Adjust to the given line a side adjacent to one of these angles, and guide the side adjacent with a straightedge. Remove the first triangle and substitute the other so that one adjacent side of the angle to be subtracted is along the guiding edge, as shown in Fig. D.33(b); then slide the triangle into position and draw along the other adjacent side.

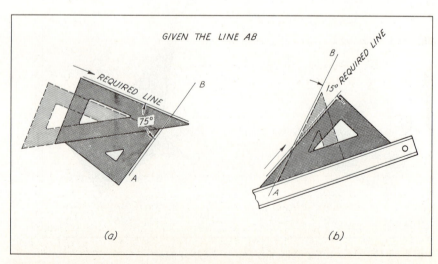

GIVEN THE LINE AB

(a)

(b)

FIG. D.33   To draw lines making 15° or 75° with a given line.

D1.24 Scales—Inches and Feet

A number of *scales* are available for various types of engineering design. For convenience, however, all scales may be classified according to their use as mechanical engineers' scales (both fractional and decimal), civil engineer's scales, architects' scales, or metric scales.

The *mechanical engineers' scales* are generally of the full-divided type, graduated proportionately to give reductions based on inches. On one form (Fig. D.34) the principal units are divided into the common fractions of an inch (4, 8, 16, and 32 parts). The scales are indicated as eighth size ($1\frac{1}{2}$ in = 1 ft), quarter size (3 in = 1 ft), half size (6 in = 1 ft), and full size.

Decimal scales are more widely used in industrial drafting rooms. The full size decimal scale shown in Fig. D.35, which has the principal units (inches) divided into fiftieths, is particularly suited for use with the two-place decimal system. The half-size, three-eighths size, and quarter-size scales (Fig. D.38) have the principal units divided into tenths.

The *civil engineers'* (chain) *scales* (Fig. D.36) are full divided and are graduated in decimal parts, usually 10, 20, 30, 40, 50, 60, 80, and 100 divisions to the inch.

Architects' scales (Fig. D.37) differ from mechanical engineers' scales in that the divisions represent a foot, and the end units are divided into inches, half

inches, quarter inches, and so forth (6, 12, 25, 48, or 96 parts). The usual scales are $\frac{1}{8}$ in = 1 ft, $\frac{1}{4}$ in = 1 ft, $\frac{3}{8}$ in = 1 ft, $\frac{1}{2}$ in = 1 ft, 1 in = 1 ft, $1\frac{1}{2}$ in = 1 ft, and 3 in = 1 ft.

The sole purpose of the scale is to *reproduce the dimensions of an object full size on a drawing or to reduce or enlarge them to some regular proportion,* such as eighth size, quarter size, half size, or double size. The scales of reduction most frequently used are as follows.

Fractional

Mechanical Engineers' Scales	
Full size	($1'' = 1''$)
Half size	($\frac{1}{2}'' = 1''$)
Quarter size	($\frac{1}{4}'' = 1''$)
Eighth size	($\frac{1}{8}'' = 1''$)

Architects' or Mechanical Engineers' Scales		
Full size	($12'' = 1'\text{-}0$)	
Half size	($6'' = 1'\text{-}0$)	
Quarter size	($3'' = 1'\text{-}0$)	
Eighth size	($1\frac{1}{2}'' = 1'\text{-}0$)	
$1'' = 1'\text{-}0$		$\frac{1}{4}'' = 1'\text{-}0$
$\frac{3}{4}'' = 1'\text{-}0$		$\frac{3}{16}'' = 1'\text{-}0$
$\frac{1}{2}'' = 1'\text{-}0$		$\frac{1}{8}'' = 1'\text{-}0$
$\frac{3}{8}'' = 1'\text{-}0$		$\frac{3}{32}'' = 1'\text{-}0$

FIG. D.34 Mechanical engineers' scale, full-divided.

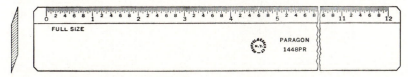

FIG. D.35 Engineers' decimal scale.

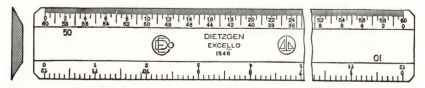

FIG. D.36 Civil engineers' scale.

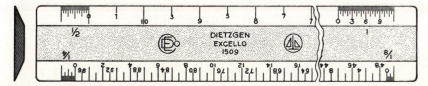

FIG. D.37 Architects' scale, open-divided.

Decimal

Mechanical Engineers' Scales	
Full size	(1.00″ = 1.00″)
Half size	(0.50″ = 1.00″)
Three-eighths size	(0.375″ = 1.00″)
Quarter size	(0.25″ = 1.00″)

Civil Engineers' Scales		
10 scale:	1″ = 1′;	1″ = 10′;
	1″ = 100′;	1″ = 1000′
20 scale:	1″ = 2′;	1″ = 20′;
	1″ = 200′;	1″ = 2000′
30 scale:	1″ = 3′;	1″ = 30′;
	1″ = 300′;	1″ = 3000′
40 scale:	1″ = 4′;	1″ = 40′;
	1″ = 400′;	1″ = 4000′
50 scale:	1″ = 5′;	1″ = 50′;
	1″ = 500′;	1″ = 5000′
60 scale:		1″ = 60′; etc.
80 scale:		1″ = 80′; etc.

The first four scales, full size, half size, quarter size, and eighth size, are the ones most frequently selected for drawing machine parts, although other scales can be used. Since objects drawn by structural draftsmen and architects vary from small to very large, scales from full size to $\frac{3}{32}$ in = 1 ft ($\frac{1}{128}$ size) are commonly encountered. For maps, the civil engineers' decimal scales having 10, 20, 30, 40, 50, 60, and 80 divisions to the inch are used to represent 10, 20, 30 ft, and so forth, to the inch.

On a machine drawing, it is considered good practice to omit the inch marks (″) in a scale specification. For example, a scale may be specified as: FULL SIZE, 1.00 = 1.00, or 1 = 1; HALF SIZE, .50 = 1.00, or $\frac{1}{2}$ = 1; and so forth.

The decimal scales shown in Fig. D.38 have been approved by the American National Standards Institute for making machine drawings when the decimal system is used.

It is essential that drafters always think and speak of each dimension as full size when scaling measurements, because the dimension figures given on the finished drawing indicate full-size measurements of the finished piece, regardless of the scale used.

The reading of an open-divided scale is illustrated in Fig. D.39 with the eighth-size ($1\frac{1}{2}$ in = 1 ft) scale shown. The dimension can be read directly as 21 in, the 9 in being read in the divided segment to the left of the zero point. Each long open division represents 12 in (1 ft).

The reading of the full-size decimal scale is illustrated in Fig. D.40. The largest division indicated in the illustration represents 1 in., which is subdivided into tenths and fifieths (.02 in). In Fig. D.38 the largest divisions on the half-size, three-eighths-size, and quarter-size decimal scales represent 1 in.

D1.25 *Metric Scales*

The *metric scale* (Figs. D41 and D42) is used in those countries where the meter is the standard of linear measurement.

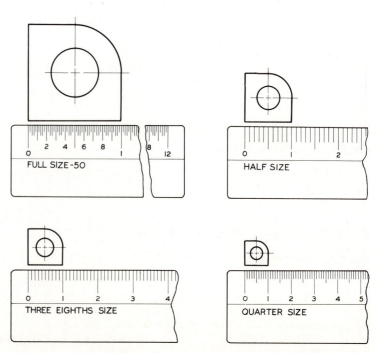

FIG. D.38 Decimal scales.

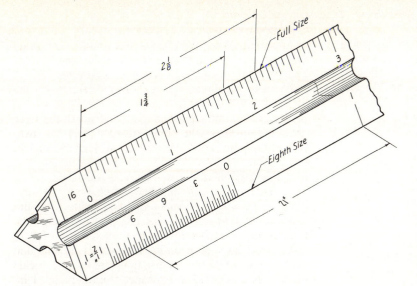

FIG. D.39 Reading a scale.

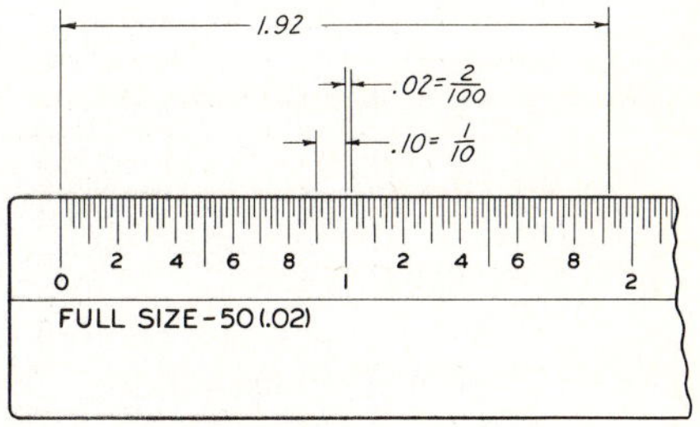

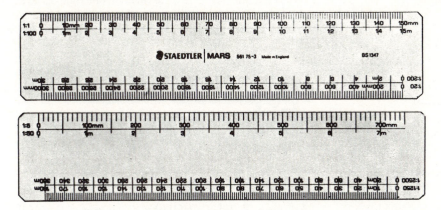

FIG. D.40 Reading a decimal scale.

FIG. D.41 Flat metric scale (front and reverse sides). (*Courtesy J. S. Staedtler, Inc.*)

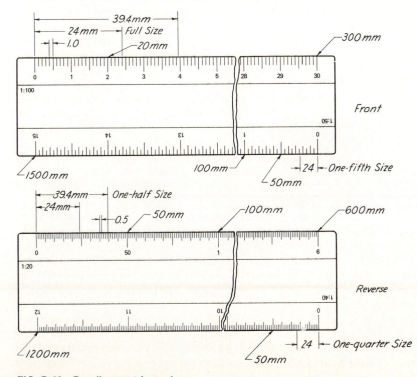

FIG. D.42 Reading metric scales.

Since the millimeter is the standard SI unit for linear dimensions, scales for drawing are marked in millimeters so that they can be read directly. The following scales for reduction and enlargement are recommended for the drawing of machine parts.

Reduced Scales	Enlarged Scales
1:2	2:1
1:3	3:1
1:5	5:1
1:10	10:1

1:2.5 and 2.5:1 scales may be used where available. The scales commonly used in the several fields are

Mechanical Engineers' Scales	
1:2.5	1:25
1:5	1:33⅓
1:10	1:50
1:15	1:80
1:20	1:100

Civil Engineers' Scales	
1:100	1:750
1:200	1:1000
1:300	1:1250
1:400	1:1500
1:500	1:2000
1:600	1:2500
1:625	1:3000

Architects' Scales	
1:1	1:125
1:2	1:200
1:5	1:250
1:10	1:300
1:20	1:400
1:25	
1:50	1:500
1:100	

The reading of distance values along the four scales of a flat scale (front and reverse sides) are shown in Fig. D.42.

To lay off a measurement, using a scale starting at the left of the rule, align the scale in the direction of the measurement with the zero of the scale being used toward the left. After it has been adjusted to the correct location, make short marks opposite the divisions on the scale that establish the desired distance (Fig. D.43). For ordinary work most draftsmen use the same pencil used for the layout. When extreme accuracy is necessary, however, it is better practice to use a sharp point and make slight indentations (not holes)

at the required points. If a regular point is not available, the dividers may be opened to approximately 60° and the point of one leg used as a substitute.

To ensure accuracy, place the eye directly over the division to be marked, hold the marking instrument perpendicular to the paper directly in front of the scale division, and mark the point. Always check the location of the point before removing the scale. If a slight indentation is made, it will be covered by the finished line; if a short mark is made and it is very light, it will be unnoticeable on the finished drawing.

To set off a measurement (say 68 mm) to half size, the scale indicated either as 1:2 or 1:20 should be used. If the measurement is to be made from left to right, place the 0 division mark on the given line, and make an indentation (or mark) opposite the 68 division point (Fig. D.43[*a*]). The distance from the line to the point represents 68 mm, although it is actually 34 mm. To set off the same measurement from right to left, place the 68 mark on the given line, and make an indentation opposite the zero division mark (Fig. D.43[*b*]).

D2 COMPUTER-AIDED DRAWING EQUIPMENT

D2.1 Introduction to Graphic Computers

Computers are being widely accepted by business, industry, science, and education as tools for problem solving and information processing. Some computers are capable of bringing major computing power to users who have not been able in the past to afford any type of computer. The computer that only a few years ago occupied an entire room now sits on a desk. In order to discuss computers, certain abbreviations are used for long and difficult terms. The first time such terms are presented in this text they are spelled out in full with their common abbreviations given. Subsequent references use only the abbreviations. (See the glossary of computer graphic terms in the Appendix.)

CADD computers may be defined by the number of users each can support. *Mainframe* CADD computers may support hundreds of users. *Minicomputers* allow up to a dozen designers to share information and divide workload. *Microcomputers* are personal design tools that may or may not be connected to other microcomputers, minicomputers, or mainframes. The system shown in Fig. D.44 supports several CADD workstations.

Within the last few years microcomputers have become widely used for CADD, CAD, and CAM. These relatively low-cost machines have been made possible by the development of the *integrated circuit* (IC). It

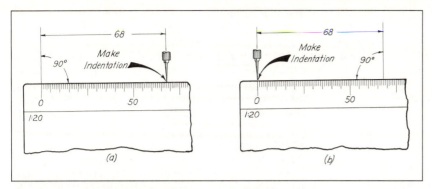

FIG. D.43 To lay off a measurement—metric scale.

FIG. D.44 Computer-aided drafting system. The unit appearing in the left foreground is the graphics processor. Behind the processor is a high-speed pen plotter. (*Courtesy Computervision Corporation*)

may be hard to believe, but it is possible for more than one million electronic components, like transistors, resistors, and capacitors, to be assembled on an integrated circuit less than half the size of a person's thumbnail.

Since the microcomputer will be the basis for most engineering workstations, it is important to understand the common components found in these units. Microcomputers are composed of the following:

• *Microprocessor* or CPU

• Several *specialized integrated circuits* that provide memory, control, sound, and graphics

• Devices that allow *interaction* with the computer (input and output, called I/O).

The CPU functions include processing data, calling data from storage, executing the instructions of a program, and transferring information between storage and I/O devices. In addition, the CPU controls the logic section which performs math functions, makes decisions, and selects and converts data. The CPU is the "smart" section of the computer.

The microcomputer has two general types of memory:

• Random-access memory (RAM)

• Read-only memory (ROM).

Information in RAM is changeable. It is lost by storing new information in the same location. Information in ROM provides permanent storage of instructions. This information cannot be changed nor erased. Instructions stored in ROM are called *firmware*. Programs stored in RAM are called *software*. There are specialized types of ROM that can be programmed (PROM) or erased and reprogrammed (EPROM) by the user.

D2.2 I/O Devices

Using a graphics computer involves the following three processes:

1. *Input* of instructions and geometric data

2. *Processing* of data

3. *Output* in a visual form that can be understood by humans.

In the case of a CADD system, input data describes the shape of the part, that is the spatial relationship of planes, holes, and other features. The *instructions* are the commands the operator gives the computer to view the geometry from different vantage points (views) or to combine, delete, modify, or move the image.

Once the data has been entered and the instructions given, the computer acts on those instructions, altering the description of the part in computer memory. The more detailed and nonlinear the design, the longer it takes the computer to do its job. Remember, part geometry is held in the computer as a set of numbers. To change the design, the computer changes the numbers and their relationship to one another.

Once this processing is completed, the operator needs a visual indication of the changes that were made. It would be too difficult (even impossible) to review the numeric data base for anything other than the most simple geometry. For this reason, graphic computers display the image defined by the data base on a display device called a monitor. If a more transportable and permanent record of the data is needed, a print of the image or a *hard copy* can be made.

The process of getting information in and out of a computer is called *I/O.*

D2.3 The Monitor

The *monitor* is the most crucial I/O device in a graphic computer system. By displaying text and the representation of graphic shapes and designs on the screen, the computer communicates with its human partner. In turn, the operator can communicate by giving instructions, verifying data, or adding new features to the design.

High-quality monitors present the image just as it would appear on a finished drawing. The sharpness of a monitor is measured in *resolution,* the number of horizontal and vertical dots that make up the screen (for example 1,024 dots vertical by 780 dots horizontal). Of more importance is the number of dots in each inch (dpi). The greater the number of dots per inch, the finer the resolution.

There are two general types of monitors, each designed for specific applications.

1. Direct view storage tube (DVST) displays are very sharp but have long redisplay times,

2. Raster displays are like TVs, with constantly changing scan lines and patterns of dots.

D2.4 CADD Workstation

CADD activity is centered around the CADD workstation. The workstation may be part of several monitors arranged in a group, sharing the same graphics computer (Fig. D.45). Or, the workstation may be a single unit connected to a *host* computer that is some distance away. More likely, the modern CADD workstation is a desktop microcomputer connected in a network to a larger CADD computer. This provides the

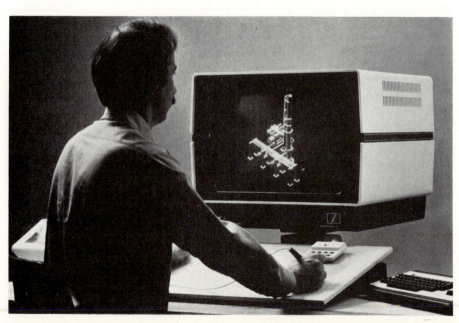

FIG. D.45 CRT terminal. (*Courtesy Computervision Corporation*)

engineer or technologist with both a personal productivity tool and an entry point (*node*) to a larger computing environment.

The key to this distributed graphics system is the sharing of *I/O peripherals:* The printers, plotters, digitizers, and scanners are not at the workstation but are on the CADD network, available when needed. The typical CADD workstation consists of the following:

1. Powerful microcomputer

2. Graphics and application software

3. Input device like a mouse or digitizing pad with pen

4. Communications hardware and software for networking.

D2.5 *Printers and Plotters*

A *printer* gives a computer the capability to create paper or hard copy of textual material such as bills of material, parts lists, and schedules. Most computer printers are *dot matrix printers* that create characters with small dots arranged in a way that forms a letter or a numeral. Many dot matrix printers can also print drawings, but at a low, 75- to 150-dpi resolution. *Laser printers* use much more sophisticated technology to print text and drawings at an acceptable 300 to 600 dpi. Some graphic computers have hard copy units attached directly to each monitor so that quick copies can be made for review. In the engineering design room, a hard copy might be requested by a designer to check the dimensions and notations on a drawing executed from a sketch. A hard copy printer can be used by a design group during the early stages of a design project. Copies can continue to be called for at later stages of the design to document the development of the project (see Chapter 12). Some of these prints may be included in both preliminary and final design reports.

When high-quality graphic prints are needed in sizes larger than that produced by a laser printer, plots are made by a *digital plotter*. Plotters use wet ink, felt tip, or ball point pens to draw on paper or polyester drafting film. Commercial plotters accommodate multiple pens, making possible varying line color. Plotters are available in several forms, commonly identified as

- Drum plotters (Fig. D.46)
- Beltbed plotters (Fig. D.47)
- Flatbed plotters (Fig. D.48).

The least expensive is the *drum plotter*, which has a drum on which paper is placed (Fig. D.46). The paper, with perforated holes along the edges, engages sprockets at both ends of the drum. A large drum plotter can take paper as wide as 36 in.

The *beltbed plotter* makes possible the use of *cut sheet* paper or polyester film, while providing the com-

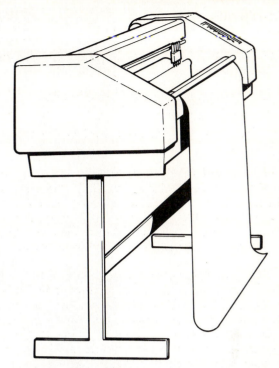

FIG. D.46 Drum plotter.

pactness of the drum plotter. Four or more pens can be resident in the plotter at one time, and users can select from 16 pen widths. All that the operator has to do is select the color and width of the pens to be installed in the pen carriage. Smaller models can handle up to ANSI size D or ISO size A1. Larger models are for bigger drawings, up to ANSI size E or ISO size AO (Fig. D.47).*

There are a number of small, inexpensive *flatbed plotters* available for CADD systems. More expensive flatbed plotters feature a carriage designed for motion in two directions (Fig. D.48). Depending on the model, a flatbed plotter can have a horizontal, vertical, or tilting table. Although the horizontal table requires more floor space than a vertical table and cannot be viewed as easily, it has advantages that cause it to be favored when very accurate work is required. A tilting table can be horizontal or can be adjusted to almost vertical.

* Standard paper sizes.

American Standard in inches	International Standard in millimeters
A 8.5 × 11.0	A4 210 × 297
B 11.0 × 17.0	A3 297 × 420
C 17.0 × 22.0	A2 420 × 594
D 22.0 × 34.0	A1 594 × 841
E 34.0 × 44.0	A0 841 × 1189

FIG. D.47   Beltbed plotters.
(*Courtesy CalComp*)

Commercial plotters often have a pen carriage that revolves, bringing the desired pen station into position. Each station can accommodate the types of pens mentioned earlier or can be loaded with pencils or scribes for cutting film.

The plotter shown in Fig. D.49 combines automatic digitizing (a process of identifying X and Y points on an existing drawing) and high-speed plotting in one complete system. Its capabilities include data and drawing management, display, editing, I/O, and numerical machining tape (NC) production (see Chapter 18). These capabilities make this system ideal for processing quantities of large-size drawings and NC machine tool tapes. The hardware components of this type of plotter-digitizer include the following:

• CPU capable of controlling the unit while drafting or digitizing

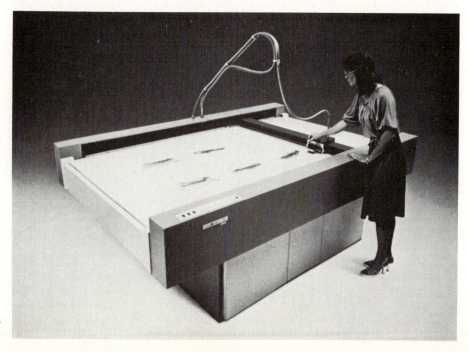

FIG. D.48   Flatbed plotter.
(*Courtesy Calcomp*)

FIG. D.49 **Automatic drafting-digitizing system** (*Courtesy The Gerber Scientific Instrument Company*)

- Punched tape reader to read existing NC tapes
- Tape punch to generate new NC machining tapes
- Keyboard for entering data and instructions
- Operator control console
- Plotting and digitizing table
- Optical line follower.

The *electrostatic printer/plotter,* shown in Fig. D.50, plots data many times faster than a conventional pen plotter. Using an electronic matrix, an electrostatic printer prints dots on charge-sensitive paper. Special paper and chemicals are required with this process. It produces prints up to 72 in wide and functions as a large-scale version of a laser printer or rasterizer.

By using a MODEM (MOdulator-DEModulator), a graphics computer may be connected to other computers using phone lines, dedicated wires, or microwave. With a MODEM, a small computer can gain access to a large data bank of drawings in another computer system.

FIG. D.50 **Electrostatic printer-plotter.** (*Courtesy CalComp*)

D2.6 *Digitizing*

If plotting is a process of taking digital or numeric information and turning it into a drawing, *digitizing* is the process that takes a drawing and turns it into a digital data base or *file*. With any CADD system, there are always some drawings that exist on paper—sketches or engineering drawings made prior to computerization or received from noncomputerized vendors. Graphic data needed for lines, points, planes,

FIG. D.51   Digitizing tablet. (*Courtesy Computervision Corporation*)

arcs, circles, and special curves must be input to the computer. The input process for taking X (width), Y (height), and Z (depth) coordinates off a drawing is known as *digitizing*.

The digitizing process requires the use of a *digitizer*, which consists of either a digitizing tablet or a board similar to a drawing board (see Figs. D.51 and D.52). In a way, digitizing is much like tracing with a tracer. The tracer in this case is an input device called a *mouse, puck*, or a *stylus* that, when traced over a drawing, feeds the coordinates of the image directly into the computer.

A *digitizing tablet* is well suited for interactive design since the designer can work naturally and freely and at the same time see results on the screen. At the user's command, the computer can straighten lines and present an accurate drawing. Figure D.53 shows the use of a digitizing tablet.

Since designers easily think in three-dimensions, three-dimensional digitizing opens many new possibilities for CAD/CAM. A three-dimensional digitizer (Fig. D.54) provides Z-axis information in addition to X and Y. It does so without complicated operations, making it extremely easy to manipulate three-dimensional data when digitizing complex and irregular shapes. The three-dimensional display shown in the monitor in Fig. D.54 was created by tracing the physical object.

Commercial digitizing equipment may contain an *optical line follower*, as shown in Fig. D.55. The line follower contains a light source for illuminating the digitizing surface, a light sensing device, a television camera, and a three-station tool holder. While the light-sensing device transmits signals to the digitizer's computer, the television camera transmits a magnified view of the area being digitized to the operator.

Another form of digitizing is called *scanning*. This uses a *raster-to-vector converter* to scan a drawing and translate the visual picture into geometric data (vectors) understood by the CADD system (Fig. D.56). This process can also go the other way, in a vector-to-raster conversion. This is done to send vector data stored in a CADD system to a raster printer, such as a laser printer, capable of printing dot resolution.

D2.7 *Storing CADD Drawings*

A CADD drawing is called a *file*. These files are arranged in hierarchial *directories* and given very specific and descriptive names. A certain number of files are stored permanently in the computer for daily use. Most drawing files, however, are stored *off line* on specialized electronic storage devices like *magnetic tape* (Fig. D.57) or *removable disks* (Fig. D.58).

Drawing files stored in central-processing unit

FIG. D.52   Digitizing. (*Courtesy Computervision Corporation*)

FIG. D.53   Microcomputer drafting system. The drafter is using the digitizing tablet. (*Courtesy T&W Systems, Inc.*)

FIG. D.54   Digitizing an object in three dimensions. (*Courtesy CADKEY, Inc.*)

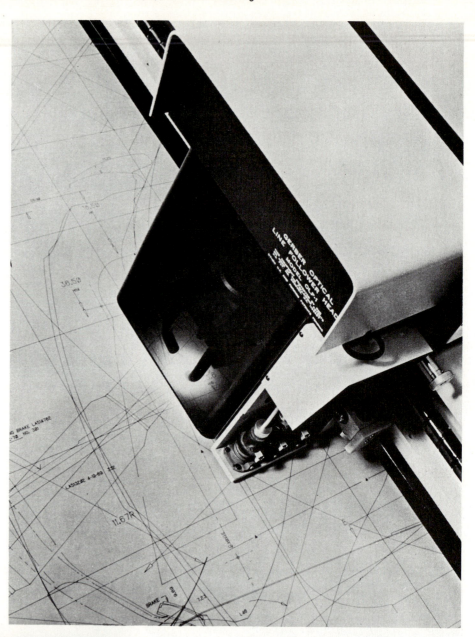

FIG. D.55   Optical Line Follower. (*Courtesy The Gerber Scientific Instrument Company*)

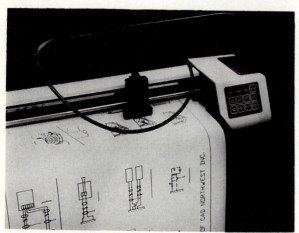

FIG. D.56   Scanning a drawing.

(CPU) memory are temporary and vanish when the computer is turned off or if the operator terminates a work session. This fact should never be forgotten. Information that needs to be retained indefinitely must be stored on disk or tape.

D2.8 *CADD Software*

The necessary sequential instructions to run a CADD system are provided by *software* programs. For discussion purposes it can be said that software falls into the following four categories:

FIG. D.57 Magnetic tape unit.

FIG. D.58 Disk storage.

1. Software for the operation of the system
2. Graphics instructions
3. Applications software
4. User-developed software.

The first three types can be purchased from producers of CADD software or original equipment manufacturers.

Operating system (OS) software makes possible the general operation of the CADD system. It provides for such tasks as memory allocation, the scheduling of the CPU, and the operation of the input and output devices, and the OS prioritizes operations and interruptions.

Graphic software enables the computer to process graphic data and prepare drawings and graphs complete with notations. To meet the requirements of designers and drafting technicians, graphic software must be designed to permit creating, editing, revising, correcting, and storing data for graphic primitives such as points, lines, planes, arcs, and circles in a way that is familiar and easy to learn. The way in which this is done is called the *user interface.*

CADD *applications software* is created for specific tasks in technical fields relating to design. Such software permits drafting technicians to perform drafting tasks like the preparation of layouts, shop drawings, and piping schematics. Applications software is available for electronic, structural, pictorial, highway, and map drafting. Some applications software *postprocesses* the data base after creation on a CADD system.

Although CADD operators rarely develop their own software, they should be familiar with the several types of software required for the operation of the total system. User software is task-specific for applications that are unique to a company. *User software* is usually prepared by the company pro-grammer, possibly assisted by the drafting technician. One common example of user software is the creation of specialized menus for input. Menu-driven programs may also be purchased from producers of software or the makers of CADD systems as part of the total system. *Macrocommands,* another form of user software, are a way of executing commonly used steps in sequence with a single command.

A CADD menu is a common input device having a pattern of squares on the digitizing surface to which CADD functions are assigned (see Fig. D.59). When a square is touched by an electronic stylus, the command assigned to that square is executed. The command may be represented in the box by a word, number, shape, value, or symbol. Because of the menu, the CADD operator finds it easy to prepare a drawing with frequently used symbols and then add all the notations to complete it. The menu is one example of user interface.

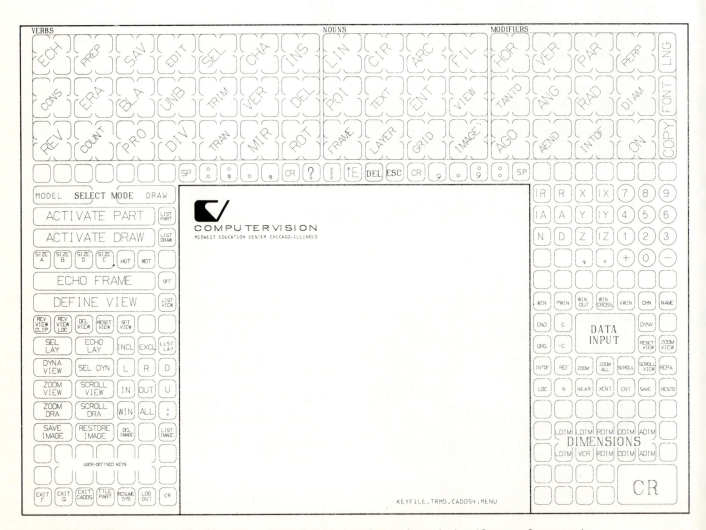

FIG. D.59 Menu form used in conjunction with a digitizing board as an input device. (*Courtesy Computervision Corporation*)

D3 TECHNICAL LETTERING—MANUAL, MECHANICAL, AND CADD

D3.1 Introduction to Manual Lettering

To present a complete *shape description* of a machine or structure, the drawing must be accompanied by *size description*—dimensions, notes, and text (Fig. D.60). On traditional engineering drawings, dimensions and notes are lettered in a plain, legible style that can be rapidly executed. Poor lettering detracts from the appearance of a drawing and often impairs its usefulness, regardless of the quality of the line work.

D3.2 Technical Lettering, Single-Stroke Letters

Single-stroke letters are used universally for technical drawings. This style is suitable for most purposes because it is legible and can be written quickly. On commercial drawings it appears in slightly variant forms since each person develops a unique style.

Single stroke means that the straight and curved lines that form the letters are the same width as the stroke of the pen or pencil.

D3.3 General Proportions of Letters

Although there is no fixed standard for the proportions of hand lettering, certain rules must be observed if the lettering is to appear neat, readable, and pleasing. The best way to acquire lettering ability is to develop good lettering practices. Study the example of letter form in Fig. D.60 and try to make your own lettering appear the same. Master the form first and then develop speed. It is advisable for the beginner, instead of relying on his untrained eye for proportions, to follow the fixed proportions shown in Figs. D.67 to D.72. Otherwise, the lettering will probably be displeasing to the trained eye of a professional. Later, after thoroughly mastering the art of lettering, individuality will be revealed naturally by light variations in the shapes and proportions of some of the letters.

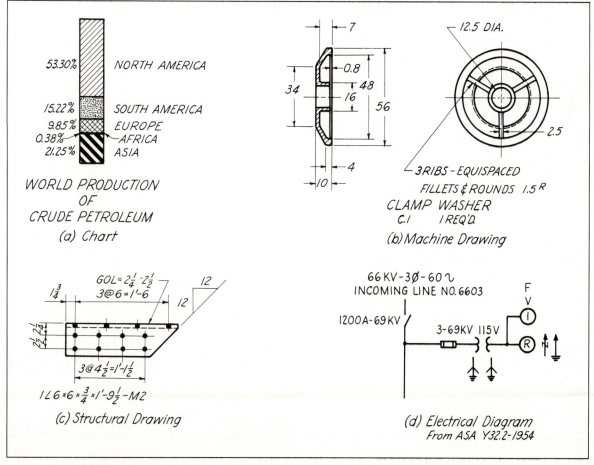

FIG. D.60   Technical drawings.

NORMAL LETTERS

COMPRESSED LETTERS

EXTENDED LETTERS

FIG. D.61 Compressed and extended letters.

It is often desirable to increase or decrease the width of letters in order to make a word or group of words fill a certain space. Letters narrower than normal are called *compressed letters;* those that are wider are called *extended letters* (Fig. D.61).

D3.4 *Uniformity and Composition in Lettering*

Uniformity in height, inclination, spacing, and strength of line are essential for good lettering (Fig. D.62). Professional appearance depends as much on uniformity as on the correctness of the proportion and shape of individual letters. Uniformity in height and inclination is assured by the use of guide and slope lines (Fig. D.63). Uniformity of weight and darkness is controlled by the type of pencil used and the pressure of its point on the paper.

In combining letters into words, the spaces for the various combinations of letters are arranged so that the areas appear to be equal (Fig. D.64). For standard lettering, this area should be about equal to one-half the area of the letter M.

The space between words should be equal to or greater than the height of a letter but not more than twice the height. The space between sentences should be somewhat greater.

Devices for drawing guide lines are available in a variety of forms. The two most popular are the *Braddock lettering triangle* (Fig. D.65) and the *Ames lettering guide* (Fig. D.66). Under no circumstance should technical lettering be attempted without the use of guide lines.

The Braddock lettering triangle is provided with sets of grouped holes that may be used to draw lines by inserting a sharp pointed pencil (4H or 6H lead) in the holes and sliding the triangle back and forth along a straight edge (Fig. D.65). The holes are grouped to give guide lines for capitals and lowercase letters. The numbers below each set indicates the height of the capitals in thirty-seconds of an inch. For example, the number 3 set of holes is for capitals $\frac{3}{32}$-in high, the number 4 set, for capitals $\frac{1}{8}$-in high, and so on. For metric drawing, dimension letters should be 3.5- to 5-mm high and the drawing number and title should be 7 mm in height.

UNIFORMITY IN HEIGHT, INCLINATION, AND STRENGTH OF LINE IS ESSENTIAL FOR GOOD LETTERING

FIG. D.62 Uniformity in lettering.

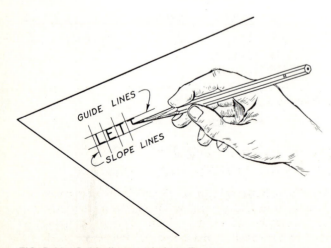

FIG. D.63 Guide lines and slope lines.

POOR

GOOD

FIG. D.64 Letter areas.

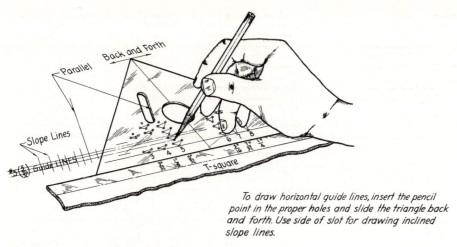

To draw horizontal guide lines, insert the pencil point in the proper holes and slide the triangle back and forth. Use side of slot for drawing inclined slope lines.

FIG. D.65 Braddock lettering triangle.

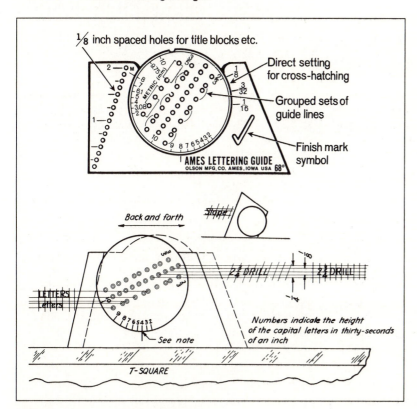

FIG. D.66 Ames lettering instrument.

D3.5 Technique of Freehand Lettering

Any prospective engineer or technologist can learn to letter by practicing intelligently and maintaining a persistent desire to improve. The necessary muscular control, which must accompany the knowledge of lettering, can only be developed through constant repetition.

Pencil letters should be formed with strokes that are dark and sharp, never with strokes that are grey and indistinct. Beginners should avoid the tendency to form letters by sketching, as strokes made in this manner vary in darkness and width.

D3.6 Inclined and Vertical Letters and Numerals

The letters shown in Figs. D.67 and D.68 have been arranged in related groups. In laying out the characters, the number of widths and strokes have been reduced to the smallest number consistent with good appearance, similarities of shape have been empha-

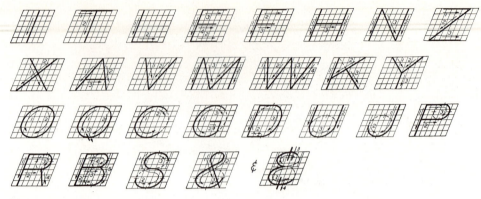

FIG. D.67 **Inclined capital letters.**

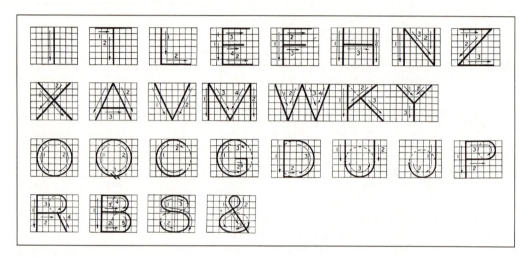

FIG. D.68 **Vertical capital letters.**

sized, and minute differences have been eliminated. Arrows with numbers indicate the direction and order of the strokes. The curves of the inclined letters are portions of ellipses, while the curves of vertical letters are parts of circles.

The numerals shown in Figs. D.69 and D.70 have been arranged in related groups in accordance with the

common characteristics that can be recognized in their construction.

Study the letterforms, noting the placement of cross bars and the proportions of upper and lower parts of each letter. Try to make your own lettering look like the example in Fig. D.62.

Single-stroke lower case letters (Figs. D.71 and

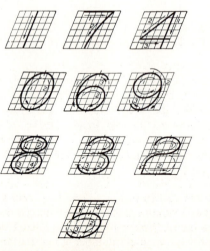

FIG. D.69 **Inclined numerals.**

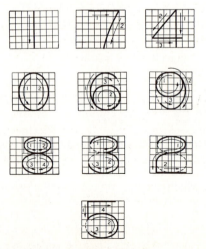

FIG. D.70 **Vertical numerals.**

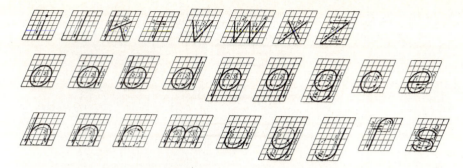

FIG. D.71 Inclined lowercase letters.

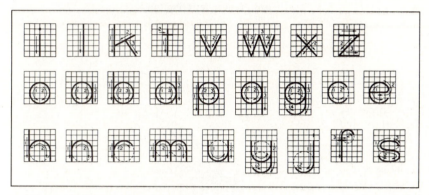

FIG. D.72 Vertical lowercase letters.

D.72), either vertical or inclined, are commonly used on map drawings, topographic drawings, structural drawings, and in survey field books. They are particularly suited for long notes and statements because they can be executed much faster than capitals and words and statements formed with them can be read more easily.

D3.7 *Large and Small Caps in Combination*

Many commercial draftsmen use a combination of large and small capital letters in forming words, as illustrated in Fig. D.73. When this style is used, the height of the small caps should be approximately three-fifths the height of the standard capital letter.

D3.8 *Fractions*

The height of each of the numbers in the numerator and demoninator is equal to three-fourths the height of a non-fractional number, and the total height of the

HANDLE PIN

C.R.S. 1 REQ'D.

FIG. D.73 Use of large and small caps.

FIG. D.74 Fraction height.

fraction is twice the height of this number. The division bar should be horizontal and centered between the fraction numerals, as shown in Fig. D.74. It should be noted that the axis of the fraction bisects both numerator and denominator and is parallel to the axis of the whole number.

D3.9 *Titles*

Every drawing, sketch, graph, chart, or diagram has some form of descriptive title to impart certain necessary information and to identify it. On machine drawings, where speed and legibility are prime requirements, titles are usually single stroke. On display drawings, maps, and the like, which call for an artistic effect, the titles are usually composed of "built-up" ornate letters.

Figure D.75 shows a title block that might be used on a machine drawing. It should be noted that the important items are made more prominent by the use of larger letters formed with heavier lines. Less important information, such as the scale, date, drafting information, and so on, are given less prominence.

MK	QTY	DESCRIPTION	PART NO.	VENDOR
43	1	BASE PLATE	A-538	—

METALTECH
DIVISION OF UNITED METALS

P.O. BOX 1471
LOS ANGELES, CA
93940

DRAWING TILE

MATCH PLATE ASSMBLY

DWN *T.E.B.* CHK *P.M.M.* DRAWING NUMBER SHEET
USED ON *1428-325* DATE *1-9-87* **567E349** *1* OF *4*

FIG. D.75   Title block.

FIG. D.76   Use of a technical fountain pen and Rapido lettering guide. (*Courtesy Koh-I-Noor, Inc.*)

To be pleasing in appearance, a title should have some simple geometric form. An easy way to ensure the symmetry of a title is to count the letters and spaces, and then, working first toward the right from the middle, sketch the title lightly in pencil before lettering the final form. An alternative is to letter a trial title along the edge of a scrap piece of paper and place it in a balanced position just above the location of the line to be lettered.

D3.10 Mechanical Lettering Devices and Templates

Up to this point our discussion of lettering has been confined to *freehand lettering,* done with a pencil or pen with only the help of guidelines. There are several mechanical aids available which improve the legibility of manually produced letters.

Although mechanical lettering devices produce letters that may appear stiff to an expert, they are used in many drafting rooms for the simple reason that they enable even the most unskilled letterers to produce satisfactory results. These mechanical aids fall into three categories.

1. Lettering templates
2. Mechanical guides with scribes
3. Electronic lettering guides.

Lettering templates are an inexpensive alternative to freehand lettering. These plastic templates are held in place and moved along a straight edge while the inside of each letterform is traced (Fig. D.76). These plastic guides are available to produce letters of $\frac{3}{32}$ to $\frac{1}{2}$ in in height.

The *Leroy* lettering guide (Fig. D.77) uses a tracer and precision-cut guide to form each letter. As with lettering templates, the user must space each letter, but generally the results are better.

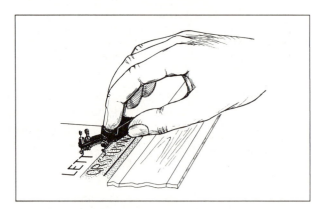

FIG. D.77   Leroy lettering device.

Electronic lettering guides work very much like the Leroy guide except that text is lettered as a complete note, and the machine takes care of letter spacing and alignment (Fig. D.78).

D3.11 Introduction to CADD Lettering

The purpose behind lettering an engineering drawing is the same for both manual and CADD drawings. Terminology and practices are different when using a computer to add text, however. A prospective draftsman or engineer should be familiar with this automated method of adding text to a drawing.

The obvious difference between manual and computer lettering is that manual lettering requires some measure of artistic skill where computer lettering requires typing skill and a knowledge of computer commands. The better the typing skill of the CADD operator, the more easily text is entered with fewer mistakes.

Text is created in two distinctly different ways in CADD. Text blocks, called *strings* can be identified by the computer as entities in the data base (like circles, lines, or arcs). As an entity, a block of text can be identified by its origin and scaled, rotated, inclined,

FIG. D.78 Electronic lettering guides.

moved, made bolder, and so on. This CADD text, however, is distinctly *different from word-processed text*. In the case of word-processed text, letters may be made larger or smaller, but they cannot be inclined, rotated, or moved independently of the text around them. There are times that word-processed text is more efficient for an engineering drawing, as for example when there are extensive bills of materials and specifications. Word-processed text requires considerably less space inside the computer than does CADD text.

D3.12 *Text Fonts*

A *text font* is a computer file of all the characters in a particular lettering style and size (Fig. D.79). The total number of characters in text fonts may vary due to specialized characters. Many CADD systems have a Leroy font that matches the lettering of the mechani-

ABCDEFGHIJKLMNOPQRSTUVWXYZ
abcdefghijklmnopqrstuvwxyz
1234567890
-_=+!@#$%^&()[]{};:'",<.>/?`~\|*
TEXT FONT(ITALIC) HEIGHT (.5 INCH)

ABCDEFGHIJKLMNOPQRSTUVWXYZ
abcdefghijklmnopqrstuvwxyz
1234567890
-_=+!@#$%^&*()[]{};:'",<.>/?`~\|
TEXT FONT(PLAIN) HEIGHT (.25 INCH)

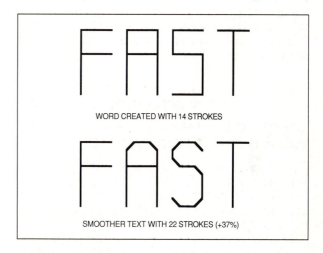

WORD CREATED WITH 14 STROKES

SMOOTHER TEXT WITH 22 STROKES (+37%)

FIG. D.80 Fast font.

cal lettering guide previously described in Sec. 2.43. Which font to use is generally a company standard.

One factor governing the choice of text font is the method by which CADD drawings will be reproduced. Digital plotters (see Sec. 2.30) produce curved letters as a series of short vector lines or strokes. The smoother the letters, the smaller and more numerous the strokes and the greater the amount of memory required to store the text. If the CADD drawing contains a considerable amount of text, it may take longer than feasible to plot. A solution to this is the choice of a *fast font* (Fig. D.80) where the minimum number of strokes are used to form each letter. For a text-intensive drawing, plotting times may be lowered by 75%. CADD drawings, electrostatically printed (like a photo copy) or laser printed, are converted from strokes or vectors to a pattern of dots called a *rasterized image*.

FIG. D.81 Stroke and raster text.

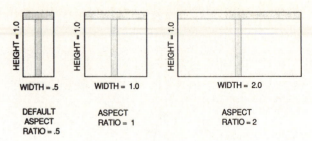

FIG. D.83 Results of changing text aspect ratio.

This process, called a vector-to-raster conversion, removes the plotting time benefit of a fast font (Fig. D.81).

D3.13 *Text Attributes*

All CADD text has assigned to it certain attributes, often called *parameters*. These attributes control how the text appears and where it is located on the drawing. All attributes have standard settings called *default parameters* which are in effect when the CADD system is started. If you want larger text with fatter lines, you have to change the default parameters. Any attribute may be changed for a particular instance of text, or every instance of text on a drawing may be changed at once. These text attributes or parameters include

1. Font
2. Size
3. Aspect ratio
4. Slant
5. Angle
6. Line font
7. Justification.

The *text size* attribute can be specified in a number of ways, but generally the height of the letter is what is important. Height can be specified as a fraction of an inch ($\frac{1}{4}$, $\frac{1}{2}$), a decimal fraction of an inch (.25, .50), in millimeters (25, 50), or by points (12, 14). The point system of text measurement is the standard used by commercial printers where 1 in = 72 points (Fig.

D.82). Because CADD computers often send their drawings to typesetting computers for the production of engineering documents, many CADD systems provide for this specification of text. The default text height may be .25 in, 12 mm, or 12 points.

The *aspect ratio* attribute controls the relationship of width to height. Text width may be 80% of its height by default. An aspect ratio of .5 would mean that each letter is 40% of its height (Fig. D.83). As with hand lettering, text that is narrower than normal is called condensed and that which is wider is called expanded. The default aspect ratio is 1, meaning that regardless of the text size, the width is automatically adjusted to 80% of its height.

The text attribute *slant* refers to the deviation of the text axis from vertical (Fig. D.84). The range of inclination can be from −45° to 45°. The default inclination is zero degrees, or vertical.

Text angle describes the deviation from horizontal of the text's *base line* (Fig. D.85). This allows text to be placed at any angle—horizontal, vertical, even upside down. The default text angle is zero degrees. This means that unless you specify otherwise, text is entered on a horizontal base line.

Line font is a number (1, 2, 3, etc.) that represents the type and thickness of the line in which the lettering is executed. Each letter stroke may be thin or fat, solid or dashed, black or in color. The default text line font is the solid black single stroke line (Fig. D.86).

Text justification determines where text will be aligned and the point on the text string that acts as its handle for identification. This identification handle is

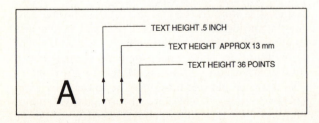

FIG. D.82 Text lettering.

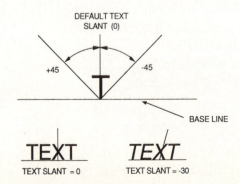

FIG. D.84 Text slants.

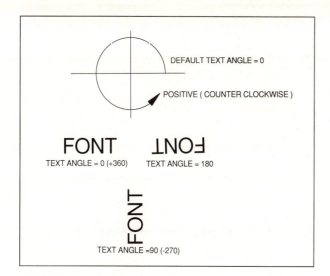

FIG. D.85   Text angle.

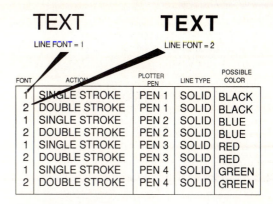

FIG. D.86   Line font.

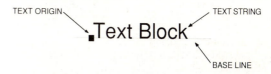

FONT	ACTION	PLOTTER PEN	LINE TYPE	POSSIBLE COLOR
1	SINGLE STROKE	PEN 1	SOLID	BLACK
2	DOUBLE STROKE	PEN 1	SOLID	BLACK
1	SINGLE STROKE	PEN 2	SOLID	BLUE
2	DOUBLE STROKE	PEN 2	SOLID	BLUE
1	SINGLE STROKE	PEN 3	SOLID	RED
2	DOUBLE STROKE	PEN 3	SOLID	RED
1	SINGLE STROKE	PEN 4	SOLID	GREEN
2	DOUBLE STROKE	PEN 4	SOLID	GREEN

referred to as the "origin" of the text and must be used to identify the piece of text for repositioning. Text may be left, right, or center justified at the base line, middle, or top (Fig. D.87). The default text justification is generally at the left base line in most CADD systems. The location of the handle, or origin, is critical because identification of the origin of a block of lettering is necessary for any or all of its attributes to be changed.

	BOTTOM	TOP	CENTER
L	■Text Block	■ Text Block	■Text Block
C	Text■Block	Text■Block	Text■Block
R	Text Block■	Text Block■	Text Block■

FIG. D.87   Text justification.

Index

A

Abbreviations, ANSI, 197–98
Adjustable curves, 210–11
Air-bag–seat-belt restraint system (Ford Motor Company), 21
Alarm, portable safety, 25
Aligned method of dimensioning, 112
American National Standards Institute (ANSI), 6, 173, 197–98
Ames lettering guide, 232, 233
Analysis, design, 26–27
Angle(s), 89
  bisecting, 73–74
  constructing, equal to given angle, 75
  dihedral, 99, 158–59
  dimensioning, 114, 115
  helix, 88
  in isometric drawings, 178–80
  multiview projection, 137–38
  oblique, 186–87
  text, 238, 239
  trisecting, 74
ANSI, 6, 173, 197–98
Anthropometric data, 18
Applications software, 230
Approximation, four-center, 180
Arc(s), 89. *See also* Circle arc(s)
  in CADD, 90
  dimensioning, 114, 115, 118
  as dimension line, 114
Archimedean screw and wheel, 12
Architects' scales, 217
Arm, Boston, 20
Arrowheads, 110
Aspect ratio, 238
Atlantis undersea habitat, 21
Attorney, patent, 33–35
Automatic dimensioning, 47–52
Automobiles, electronic control of, 14
Auxiliary lines, 208
Auxiliary views, 152–62
  partial and complete, 153, 159–60
  primary, 152–62
    bilateral, 156, 157
    constructing, 159
    curved lines in, 156–58
    dihedral angles, 158–59
    line of intersection, 160, 161–62
    projection of curved boundary, 158

    symmetrical and nonsymmetrical, 155–56
    types of, 152–54
    unilateral, 156, 157
  secondary (oblique), 161–62
  theory of projecting, 153
  use of, 152
Axis/axes, 66–67
  coordinate. *See under* Shape description
  isometric, 176, 182–83
  receding, 185, 187–88
Axonometric projection. *See* Pictorial drawing: isometric

B

Backing up drawings, 40
Ball bearings, sectioning, 169
Base-line dimensioning, 117
Basic plane theory of construction, 185–87
Beam compass, 210
Beltbed plotter, 223, 224
Belts, crossed and open, 83–84
Bezier curve, 91
Biomechanics, 18–19
Blind hole, 145
Blocking in oblique sketches, 69
Body motion, 19
Boltheads, multiview treatment of, 146, 147
Boolean operators, 93–94
Boston Arm, 20
Bow compass (large bow), 203–5, 209–10
Braddock lettering triangle, 232, 233
Brainstorming, 15–17
"Breaking down" method, 143
Breaks in drawing, 143, 149, 151
Broken section, 164–66
Built-up method, 66

C

Camera, Land, 13
Cartesian axes. *See* Axes/axis: coordinate
Cavalier projection, 184
Center lines, 142
Center of mass, 94
Centroid, geometric, 94
Chain scales, 217

Chamfers, dimensioning, 116, 117
Circle(s), 84, 89
  in CADD, 90
  center of, 79
    geometric, 90
  concentric, 85
  freehand sketching of, 64
  involute of, 86
  isometric, 67–68, 180–82
  lines tangent to, 82–84
  oblique, 186–87
  origin of, 90
  tangent, 79
  templates of, 209
  two-dimensional, 88
Circle arc(s), 89, 90
  in CADD, 90
  isometric, 180–82
  line tangent through point on, 83
  oblique, 186–87
  tangent, 79
  tangent to, having inaccessible center, 83
  tangent to circular arc and a line, 80–81
  tangent to two circular arcs, 81
  tangent to two lines, 79–80
  through three points, 91
Circular cylinder, 108, 109
Civil engineers' (chain) scales, 217
Clamp, quick-acting, 26
Command language, CADD, 43
Compass:
  beam, 210
  bow, 203–5, 209–10
Computer(s), 220–21. *See also* Computer-aided design and drafting (CADD)
  design and, 31–33
  drawing and, 6
  geometry and, 88–94
  I/O devices, 221, 222
  monitor (CRT), 32, 33, 222
Computer-aided design and drafting (CADD), 6–8, 37–57
  activities unique to, 44
  already-existing drawings, 38–40
  CAD vs., 6
  checking and correcting drawings, 53
  circles in, 90
  circular arcs in, 90
  command language, 43
  components of, 38
  construction planes in, 100–101
  crosshatching in, 47
  curves in, 90–91
  device axes in, 103–4
  digital storage in, 52–53
  digitizing process, 225–26, 227
  dimensioning in, 47–52
  equipment, 220–30
    printers and plotters, 41, 54, 223–25
    workstations, 9, 32, 222–23
  examples of, 54–57
  filleting in, 47, 49
  function of, 37–38
  geometry and, 88–94
    arcs, 90
    Boolean operators, 93–94

    circles, 90
    constructive solid geometry (CSG), 93
    curves, 90–91
    figures, 90–92
    geometric modeling, 92
    lines, 89–90
    primitives, 89
    surface modeling, 92
    wire frame modeling, 92
  grid or scale selection, 43–44
  input methods, 40–43
    digitizing tablet, 40, 41, 43, 226
    menus, 41–43, 230
  lettering in, 236–39
    text attributes, 238–39
    text fonts, 237–38, 239
  loading files, 53
  manual drafting vs., 7–8
  multiview projection in, 130–31
  new drawings, 40, 53–57
  orthographic views in, 106–7
  overlays, 44–46
  rotation in, 105–6
  software, 221, 228–30
  storing drawings, 226–28
  transformation in, 47
  use of drawings, 8
  view manipulation in, 46–47
Computer-aided design and manufacturing (CAD/ CAM), 8–9, 31, 32–33
Computer-aided design (CAD), 31–33
  CADD vs., 6
  glossary of terms, 194–96
Computer-aided drafting, 33
Computer-integrated manufacturing (CIM), 8
Computer models, 6
Computer numerically controlled (CNC) machines, 8
Concentric circle method of constructing ellipses, 85
Conceptualization, 25–26
Cones, dimensioning, 109
Conical tapers, dimensioning, 119–20
Conic sections, 84
Construction lines, 208
Construction planes, CADD, 100–101
Constructive solid geometry (CSG), 93
Consumer feedback, 29
Consumption, 29
Control points, 91
Conventional symbols, 151
Convergent (perspective) projection, 95–96, 100
Coordinate axes. *See under* Shape description
Coordinate construction method, 178, 179
Coordinate planes (2-D) projection, 96–100
  first- and third-angle, 99, 100
  orthographic (parallel), 96–99, 100
CPU (microprocessor), 221
Criticism, constructive, 22
Crossed belt, 84
Crossed-lines (diagonals) symbol, 151
Crosshatching, 47
CRT screen, 32, 33, 222
Curve(s), 89
  Bezier, 91
  in CADD, 90–91
  dimensioning, 118
  flexible (instrument), 205

Curve(s) (*cont.*)
  French and adjustable (instrument), 210–11
  involute, 86
  irregular, 89
  parallel, about a curved center line, 74
  reverse (ogee), 81–82
Curved boundary, primary projection of, 158
Curved-line auxiliary view, 156–58
Curved outline (space curve), multiview projection
    of, 140
Cut sheet paper, 223
Cutting plane, symbolic representation for, 170
Cutting-plane line, 137
Cycloids, 86
Cylinder(s):
  circular, 108, 109
  dimensioning, 115, 118

D

Dashboard panel, 22
Dashed lines, 137
Data base, 6
  multiple view from single, 130–31
  numeric, 38
  three-dimensional, 101–2
Datum/data:
  anthropometric, 18
  dimensioning from, 122
Da Vinci, Leonardo, 3, 4, 18, 61
Decimal-inch dimensioning, 111–12
Decimal inch-millimeter table, 202
Decimal scales, 217
Default parameters, 238
Delimiters, 52
Design, 11–36
  computers and, 31–33
  defined, 11
  design synthesis, 12–13
  drawing and, 5
  human engineering in, 19–21
  innovative, 14–17
  new-product creation and, 17
  patents on, 33–36
  process phases, 23, 24–30
  of systems and products, 13–14
  visual, 21–22
Design analysis, 26–27
Designers, 5–6
Design layout drawing, 30
Design records, 35–36
Design (solution) description, 28–29
Design team, 5
Detail drawing, 30
Detail (removed) section, 166, 167
Device axes, 103–4, 106–7
Difference operation, 93, 94
Digital plotter, 41, 223
Digital storage of CADD files, 52–53
Digitizing, 225–26, 227
Digitizing tablet, 40, 41, 43, 226
Dihedral angles, 99, 158–59
Dimension figures, 111, 114
Dimensioning. *See under* Size description

Dimension line, 110, 112
Dimetric projection, 96
Direction of sight vector, 104
Directories, 226
Direct view (natural) method, 128
Disk storage, 226, 229
Distribution of product, 29
Ditto lines, 150–51
Dividers, 206, 210
Dot matrix printers, 223
Drafter, 6
Drafting film, 207
Drafting machine, 206–7
Drafting templates, 205
Drawing, 2–10. *See also* Computer-aided design and
    drafting (CADD)
  breaks in, 143, 149, 151
  CAD/CAM, 8–9, 31, 32–33
  computer and, 6
  design and, 5
  design layout, 30
  detail, 30
  educational value of, 9–10
  history of, 3–4
  metric system and, 9
  today, 5–6
Drawing Exchange Format (DXF), 38
Drawing paper, 209
Drawing symbols, 124, 125
Drum plotter, 223
Duplicate geometry, 131

E

Electronic lettering guides, 236
Electrostatic printer/plotter, 225
Electro symbol template, 205
Ellipse(s), 84, 139
  concentric circle method of constructing, 85
  isometric, 67
  pictorial, 180
  templates of, 205
  trammel method of constructing, 84–85
Elliptical boundary, multiview projection of, 139–40
End view, 129, 130
Engine, Wankel (rotary), 15
Engineering, geometry. *See* Geometry
Engineering technicians, 6
Entity, 91
Environment, working, 19–21
Epicycloids, 86, 87
Equilateral triangles, 76
Equipment:
  CADD, 220–30
    printers and plotters, 41, 54, 223–25
    workstations, 9, 32, 222–23
  manual drawing, 203–13
    basic list of, 203
    bow compass (large bow), 203–5, 209–10
    dividers, 206, 210
    drawing instrument set, 203–5
    electric erasing machine, 205, 206
    erasing shield and eraser, 211
    French and adjustable curves, 210–11

pencils, 207–8
protractor, 204, 205
special instruments and templates, 205–6, 209, 236
tracing paper and drafting film, 207
triangles, 211, 213
T-square, parallel edge, and drafting machine, 206–7
Eraser, 211
Erasing machine, electric, 205, 206
Erasing shield, 211
Experimental testing, 27
Exploded illustration sketches, 72
Exploration, research and, 14
Extension lines, 110

F

Fastener(s):
multiview treatment of, 146, 147
sectioning, 169
Feedback, consumer, 29
Figures:
in CADD, 90–92
dimension, 111, 114
File name, 40
Files, CADD, 52–53, 226–28, 229
Fillet(s):
in CADD, 47, 49
conventional treatment in pictorial, 189
freehand sketching of, 71
multiview projection of, 148–49, 150
Film, drafting, 207
Final report, 28–29
Finished lines, 208
Finish marks, 111
Firmware, 221
First-angle projection, 99, 100
Flatbed plotters, 223, 224
Flat menu, 42
Flat tapers, dimensioning, 120
Flexible curves, 205
Fonts, text, 237–38, 239
Formal proposal, 23
Four-center approximation, 180
Fractional dimensioning, 111
Fractions, lettering of, 235
Freehand sketching, 59–72
circles, 64
conventional treatment of fillets, rounds, and screw threads, 71
exploded illustration sketches, 72
instructional, 60
in isometric, 66–69
lines, 62–64
materials for, 62
multiview sketches, 60, 64–66
in oblique, 69–70
overlays in, 71–72
pencil shading, 70
perspective, 70
pictorial sketches, 59, 60, 66
on ruled paper, 72
projection, 60–62

schematic, 60
thinking with a pencil, 60
value of, 60
French curves, 210–11
Frontal plane, 97, 98, 101
Front view (front elevation), 129
Full section, 163–64, 165

G

Gasket drawing, 54
Geometric center of circle, 90
Geometric centroid, 94
Geometric modeling in CADD, 92
Geometry, 73–94
angles, 89
bisecting, 73–74
constructing, equal to given angle, 75
trisecting, 74
circles, 84, 89
CADD drawing of, 90
center of, through three given points not in a single line, 79
concentric, 85
involute of, 86
line tangent to, given point on the circumference, 82–83
line tangent to, through a given point outside the circle, 83
line tangent to two, 83–84
tangent, 79
two-dimensional, 88
circular arcs, 89
CADD drawing of, 90
tangent, 79
tangent to, having inaccessible center, 83
tangent to circular arc and a line, 80–81
tangent to two circular arcs, 81
tangent to two lines, 79–80
through three points, 91
computer (CADD) and, 88–94
conic sections, 84
curves, 89
CADD drawing of, 90–91
involute, 86
parallel, about a curved center line, 74
reverse (ogee), 81–82
reverse (ogee), tangent to three given lines, 82
cycloids, 86
duplicate, 131
ellipses, 84
concentric circle method of constructing, 85
trammel method of constructing, 84–85
epicycloids, 86, 87
helix, 87–88
hyperbola, 84
hypocycloids, 87
importance of, 88
parabolas, 84, 85
offset method of constructing, 85–86
polygons, regular, 76–78
constructing, given one side, 78
hexagons, 77–78, 89
octagons, 78, 89

Geometry (*cont.*)
    pentagons, 77, 89
    transferring, 76, 77
  quadrilaterals
    squares, 76–77, 89
    trapezoids, 78–79, 89
  spiral of Archimedes, 87
  straight lines, 89
    bisecting, 73, 74
    circular arc tangent to a circular arc and a line, 80–81
    circular arc tangent to two, 79–80
    division into equal parts, 74–75
    through a given point and inaccessible intersection of two given lines, 75–76
    proportionally divided, 75
    reverse curve tangent to three, 82
    tangent through a point on circular arc having inaccessible center, 83
    tangent to a circle at a given point on circumference, 82–83
    tangent to a circle through a given point outside the circle, 83
    tangent to two given circles, 83–84
    trisecting, 73, 74
  triangles, 89
    constructing, given its three sides, 76
    division into equal parts, 78–79
    equilateral, 76
  two- and three-dimensional, 88–89
"Glass box" method, 128–30
  "second position" for side view, 130
Glossary, 191–96
  CAD terms, 194–96
  shop terms, 191–93
Graphic software, 229–30
Gravity points, 91
Grid paper, 62, 72
Grid selection in CADD, 43–44

H

Half sections, 164, 165, 172, 173
  dimensioning, 121
Handle, control, 91
Hard copy, 222
Hard leads, 207
Helix, 87–88
Helix angle, 88
Hexagons, 77–78, 89
Hierarchical menu, 42–43
Highway route plan and profile, 44
Hole(s):
  blind, 145
  dimensioning, 115, 117–18, 119, 122
  multiview treatment of, 144–45, 146, 147
  radially arranged, 148
Horizontal construction planes, 101
Horizontal lines, 132, 213
Horizontal plane, 98
Human engineering:
  in design, 19–21
  history and background of, 18–19
Hydraulic motor, 39, 48, 51

Hyperbola, 84
Hypocycloids, 87

I

IBM interactive graphics display system, 2
Idea sketch in isometric, 68
Ideation, 25
Illustration sketches, exploded, 72
Imagineering, 25
Implementation, 29
Inch-millimeter table, 199–202
  decimal, 202
Inclined lines, 132, 214–15
Inertia, moments of, 94
Initial Graphics Exchange Standard (IGES), 38
Input methods in CADD, 40–43
  digitizing tablet, 40, 41, 43, 226
  menus, 41–43, 230
Instructional sketches, 60
Integrated circuit (IC), 220–21
International Standards Organization (ISO), 6
Intersection(s):
  lines of
    multiview projection for, 149
    primary auxiliary view of, 160, 161–62
  multiview treatment of, 146, 147
  run-out, 149
Intersection operation, 93, 94
Inventor, role in obtaining patent, 35–36
Invisible lines, 136–37, 142
Involute curves, 86
I/O (input/output) devices, 40, 41, 43, 221, 222, 226
Isometric drawing. *See under* Pictorial drawing
Isometric lines, 176
Isometric paper, 72
Isometric projection, 96
Isometric sketching, 66–69

J

Justification, text, 238–39

K

Keyslots, dimensioning, 119
Keyways, dimensioning, 119
Knurls, dimensioning, 119, 120

L

Land camera, 13
Large bow (bow compass), 203–5, 209–10
Laser printers, 223
Layer number, 46
Layers in CADD, 44–46
Lead, pencil, 207
Leader, 111

Lear, William, 17
Leroy lettering guide, 236
Lettering, technical, 231–39
    CADD, 236–39
        text attributes, 238–39
        text fonts, 237–38, 239
    devices and templates for, 236
    manual, 231–36
        fractions, 235
        freehand, 233, 236
        general proportions of letters, 231–32
        inclined and vertical letters and numerals, 233–35
        large and small caps in combination, 235
        single-stroke letters, 231
        titles, 235–36
        uniformity and composition, 232–33
Libraries of figures, 91–92
Limit dimensioning, 124, 125
Line(s). *See also* Arc(s); Straight lines
    in CADD, 89–90
    center, 142
    circular arcs tangent to circular arc and, 80–81
    circular arcs tangent to two, 79–80
    conventional symbols, 211, 212
    cutting-plane, 137
    dashed, 137
    dimension, 110, 112
    extension, 110
    freehand sketching of, 62–64
    horizontal, 132, 213
    inclined, 132, 214–15
        with oblique line, 216
    invisible, 142
    isometric, 66–67, 176
    mold, 121
    multiview projection of, 131–34
        ditto, 150–51
        invisible lines, 136–37
        parallel, 138–39
        precedence of, 137
        true-length, 144
    nonisometric, 178
    oblique, 133
    origin of, 89–90
    parallel, 215
    pencil, 208
    perpendicular, 215–16
    section, 168–69
        symbols, 173
    solid, 137
    tangent to circles, 82–84
    vertical, 132, 213
Line font, 238–39
Location dimensions, 109, 113
Lugs, multiview treatment of, 147
Lunar Rover, 5

M

Macrocommands, 230
Magnetic tape, 226, 229
Mainframe, 220
Manufacturing, 29

Marketing specialists, 29
Mass, 94
Material(s). *See also* Equipment
    basic list of, 203
    for freehand sketching, 62
Material removal symbol, 111
Measurement, laying and setting off, 220
Measure of Man, The, 18
Mechanical engineers' scales, 217
Memory, computer, 221
Menus, CADD, 41–43, 230
Metric dimensioning, 112
Metric scales, 218–20
Metric system, 9
Microcomputers, 9, 220, 227
Microprocessor (CPU), 221
Minicomputers, 220
Mirroring, 47, 49
Mockups, 27
Model(s):
    computer, 6
    geometric, 92
    preliminary and scale, 28
    solid, 93
    surface, 92
    wire frame, 92
MODEM (MOdulator-DEModulator), 225
Mold lines, 121
Moments of inertia, 94
Monitor (CRT), 32, 33, 222
Motor, hydraulic, 39, 48, 51
Motor boat, remote control system for, 26
Mouse, 226
Move and duplicate function (CADD), 49
Multiview sketches, freehand, 60, 64–66
Multiview projection, 127–51
    of angles, 137–38
    CADD strategies for, 130–31
    conventional practices, 145–51
        aligned views, 147–48
        for boltheads, slots, and holes for pins, 146, 147
        breaks, 149, 151
        defined, 145
        half views and partial views, 145–46
        for nonexisting lines of intersection, 149
        for radially arranged features, 148
        representation of fillets and rounds, 148–49, 150
        for showing part in alternative position, 151
        symbols (representation), 151
        for unimportant intersections, 146, 147
    of curved outline (space curve), 140
    defined, 127
    of elliptical boundary, 139–40
    interpretation of adjacent areas of, 143–44
    of lines, 131–34
        ditto, 150–51
        invisible lines, 136–37
        parallel, 138–39
        precedence of, 137
        true-length, 144
    methods of obtaining, 127–30
    orthographic drawing of, 140–42
    points in, 133–34
    principal (front) view, 136
    principles of drawing, 130
    representation of holes, 144–45, 146, 147

Multiview projection (*cont.*)
  selection of, 134–36
  of surfaces, 133–34
    intersecting finished and unfinished, 140, 141
    tangent, 138, 139
  visualizing object from, 142–43

N

Natural (direct view) method, 128
NEMO, 15
Nonisometric lines, 178
Notebook, patent, 36
Notes, 122–25
  selection and placement of, 112–22
Numerals, inclined and vertical, 233–35
Numerically controlled (NC) machines, 8, 33
Numeric data base, 38

O

Oblique drawing. *See under* Pictorial drawing
Oblique line, 133
Oblique projection, 96, 97
Oblique (secondary) views, 161–62
Oblique sketching, 69–70
Octagons, 78, 89
Offset method, 85–86, 178, 179
Ogee (reverse) curves, 81–82
One-plane projection, 95–96, 97, 100
Open belt, 83–84
Operating system (OS) software, 229
Operators, Boolean, 93–94
Optical line follower, 226, 228
Origin, 99
  of circle, 90
  of line, 89–90
Orthographic drawing of multiview projections, 140–42
Orthographic (parallel) projection, 95, 96–99
Orthographic views, 106–7
Outline sectioning, 169
Overlays:
  in CADD, 44–46
  freehand sketching of, 71–72

P

Pan command (CADD), 47
Paper:
  cut sheet, 223
  drawing, 209
  grid, 62, 72
  isometric, 72
  standard sizes, 223
  tracing, 207
Parabolas, 84, 85–86
Parallel edge, 206
Parallel lines, 138–39, 215
Parallel (orthographic) projection, 95, 96–99

Parameters, 238
Patent attorney, 33–35
Patents on designs, 33–36
Pen, technical, 205, 206, 236
Pencil lines, 208
Pencils, 207–8
Pencil shading, 70
Pen control, 102
Pentagons, 77, 89
Perpendicular lines, 215–16
Perspective, oblique drawing vs., 187
Perspective (convergent) projection, 95–96, 100
Perspective sketch, 70
Phantom section, 166, 167
Pictorial drawing, 174–89
  conventional treatment in, 188–89
  dimensioning of, 188, 189
  divisions of, 174–76
  isometric, 96, 176–83
    angles in, 178–80
    of circle and circle arcs, 180–82
    coordinate construction method of, 178, 179
    isometric projection vs., 176, 177
    nonisometric lines in, 178
    position of isometric axes in, 182–83
    of rectangular objects, 67, 176–78
    of section views, 183
  oblique, 184–88
    of angles, circles, and circle arcs, 186–87
    basic plane theory of construction, 185–87
    oblique projection vs., 184
    perspective vs., 187
    procedure for, 184–85
    reduction of measurements in direction of receding axis, 187–88
    rules for, 186
    of section views, 188
Pictorial sketches, 58, 59, 60, 66, 72
Picturephone, 15
Piercing points, 95
Pins, multiview treatment of, 146, 147
Pioneer Satellite A-B-C-D series prototype, 28
Pipe layer, self-contained, 16
Piping installation drawing, 55
Plane(s). *See also* Geometry
  cutting, symbolic representation for, 170
  profile, 98, 101
  reference, 178
Plane surfaces, 133
Plan (top view), 129
Plot of subdivision, 45
Plotters, 41, 54, 223–25
Point(s), 89
  control, 91
  gravity, 91
  in multiview projection, 133–34
  piercing, 95
Pointer, 111
Polygons, 76–78, 89
  constructing, given one side, 78
  hexagons, 77–78, 89
  octagons, 78, 89
  pentagons, 77, 89
  transferring, 76, 77
Postprocessing, 94
Preliminary models, 28

Primitives:
  geometric, 89
  solid modeling, 93
Principal planes of projection, 96–100
Printers, 54, 223–25
Prisms, dimensioning, 108, 109
Production, design for, 29
Products:
  creation of new, 17
  design of, 13–14
  distribution of, 29
Profile dimensioning, 121
Profile plane, 98, 101
Projection(s). *See also* Multiview projection
  coordinate planes (2-D), 96–100
    first- and third-angle, 99, 100
    orthographic (parallel), 96–99, 100
  in freehand sketching, 60–62
  isometric, 176, 177
  oblique, 184
  one-plane, 95–96, 97, 100
  perspective (convergent), 95–96, 100
Projectors, 97
Proportional dividers, 206
Proportioning, 68–69
Proportions in multiview sketches, 65–66
Proposal, formal, 23
Prototypes, 28
Protractor, 204, 205
Puck, 40, 41, 226
Pyramids, dimensioning, 109

Q

Quadrilaterals:
  squares, 76–77, 89
  trapezoids, 78–79, 89

R

Radial distances, marking off, 64
Radii, dimensioning, 116
Random-access memory (RAM), 221
Rapido lettering guide, 236
Raster-to-vector converter, 226
Rays, visual, 95
Read-only memory (ROM), 221
Receding axis, 185, 187–88
Records, design, 35–36
Rectangle(s), 89, 90
  isometric, 67, 176–78
  proportioning, 65–66
Rectangle method, 66
Reference plane, isometric, 178
Removable disks, 226
Removed (detail) section, 166, 167
Report, final, 28–29
Research and exploration, 14
Reverse (ogee) curves, 81–82
Revolved section, 166, 167
Revolved triangle method, 215
Rhomboids, 69, 89

Rhombus, 89
Rib(s):
  multiview treatment of, 147
  radially arranged, 148
  in section, 172, 173
Right triangle (instrument), 211, 213
Roman architects, 3
Rotary (Wankel) engine, 15
Rotate command (CADD), 46–47
Rotate copy command (CADD), 47, 49
Rotate transformation command (CADD), 47
Rotation about coordinate axes, 104–6
Round(s):
  conventional treatment in pictorial, 189
  freehand sketching of, 71
  multiview projection of, 148–49, 150
Rounded ends, dimensioning, 119
Ruled paper, pictorial sketches on, 72

S

Scale models, 28
Scales, 217–20
  metric, 218–20
  selection in CADD, 43–44
Scaling, 7
Scanning, 40, 41, 226, 228
Schematic sketches, 60
Screen, CRT, 32, 33, 222
Screw, Archimedean, 12
Screw threads, freehand sketching of, 71
Scroll command (CADD), 47
"Second position" for side view, 130
Section(s), 163–73
  broken, 164–66
  conventional techniques, 171–72
  full, 163–64, 165
  half, 121, 164, 165, 172, 173
  isometric, 183
  oblique, 188
  outline treatment, 169
  phantom, 166, 167
  removed (detail), 166, 167
  revolved, 166, 167
  ribs in, 172, 173
  section lines, 168–69
    symbols, 173
  symbolic representation for cutting plane, 170
Semiautomatic dimensioning, 52
Shading, pencil, 70
Shafts, sectioning, 169
Shape description, 95–107
  CADD construction planes, 100–101
  coordinate axes, 101–7
    device axes and, 103–4, 106–7
    orthographic views in CADD, 106–7
    right-hand system, 103
    rotation about, 104–6
    three-dimensional data base and, 101–2
  coordinate planes (2-D) projection, 96–100
    first- and third-angle, 99, 100
    orthographic (parallel), 96–99, 100
  one-plane projection, 95–96, 97, 100
Shield, erasing, 211

Shop terms, glossary of, 191–93
Side view (side elevation, end view), 129, 130
Single-curved surfaces, 133
Size description, 108–25
   dimensioning, 108–22
      of angles, 114, 115
      of arcs, 114, 115, 118
      automatic, 47–52
      base-line, 117
      in CADD, 47–52
      of chamfers, 116, 117
      of conical tapers, 119–20
      of curves, 118
      of cylinders, 115, 118
      from datum, 122
      decimal-inch, 111–12
      of flat tapers, 120
      fractional, 111
      of half-section, 121
      of holes, 115, 117–18, 119, 122
      of internal chambers, 117
      of keyways and keyslots, 119
      of knurls, 119, 120
      limit, 124, 125
      location dimensions, 109, 113
      metric, 112
      out-of-scale, 121
      pictorial, 188, 189
      practices, 110–11, 112–22
      procedure in, 109
      profile, 121
      of radii, 116
      of repetitive features, 122
      of rounded ends, 119
      selection and placement of dimensions, 109–10,
         112–22
      size dimensions, 108–9
      of slots, 119, 122
      of spheres, 109, 115
      theory of, 108
   drawing symbols in, 124, 125
   notes, 122–25
      selection and placement of, 112–22
Sketching. *See* Freehand sketching
Skylab, 6
Slant, text, 238
Sliding triangle method, 215
Slot(s):
   dimensioning, 119, 122
   multiview treatment of, 146, 147
Snapshots, 131
Soft leads, 207
Software, CADD, 221, 228–30
Solid lines, 137
Solid modeling, 93
Solution (design) description, 28–29
Space curve, multiview projection of, 140
Specifications, 24, 33
Sphere(s)
   dimensioning, 109, 115
   isometric, 182
Spiral of Archimedes, 87
Spokes, in section, 171
Squares, 76–77, 89
Standard symbol, 145

Storage of CADD files, 52–53, 226–28, 229
Straight lines, 89
   bisecting, 73, 74
   circular arc tangent to a circular arc and a line,
      80–81
   circular arc tangent to two, 79–80
   division into equal parts, 74–75
   through a given point and inaccessible intersection
      of two given lines, 75–76
   proportionally divided, 75
   reverse curve tangent to three, 82
   tangent through a point on circular arc having
      inaccessible center, 83
   tangent to a circle at a given point on circumfer-
      ence, 82–83
   tangent to a circle through a given point outside
      the circle, 83
   tangent to two given circles, 83–84
   trisecting, 73, 74
Structural drawing, 57
Styling, 22
Stylus, 226
Subdivision, plot of, 45
Surface modeling, 92
Surfaces, multiview projection of, 133–34
   intersecting finished and unfinished, 140, 141
   tangent, 138, 139
Symbol(s):
   conventional, 151
   conventional line, 211, 212
   drawing, 124, 125
   material removal, 111
   section line, 173
   standard, 145
Symbolic representation, 59
   for cutting plane, 170
Synthesis, design, 12–13
Système international d'Unités (SI). *See* Metric
   system
Systems design, 13

T

Tangent circles, 79
Tangent circular arcs, 79
Tape, magnetic, 226, 229
Tapers, dimensioning, 119–20
Task definition, 23–24
Task specifications, 24
Technicians, engineering, 6
Technologists, 5–6
Telecopier transceiver, 13
Templates, 205–6, 209
   lettering, 236
Testing, experimental, 27
Third-angle projection, 99, 100
Threads, conventional treatment in pictorial, 189
Three-dimensional geometry, 88–89
Tilt-hex drafting template, 205
Title block, 40
Titles, 235–36
Tooling template, 205
Top view (plan), 129

Tracing paper, 207
Trammel method of constructing ellipses, 84–85
Transceiver, telecopier, 13
Transformation in CADD, 47
Translate command (CADD), 47
Translate copy command (CADD), 47, 49
Trapezium, 89
Trapezoids, 78–79, 89
Triangle(s), 89
    Braddock lettering, 232, 233
    constructing, given its three sides, 76
    division into equal parts, 78–79
    equilateral, 76
    right (instrument), 211, 213
Triangles (instrument), 211, 213
Trimetric projection, 96
T-square, 206
Two-dimensional geometry, 88–89

U

Unidirectional method of dimensioning, 112, 113
Union operator, 93–94
User software, 230

V

Vector, direction of sight, 104
Vellum, drafting, 207
Vertical line, 132, 213
View manipulation in CADD, 46–47
Vision, 19
Visual design, 21–22
Visual rays, 95

W

Wankel (rotary) engine, 15
Weight, 94
Wheel, Archimedean, 12
Wire frame modeling, 92
Working drawings, 6
Working environment, 19–21
Workstations, CADD, 9, 32, 222–23

Z

Zoom command (CADD), 46

Exercises

The following exercises provide engineering drawing practice coordinated with the text. The exercises are organized into sections which cover the following areas:

Section 1   Plates 1.1–1.7   Geometric Construction
Section 2   Plates 2.1–2.12   Multiview Drawing
Section 3   Plates 3.1–3.5   Orthographic Reading
Section 4   Plates 4.1–4.8   Isometric Sketching
                                and Drawing
Section 5   Plates 5.1–5.3   Sections
Section 6   Plates 6.1–6.6   Auxiliary Views
Section 7   Plates 7.1–7.5   Blueprint Reading
Paper   P1   Blank Sheets (5)
                         P2   Multiview Sketching (5)
                         P3   Isometric Sketching (5)
                         P4   Lettering (4)

Carefully read the instructions for each exercise. You may be required to start your solution at a specific location on the plate. Some problems will be worked at full scale while others use a reduced or enlarged scale. Or, you may be assigned one or more problems from several displayed on the sheet.

The title block on each plate should be carefully lettered and should include all appropriate information. Practice your technical lettering on P4 paper as assigned by your instructor, and in Section 7, where written answers to questions are required.

Instrument drawings should be laid out with sharp light lines and finished crisp and black. As a general rule, do not erase your construction. Your instructor can better evaluate your successes—and failures—if you show your work.

When sketching, linework should be dark and bold and follow grid lines. Some assignments normally executed with instruments can be completed on P3 paper or on clear sheets for practice in sketching without grid paper.

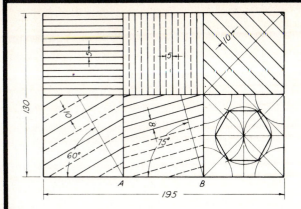

Complete one figure each from the top and bottom row as assigned by your instructor. Full scale with instruments.

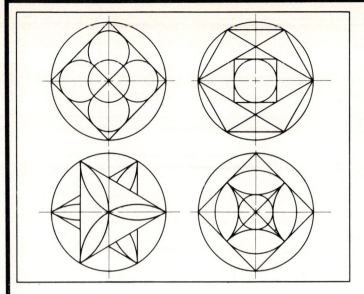

Complete one of the figures as assigned by your instructor. The circle is 5.00" diameter.

INTRODUCTION TO
ENGINEERING DRAWING

DRAWN BY .

CLASS/SEC .   DATE   SCALE   .

LAB

1.2

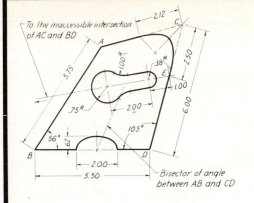

Construct the geometry of the plate at full scale. Note the position of corner 'B'.

Point B

INTRODUCTION TO
ENGINEERING DRAWING

DRAWN BY .

CLASS/SEC .   DATE   SCALE   .

LAB

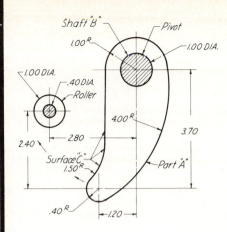

Part 'A' revolves about shaft 'B' in a clockwise direction from the position shown until surface 'C' contacts the roller. Reproduce the drawing as shown and in phantom, the revolved position of part 'A'. Note the position of the roller.

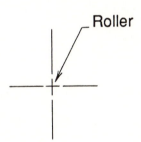

Roller

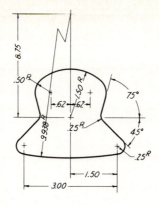

Complete the dolly block at full scale. Note the starting position of the 1.50 R arc.

INTRODUCTION TO	DRAWN BY		LAB
ENGINEERING DRAWING	CLASS/SEC	DATE SCALE	1.5

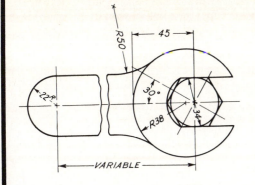

R50
45
22-R
30°
R38
34
VARIABLE

Construct the wrench at full scale. Show the broken handle and complete the "variable" dimension with note, dimension, and extension lines.

INTRODUCTION TO
ENGINEERING DRAWING

DRAWN BY .

.

LAB

CLASS/SEC .   DATE   SCALE   .

1.6

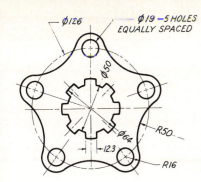

Ø126   Ø19 — 5 HOLES
EQUALLY SPACED

Ø50

Ø64

12.3

R50

R16

Complete the spline plate at half scale.

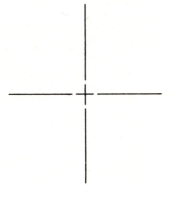

Using P2 paper, complete multiview drawings of the following pictorials as assigned by your instructor. The views of four objects may be drawn per sheet.

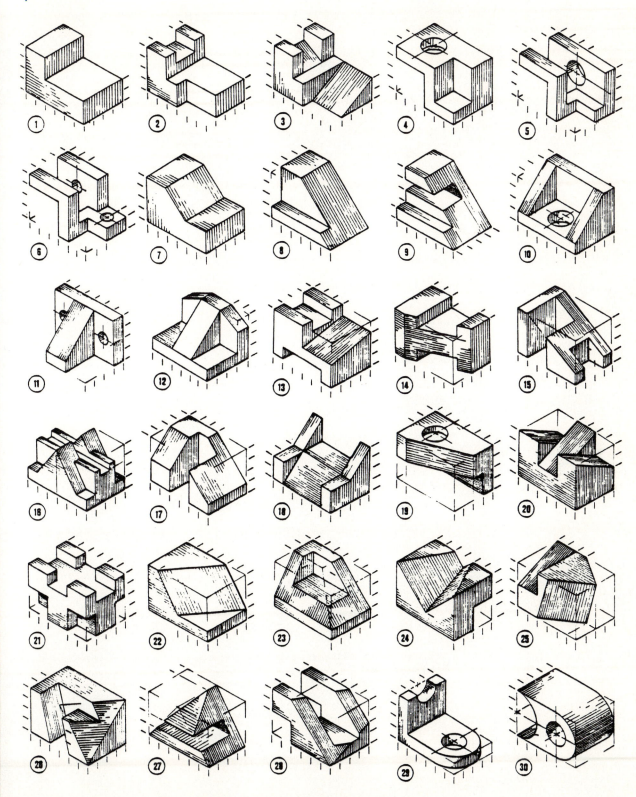

INTRODUCTION TO
ENGINEERING DRAWING

DRAWN BY

CLASS/SEC   DATE   SCALE

LAB

2.1

Use the pictorial information to complete a multiview drawing of each of the objects shown. Choose the necessary and most descriptive views.

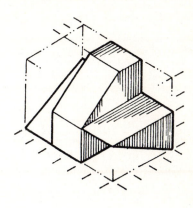

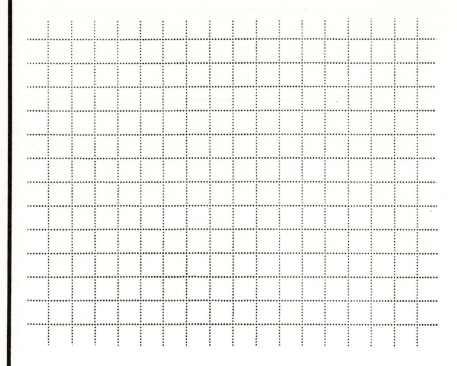

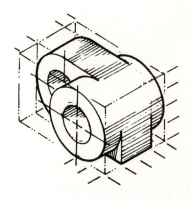

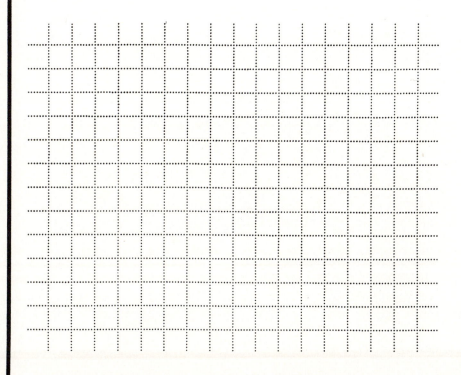

INTRODUCTION TO	DRAWN BY		LAB
ENGINEERING DRAWING	CLASS/SEC	DATE SCALE	

Use the pictorial information to complete a multiview drawing of each of the objects shown. Choose the necessary and most descriptive views.

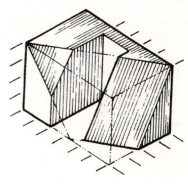

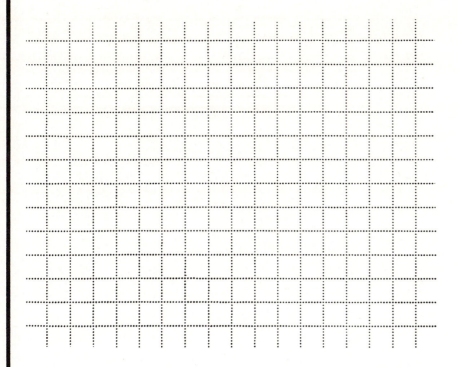

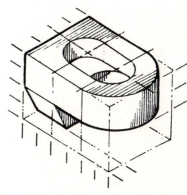

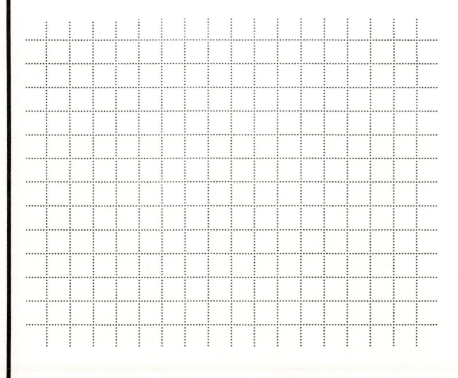

INTRODUCTION TO	DRAWN BY		LAB
ENGINEERING DRAWING	CLASS/SEC	DATE SCALE	

Use the pictorial information to complete a multiview drawing of each of
the objects shown. Choose the necessary and most descriptive views.

| INTRODUCTION TO | DRAWN BY . | . | LAB |
| ENGINEERING DRAWING | CLASS/SEC . | DATE   SCALE | . |

Use the pictorial information to complete a multiview drawing of each of the objects shown. Choose the necessary and most descriptive views.

INTRODUCTION TO	DRAWN BY .	LAB
ENGINEERING DRAWING	CLASS/SEC . DATE SCALE .	

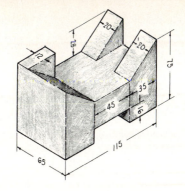

Complete a half scale multiview drawing of the rest block. Choose appropriate views, determine visibility of features, and complete the drawing with correct line weights.

INTRODUCTION TO
ENGINEERING DRAWING

DRAWN BY .

CLASS/SEC .   DATE   SCALE   .

LAB

2.2

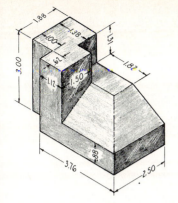

Complete a full scale multiview drawing of the angle block. Choose appropriate views, determine visibility of features, and complete the drawing with correct line weights. Orient the paper horizontally.

INTRODUCTION TO
ENGINEERING DRAWING

DRAWN BY

CLASS/SEC   DATE   SCALE

LAB

2.3

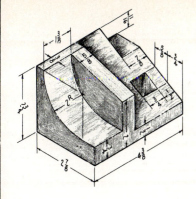

Complete a half scale multiview drawing of the stop block.
Choose appropriate views, determine visibility of features,
and complete the drawing with correct line weights.

INTRODUCTION TO	DRAWN BY		LAB
ENGINEERING DRAWING	CLASS/SEC	DATE	SCALE	2.4

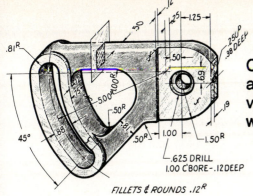

.81R

.12
.50
.25
1.25
.25 UP
.38 DEEP

.50
69

.19

.21
.75
5.00 R
1.00 R

.50 R

45°

.88

.81

.50 R
1.00
1.50 R

.625 DRILL
1.00 C'BORE -.12 DEEP

FILLETS & ROUNDS .12R

Complete a half scale multiview drawing of the
adjustment bracket. Choose appropriate views, determine
visibility of features, and complete the drawing
with correct center lines and line weights.

INTRODUCTION TO
ENGINEERING DRAWING

DRAWN BY

CLASS/SEC   DATE   SCALE

LAB

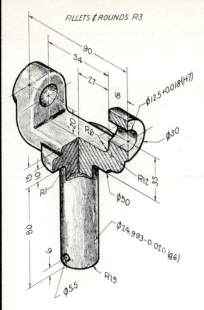

FILLETS & ROUNDS R3

90
54
27
18
φ12.5 +0.018 (H7)
φ30
R6
R12
35
20
15
R1
10
φ50
80
φ24.993 -0.010 (g6)
9
R15
φ5.5

Complete a full scale multiview drawing of the shaft guide utilizing partial or broken views as needed. Determine visibility of features, and complete the drawing with correct line weights.

Complete front and top views at full scale. Determine visibility of features, and complete the drawing with correct line selection and weights.

SMALL HOLE TO AXIS OF LARGE HOLE

1.62 CENTER OF

.406 DIA.

.38 R

1.00

.28

.38

.38R

.88R

60°

.312 DIA.
2 HOLES

.481 ± .56

.31

1.62

.75

.75

.88R

2.50

.44

2.38

.594

.609 DRILL
C BORE 1.00 x .25 DEEP

FILLETS & ROUNDS .12 R

INTRODUCTION TO
ENGINEERING DRAWING

DRAWN BY

CLASS/SEC   DATE   SCALE

LAB

2.7

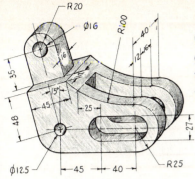

Complete a half scale multiview drawing of the pivot guide. Choose appropriate views, determine visibility of features, and complete the drawing with correct line weights.

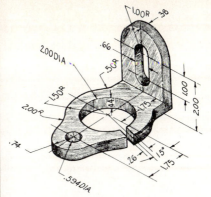

Complete a full scale multiview drawing of the index guide. Choose appropriate views, determine visibility of features, and complete the drawing with correct line weights.

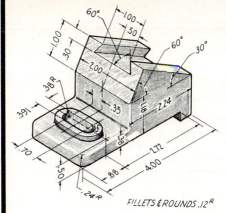

60°
1.00
.50
60°
30°
1.00
.30
2.00
.38 R
.391
.35
.18
2.24
.70
.38
1.72
4.00
.50
.88
.24 R

FILLETS & ROUNDS .12 R

Complete a full scale multiview drawing of the dove tail bracket. Choose appropriate views, determine visibility of features, and complete the drawing with correct line weights.

INTRODUCTION TO

ENGINEERING DRAWING

DRAWN BY .

CLASS/SEC .

DATE

SCALE

.

LAB

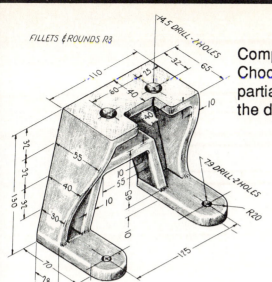

FILLETS & ROUNDS R3

14.5 DRILL-2HOLES
110
25
32
65
60
40
40
10

55
32
32
32
130
55
10
40
10
55
30
10
65
0

79 DRILL-2HOLES
R20
125
70
28

Complete a half scale multiview drawing of the lathe leg. Choose appropriate views, make use of symmetrical or partial views, determine visibility of features, and complete the drawing with correct line weights.

Complete a two view drawing of the tube support at half scale. Choose appropriate views, determine visibility of features, and complete the drawing with correct line weights.

13 DRILL-THRU

72

R15

3 SAWCUT

38

34.9 REAM

VIEW A

75

40

13

50

R65

65

3.1 DRILL

R30

10 6.4

R20

38

100

64

5

RIB
VIEW "A"

FILLETS & ROUNDS R3

38

19.04
19.06 THRU
25.4 BORE
12.7 DP

INTRODUCTION TO
ENGINEERING DRAWING

DRAWN BY

CLASS/SEC   DATE   SCALE

LAB

2.12

In the space provided, accurately sketch the missing view.

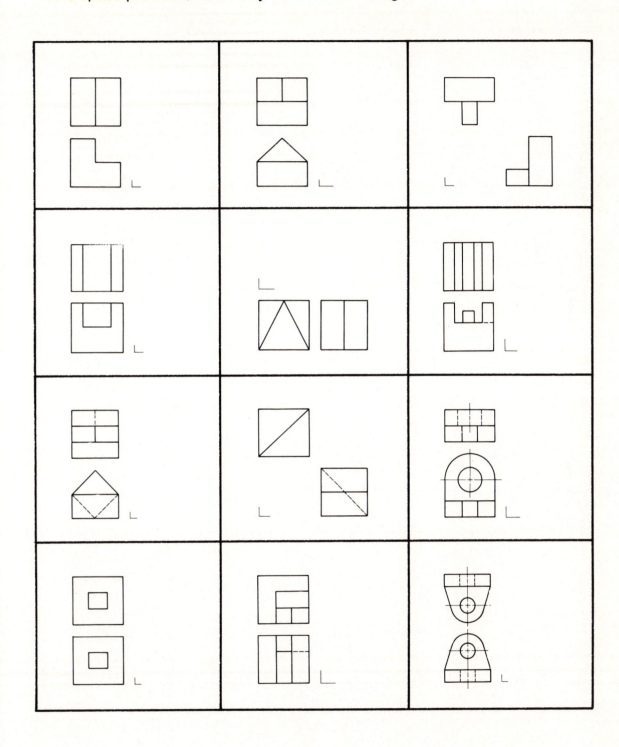

INTRODUCTION TO
ENGINEERING DRAWING

DRAWN BY .

CLASS/SEC .

DATE

SCALE

LAB

.

Two complete and correct views are given in the following problems.
Complete the missing view using the identified corner. Clearly mark all
reference and cutting planes.

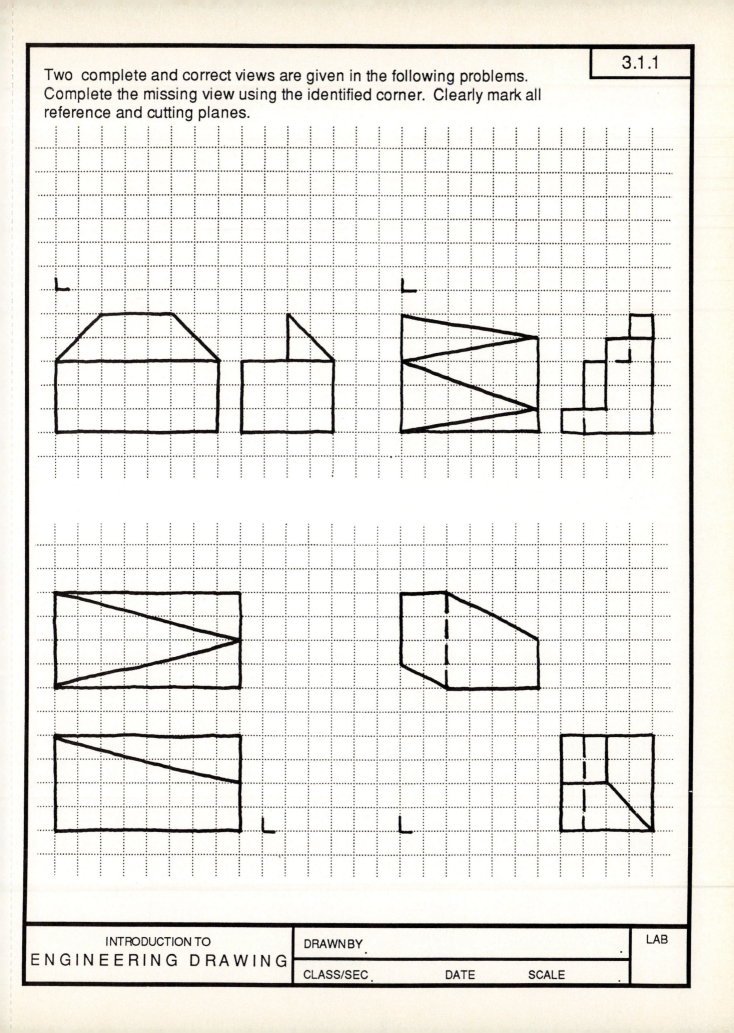

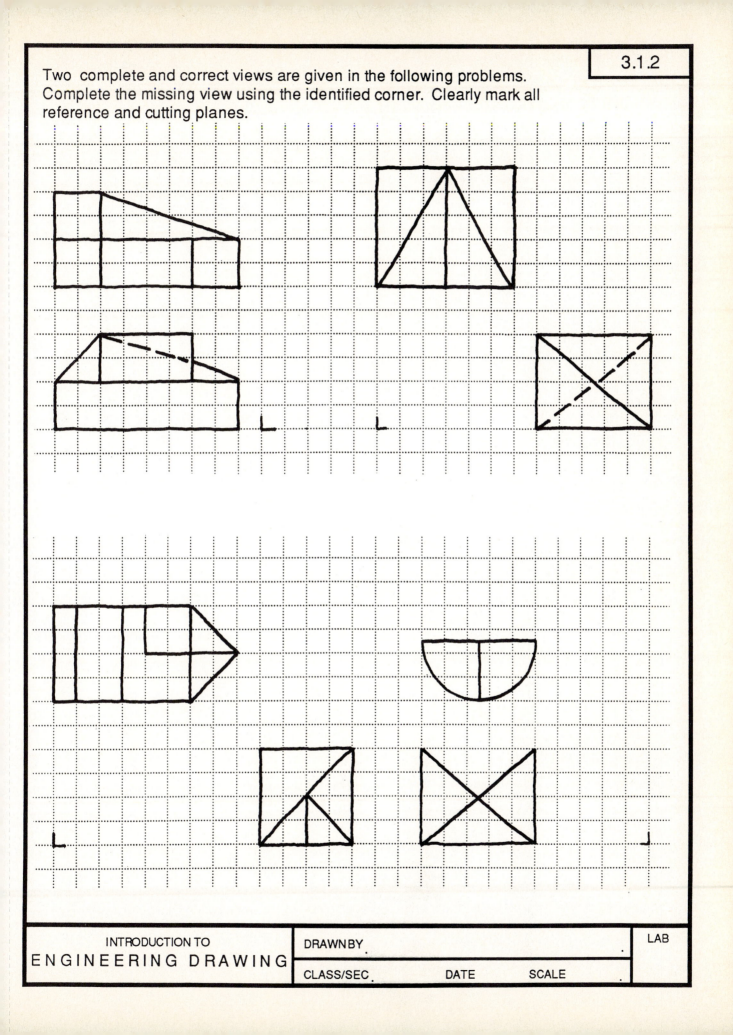

Two complete and correct views are given in the following problems. Complete the missing view using the identified corner. Clearly mark all reference and cutting planes.

3.1.2

Two complete and correct views are given in the following problems. Complete the missing view using the identified corner. Clearly mark all reference and cutting planes.

3.1.3

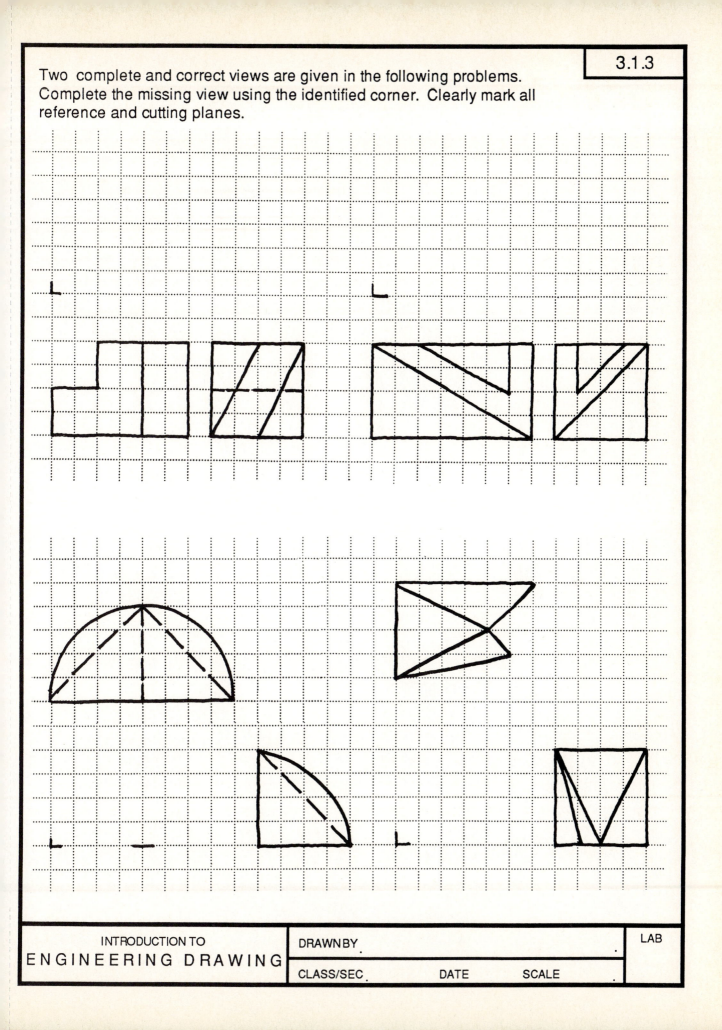

INTRODUCTION TO
ENGINEERING DRAWING

DRAWN BY .

CLASS/SEC .   DATE   SCALE .

LAB

Two complete and correct views are given in the following problems. Complete the missing view using the identified corner. Clearly mark all reference and cutting planes.

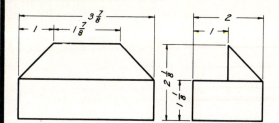

Complete the given views at full scale. Complete the required view in correct position.

INTRODUCTION TO
ENGINEERING DRAWING

DRAWN BY

CLASS/SEC   DATE   SCALE

LAB

3.2

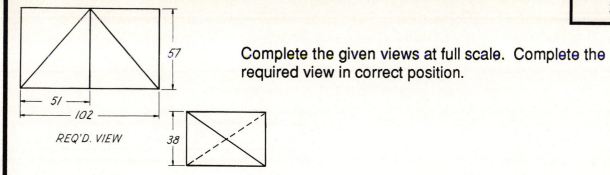

57

51

102

REQ'D. VIEW

38

Complete the given views at full scale. Complete the required view in correct position.

3.3

INTRODUCTION TO

E N G I N E E R I N G   D R A W I N G

DRAWN BY

CLASS/SEC   DATE   SCALE

LAB

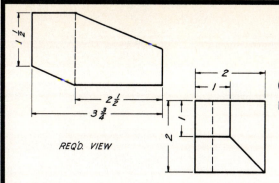

REQ'D. VIEW

Complete the given views at full scale. Complete the required view in correct position.

INTRODUCTION TO

ENGINEERING DRAWING

DRAWN BY

CLASS/SEC   DATE   SCALE

LAB

3.4

On P1 paper, complete a detail drawing of the part shown. Choose appropriate views and scale. Finish the drawing with conventional line treatment.

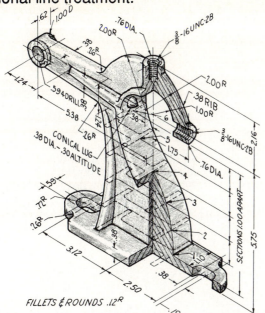

SECTION NUMBER	A	B	C	D	E
1	1.00	2.00	3.00	1.88	1.62
2	.94	1.88	2.82	1.75	1.38
3	.62	1.82	2.44	1.62	1.12
4	0.00	1.88	1.88	1.50	.88
5	.68	2.12	1.44	1.38	.62
6	1.00	—	—	1.25	—

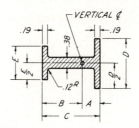

FILLETS & ROUNDS .12ᴿ

On P1 paper, complete detail orthographic views of parts as assigned. Or, complete a sectional drawing of all parts assembled. Choose appropriate views and scale.

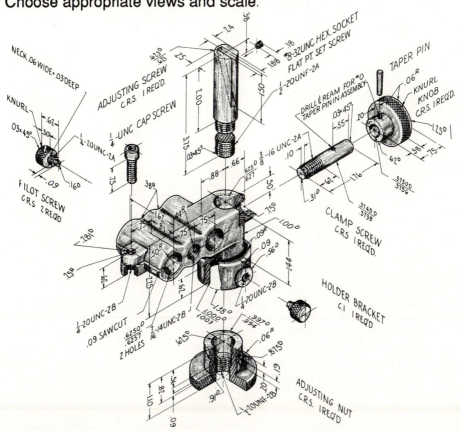

INTRODUCTION TO
ENGINEERING DRAWING

DRAWN BY

CLASS/SEC   DATE   SCALE

LAB

Complete an isometric sketch of each multiview object at
1:1 scale. Choose best orientation and show light,
accurate construction.

Complete an isometric sketch of each multiview object at
1:1 scale. Choose best orientation and show light,
accurate construction.

Complete an accurate proportional isometric sketch as assigned by your instructor. Choose an appropriate scale and finish with easily readable linework.

INTRODUCTION TO	DRAWN BY		LAB
ENGINEERING DRAWING			4.3
	CLASS/SEC	DATE SCALE	

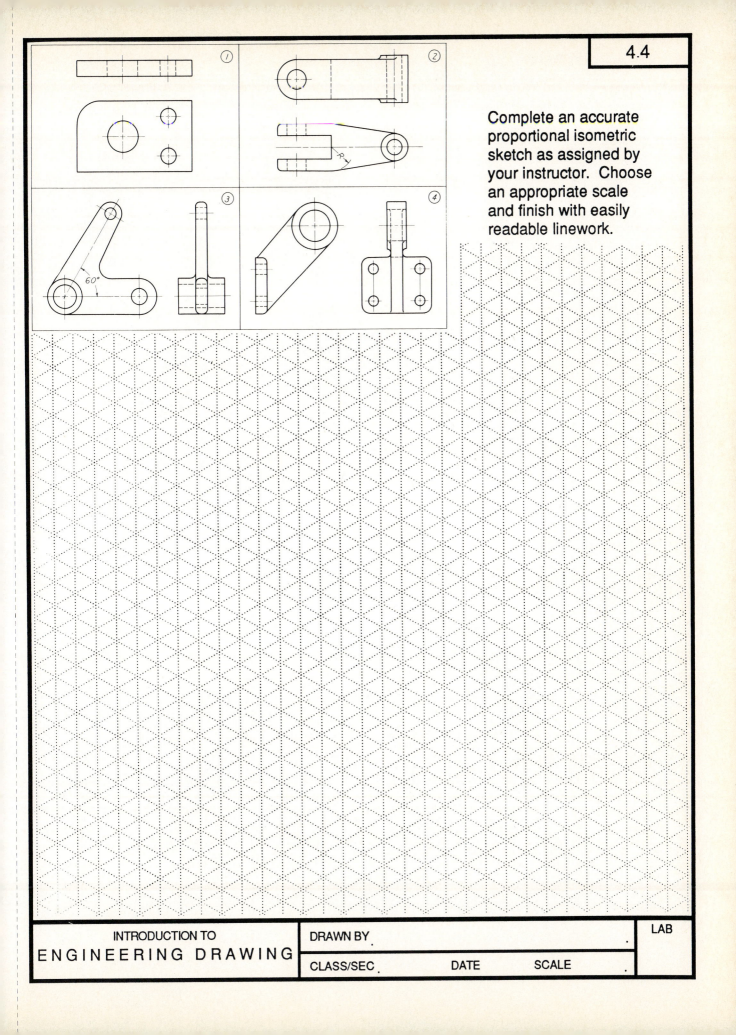

4.4

Complete an accurate proportional isometric sketch as assigned by your instructor. Choose an appropriate scale and finish with easily readable linework.

INTRODUCTION TO
ENGINEERING DRAWING

DRAWN BY .

CLASS/SEC .   DATE   SCALE   .

LAB

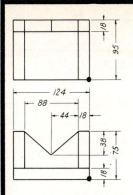

Complete a half scale isometric drawing by placing the corner identified by the black dot at the isometric axis.

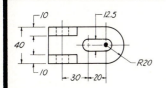

Complete a full size isometric drawing by placing the center identified by the black dot at the isometric center.

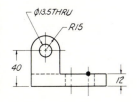

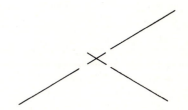

| INTRODUCTION TO | DRAWN BY . | . | LAB |
| ENGINEERING DRAWING | CLASS/SEC . | DATE | SCALE . |

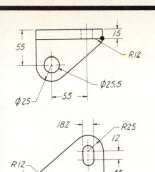

Complete a full scale isometric drawing by placing the corner identified by the black dot at the isometric axis.

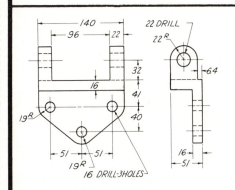

Complete a half scale isometric drawing of the object shown. Orient the bracket with three 16 mm diameter holes in a horizontal plane.

16 DRILL-3HOLES

| INTRODUCTION TO | DRAWN BY | LAB |
| ENGINEERING DRAWING | CLASS/SEC   DATE   SCALE | 4.6 |

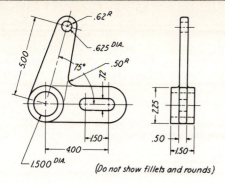

.62^R

.625 $^{DIA.}$

.500

75°

.50^R

77°

1.500 $^{DIA.}$

400

1.50

.225

.50

1.50

(Do not show fillets and rounds)

Complete a full scale isometric drawing of the crank arm. Position the pictorial such that the outside center of the 1.500 diameter hole is centered on the isometric center shown.

INTRODUCTION TO

ENGINEERING DRAWING

DRAWN BY

CLASS/SEC

DATE

SCALE

LAB

4.7

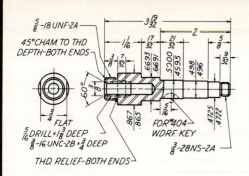

$\frac{5}{8}$ –18 UNF-2A

45° CHAM. TO THD.
DEPTH-BOTH ENDS

60°

$\frac{3}{4}$ FLAT

$\frac{5}{16}$ DRILL × $1\frac{3}{8}$ DEEP
$\frac{3}{8}$ –16 UNC-2B × $\frac{3}{4}$ DEEP

THD. RELIEF-BOTH ENDS

$3\frac{19}{32}$

2

$1\frac{1}{16}$

$\frac{17}{32}$

$\frac{21}{32}$

$\frac{5}{8}$

$\frac{9}{32}$

$\frac{3}{8}$

$\frac{7}{32}$

.6693
.6691

.5700
.5695

.498
.496

.867
.865

$\frac{5}{16}$

FOR #404
WDRF. KEY

$\frac{3}{8}$ –28NS-2A

.4725
.4722

Complete an isometric drawing of the spindle. Choose a scale larger than 1:1. Orient the spindle such that the part is vertical and the chamfered hole is on top. You may choose to show the interior detail by a broken section.

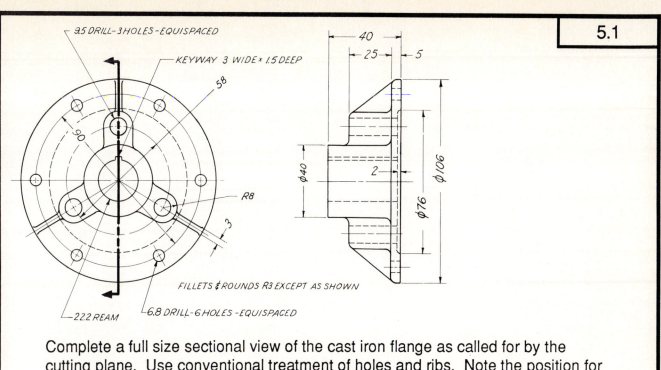

9.5 DRILL-3HOLES-EQUISPACED

KEYWAY 3 WIDE × 1.5 DEEP

58

90

R8

3

22.2 REAM

6.8 DRILL-6 HOLES -EQUISPACED

FILLETS & ROUNDS R3 EXCEPT AS SHOWN

40

25

5

φ40

φ106

φ76

2

Complete a full size sectional view of the cast iron flange as called for by the cutting plane. Use conventional treatment of holes and ribs. Note the position for the 2.22 reamed hole and the base of the flange.

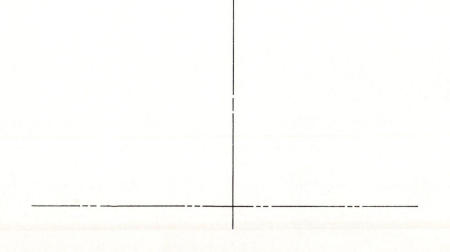

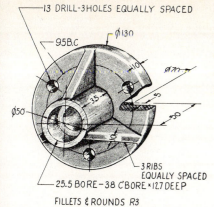

13 DRILL-3 HOLES EQUALLY SPACED

95 B.C

Ø130

Ø50

35

Ø70

50

3 RIBS
EQUALLY SPACED

25.5 BORE - 38 C'BORE × 12.7 DEEP

FILLETS & ROUNDS R3

Complete a half section at an appropriate scale and orientation. Use conventional treatment for holes and ribs. Clearly mark the cutting plane.

INTRODUCTION TO	DRAWN BY		LAB
ENGINEERING DRAWING	CLASS/SEC	DATE SCALE	5.2

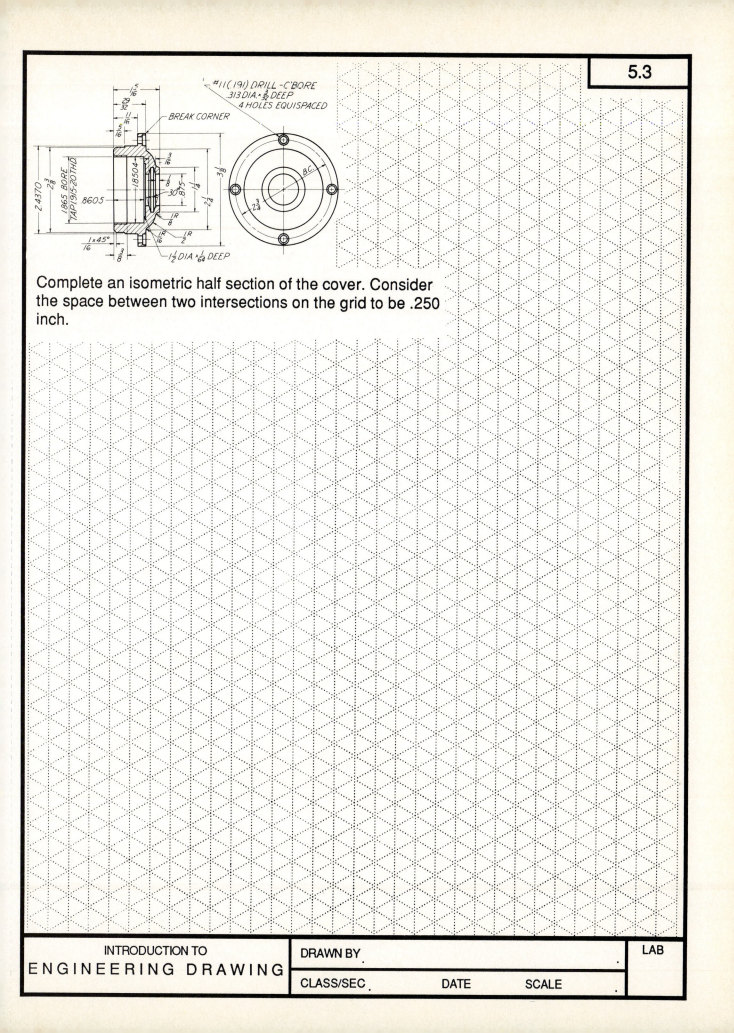

#11 (191) DRILL -C'BORE
.313 DIA.× 3/8 DEEP
4 HOLES EQUISPACED

BREAK CORNER

Complete an isometric half section of the cover. Consider the space between two intersections on the grid to be .250 inch.

Given the front and five alternative top views. Reconstruct
the views as assigned by your instructor. Complete a
normal view of the inclined surface. Clearly mark all
reference planes.

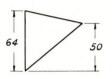

Top Views

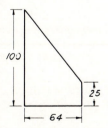

Front View

INTRODUCTION TO

ENGINEERING DRAWING

DRAWN BY

CLASS/SEC   DATE   SCALE

LAB

6.1

Given the front and five alternative top views. Reconstruct
the views as assigned by your instructor. Complete a
normal view of the inclined surface. Clearly mark all
reference planes.

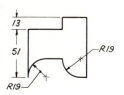

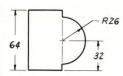

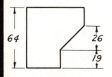

Top Views

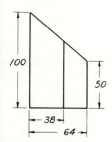

Front View

INTRODUCTION TO
ENGINEERING DRAWING

DRAWN BY

CLASS/SEC   DATE   SCALE

LAB

6.2

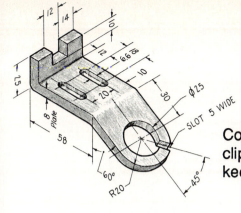

12
14
10
12
8.9.9
8
15
10
30
ø25
SLOT 5 WIDE
8
plate
20
58
60°
R20
45°

Construct the views necessary to fully describe the anchor clip. Choose an appropriate scale and object orientation to keep the drawing on the sheet.

INTRODUCTION TO

ENGINEERING DRAWING

DRAWN BY .   .

CLASS/SEC .   DATE   SCALE   .

LAB

6.3

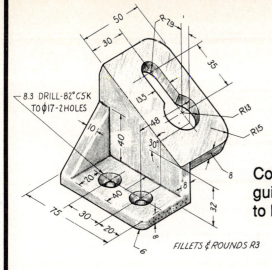

8.3 DRILL-82°CSK
TO∅17-2HOLES

50

30

R 7.9

35

13.5

48

R13

R15

30°

8

8

32

10

40

20

40

8

75

30

20

6

FILLETS & ROUNDS R3

Construct the views necessary to fully describe the offset guide. Choose an appropriate scale and object orientation to keep the drawing on the sheet.

INTRODUCTION TO
ENGINEERING DRAWING

DRAWN BY

CLASS/SEC   DATE   SCALE

LAB

6.4

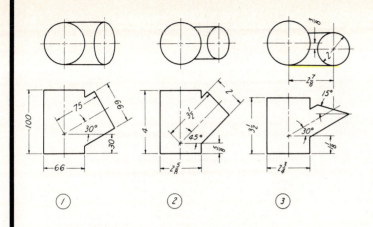

① ② ③

Reconstruct the cylinders as assigned by your instructor.
Make use of partial views if appropriate. Determine the
intersection and normal view of the inclined surface.
Scale: One Half.

INTRODUCTION TO
ENGINEERING DRAWING

DRAWN BY

CLASS/SEC   DATE   SCALE

LAB

6.5

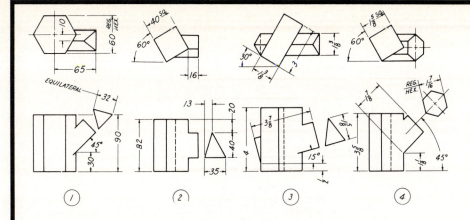

Reconstruct the prisms as assigned by your instructor.
Make use of partial views if appropriate. Determine the
intersection and normal view of any inclined surface.
Scale: One Half.

Using the assembly drawing of the bearing below, answer the questions on this sheet.

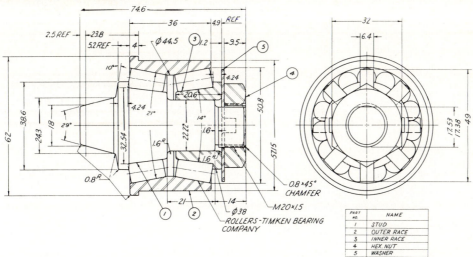

PART NO.	NAME
1	STUD
2	OUTER RACE
3	INNER RACE
4	HEX. NUT
5	WASHER

1. What are the dimensions of Part 1? ⟋_____⟋ length ⟋_____⟋ diameter

2. What is the finished length of the Bearing Assembly? ⟋_____⟋

3. How many Timken rollers are needed for the assembly? ⟋_____⟋

4. What size wrench is required to tighten the hex nut, Part 4? ⟋____⟋

5. What is the inner diameter of Part 3? ⟋____⟋ Outer diameter? ⟋____⟋

6. Study the washer, Part 5. What is its function? ⟋_____⟋

7. Sketch a proportional isometric drawing of the stud, Part 4.

Using the assembly drawing of the support bracket, answer
the questions on this sheet.

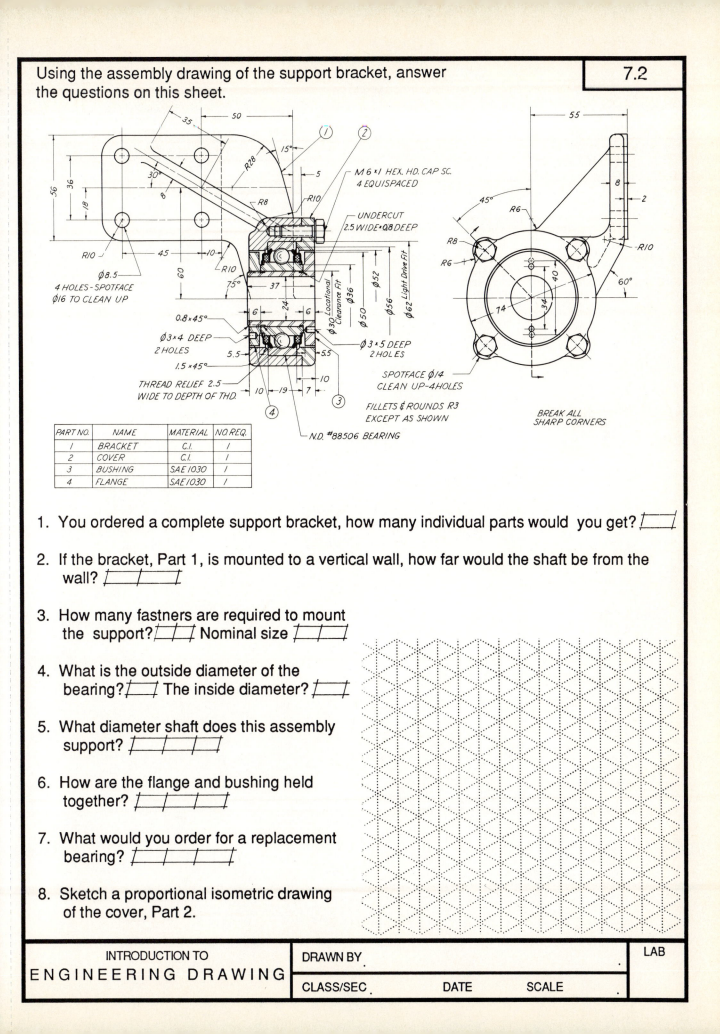

PART NO.	NAME	MATERIAL	NO. REQ.
1	BRACKET	C.I.	1
2	COVER	C.I.	1
3	BUSHING	SAE 1030	1
4	FLANGE	SAE 1030	1

1. You ordered a complete support bracket, how many individual parts would you get?

2. If the bracket, Part 1, is mounted to a vertical wall, how far would the shaft be from the wall?

3. How many fasteners are required to mount the support? Nominal size

4. What is the outside diameter of the bearing? The inside diameter?

5. What diameter shaft does this assembly support?

6. How are the flange and bushing held together?

7. What would you order for a replacement bearing?

8. Sketch a proportional isometric drawing of the cover, Part 2.

INTRODUCTION TO
ENGINEERING DRAWING

DRAWN BY

CLASS/SEC   DATE   SCALE

LAB

7.2

Using the assembly drawing of the bench press, answer
the questions on sheet 7.3b.

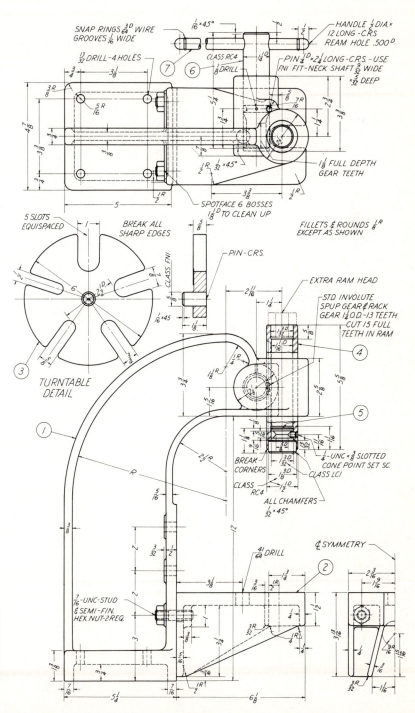

PART NO.	NAME	MATERIAL	NO. REQ.
1	BASE	C.I.	1
2	TABLE	C.I.	1
3	TURNTABLE	C.I.	1
4	RAM	S.A.E. 1045	1
5	RAM HEAD	S.A.E. 1040	1
6	SPINDLE	S.A.E. 1045	1
7	HANDLE	C.R.S.	1

INTRODUCTION TO
ENGINEERING DRAWING

DRAWN BY

CLASS/SEC   DATE   SCALE

LAB

Refer to sheet 7.3a to answer these questions.

1. What is the wall thickness of Part 1, the Base?

2. How is the Handle, Part 7, kept in the Spindle, Part 6?

3. How is the Spindle secured in the base?

4. How is the table, Part 2, secured to the base, Part 1?

5. How far is the upper surface of the Table, Part 2, above the bottom of the Base at its lowest setting? At its highest setting?

6. How many fasteners are required to mount the assembly to a horizontal surface? Are they screws or bolts? What is their nominal size.

7. How large of a "footprint" does the press make? square inches

8. What is the clearance between the turntable positioning pin and its hole in the table?

9. When installed, what is the clearance between the turntable and the base?

10. How many teeth does the spur gear on the Spindle have? The rack on the Ram, Part 4?

11. There are 6 instances of drawing conventions on sheet 7.3a. Locate and identify each by its correct name.

12. Determine the width of the teeth.

13. What is the finished length of the assembled Ram and Ram Head?

14. How is the Ram Head, Part 5, secured to the Ram?

15. Make a proportional isometric sketch of the Base.

INTRODUCTION TO	DRAWN BY	LAB
ENGINEERING DRAWING	CLASS/SEC DATE SCALE	

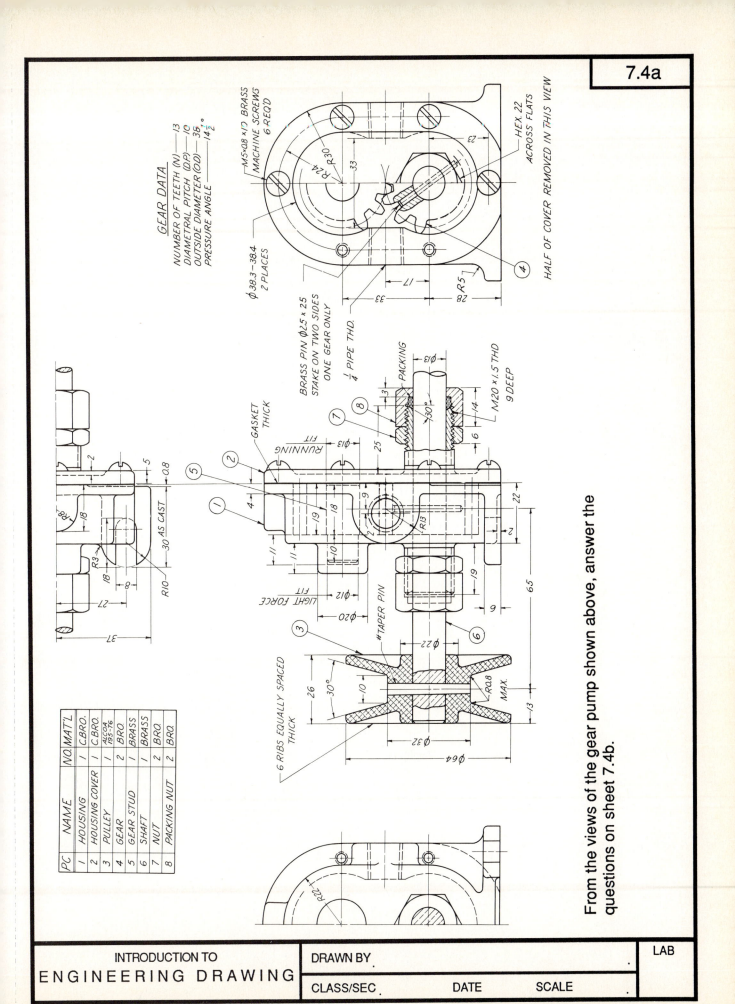

7.4a

GEAR DATA

NUMBER OF TEETH (N) — 13
DIAMETRAL PITCH (DP) — 10
OUTSIDE DIAMETER (OD) — 38⁴⁄₅
PRESSURE ANGLE — 14½°

M5×0.8 ×17 BRASS
MACHINE SCREWS
6 REQD

HEX. 22
ACROSS FLATS

HALF OF COVER REMOVED IN THIS VIEW

R30
R24
33
23
R5
Φ 38.3 – 38.4
2 PLACES
33
17
28

④

BRASS PIN Φ2.5 × 25
STAKE ON TWO SIDES
ONE GEAR ONLY

¼ PIPE THD.

GASKET
THICK

PACKING
M20 ×1.5 THD
9 DEEP
30°
3
Φ13
14
6

RUNNING
FIT
Φ13
25

⑦ ⑧

②
⑤
①
4
11
19
18
9
2
R13
22
2

30 AS CAST
R38
18
R3
18
8
R10
27
37
5
2
0.8

LIGHT FORCE
FIT
Φ12
Φ20

③ #TAPER PIN

6 RIBS EQUALLY SPACED
THICK
26
30°
10
Φ22
R0.8
MAX.
Φ32
Φ64
13
6
19
65

⑥

R22

From the views of the gear pump shown above, answer the
questions on sheet 7.4b.

PC	NAME	NO.	MAT'L
1	HOUSING	1	C.BRO.
2	HOUSING COVER	1	C.BRO.
3	PULLEY	1	ALCOA 195-T6
4	GEAR	2	BRO
5	GEAR STUD	1	BRASS
6	SHAFT	1	BRASS
7	NUT	2	BRO
8	PACKING NUT	2	BRO.

INTRODUCTION TO
ENGINEERING DRAWING

DRAWN BY

CLASS/SEC   DATE   SCALE

LAB

Refer to sheet 7.4a to answer these questions.

1. How is the Pulley, Part 3, secured to the Shaft, Part 6?

2. How is the lower Gear, Part 4, secured to the Shaft?

3. What is the diameter of the Shaft?

4. How is the Cover, Part 2, secured to the Housing, Part 1?

5. What dimension is the most critical in the pump assembly? Is there provision made to adjust this dimension?

6. What is the length of the Shaft?

7. What is the difference between the bottom of the Pulley and the bottom of the Housing?

8. What is the clearance between each Gear and the inside of the Housing?

9. If you were to drill two holes to firmly mount the pump, what would be the spacing of the holes?

10. Ditto lines are used on the pump drawing for what purpose?

11. What is the function of Part 7, the Nut?

12. Why are the slots on the mounting screws shown out of projection?

13. What is the overall height of the Housing?

14. Sketch an isometric full section of the Pulley, Part 3.

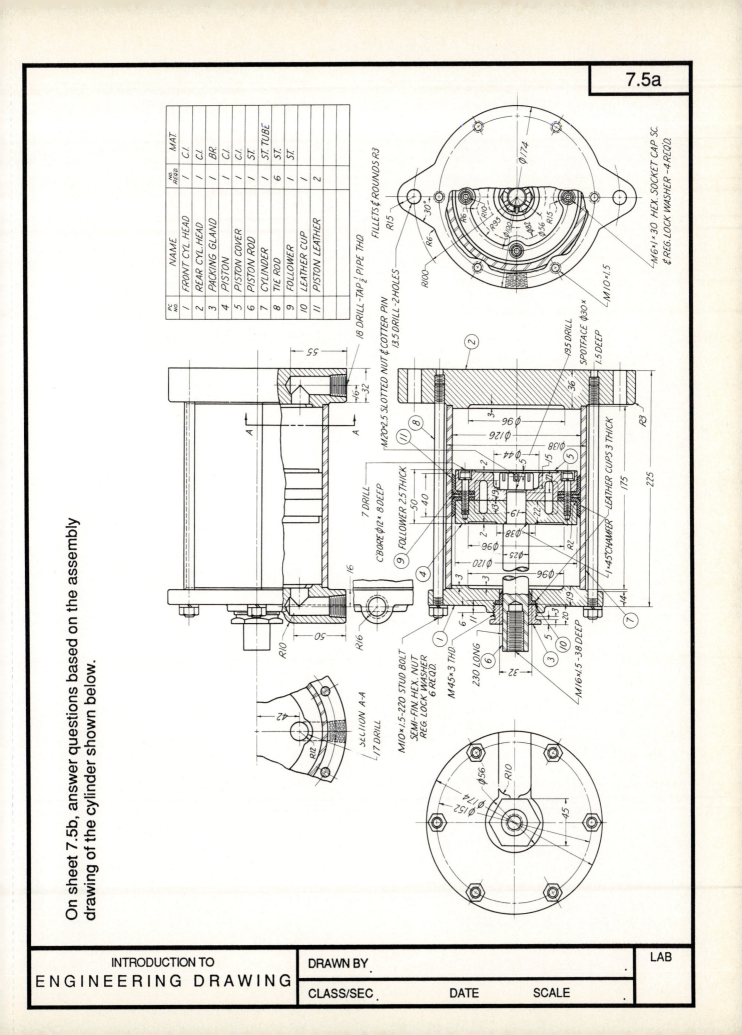

On sheet 7.5b, answer questions based on the assembly drawing of the cylinder shown below.

7.5a

PC NO	NAME	NO REQD	MAT.
1	FRONT CYL. HEAD	1	C.I.
2	REAR CYL. HEAD	1	C.I.
3	PACKING GLAND	1	BR.
4	PISTON	1	C.I.
5	PISTON COVER	1	C.I.
6	PISTON ROD	1	ST.
7	CYLINDER	1	ST. TUBE
8	TIE ROD	6	ST.
9	FOLLOWER	1	ST.
10	LEATHER CUP	1	
11	PISTON LEATHER	2	

INTRODUCTION TO
ENGINEERING DRAWING

DRAWN BY

CLASS/SEC.   DATE   SCALE

LAB

Refer to sheet 7.5 a to answer these questions.

1. How is the Piston, Part 4, secured to the Piston Cover, Part 5?

2. How is the assembly of piston ports secured to the Piston Rod, Part 6?

3. To mount the cylinder assembly by its two legs, how far apart must the two mounting holes be?

4. What is the outside diameter of the Piston?

5. What is the thickness of the Leather Cups?

6. What is the maximum travel of the Piston in one direction?

7. What is the length of the Cylinder, Part 7? The wall thickness of the Cylinder?

8. What is the inner diameter of the Packing Gland, Part 3?

9. What is the distance between the inlet and outlet orifices?

10. What size wrench would be required to tighten the Packing Gland?

11. Sketch a pictorial exploded isometric assembly drawing of the piston assembly including the Piston, Leather cups, Follower, Piston cover, and required fasteners.

INTRODUCTION TO
ENGINEERING DRAWING

DRAWN BY .

CLASS/SEC .   DATE   SCALE   .

LAB

P1

P1

INTRODUCTION TO
ENGINEERING DRAWING

DRAWN BY .   .   LAB

CLASS/SEC .   DATE   SCALE   . P1

INTRODUCTION TO
ENGINEERING DRAWING

DRAWN BY .   .

CLASS/SEC .   DATE   SCALE   .

LAB

P1

INTRODUCTION TO
ENGINEERING DRAWING

DRAWN BY

CLASS/SEC

DATE

SCALE

LAB

P2

P2

INTRODUCTION TO
ENGINEERING DRAWING

DRAWN BY

CLASS/SEC   DATE   SCALE

LAB

INTRODUCTION TO

ENGINEERING DRAWING

DRAWN BY

CLASS/SEC   DATE   SCALE

LAB

P2

P2

INTRODUCTION TO

ENGINEERING DRAWING

DRAWN BY

CLASS/SEC

DATE

SCALE

LAB

P3

INTRODUCTION TO
ENGINEERING DRAWING

DRAWN BY .

CLASS/SEC .   DATE   SCALE

LAB

P3

INTRODUCTION TO
ENGINEERING DRAWING

DRAWN BY

CLASS/SEC   DATE   SCALE

LAB

P3

P3

INTRODUCTION TO
ENGINEERING DRAWING

DRAWN BY .

LAB

CLASS/SEC .   DATE   SCALE   .

| INTRODUCTION TO | DRAWN BY | LAB |
| ENGINEERING DRAWING | CLASS/SEC   DATE   SCALE | P4 |

| INTRODUCTION TO | DRAWN BY . | . | LAB |
| ENGINEERING DRAWING | CLASS/SEC . | DATE   SCALE . | P4 |

INTRODUCTION TO
ENGINEERING DRAWING

DRAWN BY		LAB
CLASS/SEC	DATE	SCALE	P4

INTRODUCTION TO
ENGINEERING DRAWING

DRAWN BY .

CLASS/SEC .   DATE   SCALE   .

LAB

P4